PSYCHOLOGY
AND
PERSONAL
GROWTH

FIFTH EDITION

PSYCHOLOGY AND PERSONAL GROWTH

Nelson Goud

INDIANA UNIVERSITY-PURDUE UNIVERSITY
AT INDIANAPOLIS

Abe Arkoff

UNIVERSITY OF HAWAII AT MANOA

Allyn and Bacon
BOSTON LONDON TORONTO SYDNEY TOKYO SINGAPORE

Vice President/Director of Field Marketing: Joyce Nilsen
Senior Editor: Carolyn Merrill
Series Editorial Assistant: Amy Goldmacher
Production Administrator: Christopher H. Rawlings
Editorial-Production Service: Omegatype Typography, Inc.
Composition and Prepress Buyer: Linda Cox
Manufacturing Buyer: Suzanne Lareau
Cover Administrator: Linda Knowles

Copyright © 1998 by Allyn & Bacon
A Viacom Company
160 Gould Street
Needham Heights, MA 02194

Internet: www.abacon.com
America Online: Keyword: College Online

Library of Congress Cataloging-in-Publication Data

Goud, Nelson.
     Psychology and personal growth / Nelson Goud. Abe Arkoff. —5th ed.
          p.   cm.
     Includes bibliographical references.
     ISBN 0–205–26102–7 (pbk.)
     1. Psychology. 2. Maturation (Psychology) 3. Self-actualization (Psychology) I. Arkoff, Abe. II. Title.
BF149.P835   1997
158—DC21   96–40313
                                                          CIP

Printed in the United States of America

10 9 8 7 6 5 4 3 2 1   02 01 00 99 98 97

To the memory of my parents and
for my children, David and Debbie.
—Nelson Goud

For my fellow growers
Susan, Amy, and Ty.
—Abe Arkoff

CONTENTS

SECTION five   HUMAN RELATIONSHIPS   245

SECTION six   A QUALITY LIFE   317

PREFACE

The focus of this book is your life. Given this premise, it should be very unlikely that the reading will be boring. Over six dozen articles, drawings, and photo-essays have been written and selected to apply psychology to your development as a person. These selections explore six themes: identity, human communication, growth dynamics, feelings and emotions, human relationships, and a quality life.

Some of the selections will have immediate relevance and application. Others may take some thought, discussion, or writing to fully comprehend their message. Each article has a Follow-Up section which provides guidance in interpreting the ideas. You are strongly urged to answer at least one of these questions for each assigned article.

Applied Activities are offered at the end of each of the six sections. These exercises apply and extend the main ideas of the section. Completing these activities will aid in integrating what you've learned into your life.

To Instructors

This book is designed so that most of the articles can be read within a semester. Depending on your teaching style, the articles can be used for small and large group discussion, student journal assignments, or as launching pads for related topics. Some students need little or no guidance and others need a great deal of structure in interpreting a reading.

I have found it helpful to have students complete at least one of the Follow-Up items for every assigned article. I would also recommend that at least one Applied Activity be assigned per section. If you use small groups as part of your instruction, it is suggested that students read Section 2 (Human Communication) prior to any group interaction. Additional teaching suggestions are offered in the supplemental Instructor's Manual and Test Bank.

I have used the four earlier editions of this book since 1975 in a class entitled *Developing Human Potential*. Those of you who have used the earlier versions will note both similarities and changes. Approximately two-thirds of the selections are new. An attempt has been made to shorten the length of articles and the whole book. Abe and I are very interested in your reaction to this edition.

An Invitation

Readers, both students and instructors, are invited to share your comments, reading suggestions, or other ideas with me at the address below:

Nelson Goud, Ph.D.
School of Education
Indiana University-Purdue University at Indianapolis
902 W. New York Street
Indianapolis, IN 46202

THANKS

A note of thanks to those who made it possible to complete this book.

Section one   Identity

Carl Rogers. "The Search for Identity." From *Freedom To Learn* by Carl Rogers & H. Jerome Freiberg. Copyright © 1994, 3rd ed., 52, 53, 56, 57, 65. Reprinted by permission of Prentice Hall.

Kurt Vonnegut, Jr. "Harrison Bergeron." From *Welcome To the Monkey House* by Kurt Vonnegut, Jr. Copyright © 1961. Used by permission of Delacorte Press/Seymour Lawrence, a division of Bantam Doubleday Dell Publishing Group, Inc.

Richard Cohen. "Suddenly I'm the Adult?" Permission granted by Richard Cohen of *The Washington Post*.

Katherine Davis. "I'm Not Sick, I'm Just In Love." From *Newsweek*, July 24, © 1995, Newsweek, Inc. All rights reserved. Reprinted by permission.

Rosalind C. Barrett and Caryl Rivers. "The Myth of the Miserable Working Woman." First appeared in *Working Woman* in Feb., 1992. Reprinted with the permission of *Working Woman Magazine*, Copyright © 1992 by *Working Woman Magazine*.

Sam Keen. "On Being A Man." Excerpts from *Fire In the Belly* by Sam Keen. Copyright © 1991 by Sam Keen. Used by permission of Bantam Books, a division of Bantam Doubleday Dell Publishing Group, Inc.

Excerpt by Lillian Rubin taken from her book, *Intimate Strangers: Men and Women Together*, 1983, Harper & Row.

Denise Karuth. "If I Were A Car, I'd Be A Lemon." Originally published in *Ordinary Moments: The Disabled Experience*, 1984, Ed. Alan J. Brightman, by University Park Press. Reprinted through the permission of Alan J. Brightman.

The Think "People First" list was developed by Ohio Public Images/Public Images Network.

Section two   Human Communication

Warner Burke. "Interpersonal Communication." Reprinted with permission from NTL Institute, 78–84. From the Selected Series Reading Nine, *Behavioral Science and the Manager's Role*, edited by Warner Burke, Copyright © 1969.

Carl Rogers. "To Hear and To Be Heard." From *Freedom To Learn* by Carl Rogers, Copyright © 1969, 222–227. Reprinted by permission of Prentice Hall.

Section six   A Quality Life

AND MORE THANKS

There are several pieces in this book which have unnamed authors. These contributions are from students in the senior author's Developing Human Potential course. They wish to remain anonymous but are willing to share their thoughts. I applaud their articulate and caring excerpts, all of which provide a personalized perspective of the book's themes.

All of the illustrations were drawn by Tom McCain, a professional cartoonist, illustrator and old friend. Copyright © 1996 by Tom McCain and printed with permission. Thanks "½" for the usual outstanding work.

Thanks to photographer Mr. Greg Mason for the photo of the triplets and of the two brothers. Copyright © 1996. Reprinted with permission.

Unless otherwise indicated, all photos by Nelson Goud, Copyright © 1996.

Thanks to the following individuals who gave permission to print the sibling photos: Ms. Debra Townsend, Ms. Tamara A. Beachler, David and Deborah Goud.

A statement of gratitude is in order for the efforts of the following persons who greatly assisted in the preparation of the manuscript: Ms. Marcia Makarenko, Dr. Barbara Wilcox, Ms. Dottie Swinney, Ms. Margo Barrick, and Ms. Bonnie Beaumont. Also, I'm grateful to the skilled staff of Omegatype Typography, Inc.—especially to those masters of the red pencil—Ms. Barbara Cook and Ms. Kathy Robinson.

An earnest and systematic attempt has been made to trace copyrighted material and to secure permissions. If errors have been made, it is unintentional. If the latter occurred, necessary corrections will be made in any future editions.

PSYCHOLOGY
AND
PERSONAL
GROWTH

IDENTITY

What am I? Where am I? Who am I?
No one can answer these questions—
Why have I been so afraid to try?
I know if I look it's all there to see;
So I opened one small door to look inside,
And from out of that door a small voice cried,
"Have you come to set me free?"
It scared me a bit—Should I close the door?
No, I had to find out whose voice had cried,
Should I step inside and ask the voice to say more?
Perhaps if I took just one small glance inside—
So I peered through the door, but all was dim;
Could I summon the courage to step within—
And find the voice before its echo died?

—Anonymous

Who am I? This is the essential question of identity. It is rarely asked in public (thankfully), but is almost always raised during times of personal change. Throughout our lifetime we will be redefining who we think we are. Our identity, or sometimes called our self-concept, is crucial for positioning ourselves in life. It is the center of how we view others and the world. For a brief check of the current status of your identity, provide 10 answers to this question "Who are you?" Just list your answers as quickly as you can.

_____   _____

_____   _____

_____   _____

_____   _____

_____   _____

Your answers may offer some helpful clues about your identity. You may define yourself primarily by *roles* such as age, gender, race, major or occupation, marital status, organizational membership, and so on. You may define yourself by *individual qualities* such as how you think, believe, or feel. Imagine yourself ten years ago looking at the list you just wrote. You probably would have wondered—Who is this person? Our identity both initiates and reflects our development as a person.

The confidence you have in your identity will vary. Sometimes there will be a strong sense of who you are and where you are going in life. Then there are times of questioning and doubt about who this person is inside your skin. Identity changes can occur rapidly or gradually. Some identity changes are forced upon a person, while others are natural developmental shifts, and even others are the product of deliberate effort. Most identity change does not occur in the manner hoped for by this undergraduate student:

I am very confused. I am glad I decided to go to a therapist so I can know who I am and where I should be going career-wise. I am glad there is a break before next semester so I can spend time with God and discover who I am and where I am going. I hope I will know before next semester starts.

Possibly this student found her identity during the holiday break—it *could* happen—but it's unlikely. This student, however, stated what most of us want when confronted with an identity crisis—a quick solution because it is so unsettling.

This section focuses on major issues in identity formation. The articles selected examine identity from several perspectives:

- In "The Search for Identity," Carl Rogers, a major theorist and therapist, discusses how the struggle to discover an identity is a modern problem. He explains how finding and creating an identity is a lifetime journey. His account of how artist Georgia O'Keeffe discovered her artistic identity has relevance for us all.

- In "The Basic Relationship," Abe Arkoff suggests that the way we come to see and regard ourselves is our most fundamental relationship. Included in this piece are explanations of the various forms of self-image and multiple subpersonalities.

- We are treated to Kurt Vonnegut's short story, "Harrison Bergeron." Here we observe what it would be like if all persons were equal in all ways. There are no individual identities—except for the case of Harrison Bergeron.

- Nelson Goud elaborates on a little known concept of the pioneering psychologist Abraham Maslow called "Rubricizing." He discusses how we place people, including ourselves, into identity categories, and how rubricizing helps or hinders.

- In "Suddenly I'm the Adult?" Richard Cohen provides a personalized history of his identity milestones. Of particular emphasis is how he became an adult. Most of us will quickly spot parallels in our own lives.

- In "I'm Not Sick, I'm Just in Love," Katherine Davis poses some basic questions about identity choices regarding marriage and career. Choosing to marry earlier than her peers, she encounters multiple resistances from friends and family.

- Much has been discussed and written on the effects of a woman working in relation to marriage, raising children, and levels of personal stress. In "The Myth of the Miserable Working Woman" by Rosalind C. Barnett and Caryl Rivers, this issue is examined with some surprising conclusions.

- A prominent psychologist/philosopher, Sam Keen, highlights both historical and modern problems associated with the male role. "On Being A Man" contains excerpts from Keen's best selling *Fire In the Belly.*

- Sometimes a major part of one's identity is forced on a person. Such is the case with Denise Karuth. She discusses how she views her world and herself as a physically disabled person in "If I Were a Car, I'd Be A Lemon." Karuth reveals how her life has been drastically affected, but also shows how her personhood is essentially no different from yours or mine.

- Occupational choices comprise a major portion of our identity. Nels Goud tells about encountering people with perfect jobs in "Don't Look Too Closely." Christopher Schaefer also offers a brief account of an occupational odyssey to show how one person finally matched work and his personal identity.

- Body image as it relates to one's identity is explored in Abe Arkoff's "To A Body, With Love." He demonstrates a unique way of communicating with your body in this piece.

You are urged to attempt one or all of the Follow-Up questions at the end of each article. They are designed to personalize the ideas mentioned in the articles. At the end of the section are some Applied Activities that extend and apply the concepts presented.

The Search for Identity: A Modern Problem

Carl Rogers

We are, perhaps all of us, engaged in a struggle to discover our identity, the person we are and choose to be. This is a very pervasive search; it involves our clothes, our hair, our appearance. At a more significant level, it involves our choice of values, our stance in relation to parents and others, the relationship we choose to have to society, our whole philosophy of life. It is, in these days, a most perplexing search. As one college woman says:

I'm confused. Just when I think I'm getting my head together, I talk with some fellow who's sure he knows what life is all about. And because I'm uncertain, I'm really impressed. And then when I get away I realize that's his answer. It can't be the answer for me. I've got to find my own. But it's hard when everything is so loose and unsure.

I see this search for one's real self, for identity, as much more of a problem today than it was in the historical past. During most of history, it made little difference whether the individual discovered himself. Perhaps he lived a more comfortable life if he did not because the identity he lived was defined for him. It is interesting to imagine ourselves back in feudal times. The serf was expected to be a serf throughout his life, as were his children after him. In return he was permitted to eke out a meager living, most of his work going to support the lord of the manor, who in turn protected him. The nobleman was, in a more luxurious way, also constricted. He was the lord, responsible for his followers, and his children would continue the role of the nobleman. In our own country, during one dark pe-

riod of our history, the slave was always the slave and the master always the master. The difficulties of abandoning these role identities are still painfully with us. While the rigidity of the defined role seems incredibly restrictive to us now, it should not blind us to the fact that such rigidity made life simpler in many ways. The cobbler knew that he and his sons would always be cobblers; his wife knew that she and her daughters would always be primarily servants of their husbands. There were almost no options, and peculiarly enough this gave people a type of security that we have left behind. Perhaps one of the few analogies that are comprehensible to us is the peacetime army. Many men and women have come to accept army life with more satisfaction than they had supposed possible. There are almost no decisions: they are told what to wear, how to behave, where to live, and what to do. They can gripe as freely as they wish, without any responsibility for their lives. They are given an identity, told who they are; and the agonizing personal search that most of us must go through is at least temporarily abrogated.

It is for reasons of this sort that I say the search for one's real self is a peculiarly modern problem. The individual's life is no longer defined (though it may be influenced) by one's family, social class, color, church, or nation. We carry the burden ourselves of discovering our identity. I believe the only person today who does not suffer this painful search for self is the person who voluntarily surrenders his or her individual identity to some organization or institution that defines the purposes, the values, the philosophy to be followed. Examples include people who completely commit themselves to some strict religious sect that is sure of all the answers; those who commit themselves to a rigorous ideology (whether revolutionary or reactionary) that defines their philosophy, their life-style, and their actions; those who give themselves completely to science or industry or traditional education (though there are large cracks in the certainties of all these institutions); or, as I mentioned, those who give their lives to the military. I can thoroughly understand the satisfactions and securities that cause individuals to make such commitments, one of which is to gain a certain comfort.

The transition from conformity to freedom creates a strong sense of disequilibrium and discomfort. Yet I suspect that the majority of young people prefer the more painful burden of choosing the uniqueness that is involved in discovering the real self. I know that is my choice. Still, one of the most common fears of people trying to discover who they really are inside is that this undiscovered "me" will turn out to be a worthless, bizarre, evil, or horrible creature. Something of this fear is expressed by a searching student:

I feel my mind is open, kind of like a funnel, and on top there are sparks and exciting things, but down deeper in the funnel it's dark, and I'm afraid to go down in there because I'm scared of what I might find. I'm not going to do it just now.

This attitude is a very common one indeed. There are a number of ways in which individuals pursue this goal of becoming themselves. Some lives have been badly distorted or warped by early childhood. For them, the search for solidity in themselves, for their own real self, may be a long or painful one. Others more fortunate are already in the process of discovery and have an easier time. Some are sufficiently frightened by the risks involved in the search that they endeavor to freeze themselves as they are, fearful of any road that would lead into unknown territory. I will briefly describe several of the ways in which people venture, as they search for the real self.

THE LIFETIME JOURNEY OF SELF-DISCOVERY

This process of self-discovery, self-acceptance, and self-expression is not something that goes on only in therapy or in groups. Many people have neither of these experiences. For those who do, the therapy or the group exists for only a limited time. But for all of us, the search to become the person we most uniquely are is a lifetime process. I believe this is one reason why biography holds a fascination for so many readers. We like to follow the struggle of individuals to become what they are capable of becoming. For me, this is illustrated by the book I have just finished reading: the life story of artist Georgia O'Keeffe [*Portrait of An Artist: A Biography of Georgia O'Keeffe,* by L. Lisle (1980)]. There are many steps in her development. At fourteen, the inwardly independent but outwardly conforming girl won a gold medal for her ladylike deportment at a strict Catholic school. But by the age of sixteen, she was beginning to dress in a "tailored, midwestern corsetless style" (in 1903!), which was to be a characteristic throughout her many years. And at age twenty-nine she locked herself into her studio and analyzed all her work up to that point with "ruthless detachment." She could tell which paintings had been done to please one professor and which to please another. She could tell which had been influenced by well-known artists of the day.

> Then an idea dawned on her. There were abstract shapes in her mind integral to her imagination, unlike anything she had been taught. 'This thing that is your own is so close to you, often you never realize it's there,' she later explained. . . . 'I could think of a whole string of things I'd like to put down but I'd never thought of doing it because I'd never seen anything like it.' . . . She had made up her mind. This was what she would paint. (p. 81)

As you can imagine, this decision was the initial step toward becoming the great artist of her mature years. Even in her nineties, she relentlessly pursued that goal of painting her own unique perceptions of the desert, of bleached bones, of huge and gorgeous flowers—to the point that one has only to look at one of her paintings to realize "That's an O'Keeffe."

Like Georgia O'Keeffe, each of us is the artist or the architect of his or her own life. We can copy others, we can live to please others, or we can discover what is unique and precious to us and paint that, become that. It is a task that takes a lifetime.

YOU CAN BE YOURSELF

Let me try to summarize what it means to me to find one's real self. In the first place it is a process, a direction, not some static achievement. In my estimation no one is ever completely successful in finding all her real (and ever-changing) self. But there are certain characteristics of this process. Persons move away from hiding behind facades and pretenses, whether these have been held consciously or unconsciously. They move toward a greater closeness to and awareness of their inward experiences. They find this development exceedingly complex and varied, ranging from wild and crazy feelings to solid, socially approved ones. They move toward accepting all of these experiences as their own; they discover that they are people with an enormous variety of reactions. The more they own and accept their inner reactions—and are unafraid of them—the more they can sense the meanings those reactions have. The more all this inner richness belongs to them, the more they can appropriately *be* their own experiences. An individual may become aware of a childish need to depend on someone, to be cared for and protected. In appropriate situations she can let herself be that childish, dependent self. She may discover that certain situations anger her.

When you are very young, life, like these railroad tracks, appears to go on forever. We wonder and dream about what awaits us down the way. If there is an end, it is too distant to even think about. Sometimes our lifetrack feels just right. Other times we may have doubts about our lifetrack. Something isn't right, something is missing in our travels. Bernard Malamud's words begin to make sense—"If your train's on the wrong track every station you come to is the wrong station." If this happens, it is often wise to choose another lifetrack. But just switching tracks is not sufficient because, as Will Rogers warned, "Even if you're on the right track, you'll get run over if you just sit there."

"The Right Track" by Nelson Goud. Copyright © 1996.

She can more easily express that anger as it arises in the situation that arouses it, rather than suppress it until it pours out explosively onto some innocent victim. A man can discover soft, tender, loving feelings (which are especially difficult for men to own) and can express them with satisfaction, not shame. These people are becoming involved in the wider range of their feelings, attitudes, and potential. They are building a good relationship with what is going on within themselves. They are beginning to appreciate and like, rather than hate and mistrust, all their experiences. Thus, they are coming closer to finding and being all of themselves in the moment. To me this is the way that the person moves toward answering the question, "Who am I?"

Follow-Up

1. *Rogers quotes a college woman who is easily impressed with someone who knows for sure about life and his identity. Then she realizes that this is his answer, not hers. But she is confused on how to find her answers. When you are not sure of who you are, are you also easily influenced by confident and seemingly authoritative persons? Provide an example, if possible. Have you, like the above student, chosen to find your way and answers, even though this approach is loaded with doubts and uncertainties? If yes, try to give a real life example.*

2. *Rogers discusses how even some modern day groups offer ready-made identities in which few decisions have to be made. He mentions the military as well as political and religious sects. Do these kinds of identity solutions appeal to you? Why or why not? For further reading on this topic try the classic small book,* True Believers, *by the longshoreman philosopher Eric Hoffer.*

3. *Rogers explains how the artist Georgia O'Keeffe found her artistic voice. She said that she locked herself in her studio and looked at her work with "ruthless detachment." She then realized that she had not been painting the images which seemed to exist only in her mind. These images became her artistic identity. She concluded that "this thing that is your own is so close to you, often you never realize it's there."*

   Try looking at your own life with "ruthless detachment" to discover which parts are direct results of others' influence and which parts are uniquely yours. How can you blend the most significant of each into your own voice?

4. *Rogers mentions that biography appeals to many because it provides some hints on how others struggle with identity issues. Have you experienced this effect? Consider reading a biography of someone you admire.*

5. *In the last paragraph of his article, Rogers talks about several characteristics of the process of becoming one's real self. One characteristic is moving away from facades and pretenses. Have you found that you become truer to your identity when you drop false fronts? Consider trying out some of the ideas in this paragraph. If you're interested in a fuller discussion of these characteristics, you will find them in* On Becoming a Person *by Carl Rogers.*

The Basic Relationship

Abe Arkoff

John Vasconcellos is a highly esteemed member of the California legislature, but he speaks candidly about his own early failure to value himself and of many later years of therapy to develop his self-esteem and personhood. Recently, recalling his own long trek to a better sense of self, he wrote,

> In school, I was a high-achiever, receiving awards and excellent grades. In adulthood, I became a prominent lawyer in a prestigious firm. My first campaign for a seat in the state legislature in 1966 was successful, and I have now been reelected eleven times.
>
> Yet, through it all, I had almost no sense of my self, no self-esteem. I worked for my successes only in a constant attempt to please others. My intellect functioned superbly, but the rest of my self barely functioned at all. I had been conditioned to know myself basically as a sinner, guilt-ridden and ashamed, constantly beating my breast and professing my unworthiness. I had so little self-esteem that I lost my first election (running for eighth-grade president) by one vote—my own (Vasconcellos, 1989, pp. xiv–xv).

Vasconcellos notes that personal experience has taught him the importance of valuing oneself. He has increasingly focused on the issue of self-esteem both to help himself and others develop "a strong sense of self." He is the author of legislation creating the California Task Force to Promote Self-Esteem and Personal and Social Responsibility whose aim is to promote the well-being of the individual and society as a way of preventing rather than just reacting to serious social ills.

As a clinical psychologist, I have worked with many people who have come to me for help. Some were deeply troubled. Of these, I cannot recall a single one who had a good relationship with herself or himself. Not one was her or his own best friend. When they began to like themselves and trust themselves, I knew they were getting better. When they began to take some pride in themselves, I knew they were getting well.

Not long ago I heard a comedienne ask a group this question: "How many of you know how it feels to be the only person in a relationship?" This got a laugh, but thinking back on my clinical experience with human beings, it seems clear to me that the most important relationship we each have is the one with ourselves. How strange that most of us do not think of this as a relationship at all. How strange that this is the relationship in which we sometimes appear least humane, treating ourselves in a way we would never treat somebody else.

Think about this with reference to your own self. You are always in your own presence, and just as you are aware of the world around you, you are aware of yourself. You think, you feel, you act. You also observe yourself thinking and feeling and acting. You reflect on yourself and come to know yourself. You have *reflective awareness*—the ability to consider your behavior as you observe it.

Because you have the power of reflective awareness, you are both actor and audience in your life. You perform and at the same time watch yourself perform. But you are not a passive audience. You, the audience, attend and consider. You weigh and evaluate. Sometimes you applaud, sometimes you hiss or jeer, sometimes rise and command. You (the actor) are influenced by you (the audience) just as you (the audience) are influenced by you (the actor).

Of course, there are other people in the audience too. In their response to you, they tell you who they think you are and what you can and can't do and should and shouldn't do. You observe these others and observe them observe you and observe yourself. Out of all these observations you shape and reshape the idea of who you are, and you shape and reshape your relationship to yourself. Your relationship to yourself could be called "the basic relationship" because how you come to see and regard yourself becomes such a fundamental force in your life.

THE DYNAMIC SELF-IMAGE

Our self-image is influenced by all that is happening in our life, and at the same time it is involved in making things happen—in guiding and controlling our behavior. It is dynamic, that is, active, changing, forceful (Markus & Wurf, 1987). Among its powers are those affecting the way we see our world, how we function in it, and how we relate to those with whom we come in contact.

The Self-Image and Perception

The way we perceive or view ourselves affects the way we view our world. We are the center of our universe. Perceptual psychologists Combs, Avila, and Purkey (1978) note that the self is the yardstick used to make judgments. They write, "Others are regarded as taller, shorter, smarter, more unscrupulous, older, or younger than ourself. As the self changes, the yardstick changes, and what we believe to be true changes with it. What is considered 'old' is likely to be quite differently defined at ages six, sixteen, thirty-six, or sixty" (p. 19).

In any situation the things possible for us to perceive are almost limitless. What we select to perceive and the meaning we attach to these perceptions relate closely to the picture we have of ourselves. By way of example, Don Hamachek (1978) writes, "Depending on one's concept of self, an exam is perceived as either something to avoid failing or something to pass with as high a grade as possible; a class discussion is viewed as either something to actively engage in or something to sit quietly through for fear of saying the wrong thing; front seats of classrooms are seen as either vantage points for better seeing or potentially dangerous spots where one could be more easily seen and, heaven forbid, called on!" (pp. 44–45).

The Self-Image and Behavior

Because of its influence on our perceptions, our self-image influences our behavior in many ways. Some psychologists believe that the basic human force is the striving to maintain and enhance our conception of ourselves (Combs, Richards, & Richards, 1976). We present ourselves to others in ways calculated to enhance our image in their eyes and in our own. We defend our image from attack, whether this be assault from without or doubts arising from within.

Our self-image serves us as a basic frame of reference—as a foundation or guide for our actions. We would be lost without it, and therefore we defend it against change. Some of us seem to be resistant to growth or positive movement in our lives, but this may be our way of being true to our picture of ourselves (Rosenberg, 1979).

Psychologists have suggested that when a person believes something to be so, he or she tends to behave in a way that makes it so; this is called a "self-fulfilling prophecy." If we see ourselves in a positive light, we are apt to try harder because we think our efforts will pay off, and we are more likely to succeed or define the outcome as successful. If we have a

Date 9

low opinion of ourselves, we may avoid a situation or approach it halfheartedly, and we are more likely to fail or to interpret the results as failure (Langer & Dweck, 1973).

The Self-Image and Relationships with Others

Our self-image influences our perceptions of others and our relationships with them. There is considerable evidence that we tend to see others as we see ourselves. Emerson wrote, "What we are, that only can we see." Hamachek (1978) adds, "When we think we are looking out a window, it could be that we are merely gazing into a looking-glass" (p. 47). He suggested that a good way to find out what a person is really like is to find out what this person thinks others are like. He writes, "The man who tells us that people are basically trustworthy and kind—ignoring the plain fact that they can also be devious and cruel—may be saying more about himself than about the world" (p. 47).

People who like and accept themselves tend to accept others (Berger, 1952; Pirot, 1986). Research shows that individuals who hold themselves in high esteem tend to take a favorable view of others and also expect more acceptance and less rejection (Baron, 1974; Walster, 1965). And, of course, when others are approached in this light, they are more likely to respond favorably.

If we dislike or reject ourselves, we are more likely to view and treat others in the same way, and consequently our relations with others will suffer. Oscar Wilde observed that "all criticism is a form of autobiography." Hamachek suggests some personal research that one can do on this point. He writes, "Pay particular attention to your feelings about yourself for the next three or four days and note how they influence your behavior toward others. It may be that it is not our friend or our loved one or our children we are mad at; it is ourselves. What we feel toward ourselves gets aimed at others, and we sometimes treat others not as persons, but as targets" (p. 46).

We tend to form relationships with persons who are similar to us, who see us as we see ourselves and who confirm our own positive self-impressions (Swan, 1984; Taylor & Brown, 1988). It's hard for us to rest easy in the company of those who don't see us as we wish to be seen (Lang, Phillipson, & Lee, 1966). Joseph Joubert understood this prime requisite of friendship when he wrote, "When my friends are one-eyed, I look at their profile."

THE MULTIPLE SELF

One of Shakespeare's most famous lines (part of the counsel that Polonius gives his son Laertes in *Hamlet*) reads, "This above all: to thine own self be true." Kenneth Gergen (1972), a psychologist, who has made an extensive study of the self-concept, calls this advice "poor psychology." He believes we are unlikely to find a single self to be true to.

Gergen's research suggests that we are considerably affected by the situations in which we find ourselves—the self we are in one situation may be very different from the self we are in another. Different environments may prompt different thoughts and feelings about ourselves and therefore different behaviors. When we are talking to someone who is in a superior position, our self-relevant thoughts and feelings may be quite different from when we are with a subordinate. When we are standing up to a group, we may see ourselves differently from when we have reluctantly decided to go along with it (Markus & Kunda, 1986).

Gergen questions the assumption that many psychologists and laypersons make that it is good—or even normal—to have a firm and coherent sense of self. In fact, he suggests that we should become concerned when we become too comfortable with a self or set in a particular identity. This may simply mean we have settled into a routine of the same situations ("a rut") that calls forth the same old responses.

Gergen concludes that "we are made of soft plastic and molded by social circumstances," but other research suggests that the self-concept is not all that malleable. Taken together, the evidence supports the conclusion that the self-concept is *both* stable and malleable. We have a certain core of ideas about ourselves, and we resist information that challenges this core. At the same time, we are influenced by the situations in which we find ourselves. How we see ourselves in a particular situation results from the reconciliation of self-conceptions prompted by this core and those called forth by that situation (Markus & Kunda, 1986). It can be trying when a core conception is challenged—for example, when we pride ourselves on our honesty but also see we are sorely tempted to lie or cheat to gain an important end.

Subpersonalities

Another psychologist, John Vargiu (1977), also believes that we may not be a single self, but he doesn't agree with Gergen that we shouldn't be. Where Gergen attributes our variability to the varying situations in which we find ourselves, Vargiu attributes it to a number of *subpersonalities*—semi-autonomous personages within us all striving for expression. He holds that we need to understand these subpersonalities better and bring them into harmony with each other; doing so, we become a single harmonized self.

St. Augustine eloquently described the struggle between two of his subpersonalities —the "animal man" and the "spiritual man." Recalling this struggle in his *Confessions,* he wrote, "My inner self was a house divided against itself." Ted Kennedy was described in a 1991 *Time* magazine profile as seemingly a person of several sets of selves. One set: statesman, serious lawmaker, family patriarch. The other set: over-age, drunken frat-house boor and party animal. The profiler suggested, "A man with Kennedy's temperament and past

may need a sort of unofficial self that he can plunge back into now and then—a rowdy, loutish oblivion where he feels easy, where he takes a woozy vacation from being a Kennedy" (Morrow, 1991, p. 27).

You may recall seeing an acquaintance behave in a quite uncharacteristic way. You wonder, what's got into him? Or you think, she's not herself today. Of course, she *is* herself—but a different one of her selves or subselves or subpersonalities.

Consider the inconsistencies or subpersonalities that may exist within yourself. Have you noted that you sometimes seem to get caught up in a particular way of being and behaving? You recognize it and could even give it a label since it is so salient and you have been caught up in it before. When you are under its spell, you see yourself and your world differently and behave differently, perhaps in a way you like or don't like. You may be able to identify a number of these subpersonalities in yourself, some in harmony and some in conflict with each other.

It may be useful to identify and study the subpersonalities in yourself. When I did so recently, these subselves were most salient: The Creative but Tiring Soul (a subself that enjoyed creating something new or different and watching it develop—for awhile), Dad (a caring, helpful subself), The Relentless Searcher (a subself that was always looking for something better but never quite finding it), and The Wise Old Man (an emerging subself, one with the ability to understand, accept and enjoy things as they are). I was pleased to note that The Examiner (a subself that was constantly scrutinizing things to see if they measured up) had been largely decommissioned.

It is important not to confuse the concept of "subpersonalities," which applies to normal behavior, with that of "multiple personality," which is a serious and disabling disorder (Rowan, 1990). This latter condition is quite rare and better known to Hollywood and television script writers than to psychiatrists or psychologists. The added personalities in multiple personality disorder are quite autonomous, even with differences in handedness (left or right dominance) and in patterns of handwriting and brain waves (Putnam, 1984) and usually operate without the awareness of the original personality.

Possible Selves

Markus and her colleagues (Markus & Kunda, 1986; Markus & Nurius, 1986) have been interested in the concept of *possible selves*—the images we have concerning the persons we might be in the future. These include the selves we expect to be, the selves we hope to be, and also those we fear we might become. These images function as incentives and serve to guide us toward certain kinds of behaviors and away from others.

Markus (Possible selves, 1987) points out that our possible selves are influenced by our individual histories and also by developments in society. Social advances such as increased opportunities for women and blacks create new hoped-for possible selves among these groups. New or exacerbated social problems create new dreaded possible selves such as the AIDS-afflicted self, the drug-dependent self, the bag lady, and the street person.

The most striking finding of a study that compared possible selves in delinquent and nondelinquent boys (Oyserman & Markus, 1986) was the intensely negative set of feared selves among the delinquents (for example, being alone, poor, depressed, flunking out of school, junkie, drug pusher, criminal). Unwanted possible selves are not necessarily a negative influence because they can motivate the person to avoid them or to prepare to cope with them. However, for this process to be fully effective, the negative possible self must be countered by a positive possible self or direction that suggests what might be done. Not surprisingly, delinquent boys proved to have fewer matched pairs of negative and positive selves.

Approaches to Self-Knowledge

A useful way to gain more self-knowledge is to make ourselves the object of study just as though we were a course in which we had enrolled. During one period of his life, Sigmund Freud spent the last half-hour of each working day analyzing himself. In one of my workshops, I share some things I have learned about myself from living with myself all these years and then ask my students to write a list of things they have learned about themselves. Some are a bit dumbfounded, but once they have set themselves to the task, most find they have quite a lot to write down.

One master at the art of self-reflection is Hugh Prather. In his notebooks, he carefully observes himself and candidly shares these observations with his readers. The following brief example from his book *Notes to Myself* shows him in his watchful but positive, nurturant pursuit of self-knowledge:

> One kind of lie that I tell pops out in conversation and takes me by surprise. Sometimes I like to correct these lies right on the spot, and when I do I find that most people don't think less of me. This kind of lie, when I notice it, usually helps me see where I feel inadequate—the areas where I could be more acceptant of myself.

Wilson Van Dusen (1972), a pioneer of inner space, notes that we are constantly generating fantasies, images, and feelings that tell us who we are. He writes that "we are almost overburdened with clues to our own nature" (p. 4). But he concludes that we scarcely make use of these clues and, therefore, remain strangers to ourselves.

Van Dusen pictures our inner life as a "mind-castle," but one that is lamentably underesteemed and unexamined. He writes, "If one were locked up in an ancient castle for one's whole life—a castle full of artifacts, dungeons, endless rooms, art, and books—one would spend much time exploring and recreating the lives of the inhabitants" (p. 1). Van Dusen maintains that indeed we are ensconced in such a mind-castle, but we don't avail ourself of the opportunity to explore. He continues, "Many know little more than a sitting room in the east wing and assume this is the whole. The size of the mind-castle is little appreciated. It includes all you have experienced, will experience, and in the remote corners, all you can experience" (p. 1). Van Dusen recommends cultivation of the "lost art" of self-reflection, which he describes as "a gazing at one's life and circumstances as though it were a painting to be examined, felt, appreciated" (p. 49). To do this, he says, requires (1) some minutes of peaceful leisure, (2) the experiencing of what is, and (3) mulling this over or reflecting upon it. He also recommends that one does this regularly and writes it down afterward in a personal journal.

Accepting Ourselves

Some of the dictionary's definitions of the word *accept* are "to be favorably disposed toward," "to believe in," and "to receive as adequate or satisfactory." If we accept ourselves or show *self-acceptance*, we are favorably disposed toward ourselves and believe we are okay. That doesn't mean we don't want to be better, but it does mean whatever we are right now, it's all right to be. If we reject ourselves or show *self-rejection*, we don't like or believe in ourselves, and we feel inadequate.

Before considering self-acceptance more fully, it may be helpful to look at self-rejection— all the things self-acceptance is not. Following is a checklist of behaviors seen in those who find themselves personally unacceptable, which is adapted from larger listings by Wayne Dyer (1976) and by Bloomfield and Kory (1980). The list is presented here just to get you thinking about yourself—it's not a deep and definitive device. As you think, answer each item "yes" or "no."

_____ 1. Do you feel embarrassed by your abilities or accomplishments?

_____ 2. Do you give credit to others when you really deserve it yourself?

_____ 3. Do you put others above you when you are really their equal or superior?

_____ 4. Do you fail to stand up for the things you really believe in?

_____ 5. Do you put yourself down when you have made a mistake?

_____ 6. Do you let others put you down?

_____ 7. Do you have a cute name for yourself that reduces you in some way?

_____ 8. Do you depend on others to bolster your opinions?

_____ 9. Do you believe that others cannot possibly find you attractive?

_____ 10. Do you believe that others are being kind out of charity or some ulterior motive?

_____ 11. Do you find it hard to say no to a request because of what the person might think of you?

_____ 12. Do you find it hard to complain about poor treatment because you are afraid of making a fuss?

Because the items in the preceding list reflect self-rejection, each item that you answered "yes" suggests an area for you to work on to change the "yes" to "no." But don't put yourself down for your "yeses"—that would be another bit of self-rejecting behavior.

Showing one's "true face" even to oneself can be a difficult task when it is a face one has somehow come to think is wrong or even evil. Some lesbians and gays have written of their confusion or consternation at discovering their sexual orientation and of their struggle to "come out of the closet" and be who they truly were. In one study (Jay & Young, 1979), a woman reported that she didn't realize she was a lesbian until she was 20, and her coming out was traumatic. "I used to look at myself in the mirror and cry. I couldn't believe what I was. How could a good girl like me be something as wicked as a lesbian? Once I found the gay bars and gay community I found that there were many 'good girl' lesbians" (pp. 55–56). She noted that since then, her self-image had improved each year, and now she wouldn't want to be anyone other than who she is.

We must constantly seek to understand ourselves if we are to become ourselves, but the understanding does not come once and for all. It comes little by little as we observe ourselves in every new situation. In every situation, we can learn to tell whether we are being genuine and true to ourselves, or phony and unauthentic (Friedman, 1958).

For ten years, I was a volunteer working with hospice patients and those with life-threatening illness. Being with a number of persons as they faced death, I've come to believe that dying has been hardest for those who never really lived their lives—those who were losing both life and their last chance to become themselves. I am reminded of the story told about Rabbi Zusya as he approached death. Rabbi Zusya said that when he met the Holy One, he would not be asked, "Why were you not like Moses?" No, he would be asked, "Why were you not like Zusya?" Zusya added, "It is for this reason that I tremble."

References

Baron, P. (1974). Self-esteem, ingratiation, and evaluation of unknown others. *Journal of Personality and Social Psychology, 30,* 104–109.

Berger, E. (1952). The relation between expressed acceptance of self and expressed acceptance of others. *Journal of Abnormal and Social Psychology, 47,* 778–782.

Bloomfield, H. H., & Kory, R. B. (1980). *Inner joy: New strategies to put more pleasure and satisfaction in your life.* New York: Wyden.

Combs, A. W., Avila, D. L., & Purkey, W. W. (1978). *Helping relationships: Basic concepts for the helping professions* (2nd ed.). Boston: Allyn and Bacon.

Combs, A. W., Richards, A. C., & Richards, F. (1976). *Perceptual psychology: A humanistic approach to the study of persons.* New York: Harper & Row.

Dyer, W. W. (1976). *Your erroneous zones.* New York: Funk & Wagnalls.

Friedman, M. (1958). *To deny our nothingness: Contemporary images of man.* London: Macmillan.

Gergen, K. J. (1972, May). The healthy, happy human wears many masks. *Psychology Today,* pp. 31–35, 64, 66.

Hamachek, D. E. (1978). *Encounters with the self* (2nd ed.). New York: Holt, Rinehart and Winston.

Jay, K., & Young, A. (1979). *The gay report.* New York: Summit Books.

Kazantzakis, N. (1952). *Zorba the Greek.* New York: Simon & Schuster.

Kopp, S. B. (1971). *Guru.* Palo Alto, CA: Science and Behavior Books.

Lang, R. D., Phillipson, H., & Lee, A. R. (1966). *Interpersonal perception: A theory and method of research.* New York: Springer.

Langer, E. J., & Dweck, C. S. (1973). *Personal politics: The psychology of making it.* Englewood Cliffs, NJ: Prentice-Hall.

Markus, H., & Kunda, Z. (1986). Stability and malleability of the self-concept. *Journal of Personality and Social Psychology, 51*(4), 858–866.

Markus, H., & Nurius, P. (1986). Possible selves. *American Psychologist, 41*(9), 954–969.

Markus, H., & Wurf, E. (1987). The dynamic self-concept: A social psychological perspective. *Annual Review of Psychology, 38,* 299–337.

Morrow, L. (1991, April 29). The trouble with Teddy. *Time,* pp. 24–27.

Oyserman, D., & Markus, H. (1986). *Possible selves, motivation, and delinquency.* Unpublished manuscript, University of Michigan.

Pirot, M. (1986). The pathological thought and dynamics of the perfectionist. *Journal of Individual Psychology, 42*(1), 51–58.

Possible selves. (1987, Spring/Summer). *ISR Newsletter,* pp. 5–7.

Prather, H. (1970). *Notes to myself.* Moab, UT: Real People Press.

Putnam, F. W. (1984). The psychophysiologic investigation of multiple personality disorder: A review. *Psychiatric Clinics of North America, 7*(1), 31–39.

Rosenberg, M. (1979). *Conceiving the self.* New York: Basic Books.

Rowan, J. (1990). *Subpersonalities: The people inside us.* New York: Routledge.

Swan, W. B., Jr. (1984). Quest for accuracy in person perception: A matter of pragmatics. *Psychological Review, 91,* 457–477.

Taylor, S. E., & Brown, J. D. (1988). Illusion and well-being: A social psychological perspective on mental health. *Psychological Bulletin, 103*(2), 193–210.

Van Dusen, W. (1972). *The natural depth in man.* New York: Harper & Row.

Vargiu, J. G. (1975). Subpersonalities. In A. Arkoff (Ed.), *Psychology and personal growth* (3rd ed., pp. 22–27). Boston: Allyn & Bacon.

Vasconcellos, J. (1989). Preface. In A. M. Mecca, N. J. Smelser, & J. Vasconcellos (Eds.), *The social importance of self-esteem* (pp. xi–xxi). Berkeley: University of California Press.

Walster, E. (1965). The effect of self-esteem on romantic liking. *Journal of Experimental Social Psychology, 1,* 184–197.

Follow-Up

1. *Do you have a good relationship with yourself? Describe this relationship as it seems to you.*

2. *What subpersonalities can you detect in yourself? Name and describe each one and its influence on you.*

3. *How much insight into yourself do you have? How much of a puzzle are you? Discuss an important aspect of yourself that remains a mystery to you.*

4. *Is your life right for you? Are you on the way to becoming yourself? Give your evidence.*

Harrison Bergeron

Kurt Vonnegut, Jr.

The year was 2081, and everybody was finally equal. They weren't only equal before God and the law. They were equal every which way. Nobody was smarter than anybody else. Nobody was better looking than anybody else. Nobody was stronger or quicker than anybody else. All this equality was due to the 211th, 212th, and 213th Amendments to the Constitution, and to the unceasing vigilance of agents of the United States Handicapper General.

Some things about living still weren't quite right, though. April, for instance, still drove people crazy by not being springtime. And it was in that clammy month that the H-G men took George and Hazel Bergeron's fourteen-year-old son, Harrison, away.

It was tragic, all right, but George and Hazel couldn't think about it very hard. Hazel had a perfectly average intelligence, which meant she couldn't think about anything except in short bursts. And George, while his intelligence was way above normal, had a little mental handicap radio in his ear. He was required by law to wear it at all times. It was tuned to a government transmitter. Every twenty seconds or so, the transmitter would send out some sharp noise to keep people like George from taking unfair advantage of their brains.

George and Hazel were watching television. There were tears on Hazel's cheeks, but she'd forgotten for the moment what they were about.

On the television screen were ballerinas.

A buzzer sounded in George's head. His thoughts fled in panic, like bandits from a burglar alarm.

"That was a real pretty dance, that dance they just did," said Hazel.

"Huh?" said George.

"That dance—it was nice," said Hazel.

"Yup," said George. He tried to think a little about the ballerinas. They weren't really very good—no better than anybody else would have been, anyway. They were burdened with sashweights and bags of birdshot, and their faces were masked, so that no one, seeing a free and graceful gesture or a pretty face, would feel like something the cat drug in. George was toying with the vague notion that maybe dancers shouldn't be handicapped. But he didn't get very far with it before another noise in his ear radio scattered his thoughts.

George winced. So did two out of the eight ballerinas.

Hazel saw him wince. Having no mental handicap herself, she had to ask George what the latest sound had been.

"Sounded like somebody hitting a milk bottle with a ball peen hammer," said George.

"I'd think it would be real interesting, hearing all the different sounds," said Hazel, a little envious. "All the things they think up."

"Um," said George.

"Only, if I was Handicapper General, you know what I would do?" said Hazel. Hazel, as a matter of fact, bore a strong resemblance to the Handicapper General, a woman named Diana Moon Glampers. "If I was Diana Moon Glampers," said Hazel, "I'd have chimes on Sunday—just chimes. Kind of in honor of religion."

"I could think, if it was just chimes," said George.

"Well—maybe make 'em real loud," said Hazel. "I think I'd make a good Handicapper General."

"Good as anybody else," said George.

"Who knows better'n I do what normal is?" said Hazel.

"Right," said George. He began to think glimmeringly about his abnormal son who was now in jail, about Harrison, but a twenty-one-gun salute in his head stopped that.

"Boy!" said Hazel, "that was a doozy, wasn't it?"

It was such a doozy that George was white and trembling, and tears stood on the rims of his red eyes. Two of the eight ballerinas had collapsed to the studio floor, were holding their temples.

"All of a sudden you look so tired," said Hazel. "Why don't you stretch out on the sofa, so's you can rest your handicap bag on the pillows, honeybunch." She was referring to the forty-seven pounds of birdshot in a canvas bag, which was padlocked around George's neck. "Go on and rest the bag for a little while," she said. "I don't care if you're not equal to me for a while."

George weighed the bag with his hands. "I don't mind it," he said. "I don't notice it any more. It's just a part of me."

"You been so tired lately—kind of wore out," said Hazel. "If there was just some way we could make a little hole in the bottom of the bag, and just take out a few of them lead balls. Just a few."

"Two years in prison and two thousand dollars fine for every ball I took out," said George. "I don't call that a bargain."

"If you could just take a few out when you came home from work," said Hazel. "I mean— you don't compete with anybody around here. You just set around."

"If I tried to get away with it," said George, "then other people'd get away with it—and pretty soon we'd be right back to the dark ages again, with everybody competing against everybody else. You wouldn't like that, would you?"

"I'd hate it," said Hazel.

"There you are," said George. "The minute people start cheating on laws, what do you think happens to society?"

If Hazel hadn't been able to come up with an answer to this question, George couldn't have supplied one. A siren was going off in his head.

"Reckon it'd fall all apart," said Hazel.

"What would?" said George blankly.

"Society," said Hazel uncertainly. "Wasn't that what you just said?"

"Who knows?" said George.

The television program was suddenly interrupted for a news bulletin. It wasn't clear at first as to what the bulletin was about, since the announcer, like all announcers, had a serious speech impediment. For about half a minute, and in a state of high excitement, the announcer tried to say, "Ladies and gentlemen—"

He finally gave up, handed the bulletin to a ballerina to read.

"That's all right—" Hazel said of the announcer, "he tried. That's the big thing. He tried to do the best he could with what God gave him. He should get a nice raise for trying so hard."

"Ladies and gentlemen—" said the ballerina, reading the bulletin. She must have been extraordinarily beautiful, because the mask she wore was hideous. And it was easy to see that she was the strongest and most graceful of all the dancers, for her handicap bags were as big as those worn by two-hundred-pound men.

And she had to apologize at once for her voice, which was a very unfair voice for a woman to use. Her voice was a warm, luminous, timeless melody. "Excuse me—" she said, and she began again, making her voice absolutely uncompetitive.

"Harrison Bergeron, age fourteen," she said in a grackle squawk, "has just escaped from jail, where he was held on suspicion of plotting to overthrow the government. He is a genius and an athlete, is under-handicapped, and should be regarded as extremely dangerous."

A police photograph of Harrison Bergeron was flashed on the screen-upside down, then sideways, upside down again, then right side up. The picture showed the full length of Harrison against a background calibrated in feet and inches. He was exactly seven feet tall.

The rest of Harrison's appearance was Halloween and hardware. Nobody had ever born heavier handicaps. He had outgrown hindrances faster than the H-G men could think them up. Instead of a little ear radio for a mental handicap, he wore a tremendous pair of earphones, and spectacles with thick wavy lenses. The spectacles were intended to make him not only half blind, but to give him whanging headaches besides.

Scrap metal was hung all over him. Ordinarily, there was a certain symmetry, a military neatness to the handicaps issued to strong people, but Harrison looked like a walking junkyard. In the race of life, Harrison carried three hundred pounds.

And to offset his good looks, the H-G men required that he wear at all times a red rubber ball for a nose, keep his eyebrows shaved off, and cover his even white teeth with black caps at snaggle-tooth random.

"If you see this boy," said the ballerina, "do not—I repeat, do not—try to reason with him."

There was the shriek of a door being torn from its hinges.

Screams and barking cries of consternation came from the television set. The photograph of Harrison Bergeron on the screen jumped again and again, as though dancing to the tune of an earthquake.

George Bergeron correctly identified the earthquake, and well he might have—for many was the time his own home had danced to the same crashing tune. "My God—" said George, "that must be Harrison!"

The realization was blasted from his mind instantly by the sound of an automobile collision in his head.

When George could open his eyes again, the photograph of Harrison was gone. A living, breathing Harrison filled the screen.

Clanking, clownish, and huge, Harrison stood in the center of the studio. The knob of the uprooted studio door was still in his hand. Ballerinas, technicians, musicians, and announcers cowered on their knees before him, expecting to die.

"I am the Emperor!" cried Harrison. "Do you hear? I am the Emperor! Everybody must do what I say at once!" He stamped his foot and the studio shook.

"Even as I stand here—" he bellowed, "crippled, hobbled, sickened—I am a greater ruler than any man who ever lived! Now watch me become what I *can* become!"

Harrison tore the straps of his handicap harness like wet tissue paper, tore straps guaranteed to support five thousand pounds.

Harrison's scrap-iron handicaps crashed to the floor.

Harrison thrust his thumbs under the bar of the padlock that secured his head harness. The bar snapped like celery. Harrison smashed his headphones and spectacles against the wall.

He flung away his rubber-ball nose, revealed a man that would have awed Thor, the god of thunder.

"I shall now select my Empress!" he said, looking down on the cowering people. "Let the first woman who dares rise to her feet claim her mate and her throne!"

A moment passed, and then a ballerina arose, swaying like a willow.

Harrison plucked the mental handicap from her ear, snapped off her physical handicaps with marvelous delicacy. Last of all, he removed her mask.

She was blindingly beautiful.

"Now—" said Harrison, taking her hand, "shall we show the people the meaning of the word dance? Music!" he commanded.

The musicians scrambled back into their chairs, and Harrison stripped them of their handicaps, too. "Play your best," he told them, "and I'll make you barons and dukes and earls."

The music began. It was normal at first—cheap, silly, false. But Harrison snatched two musicians from their chairs, waved them like batons as he sang the music as he wanted it played. He slammed them back into their chairs.

The music began again and was much improved.

Harrison and his Empress merely listened to the music for a while—listened gravely, as though synchronizing their heartbeats with it.

They shifted their weights to their toes.

Harrison placed his big hands on the girl's tiny waist, letting her sense the weightlessness that would soon be hers.

And then, in an explosion of joy and grace, into the air they sprang!

Not only were the laws of the land abandoned, but the law of gravity and the laws of motion as well.

They reeled, whirled, swiveled, flounced, capered, gamboled, and spun.

They leaped like deer on the moon.

The studio ceiling was thirty feet high, but each leap brought the dancers nearer to it.

It became their obvious intention to kiss the ceiling.

They kissed it.

And then, neutralizing gravity with love and pure will, they remained suspended in air inches below the ceiling, and they kissed each other for a long, long time.

It was then that Diana Moon Glampers, the Handicapper General, came into the studio with a double-barreled ten-gauge shotgun. She fired twice, and the Emperor and the Empress were dead before they hit the floor.

Diana Moon Glampers loaded the gun again. She aimed it at the musicians and told them they had ten seconds to get their handicaps back on.

It was then that the Bergerons' television tube burned out.

Hazel turned to comment about the blackout to George. But George had gone out into the kitchen for a can of beer.

George came back in with the beer, paused while a handicap signal shook him up. And then he sat down again. "You been crying?" he said to Hazel.

"Yup," she said.

"What about?" he said.

"I forget," she said. "Something real sad on television."

"What was it?" he said.

"It's all kind of mixed up in my mind," said Hazel.

"Forget sad things," said George.

"I always do," said Hazel.

"That's my girl," said George. He winced. There was the sound of a rivetting gun in his head.

"Gee—I could tell that one was a doozy," said Hazel.

"You can say that again," said George.

"Gee—" said Hazel, "I could tell that one was a doozy."

Follow-Up

1. *Think of an instance where you have been in a situation or group where everyone is treated the same and where you are expected to act the same as everyone else. One such example would be an Army boot camp. Some social*

organizations—performing groups, athletic teams—often have this norm of sameness. Describe what you liked and disliked about this experience in reference to developing your true identity.

2. *In Vonnegut's story, equality and sameness were ideals. A Handicapper General masked all excellence by imposing selective handicaps. Psychologically there are parallels for us. Many people have a wariness about showing excellence. They do not want to be seen as being an elitist or a person who likes to show off their superiority. Like Harrison Bergeron, showing their true identity will result in being "shot down" by others. Major parts of their identity are not developed. They become their own Handicapper General.*

   Do you feel any social pressure to not *express a part of your identity because it would show that you have greater skill or knowledge than others? Or if you do show a form of excellence, do you feel compelled to dismiss it or make efforts to show that you are "not better than they are"? Do you know anyone who tends to hide their excellence because of these fears of disapproval?*

3. *Most people do not like braggarts or arrogant show-offs. However, one can demonstrate excellence without these traits. For yourself and/or others you know, think of an instance or two where the expression of excellence was valued by others and genuinely encouraged.*

4. *At one point Harrison exclaims "Now watch me become what I can become!" Think of a time when you said to yourself, "This isn't me," so you changed your actions to better fit your sense of yourself. This change may have been expressed smoothly or awkwardly at first. These kinds of changes can occur in a school or work setting, in human relationships, or in the form of decisions that influence the direction of your life. What were the results of these identity changes? Are you faced with any similar choices at this time?*

Rubricizing

Nelson Goud

She was standing in line waiting to board the Denver to Seattle flight. In her 70's, she had gray-blue hair, a red dress, and a satchel clutched under her right arm. What she did not have was a left arm. I became immediately sympathetic as the old lady negotiated the movements necessary to board the plane. On the plane she was two seats away in the same row. About 30 minutes into the flight she pulled out a paperback novel, opened to a marked page, and held the book in her only hand. I snuck a look—readers cannot seem to help but check out what other readers read—and saw *Lake Wobegon Days* on the cover. I had read it a couple of months ago and could not resist the urge to ask how she liked it. Besides, this one-armed old lady just had to be lonely and probably experienced life on the fringe, a human satellite. "How's it going in Lake Wobegon lately?" I asked while eating lunch. She talked about the book a bit and seemed quite friendly. We kept chatting and somewhere in there music was mentioned. We discovered we were big band fans. I droned on about my favorites and how I played the trumpet. She was politely attentive and when I finally took a breath she said, "I played in a big band once." This surprised me. "What did you play?" I asked. "Sax," she said. I asked if this was in high school. "Oh, no. I was 17 though. I played in an all-female professional big band which toured all the USO places in the U.S. and Europe in WWII." Not only did she know of my favorite big band leaders, but saw and talked with them in their prime. After many minutes of answering my eager questions, I noticed that the one-armed old lady had "disappeared." She had become a different person. I even for-

got about her loss of an arm and asked if she still played the sax. She just smiled and said she hadn't picked it up in a while. We deplaned and she met her daughter and two friends and I knew then I was a better reader of books than people.

At a meeting during a national convention, I found myself seated next to a counselor dressed in the garb of a 1960's throwback—Army fatigues, long hair, beard, and a detached, peaceful gaze.

"I'm having a most fascinating time at this convention," he said during a break.

"Why is that?" I asked.

"Take a look at my nametag," he motioned.

It read "Rev. Bill Smith." He then explained that prior to reading his nametag, conventioneers react to him like they would to a hippie—i.e., either ignoring him, staring, or engaging in the hippie lingo.

"The thing is," he continued, "I am not a man of the cloth. When they finally see the nametag they stop talking for a few seconds. You can sense the confusion going on as they try to figure out how to act with a 'hippie preacher.' Most people do not have that category and do not know what to say or do. I need the nametag to get into the workshops so I keep it on. So far I have learned more about people with my nametag than from the workshops."

Peace, brother, love, and that's a far out story, Reverend.

These are examples of "rubricizing" (pronounced roo-bri-sigh-zing), a term coined by Abraham Maslow. He believed that there are two major ways to perceive any experience.

One is to observe its unique essence, how the experience is truly different and individualistic. The second, rubricizing, is to respond to an experience as a representative of a category (rubric). Rubricizing perception is similar to the actions of a file clerk who recognizes only what is minimally necessary to place a paper under A, B, Y, etc. When we rubricize people, we quickly scan them for certain characteristics (often subconsciously) and place them into one of our mental file folders. A rubricized person becomes a member of a grouping: waiter, teenagers, a Johnson kid, math major, jock, married, female, southerner, sorority type, and so on. Rubrics are literally "categories of the mind."

RUBRICIZING CONTINUUM

Rubrics range from the stereotypic to the highly individualistic. A stereotype is a rubric with a pre-packaged set of meanings. Common stereotype subjects are race, religion, occupations, gender, age, marital status, residence, and geographical locale. At the other end of the rubricizing continuum is the individualistic rubric which has meaning only for the perceiver (or possibly just a few others). For instance, I know a person who can glance at the shoes of a person and then tell you his/her food and clothing tastes, social status, and several personality characteristics. To her, people have an astrology chart on their feet. There are also rubrics which fall between these extremes.

POSITIVE AND NEGATIVE ASPECTS

Rubrics can have negative or positive meanings. It is easy to understand why one dislikes being placed in a negative rubric (e.g., "she comes from ———— and you know they never amount to much"). It is also a burden to be rubricized into a positive rubric. This is common for those who stand out in some valued quality like "outstanding student," "talented musician/dancer/artist," "really good looking." Many of the latter also resist being

rubricized. Some find the pressure to uphold this image too daunting over the long haul. But the major resistance comes from the reason that every person has multiple dimensions to his/her identity which also call for expression and recognition. To always be seen characterized in reference to the outstanding quality becomes a constraining and limiting existence.

Rubricizing can be either an enhancing or hindering form of perception. It enhances one's life whenever one is required only to respond to familiar, repetitive tasks or to quickly recognize a single feature. By having only to exert partial attention to a situation, one is then freed to devote more energy to a more difficult activity (or several low challenge activities at one time). One can, for example, plan other activities during a boring committee meeting without missing a key point if it occurs, or one can watch TV and talk to another on surface topics simultaneously.

Rubricizing is a hindrance whenever a situation calls for attention to uniqueness, complexity, wholeness, and change. Trying to understand another person's life, solving a difficult problem, creating something, self-examination—these are kinds of actions which demand more than a quick, cursory scan. One must be open to the shifting multiple dimensions of what is being presented. Carl Rogers explains that this kind of perception requires an "openness to experience" and provides an example:

One of the most satisfying experiences I know—is just fully to appreciate an individual in the same way that I appreciate a sunset. When I look at a sunset . . . I don't find myself saying, "Soften the orange a little on the right hand corner, and put a bit more purple along the base, and use a little more pink in the cloud color" . . . I don't try to control a sunset. I watch it with awe as it unfolds. It is this receptive, open attitude which is necessary to truly perceive something as it is.

It is important to know that rubricizing is usually our *first* perceptual response. One must therefore be especially vigilant in the situations described above where rubricizing is a hindrance. In addition, once something is rubricized it tends to keep this meaning unless a stronger, countering experience changes this perception.

Rubricizing can freeze how a person is perceived, so that if major changes occur, they go unnoticed. You may be a significantly different person compared to earlier years, but upon a visit back home or reuniting with friends, find that they treat you as you were back then. Those very close to us are not immune to rubricizing. We have very strong rubrics about our parents (and they of us). I realize I had rubricized my grandmother. Although we had an affectionate relationship, I noticed at the age of 30 that I was acting toward her the same way as I did at 13. It was ritualistic, she was "Grandma" and I was "Grandson." I happened to ask her about her decision to come to America (she was a Dutch immigrant). Telling her life story as a young girl and woman revealed whole new dimensions of her as a person besides being a grandmother. A rubric has been broken whenever you hear or say, "You surprised me by your interest (or background) in . . ." or "I didn't know you had that in you." Take another look at those close to you to see if some rubricizing is going on.

If you value someone or something, then rubricizing diminishes that which you value. Rubricizing can be accurate or inaccurate, but it is always an *incomplete* form of perception. Everything has multiple facets of which we only perceive a portion. Sometimes we unintentionally slip into a rubricizing mode. I know a physical therapist who was talking to a friend who had to have some surgery to heal a fracture. The physical therapist said to her friend, "I have been learning about patients just like you." Her friend replied, "You have not been learning about patients just like me because there is no one like me. You probably mean that you have been learning about injuries similar to mine." The friend naturally resisted being totally classified by a type of injury.

APPLICATIONS

Here are some guidelines for lessening negative rubricizing:

- Be alert to the *language* signals of rubricizing—"She is the *type* who. . . ," "He's that *kind*," "I can *peg* a person by how. . . ."
- Probably the most frequent rubricizing questions is, "What do you do?" or "What is your major?" If answered, it is very likely that this will be the only dimension of your life that is discussed. It becomes the central identity rubric. Some prefer to be perceived primarily in this rubric. However, there are other choices if you desire to place your occupational identity in a larger context. You can refrain from initially asking a new person, "What do you do?" When introducing or meeting someone for the first time, guide the conversation first to other life activities. You can do the same if asked by someone else. I find it helpful to reply "I do quite a few things. I know you're asking about what I do for a living, but I'd like to talk first about . . . (a new book, jazz, a recent trip, a new idea). . . ." Some of my best conversations started this way; sometimes, though, others persist on finding out my occupational identity (or even shift to another rubric ritual—"What is your sign?").

  During the first weeks of a graduate course I request that students refrain from revealing their occupation or major, age, marital status, religion, and residence. Their ideas and feeling on course topics become the central focus rather than their rubrics. Only later, in the larger context of telling life stories, do the above identity markers emerge.
- Start to observe your system of "rubric triggers"—e.g., appearance, occupational / major categories, residence, mannerisms, clothing, names, family

background, social interaction style, language usage, etc. Stereotypic rubrics are relatively easy to spot. Try also to uncover the individual system of rubrics which exist primarily for you.

- Check the accuracy of initial rubricizing. Through observation and interaction one can find out if the first impressions are erroneous or too restrictive. Rubricizing is counteracted by discovering new facets of a person. Even if it is not realistic to look for new facets (e.g., being served by a waiter), basic human respect is enhanced in just knowing that this person, like you, has many dimensions that are not seen.
- Try to thaw out a frozen rubric you have of someone close to you. This usually means to talk about new topics, or to do different activities than what is customarily done.
- Develop further skills in non-rubricizing, receptive perception. Kazantzakis' Zorba seemed to have the secret—"Like the child, he sees everything for the first time. He is forever astonished and wonders why and wherefore . . . each morning when he opens his eyes he sees trees, sea, stones and birds, and is amazed. 'What is this miracle?' he cries." Unless we are alert, rubricizing can gradually erode experiences which were previously delightful. A pretty flower loses its appeal because we see it several times or find out its name. A favorite song, painting, book, poem are now given a glance instead of the full absorption which made them delightful in the first place.

One simple idea to try is to focus on a common rubricized object you see each day. Maybe a tree on the way to work. Try to discover how it is different from other trees, whether it has lost or grown leaves, how the bark looks different after a rain, and is it a home to a bird or two?

- Have you considered that you can rubricize yourself? It is possible to freeze your own identity so that all is left is repeating familiar patterns. Here are some typical self-rubricizing statements: "I am a methodical and prudent type so it is almost impossible to be spontaneous," "As a teacher I am really not qualified to do anything else but teach children," "People from my (family, school, town, etc.) don't try to do . . . , they'll fail."

All the concepts of rubricizing others also apply to ourselves. Self-rubricizing blunts the adventuring edge so necessary for realizing one's potentialities. Ask yourself. What do *you* do?

Follow-Up

1. *Describe an instance where you:*
   a. *Have been rubricized*
   b. *Rubricized another*
   c. *Rubricized yourself*
2. *Choose two statements from the article that have meaning for you and tell why.*
3. *Attempt one or more of the applications explained in the final section of the article.*

Suddenly I'm the Adult?

Richard Cohen

Several years ago, my family gathered on Cape Cod for a weekend. My parents were there, my sister and her daughter, too, two cousins and, of course, my wife, my son and me. We ate at one of those restaurants where the menu is scrawled on a blackboard held by a chummy waiter and had a wonderful time. With dinner concluded, the waiter set the check down in the middle of the table. That's when it happened. My father did not reach for the check.

In fact, my father did nothing. Conversation continued. Finally, it dawned on me. Me! I was supposed to pick up the check. After all these years, after hundreds of restaurant meals with my parents, after a lifetime of thinking of my father as the one with the bucks, it had all changed. I reached for the check and whipped out my American Express card. My view of myself was suddenly altered. With a stroke of the pen, I was suddenly an adult.

Some people mark off their life in years, others in events. I am one of the latter, and I think of some events as rites of passage. I did not become a young man at a particular year, like 13, but when a kid strolled into the store where I worked and called me "mister." I turned around to see whom he was calling. He repeated it several times—"Mister, mister"—looking straight at me. The realization hit like a punch: Me! He was talking to me. I was suddenly a mister.

personal goals

There have been other milestones. The cops of my youth always seemed to be big, even huge, and of course they were older than I was. Then one day they were neither. In fact, some of them were kids—short kids at that. Another milestone.

The day comes when you suddenly realize that all the football players in the game you're watching are younger than you. Instead of being big men, they are merely big kids. With that milestone goes the fantasy that someday, maybe, you too could be a player—maybe not a football player but certainly a baseball player. I had a good eye as a kid—not much power, but a keen eye—and I always thought I could play the game. One day I realized that I couldn't. Without having ever reached the hill, I was over it.

For some people, the most momentous milestone is the death of a parent. This happened recently to a friend of mine. With the burial of his father came the realization that he had moved up a notch. Of course, he had known all along that this would happen, but until the funeral, the knowledge seemed theoretical at best. As long as one of your parents is alive, you stay in some way a kid. At the very least, there remains at least one person whose love is unconditional.

For women, a milestone is reached when they can no longer have children. The loss of a life, the inability to create one—they are variations on the same theme. For a childless woman who could control everything in life but the clock, this milestone is cruel one indeed.

I count other, less serious milestones—like being audited by the Internal Revenue Service. As the auditor caught mistake after mistake, I sat there pretending that really knowing about taxes was for adults. I, of course, was still a kid. The auditor was buying none of it. I was a taxpayer, an adult. She all but said, Go to jail.

There have been others. I remember the day when I had a ferocious argument with my son and realized that I could no longer bully him. He was too big and the days when I could just pick him up and take him to his room/isolation cell were over. I needed to persuade, reason. He was suddenly, rapidly, older. The conclusion was inescapable. So was I.

One day you go to your friends' weddings. One day you celebrate the birth of their kids. One day you see one of their kids driving, and one day those kids have kids of their own. One day you meet at parties and then at weddings and then at funerals. It all happens in one day. Take my word for it.

I never thought I would fall asleep in front of the television set as my father did, and as my friends' fathers did, too. I remember my parents and their friends talking about insomnia and they sounded like members of a different species. Not able to sleep? How ridiculous. Once it was all I did. Once it was what I did best.

I never thought that I would eat a food that did not agree with me. Now I meet them all the time. I thought I would never go to the beach and not swim. I spent all of August at the beach and never once went into the ocean. I never thought I would appreciate opera, but now the pathos, the schmaltz and, especially, the combination of voice and music appeal to me. The deaths of Mimi and Tosca move me, and they die in my home as often as I can manage it.

I never thought I would prefer to stay home instead of going to a party, but now I find myself passing parties up. I used to think that people who watched birds were weird, but this summer I found myself watching them, and maybe I'll get a book on the subject. I yearn for a religious conviction I never thought I'd want, exult in my heritage anyway, feel close to ancestors long gone and echo my father in arguments with my son. I still lose.

One day I made a good toast. One day I handled a headwaiter. One day I bought a house. One day—what a day!—I became a father, and not too long after that I picked up the check for my own. I thought then and there it was a rite of passage for me. Not until I got older did I realize that it was one for him, too. Another milestone.

Follow-Up

1. *See the Applied Activity titled "Are You An Adult?" at the end of this readings section.*

2. *In this article, Richard Cohen describes several life events that he called milestones. These milestones caused shifts in how he viewed himself as a person. His identity had added another dimension. We all have these identity milestones, little or great, which tell us that we have changed, that we have entered another phase of life, or that we have shifted some basic way of seeing and being in the world.*

    What have been some of your identity milestones?

admitting I have a drinking problem.
getting out of an abusive relationship.
becoming stable on my own.
becoming me!

3. *Complete the statement "I know I'm getting older when . . ."?*

   ### Samples
   - *I cannot name or tolerate the top 3 rock groups*
   - *I am referred to as* sir *or* ma'am
   - *I read or watch the news*
   - *Cops are my age or younger*
   - *I hear my parent's voice coming out of my mouth*
   - *I really need consistent sleeping hours*
   - *I have a high school reunion*

   Your turn—what are some other indicators that you're getting older?

I'm Not Sick, I'm Just in Love

Katherine Davis

A couple of months ago, I received a phone call from one of my college roommates. We hadn't spoken since our graduation from Barnard College a year ago, and we both had big news to share. Her boyfriend of five years had proposed. I was thrilled for her, but not surprised. Marriage seemed inevitable for two people who have been inseparable for as long as they have. I *was* surprised to hear that they won't be getting married for at least five years. She wants to concentrate on her career.

I, too, am engaged to be married. Unlike my friend, my big news included the start of wedding plans: designing a dress, invitations, menus, engagement parties and bridal showers. While I've probably picked up more copies of brides' magazines than *The Economist* lately, I also want to focus on my career. But since I decided to marry at the age of 23, I've been made to feel as if a career is no longer a viable option. Once I was viewed as a bright young woman with promise. Now I'm dismissed by acquaintances and strangers as being sentenced to an insignificant life. I *am* young, but no younger than women who married a generation ago. The distress and hostility I've encountered has more to do with changing attitudes toward the *role* of wife. When everyone is touting "family values," why does marriage have such a bad rap?

I certainly didn't plan on an early marriage. I didn't intend to get married, ever. I envisioned my future as a broadcast journalist, traveling, meeting international leaders and, more realistically, long days and deadlines—not a husband and kids. Friends predicted I'd be a real-life Murphy Brown: ambitious, self-serving and single.

My quest to become a reporter began at MTV News, where I interned during my last semester at college, and started working as a desk assistant upon graduation. That's where I met my fiancé. Eight years my senior, Wilson has spent most of his adult life abroad and is well versed in everything from Russian literature to motorcycle repair. We found common ground in our career ambitions and agreed to a get-together some night after work to discuss them. Then I avoided him. I convinced myself I was too busy with my senior thesis and job interviews. There was no room for another commitment.

Room *was* made. By the end of last year, we were in love—and engaged. At work, since we'd kept our relationship under wraps, the news of our engagement came as a shock. Wilson was treated to some pats on the back and a celebratory night on the town. Few congratulations were addressed to me, however. I received comments like "You're so young!" or "What about your career?" When I left MTV for print journalism, some co-workers assumed I'd quit to plan my wedding. Others made me feel, as a woman, I was ceding my place in the newsroom to Wilson. One suggested that I not mention my pending nuptials to prospective employers. It might suggest lack of motivation for hard work.

My plans also touched off panic among my girlfriends. It's a return of the domino theory and, to protect themselves, some have chosen not to sympathize with the enemy. I've been taunted that my days of "sowing my wild oats" are over and reproached for secretly wanting a baby right away. (There's even a bet I'll become pregnant by Jan. 31, 1998.) I've been accused of misrepresenting myself during college as someone trying to earn a MRS. degree rather than an education. When "feminist" friends hear that I am taking my husband's name, they act as if I'm forsaking "our" cause. One Saturday afternoon, a friend phoned and I admitted I was spending the day doing laundry—mine and his. Her voice resonated with such pity that I hung up.

New York City, where we live, breeds much of this antagonism toward marriage. I've read that half of Manhattan households consist of single people. Home to the worlds of "Friends" and "Seinfeld," marriage is sort of an anomaly here. One fifth of women in this town over the age of 45 have never been married. Manhattanites aren't exactly diving to catch the bouquet.

I've also experienced prejudice in my hometown in Colorado. At a local store's bridal registry, I walked in wearing a Columbia University sweatshirt and the consultant asked if I'd gone to school there. On hearing that I'd graduated 10 months earlier, she explained that she had a daughter my age. "But she is very involved in her career," she added, presuming that I, selecting a silverware pattern, was not.

Registering at another store brought my mother and me to tears. As I perused the housewares, my mom mistook my interest in cookware to be a sign of impending domesticity and wondered where she'd gone wrong. A former home-ec teacher, my mom always joked that my lowest grade in junior high was earned in her field of expertise. It's not funny when your career-bent daughter wants a Crockpot.

It's been difficult for my mom to watch her daughter choose a husband before establishing a career—as she once did. Throughout my education, she has seen the opportunities made available to me, some that weren't imaginable when she was young. She and my father strove to provide me with the skills to take advantage of these new avenues. In the process, she grew attached to the idea of my becoming a successful professional.

I have no intention of dropping my career goals for marriage. While I'm excited by the prospect of having children, motherhood will not necessarily be the defining feature of my life. And I'll be no worse a wife for having a career. My engagement has made me no less ambitious, hardworking—or a feminist.

During our conversation, my old roommate described her engagement ring, which sits in her jewelry box because she feels people treat her differently when she wears it. I thought she was being a bit foolish. Now I understand her insecurities. Presented with an array of career options, young women today are pressured to reject "traditional" roles.

Wilson and I are fortunate to have a relationship that allows us to be as committed to our professions as we are to each other. Soon I'll be his blushing bride. And my rosy complexion will be from exuberance—not embarrassment.

Follow-Up

1. *Give your ideas on one or more of these statements Davis made:*
   - *Presented with an array of career options, young women today are pressured to reject "traditional" roles.*
   - *The distress and hostility I've encountered has more to do with changing attitudes toward the role of wife. . . . Why does marriage have such a bad rap?*
   - *Since I decided to marry at the age of 23, I've been made to feel as if a career is no longer a viable option.*

- *I have no intention of dropping my career goals for marriage. While I'm excited by the prospect of having children, motherhood will not necessarily be the defining feature of my life. And I'll be no worse a wife for having a career.*
- *I've been accused of misrepresenting myself during college as someone trying to earn a MRS. degree rather than an education.*

2. *Are males faced with these issues if they marry in their early 20's? What, if anything, is different for the male under these same circumstances?*

3. *Davis feels she may be disappointing her parents by marrying before establishing a career. Is this true for most young adult women you know? Young adult males?*

4. *Some facts from the U.S. Census Bureau are listed below. Share your reactions to as many as you want.*
   - *In 1994 the median age of first marriages for women was 24.5; for males, 26.7.*
   - *About 80% of all Americans marry at some point in their lives, and 50% of divorced persons marry a second time.*
   - *In 1993, for the 30–34 group, approximately 30% of the men had never married; approximately 20% of the women had never married.*
   - *There are 6 unmarried couple households for every 100 married couple households.*

The Myth of the Miserable Working Woman

Rosalind C. Barnett
and Caryl Rivers

"You Can't Do Everything," announced a 1989 USA Today *headline on a story suggesting that a slower career track for women might be a good idea.* "Mommy Career Track Sets Off a Furor," *de-claimed the* New York Times *on March 8, 1989, reporting that women cost companies more than men.* "Pressed for Success, Women Careerists Are Cheating Themselves," *sighed a 1989 headline in the* Washington Post, *going on to cite a book about the "unhappy personal lives" of women graduates of the Harvard Business School.* "Women Dis-covering They're at Risk for Heart Attacks," *Gan-nett News Service reported with alarm in 1991.* "Can Your Career Hurt Your Kids? Yes, Say Many Experts," *blared a* Fortune *cover just last May, adding in a chirpy yet soothing fashion, "But smart parents—and flexible companies—won't let it happen."*

If you believe what you read, working women are in big trouble—stressed out, depressed, sick, risking an early death from heart attacks, and so overcome with problems at home that they make inefficient employees at work.

In fact, just the opposite is true. As a re-search psychologist whose career has focused on women and a journalist-critic who has studied the behavior of the media, we have ex-tensively surveyed the latest data and research and concluded that the public is being en-gulfed by a tidal wave of disinformation that has serious consequences for the life and health of every American woman. Since large numbers of women began moving into the work force in the 1970s, scores of studies on their emotional and physical health have painted a very clear picture: Paid employment provides substantial health *benefits* for women. These benefits cut across income and class lines; even women who are working because they have to—not because they want to—share in them.

There is a curious gap, however, between what these studies say and what is generally reported on television, radio, and in newspa-pers and magazines. The more the research shows work is good for women, the bleaker the media reports seem to become. Whether this bizarre state of affairs is the result of a backlash against women, as *Wall Street Journal* reporter Susan Faludi contends in her new book, *Back-lash: The Undeclared War Against American Women,* or of well-meaning ignorance, the ef-fect is the same: Both the shape of national pol-icy and the lives of women are at risk.

Too often, legislation is written and poli-cies are drafted not on the basis of the facts but on the basis of what those in power believe to be the facts. Even the much discussed *Work-force 2000* report, issued by the Department of Labor under the Reagan administration—hardly a hotbed of feminism—admitted that "most current policies were designed for a so-ciety in which men worked and women stayed home." If policies are skewed toward solu-tions that are aimed at reducing women's commitment to work, they will do more than harm women—they will damage companies, managers and the productivity of the American economy.

THE CORONARY THAT WASN'T

One reason the "bad news" about working women jumps to page one is that we're all too willing to believe it. Many adults today grew up at a time when soldiers were returning home from World War II and a way had to be found to get the women who replaced them in industry back into the kitchen. The result was a barrage of propaganda that turned at-home moms into saints and backyard barbecues and station wagons into cultural icons. Many of us still have that outdated postwar map inside our heads, and it leaves us more willing to believe the horror stories than the good news that paid employment is an emotional and medical plus.

In the 19th century it was accepted medical dogma that women should not be educated because the brain and the ovaries could not develop at the same time. Today it's PMS, the wrong math genes or rampaging hormones. Hardly anyone points out the dire predictions that didn't come true.

You may remember the prediction that career women would start having more heart attacks, just like men. But the Framingham Heart Study—a federally funded cardiac project that has been studying 10,000 men and women since 1948—reveals that working women are not having more heart attacks. They're not dying any earlier, either. Not only are women not losing their health advantages; the lifespan gap is actually widening. Only one group of working women suffers more heart attacks than other women: those in low-paying clerical jobs with many demands on them and little control over their work pace, who also have several children and little or no support at home.

As for the recent publicity about women having more problems with heart disease, much of it skims over the important underlying reasons for the increase: namely, that by the time they have a heart attack, women tend to be a good deal older (an average of 67, six years older than the average age for men), and thus frailer, than males who have one. Also, statistics from the National Institutes of Health show that coronary symptoms are treated less aggressively in women—fewer coronary bypasses, for example. In addition, most heart research is done on men, so doctors do not know as much about the causes—and treatment—of heart disease in women. None of these factors have anything to do with work.

But doesn't working put women at greater risk for stress-related illnesses? No. Paid work is actually associated with *reduced* anxiety and depression. In the early 1980s we reported in our book, *Lifeprints* (based on a National Science Foundation–funded study of 300 women), that working women were significantly higher in psychological well-being than those not employed. Working gave them a sense of mastery and control that homemaking didn't provide. More recent studies echo our findings. For example:

- A 1989 report by psychologist Ingrid Waldron and sociologist Jerry Jacobs of Temple University on nationwide surveys of 2,392 white and 892 black women, conducted from 1977 to 1982, found that women who held both work and family roles reported better physical and mental health than homemakers.
- According to sociologists Elaine Wethington of Cornell University and Ronald Kessler of the University of Michigan, data from three years (1985 to 1988) of a continuing federally funded study of 745 married women in Detroit "clearly suggests that employment benefits women emotionally." Women who increase their participa-

tion in the labor force report lower levels of psychological distress; those who lessen their commitment to work suffer from higher distress.

- A University of California at Berkeley study published in 1990 followed 140 women for 22 years. At age 43, those who were homemakers had more chronic conditions than the working women and seemed more disillusioned and frustrated. The working mothers were in good health and seemed to be juggling their roles with success.

In sum, paid work offers women heightened self-esteem and enhanced mental and physical health. It's unemployment that's a major risk factor for depression in women.

DOING IT ALL—AND DOING IT FINE

This isn't true only for affluent women in good jobs; working-class omen share the benefits of work, according to psychologists Sandra Scarr and Deborah Phillips of the University of Virginia and Kathleen McCartney of the University of New Hampshire. In reviewing 80 studies on this subject, they reported that working-class women with children say they would not leave work even if they didn't need the money. Work offers not only income but adult companionship, social contact and a connection with the wider world that they cannot get at home.

Looking at survey data from around the world, Scarr and Phillips wrote that the lives of mothers who work are not more stressful than the lives of those who are at home. So what about the second shift we've heard so much about? It certainly exists: In industrialized countries, researchers found, fathers work an average of 50 hours a week on the job and doing household chores; mothers work an average of 80 hours. Wethington and Kessler found that in daily "stress diaries" kept by husbands and wives, the women report more

stress than the men do. But they also handle it better. In short, doing it all may be tough, but it doesn't wipe out the health benefits of working.

THE ADVANTAGES FOR FAMILIES

What about the kids? Many working parents feel they want more time with their kids, and they say so. But does maternal employment harm children? In 1989 University of Michigan psychologist Lois Hoffman reviewed 50 years of research and found that the expected negative effects never materialized. Most often, children of employed and unemployed mothers didn't differ on measures of child development. But children of both sexes with working mothers have a less sex-stereotyped view of the world because fathers in two-income families tend to do more child care.

However, when mothers work, the quality of non-parental child care is a legitimate worry. Scarr, Phillips and McCartney say there is "near consensus among developmental psychologists and early-childhood experts that child care per se does not constitute a risk factor in children's lives." What causes problems, they report, is poor-quality care and a troubled family life. The need for good child care in this country has been obvious for some time.

What's more, children in two-job families generally don't lose out on one-to-one time with their parents. New studies, such as S. L. Nock and P. W. Kingston's *Time with Children: The Impact of Couples' Work-Time Commitments,* show that when both parents of pre-schoolers are working, they spend as much time in direct interaction with their children as families in which only the fathers work. The difference is that working parents spend more time with their kids on weekends. When only the husband works, parents spend more leisure time with each other. There is a cost to two-income families—the couples lose personal time—but the kids don't seem to pay it.

One question we never used to ask is whether having a working mother could be *good* for children. Hoffman, reflecting on the finding that employed women—both blue-collar and professional—register higher life-satisfaction scores than housewives, thinks it can be. She cites studies involving infants and older children, showing that a mother's satisfaction with her employment status relates positively both to "the quality of the mother-child interaction and to various indexes of the child's adjustment and abilities." For example, psychologists J. Guidubaldi and B. K. Nastasi of Kent State University reported in a 1987 paper that a mother's satisfaction with her job was a good predictor of her child's positive adjustment in school.

Again, this isn't true only for women in high-status jobs. In a 1982 study of sources of stress for children in low-income families, psychologists Cynthia Longfellow and Deborah Belle of the Harvard University School of Education found that employed women were generally less depressed than unemployed women. What's more, their children had fewer behavioral problems.

But the real point about working women and children is that work *isn't* the point at all. There are good mothers and not-so-good mothers, and some work and some don't. When a National Academy of Sciences panel reviewed the previous 50 years of research and dozens of studies in 1982, it found no consistent effects on children from a mother's working. Work is only one of many variables, the panel concluded in *Families That Work,* and not the definitive one.

What is the effect of women's working on their marriages? Having a working wife can increase psychological stress for men, especially older men, who grew up in a world where it was not normal for a wife to work. But men's expectations that they will—and must—be the only provider may be changing. Wethington and Kessler found that a wife's employment could be a significant buffer *against* depression for men born after 1945. Still, the picture of men's psychological well-being is very mixed, and class and expectations clearly play a role. Faludi cites polls showing that young blue-collar men are especially angry at women for invading what they see as their turf as breadwinners, even though a woman with such a job could help protect her husband from economic hardship. But in highly educated, dual-career couples, both partners say the wife's career has enhanced the marriage.

THE FIRST SHIFT: WOMEN AT WORK

While women's own health and the well-being of their families aren't harmed by their working, what effect does this dual role have on their job performance? It's assumed that men can compartmentalize work and home lives but women will bring their home worries with them to work, making them distracted and inefficient employees.

The only spillover went in the other direction: The women brought their good feelings about their work home with them and left a bad day at home behind when they came to work. In fact, Wethington and Kessler found that it was the *men* who brought the family stresses with them to work. "Women are able to avoid bringing the contagion of home stress into the workplace," the researchers write, "whereas the inability of men to prevent this kind of contagion is pervasive." The researchers speculate that perhaps women get the message early on that they can handle the home front, while men are taking on chores they aren't trained for and didn't expect.

THE PERILS OF PART-TIME

Perhaps the most dangerous myth is that the solution to most problems women suffer is for them to drop back—or drop out. What studies actually show is a significant connection between a reduced commitment to work and increased psychological stress. In their Detroit study, Wethington and Kessler noted that women who went from being full-time employees to full-time housewives reported increased symptoms of distress, such as depression and anxiety attacks; the longer a woman worked and the more committed she was to the job, the greater her risk for psychological distress when she stopped.

What about part-time work, that oft-touted solution for weary women? Women who work fewer than 20 hours per week, it turns out, do not get the mental-health work benefit, probably because they "operate under the fiction that they can retain full responsibility for child care and home maintenance," wrote Wethington and Kessler. The result: Some part-timers wind up more stressed-out than women working full-time. Part-time employment also provides less money, fewer or no benefits and, often, less interesting work and a more arduous road to promotion.

That doesn't mean that a woman shouldn't cut down on her work hours or arrange a more flexible schedule. But it does mean she should be careful about jumping on a poorly designed mommy track that may make her a second-class citizen at work.

Many women think that when they have a baby, the best thing for their mental health would be to stay home. Wrong once more. According to Wethington and Kessler, having a baby does not increase psychological distress for working women—*unless* the birth results in their dropping out of the labor force. This doesn't mean that any woman who stays home to care for a child is going to be a wreck. But leaving the work force means opting out of the benefits of being in it, and women should be aware of that.

As soon as a woman has any kind of difficulty—emotional, family, medical—the knee-jerk reaction is to get her off the job. No such solution is offered to men, despite the very real correlation for men between job stress and heart attacks.

What the myth of the miserable working woman obscures is the need to focus on how the *quality* of a woman's job affects her health. Media stories warn of the alleged dangers of fast-track jobs. But our *Lifeprints* study found that married women in high-prestige jobs were highest in mental well-being; another study of life stress in women reported that married career women with children suffered the least from stress. Meanwhile, few media tears are shed for the women most at risk: those in the word-processing room who have no control at work, low pay and little support at home.

Women don't need help getting out of the work force; they need help staying in it. As long as much of the media continues to capitalize on national ignorance, that help will have to come from somewhere else. (Not that an occasional letter to the editor isn't useful.) Men need to recognize that they are not just occasional helpers but vital to the success of the family unit. The corporate culture has to be reshaped so that it doesn't run totally according to patterns set by the white male workaholic. This will be good for men *and* women.

Follow-Up

1. *Give your reactions to one or more of these statements:*
   - *Paid work is actually associated with reduced anxiety and depression . . . heightened self-esteem and enhanced mental and physical health. It's unemployment that's a major risk factor for depression in women.*
   - *Children of employed and unemployed mothers didn't differ on measures of child development.*

- *Having a working wife can increase psychological stress for men, especially older men (born before 1945). . . . Young blue-collar men are especially angry at women for invading what they see as their turf as breadwinners. . . .*
- *Women brought their good feelings about their work home with them and left a bad day at home behind when they came to work.*
- *Women don't need help getting out of the work force; they need help staying in it. The authors found that the women most at risk mentally and physically were those in low-paying clerical jobs of many demands, having little control over a work pace, having several children, and little home support.*
- *Women who went from being full-time employees to full-time housewives reported increased symptoms of distress. . . .*

Choose any other statement that strikes you, and comment on it.

2. *Talk to women who do not work, who work part-time, and who work full-time. See if their views match those of this article.*

3. *For women: What are your preferences regarding work/career choices throughout your life? For men: If you have (or will have) a wife or companion, what are your preferences regarding her work/career?*

On Being a Man

Sam Keen

The year I was seventeen I received many messages from my classmates, my family, and my culture about what was required to be a *real man*:

> *Join the fraternity.*
> *Get a letter in football, baseball, or basketball.*
> *Screw a lot of girls.*
> *Be tough; fight if anybody insults you or*
> *   your girl.*
> *Don't show your feelings.*
> *Drink lots of beer (predrug era).*
> *Be nice—don't fight or drink.*
> *Dress right—like everybody else: penny*
> *   loafers, etc.*
> *Get a good job, work hard and make a lot of*
> *   money.*
> *Get your own car.*
> *Be well liked, popular.*

My grandmother gave me a Bible with a note that said: "Read this every day, Big Boy—it will make you a *real man*." I felt I was probably destined to fail at being a man. I didn't drink, smoke, or swear. I was the only one in P.S. duPont High School in Wilmington, Delaware, who wore cowboy boots. I did not shave, had only a sparse crop of pubic hair, and was embarrassed in the locker room. I never got a letter in a major sport. To this day I avoid anyone who was in my high school class, especially old football heroes. I hated fraternities. The only thing that saved me from being a complete geek was that I had a car and a girlfriend, although the car was only a Model A Ford and the girlfriend was not a cheerleader.

Today I look at an old picture of that seventeen-year-old boy. He is dressed for the senior prom in a rented white dinner jacket—lanky, loose-jointed, too-large hands on hips, the pose clearly adopted from Gary Cooper. Next to him stands his girlfriend, Janet, already looking mature, dressed in the traditional white gown with the traditional purple orchid, filled with the traditional dreams of settling down. They are both virgins. I see hints in his ungainly adolescent body of the man he will become. In the forward-leaning head, slightly sunken chest, and forward-curved shoulders is the form of a question mark. In the awkwardness of his pose I see him trying to be suave for the occasion and play the man while he still feels himself to be a boy. I know he will feel boyish, not a man among men, well into his mature years.

But it is his face that moves me most. Open. Shining. Filled with a strange power of innocence and strong dreams. His mask of sophistication hides the painful sensitivity he fears is a mark of his inadequacy as a man. I do not see, but remember well, the loneliness, the uncertainty, the feeling of being both proud and embarrassed by the secret life the boy was living.

His clandestine life included many activities not on any list of requirements for being a *real man*: keeping a diary; exploring nearby woods and longing for the wilderness; sleeping under the stars; taking long walks alone; waiting and watching to see what would happen when a cowbird laid its eggs in a vireo's nest; masturbating and imagining the woman of his dreams; wondering about the limits of his mind; exploring his dark moods; writing poetry; reading books and playing with ideas; loving his parents; agonizing about war, poverty, injustice, torture; wanting to do something to make the world better.

Today I honor the boy, knowing that he knew far more about manhood than he thought he knew. For instance, the week after the prom, he set out on his walkabout, a trip across the U. S., working on a wheat harvest, ranches, carnivals, etc. Hidden in his young heart was a craving to discover his own definition of manhood. Father to the man who is writing this book, he did not know it but he had already set out on a pilgrimage, a quest to find the Grail.

Ask most any man, "How does it feel to be a man these days? Do you feel manhood is honored, respected, celebrated?" Those who pause long enough to consider their gut feelings will likely tell you they feel blamed, demeaned, and attacked. But their reactions may be pretty vague. Many men feel as if they are involved in a night battle in a jungle against an unseen foe. Voices from the surrounding darkness shout hostile challenges: "Men are too aggressive. Too soft. Too insensitive. Too macho. Too power-mad. Too much like little boys. Too wimpy. Too violent. Too obsessed with sex. Too detached to care. Too busy. Too rational. Too lost to lead. Too dead to feel." Exactly what we are supposed to become is not clear.

Men have only recently begun to explore new visions and definitions of manhood. At no time in recent history have there been so many restless, questioning men. Granted, this yeasty brotherhood is still a minority, but it is a powerful ferment. As yet, there is little literature that speaks to these questing men. The most spiritually adventurous men of our time have moved out on the frontier beyond the reporters, the popularizers, the psychologists, the so-called "experts" about men. Go into a good bookstore and ask if they have a section on women's studies and you will be shown a rich variety of books on social theory, linguistics, biographies of forgotten heroines, women's poetry, studies of the goddess, histories of feminism, etc. Ask if they have a

men's studies section and you will be shown a small one with titles relating to (1) gay experience; (2) diatribes about men's inadequacies and failures (*Men Who Hate Women and the Women Who Love Them, What to Do When He Won't Change, The Peter Pan Syndrome,* etc., ad nauseam); or (3) something called "men's liberation," which sounds suspiciously like warmed-over feminism with a reverse twist. Not much here to stir the head, the heart, or the gonads.

I would guess that a majority of men never break free, never define manhood by weighing and testing their own experience. And the single largest reason is that we never acknowledge the primal power WOMAN wields over us. The average man spends a lifetime denying, defending against, trying to control, and reacting to the power of WOMAN. He is committed to remaining unconscious and out of touch with his own deepest feelings and experience.

The chains that bind us most tightly are those we refuse to acknowledge.

We begin to learn the mysteries unique to maleness only when we separate from WOMAN'S world. But before we can take our leave we must first become conscious of the ways in which we arc enmeshed, incorporated, inwombed, and defined by WOMAN. Otherwise we will be controlled by what we haven't remembered.

The secret men seldom tell, and often do not know (consciously) is the extent to which our lives circle around our relationships to WOMAN. It takes half a lifetime of struggle for us to win a separate identity. We are haunted by WOMAN in her many manifestations. She is the center around which our lives circle. WOMAN is the mysterious ground of our being that we cannot penetrate. She is the audience before whom the dramas of our lives are played out. She is the judge who pronounces us guilty or innocent. She is the Garden of Eden from which we are exiled and the paradise for which our bodies long. She is the goddess who can grant us salvation and the frigid mother who denies us. She has a mythic power over us. She is at once terrifying and fascinating.

We have invested so much of our identity, committed so much of our energy, and squandered so much of our power in trying to control, avoid, conquer, or demean women because we are so vulnerable to their mysterious power over us. Like sandy atolls in a monsoon-swept ocean, the male psyche is in continual danger of being inundated by the feminine sea. And this fragility is not psychological, not neurotic, not a symptom of abnormality, but is an ontological fact rooted in our being. Those men who allow themselves to feel it are stronger, not weaker, than those who pretend they are self-sufficient and autonomous. We emerged from WOMAN and we naturally fear that the individual self we have managed to erect, like a makeshift seawall, may be lost.

At this point the voice of common sense is likely to intrude and object. "Who is this female monster you portray as a black hole into which the male psyche disappears? WOMAN a threat? How? Be clear!" But herein lies the problem. Clarity about WOMAN and women is a hard-won prize that comes near the end, not at the beginning, of a man's journey. Before a man struggles to become conscious of the nature and limits of his virility, *the essence of the threat he feels from WOMAN lies in its vagueness.* She is the soft darkness at the core of his psyche, part of him, not a stranger. We are linked to her in our deepest being, but she remains hidden in a haze just beyond the horizon of our reason and never comes out of the shadows to meet us face to face.

One of the major tasks of manhood is to explore the unconscious feelings that surround our various images of WOMAN, to dispel false mystification, to dissolve the vague sense of threat and fear, and finally to learn to respect and love the strangeness of womankind. It may be useful to think about sexual-spiritual maturation—the journey of manhood—as a process of changing WOMAN into women into Jane (or one certain woman), of learning to see members of the opposite sex not as archetypes or members of a class but as individuals. It is the WOMAN in our heads, more than the women in our beds or boardrooms, who causes most of our problems. And these archetypical creatures—goddesses, bitches, angels, Madonnas, castrators, witches, Gypsy maidens, earth mothers—must be exorcised from our minds and hearts before we can learn to love women. So long as our house is haunted by the ghost of WOMAN we can never live gracefully with any woman. If we continue to deny that she lives in the shadows she will continue to have power over us.

The popular cliché says that men think and do, women feel and emote. It's a half-truth worth playing with. Most of us learned that real men were supposed to control their feelings. From childhood onward we heard that "men don't cry." We learned to work hard, take a lot of punishment, and not bitch about it. Remember the pride we took in climbing mountains, ignoring the cold, running until we were exhausted, taking hard punches, pushing the limits, driving all night? No pain, no gain. That's the right stuff.

Little did we understand that by doing the manly thing, girding up our loins, pulling in our guts, pushing out our chests, tightening our jaws, and constricting our breathing, we forced most feelings into exile in our unconscious. It is hard to experience a lot of emotion when the body's potential for motion is constricted.

Don't ask me to make logical sense of this, but I know it to be a psychological fact that aging and death come as a terrible surprise to men. "Old age is the most unexpected of all the things that can can happen to a man," Leon Trotsky said. In his eighties, Joseph Campbell told me, "I don't feel like an old man. I feel like a young man who has something wrong with him." Listen and you will hear men talk about their rebellion against aging. We "do not go gentle into that good night." Perhaps this feeling is uniquely American, a product of a youth-worshiping, obsessively optimistic culture. Or maybe men find it difficult to grow old because we were never allowed to be young.

And then there is the grief over our lost innocence. The world into which most men were initiated and indoctrinated required us prematurely to put away childish things—play, imagination, sensuality, carefree wandering, experimenting with different roles, adventure. By our midtwenties we had manfully shouldered the load of work and family.

As we push deeper into the interior of a man's psyche, we discover that in back of the facade of toughness and control there is an entire landscape of undifferentiated fears, with all manner of beasts, demons, and ghosts lurking in the shadows. And to win our soul or rescue our self from its entrapment in our personality, we have to do battle with a legion of fears we never knew we had.

How long ago was it that we men forced our fear into exile and condemned it to live in the shadow? Evolution demanded that the male be tough enough to repel the onslaught of saber-toothed tigers, or more recently, corporate raiders. If you want the no-nonsense definition of a man, skip the claim that we are *Homo sapiens* and go directly to "fearless" and its synonyms—undaunted, bold, intrepid, audacious, brave, courageous, valiant, valorous, doughty, daring, adventurous, heroic, gallant, plucky, gritty.

I can hardly remember a time when I wasn't working at being fearless. Can you? It started with seemingly innocent advice and guidance from grown men, big brothers, and sometimes mothers: "Don't be a scaredy-cat. There is nothing to be afraid of." Early on, we learned that fear could be controlled in the same way as grief: Lock your jaw to prevent it from quivering, tighten your chest, and push yourself to the edge of danger to prove yourself. We flirted with fearful things: walking

through graveyards at midnight; running through the turf of rival gangs; sneaking into a haunted house; stealing a car; jumping from the cliff high above the swimming hole; taking a dare; going to the whorehouse. And, finally, we went to war—without ever acknowledging the depths of our terror. Every time we resisted yielding to the seduction of fear, we fell more deeply in love with our own image of ourselves as heroes. We are men; we are unafraid. We can do what must be done.

But we paid a terrible price for our conquest of fear, for viewing ourselves as actual or potential heroes.

For starters, we reduced our world to an arena within which courage is constantly demanded, and other virtues—patience, honesty, kindness, contentment, intelligence, wisdom—are not cultivated.

Perhaps the greatest price men have paid for their obsession with fearlessness is to have become tough on the outside but empty within. We are hollow men. The connection between fearlessness and feelinglessness should be obvious. Fear, along with grief, joy, and anger, is one of the primal feelings. And the ability to feel is indivisible. Repress awareness of any one feeling and all feelings are dulled. When we refuse to allow fear we correspondingly lose the ability to wonder. When we repress our grief we blunt our capacity to experience joy. The same nerve endings are required for weeping and dancing, fear and ecstasy.

Men and women seem to have different styles of fearing. Men's fears focus around loss of what we experience as our independence, and women's around the loss of significant relationships. We most fear engulfment, anything that threatens to rob us of our power and control. Women most fear abandonment, isolation, loss of love. Traditionally, women have been expected to be more fearful than men. But experience and hearsay have convinced me that men are more fearful of death than women. When we get sick and our flesh no longer rises to the dictates of our will, we feel the Reaper, the Raper, coming for us and we panic. Men make lousy patients. Ask any doctor. Disease and disability frighten us more than they do women, who have known from first menstruation and childbirth that mortality is often accompanied by cramping and pain and that we are born in order to lose control. Sickness raises the specter of all that men have been taught to fear: weakness, dependency, passivity.

Men usually do not talk much about their sexual fears and disappointments. Sex is a big thing for us. And we judge it in more absolute terms than women do. It is either/or. Up or down. And should our erector set fail or collapse in the middle of the job, the most sophisticated of us still suffers a degree of em-

CARRYING TO MANY BURDENS

"Carrying Too Many Burdens" by Tom McCain. Copyright © 1996.

barrassment. Liberated women a generation ago were confessing in *Ms.* magazine how often they faked orgasm. But no man has yet been able to write an article, "How I Faked an Erection." And no matter how many times women have told us it is the tenderness and sensuality that counts, we still carry around scorecards and rating systems in our minds.

There is no how-to guide to the process of becoming a full-summed and spirited man. To suggest there are techniques to achieve authentic manhood would be to devalue the dignity we can achieve only by struggling to become conscious and compassionate. We win our souls after long years of practicing the discipline of awareness and abiding in fear and trembling until we learn, at last, to rest content with our grandeur and baseness.

Men who are beginning to nibble on the apple of consciousness often ask "Where do we start? How do we do it?" The answer is simple: Begin where you are. No esoteric cult, enlightened guru, holy ashram, secret gnostic practice, or all-knowing psychotherapist is necessary. Once a man or a woman crosses the great divide that separates unconscious living from the quest to become more conscious, any event is an invitation to awareness. In India there is an old saying: "When the student is ready the guru appears." To a man who wants to know who he is, and is willing to change in accordance with what he learns, the world and everyday experience are his teachers. If I have a fight with my wife, it is an occasion to reflect on the way I deal with womankind, conflict, anger, violence, resentment, blame, or guilt. If I find myself marooned in a blizzard at a truck stop in Wyoming, it is an opportunity to meditate on how I cope with captivity, boredom, and the inability to control circumstances.

Although there are no techniques that can guarantee us certain and safe passage, valuable assistance, and companionship in sharing the lore of the journey are available from fellow travelers.

Reflection without social action, the inner journey without the practice of virtue, is sterile. And vice versa. Introversion and extroversion are the yin and yang of a balanced life.

There is no end to the ways we can express a spirited and careful sense of manhood. Recently I have come across men who have chosen to exercise their care by: becoming big brothers to fatherless boys; creating a breeding program that rescued Peregrine falcons from extinction; going into hospitals and holding abandoned babies born to drug-addicted mothers; helping to finance a shelter for battered women; working as a volunteer in a hospice; teaching English to recent immigrants; growing gardens in vacant city lots; creating a computerized system of communication for mute children; rejuvenating a local Democratic party; lobbying to make television more interactive and responsive to community needs.

Find an appropriate vehicle for your passion. In general, it seems best to focus your attention and energy on one social ill so you may become effective.

In the end, there are only two rules: Remember yourself. Practice compassion. And, now that I think about it, they amount to the same thing.

Follow-Up

1. *Keen lists the qualities his culture said were necessary for being a real man. Are these still important today for men? He also talks about hiding some of his traits because they did not fall into the ways of being a real man. If you*

*are a man, have you experienced this also? If you are a woman, have you no-
ticed this hiding of certain traits in men you know? See also the "Gender
Role: Positive and Negative" applied exercise at the end of this section.*

2. *Give your reactions to one or more of these statements:*
   - *Aging and death come as a terrible surprise to men.*
   - *For many men the path to vital manhood involves first grieving the ab-
     sence of fathers and then, if their fathers are living, making a renewed ef-
     fort to establish a new relationship.*
   - *Perhaps the greatest price men have paid for their obsession with fearless-
     ness is to have become tough on the outside but empty within. We are hol-
     low men. . . . Repress awareness of any one feeling and all feelings are
     dulled."*
   - *Men's fears focus around loss of what we experience as our independence,
     and women's around the loss of significant relationships.*
   - *Men usually do not talk much about their sexual fears and disappointments.*

3. *Keen says that many men feel blamed, demeaned, and attacked. Men are criticized for contradictory qualities, e.g., too aggressive and too soft, too macho
   and too much like little boys, too interested in sex and not interested enough
   (see the article for other examples). For men: Do you agree with this contention? For women: Ask the men you know if they agree with this argument.*

4. *Keen argues that to learn the unique male essence, a man must first learn
   how his life is and has been influenced by the idea of WOMAN. Then he must
   separate from WOMAN's world to explore what it means to be male, and
   how to relate to real women (see the article for more discussion). What are
   your reactions to this belief?*

From Both Sides

Stop a woman in mid-sentence with the question, "What are you feeling right now?" and you might have to wait a bit while she reruns the mental tape to capture the moment just passed. But, more than likely, she'll be able to do it successfully. More than likely, she'll think for a while and come up with an answer.

The same is not true of a man. For him, a similar question usually will bring a sense of wonderment that one would even ask it, followed quickly by an uncomprehending and puzzled response. "What do you mean?" he'll ask. "I was just talking," he'll say.

To a woman, the world men live in seems a lonely one—a world in which their fears of exposing their sadness and pain, their anxiety about allowing their vulnerability to show, even to a woman they love, is so deeply rooted inside them that, most often, they can only allow it to happen "late at night in the dark."

Yet, if we listen to what men say, we will hear their insistence that they *do* speak of what's inside them, *do* share their thoughts and feelings with the women they love. "I tell her, but she's never satisfied," they complain. "No matter how much I say, it's never enough," they grumble.

From both sides, the complaints have merit. The problem lies not in what men don't say, however, but in what's not there—in what, quite simply, happens so far out of consciousness that it's not within their reach. For men have integrated all too well the lessons of their childhood—the experiences that taught them to repress and deny their inner thoughts, wishes, needs, and fears; indeed, not even to notice them. It's real, therefore, that the kind of inner thoughts and feelings that are readily accessible to a woman generally are unavailable to a man. When he says, "I don't know what I'm feeling," he isn't necessarily being intransigent and withholding. More than likely, he speaks the truth.

Note: From *Intimate Strangers: Men and Women Together,* by L. Rubin, 1983, New York: Harper & Row.

If I Were a Car, I'd Be a Lemon

Denise Karuth

This morning the plumber for my building stopped by. I assured him that my barking Labrador retriever wouldn't bite by explaining that she was a seeing eye dog.

"You aren't blind are you?"

"Yes, but I used to be able to see better."

"But you're . . . you're in a wheelchair . . . You're not," he hesitated, "a cripple, too, are you?"

"I have multiple sclerosis," I answered. "Some of us just have all the luck."

"Holy Jesus! God bless you, ma'am. I'm really sorry. God bless you. If you ever have any trouble with your sink or electricity you just call this number." He placed his card on the arm of the couch. "Call any time, even at night. Just tell them you're a handicapped apartment and they'll come right out. God bless you. Jesus God!"

Sometimes the reactions are even stronger.

I would never willingly cause pain to anyone, so it makes me sad when perfect strangers walk up to me and burst into tears. My first reaction is to think that their tears are somehow my fault. As it happens, some of the people who cry have lost family members or friends to disabling illness, and in two instances, deaf senior citizens cried from a sense of empathy and community with me. In most cases, though, the tears are shed because of peoples' bleak notions of what life must be like for me, the "helpless blind cripple."

I'm not talking only about "the man in the street." The same misconceptions are held as well by students and professionals. Back when I was "just" blind, a middle-aged man passed me on campus and remarked to his companion, "Oh my God, Martha. Look at that. She's blind!"

"Yes," I replied, "but she isn't deaf!"

Then, of course, there are the rehabilitation counselors and the doctors, professionals who deal with disabled people *on a regular basis*. How much they, too, have yet to learn. For example, during my last eye exam at a leading teaching hospital in Boston, one of the top ophthalmologists said (in my presence) to three of his students: "When the retinal damage is not too severe, many of these patients can lead a normal life. But in a case like this, a normal life is impossible."

This pro may have known about my eyes. He knew very little about me.

Another doctor once told me, "You can't possibly have MS. Lightning just doesn't strike twice in the same place." Would that he had been right.

I would like to be able to sit people down and say, "Look, I appreciate your concern, but my life isn't that bad. Sure, it's not quite uninterrupted bliss, but whose life is? It's a good life. I work and play and have friends and make love and mistakes and get bored now and again just like you. So put your handkerchiefs away. First impressions aside, I'm a lot more like you than you probably imagine."

MORNING THOUGHTS

It's 6:30 a.m., and the solar alarm clock beckons through the patio doors; it refuses to be ignored. I savor a few last moments of rest and begin to plan the day ahead. It's Saturday. My weekend shower and hairwash are behind me, as are bladder irrigation and bowel care; with regard to personal care, this should be an easy day. I read over a long list of ongoing projects and responsibilities compiled over the last 2 days and select several items to work on. (With MS, memory can be affected, and mine needs all the help it can get; hence, the list.)

What's this? A Stravinsky attack! I am back at Symphony Hall where last night I heard the Dumbarton Oaks Concerto, a piece long familiar to me from my years as a music major and an orchestral musician. I must hear it again—now—and am compelled to roll over in bed to search for it in a small box of cassettes. I find it and slip it in the deck.

Having been an orchestral musician was one of the high points of my life. Orchestral playing has to be one of the most complex and beautiful group endeavors (a team sport, if you will) yet devised by humanity. Football pales to insignificance in comparison.

As a 17 year old who had been ardently playing double bass for only 2 years, Chamber Orchestra helped me discover the exhilaration of overcoming overwhelming inexperience, the joy of sharing in the creation of something unsurpassingly wonderful, and of intimate involvement with a plane of music that I would have thought far beyond my understanding.

My intense involvement with music was like an express train to enlightenment: Regardless of what happens at the end of the line, one is always grateful for the ticket. People often wonder that I am not bitter about having to give up my orchestral playing. Sometimes I miss it so much that I cry. Mostly, though, I am grateful for having had the opportunity and for having learned, importantly, from it. So I cannot complain. My life now presents me with many of the same challenges and opportunities as did Stravinsky's music. The stakes, of course, are higher, but the price of defeat is more than I am willing to pay.

The joy of living with meaning and with purpose is worth considerable effort. In the long run, I do not have a great deal of control over what is happening to me physically. But if I let my physical disability paralyze my spirit, my life would become a well of self-pity, anger, and despair. I cannot allow that to happen.

THE NORMAL ASPECTS

What's my life been like? I was born 2 months prematurely in November 1954, the middle child of three. My family lived in the Adirondack Mountains and in Buffalo, New York. I attended public schools in Cheektowaga and Amherst, both neighbors to Buffalo. In 1972 I won a New York State Regents' Scholarship that paid my tuition to the State University of New York at Buffalo. In 1976 I graduated magna cum laude with a degree in music. That September, my brother Ed, our closest friend Fred, and I moved to Boston where I attended graduate school and received a master's degree in rehabilitation counseling,

My faith education stressed the importance of serving others and working for justice and peace. I am a member of the local chapters of the American Friends' Service Committee, Mobilization for Survival, Amnesty International, and IMPACT, a national ecumenical political action network. I have also lobbied at both state and national levels concerning U.S. involvement in Latin America, U.S. food policy, nuclear disarmament, civil rights for the disabled, and human services legislation and cutbacks. I have supported the Infant Formula Action Coalition, INFACT, which fights the unethical promotion of infant formula in Third World countries and helped organize a Legal Defense Fund for a friend who was unjustly arrested at the Seabrook nuclear power plant site in New Hampshire (all charges against him were later dropped). I have written a review of an accessible art exhibit for the Cambridge women's magazine *Sojourner*, and have had requests to do further writing. I also have been involved with two area food co-ops.

For fun, I run Irene, my black Labrador retriever, around Jamaica Pond every week in good weather. I entertain and visit friends, play some piano and recorder, and take walks in my motorized wheelchair either with friends or on my own.

So much for the many "normal" aspects of my life. As I focus on my experience as a disabled individual, I hope that you, the reader, will not lose sight of the similarity of the life we share.

COUSIN CAROL'S PREGNANT?

Being legally blind, with a small amount of residual vision, is like living in a bizarre fun house where what you see is not necessarily what you get. First off, I can see things up close far better than things any distance away. I can see my fingers, for example, if I hold them 2 inches from my face, but I cannot see my toes (although, when the lighting is right, I can see a blur where my foot is). If the contrast is right, I can make out Irene's dark shape; but, then, I have also mistaken a low stool or my black skirt or my black coat lying on the bed for Irene, even in the best light.

As my sight deteriorated, I found myself asking questions of store mannequins, I mistook full-length mirrors for doorways, and I tried to find the "Push for Walk" button on trees.

Many people think that either you can see or you can't. How difficult it is to write about vision, since no common vocabulary exists that adequately explains the variability of sight.

Being blind with residual vision means that you "see" your relatives and friends on the Boston trolleys and busses . . . even though those relatives never left Buffalo. It means looking both ways before crossing the street and then walking out into the side of a schoolbus. It means entering an unfamiliar room and being visually bombarded by confusing patterns of light and dark. It means getting so accustomed to familiar places that your friends accuse you of being able to see, or worse, they forget to warn you about newly placed obstacles.

Being blind means getting so thoroughly lost that sometimes you have no idea where you are, much less how to get where you're going. It means having people come up to you in the street, say "Hi!" and disappear, before you can figure out who they were. (*Always* identify yourself to your blind friends, especially if your meeting occurs in a place where they're not used to seeing you.)

Being blind means not knowing that Aunt Trudy has lost weight, or that cousin Carol is 8 months pregnant (until you embrace them). It means brushing up against wet paint, waltzing down the street with silver-streaked coat and hair, and wondering why people are taking notice of you. It means being the only person in the theater who does not dive under a chair when Audrey Hepburn's ankle is grabbed by her assailant in "Wait Until Dark." It means being utterly confused by cars making right and left turns on red. It means spending too much time looking for housekeys, dark glasses, the checkbook, or the vegetable steamer. And it means knowing how to take notes into exams by a method so wonderfully clever that I will not reveal it here.

In my case being blind is compounded by poor memory, difficulty with sense of touch, and the fact that I rely on others to do so much for me that things are often put away without my knowing where to find them again.

In short, being blind means having to become adept at assembling an image of reality from a jumble of jigsaw puzzle pieces—and doing so in the shortest possible time.

MS. It stands for multiple sclerosis, a chronic, disabling, neurologic disease. In my book it also stands for the Marquis de Sade, who, if given the chance to invent a disease, would have been hard pressed to come up with anything more diabolical.

No one knows what causes MS or how to cure it. There isn't even a fool-proof diagnostic test to see if you've got it. Many MS'ers are told that their symptoms are caused by depression, anxiety, hysteria, and even conversion reaction. It's not uncommon for as many as 8 years to elapse before the diagnosis is confirmed.

MS presents with dozens of different symptoms and affects each individual who has it quite differently. Textbook cases of MS are found only in textbooks.

One of the most disabling aspects of the disease is fatigue. There are 168 hours in a week. In a good week I can spend about 15 hours away from home in a wheelchair doing things like working, socializing, attending meetings and church, and the like. About 85% of my time is spent in bed in a mixture of work, resting up, and planning ahead. Being able to condense much of life into 15 hours a week and developing strategies for a constructive invalidism should earn me an honorary degree as a management consultant.

When I finally moved into an accessible apartment and acquired my two electric wheelchairs (the second because my first was unsuitable for outdoor use), the sense of freedom came rushing in like a wave. The second day I had my outdoor chair, I took it and Irene on an 8 mile walk, four times longer than any walk I'd been able to take in 5 years! The wheelchair had liberated me from the limits of my walking, and from a fair amount of the pain that walking and standing had intensified.

There are times now when I almost take for granted my ability to glide down streets for distances that were formerly unthinkable. I pass places where I spent hours waiting for buses to go distances I can now wheelchair in minutes. I remember how much it hurt to stand and wait for trains and buses, how I sat down on curbs and on floors of trolleys, banks, and supermarkets in an attempt to lessen the overwhelming pain and fatigue. I remember the times I cried walking down the street, doing dishes, or waiting for transit.

Whose turn is it to ask for a ride to church? (My dislike of asking people for rides to church is outmatched only by my love of choir, which rehearses earlier than the local wheelchair transit service can get me there.) Some would think that dependency and illness simplify life in that one is no longer faced with the burdens of work and self-reliance. On the contrary, a severely disabled person generally has more details to keep track of and a harder time doing it.

An able-bodied person does not have to:

- Know exactly where everything is in the house (from Elmer's Glue and electrical tape to hair barrettes and catheter clamps) because the able-bodied person can easily get up and search for things. A disabled person who spends a great deal of time in bed has to be able to tell others where things can be found.
- Set aside substantial amounts of time or plan in advance for things like bowel movements and catheter irrigation.
- Plan activities 5 business days in advance to meet the requirements of the wheelchair transit system.
- Make sure that a list of approximately 20 medical and surgical supplies are in stock and close at hand, along with whatever prescription drugs are required.
- Keep a particularly close watch on the budget so he or she can afford to pay attendants even when the reimbursement checks from Medicaid are 3 to 4 months behind.
- Budget time so that not more than 5 hours a day are spent out of bed.
- Hassle with things like wheelchair acquisition, maintenance, and repair or bills that providers did not submit to Medicaid.

In general, the less you are able to do for yourself, the more health problems you have that require specialized care. Also, as it gets harder to remember things, the more things there are to be remembered, planned, and kept track of.

The more disabled you are, the more of a magician you have to be simply to lead a normal life.

My best friend is most remarkable. She has congenital deformities of both hands, no intelligible speech, and she functions at a 3- to 4-year level. She is nearsighted, color blind, short statured, and dependent on others for assistance with personal care. She is also black, which many would agree is an additional handicap in today's society.

Yet, after a 3-month vocational training program, and with only a minimum of adaptive equipment, my best friend is now successfully employed in a skilled job that many able-bodied individuals would find daunting.

My best friend's name is Irene. Irene is my guide dog.

She has a black silky coat that looks like it's been polished, and a wonderfully expressive face with big brown eyes that could melt glaciers. Her favorite pastimes are eating, sleeping, playing, and being lovable. Her favorite food is virtually anything organic.

Irene, I am told, is a Greek word meaning peace. My best friend couldn't have a better name.

Irene is loyalty incarnate. She even goes with me into the too-little stalls in public bathrooms. As I write this, she is sleeping in a chair at the foot of my bed. The space is much too cramped for her, but she prefers to stay there, close to me, rather than stretching out comfortably on the double bed or the couch in the other room.

Irene and I have been together for the past 5½-years. Twenty-four hours a day. Seven days a week. We've enjoyed a truly symbiotic relationship.

How does Irene guide me? In the wheelchair I am so close to the ground that I can hold the leather leash very near to her collar. In this way, I'm able to follow her moves without having to hold the metal harness. She, of course, stops for curbs and steps, just as she did when I could walk. But now, in addition, she aims for curb-cuts and driveways.

Oh love of my life, dog of my dreams, hound of my heart. How car I possibly describe this relationship of ours? Should I write of our first week in training school when we were waiting to cross Massachusetts Avenue? You were eager and pulling my arm, but I told you that the light was against us. "Relax," I said. You looked up at me as if to say, "You mean that?" and promptly lay down (in complete disregard of standard guide dog behavior). Or should I tell about the time we went to see the Boston Ballet and you reacted to a bizarre, musically dissonant piece by climbing in terror upon my lap? Or should I write about the 160 or more days we've spent together in various hospitals? How you always knew when to put on the "Lassie act" to impress administrators and Nursing Supervisors.

Remember the time we walked on the subway platform and a disturbed lady greeted us with a cry of "Lord, strike down this demon dog led by a demon!"? Or when you had a gland infection and couldn't wag your tail? Or when you held your ground, even after I'd given the "Forward" command, and saved me from being hit by a car on Newbury Street?

Maybe I should write about how you joyously proceed with choir on Sunday mornings, snore during the sermon, and always know when the worship is over. Or about all the great romps we've had together. (How you love to play and make friends.) Or about how I'm convinced I can tell what you're thinking at any point in time.

I should write about your talent for being able to remember routes we've taken or people we've met only once before. Or about your adaptability in learning to locate curb-cuts, driveways, and elevators. Or your eagerness to shepherd others who travel with me. Maybe I should even mention that I've only run over your paws once in the 2 years I've been in a wheelchair.

I'm so proud of you that I don't care if people stare as we glide together down the street with your leash in my left hand and the wheelchair control in my right.

All in all, you are my pride, my love, and my joy. I can't conceive of life without you. If someone gave me a choice between losing my right arm or losing you permanently, I would part, reluctantly, with my right arm.

But then, what are best friends for?

MY BODY, MY WIMP

Right now it is 8:45 on a Sunday night, and I've been in bed for 5 hours. I want to continue to write, but my body wants to sleep. Can you remember being a little kid and wanting to stay up late, but your mother wouldn't let you? It's frustrating and aggravating to have a mother who never gives in, not even once. Sometimes I want to shout: "I'm 27 years old! Can't I even stay up until 10:00?" But I know from long experience that my protests are of no avail, that my only option is to give in. But not before I negotiate.

"Give me just 20 minutes," I say. "Maybe even 15." I find that I negotiate with my body a lot. "If we go to Jamaica Pond this afternoon and to choir this evening, I promise to stay in all day tomorrow." Or, "I know you're tired, but it's an important meeting, and I really should be there." I even apologize to it: "Chastity (one of my nicknames for my genital area), I'm sorry. Being catheterized is a bitch. What can I say? Let's hope we don't have to do it again for awhile."

For years before it became irrefutably clear that my increasing weakness, fatigue, and pain were the result of illness, I was at war with my body, always pushing it beyond its limits. Now I realize that I treated it like a traitor instead of a besieged ally. I gave it years of grief that it did nothing to deserve,

Time's up. It's 9:00. I got my 15 minutes in. Now I'm negotiating with a body that is busy spacing out. "Let's put the writing board away, take our evening medications, pull up the covers, and go to sleep."

I'll have to leave the lights on since Fred is out. I used to feel badly that I had to trouble someone else to close doors and turn out lights that I couldn't get to. The paradox of their physical closeness and inaccessible distance hit home. Now I rarely think about it. I guess that's adjustment.

It's 9:05, and I'm reluctantly going to sleep. That's adjustment, too. "You know, body," I tease affectionately, "you're really a wimp."

Follow-Up

1. *If you are not physically disabled to a marked degree: Think of actual instances in your life when you have seen or interacted with physically disabled persons. Describe your thoughts and feelings from these encounters. Are you confused on how to talk to a physically person or to know what is "proper"?*

   For the physically disabled individual: What have been your experiences with abled persons? Were they similar to those described by Denise Karuth?
2. *Select one or more of these statements and offer your reactions:*
   - *I do not have a great deal of control over what is happening to me physically. But if I let my physical disability paralyze my spirit, my life would become a well of self-pity, anger, and despair.*

- *As I focus on my experience as a disabled individual, I hope that you, the reader, will not lose sight of the similarity of the life we share.*
- *To her 'best friend' Irene, Denise says "If someone gave me a choice between losing my right arm or losing you permanently, I would part, reluctantly, with my right arm."*
- *I was at war with my body, always pushing it beyond its limits. Now I realize that I treated it like a traitor instead of a besieged ally.*

3. *In another section of the article, Denise Karuth says that the biggest environmental barriers faced by individuals who use wheelchairs are, of course, architectural. She estimates that 60% of "accessible" architecture is flawed, with about 20% posing insurmountable difficulties. If you do not use a wheelchair, as you go through your day imagine doing your activities in a wheelchair. If you know someone who has to use a wheelchair, ask about the challenges to getting around. If you do use a wheelchair, would you agree or disagree with Karuth?*

4. *Karuth could spend a maximum of 15 hours away from home in a wheelchair. Faced with similar constraints, what would your life be like?*

5. *Try one or more of the suggestions in the accompanying piece titled "Think People First."*

6. *See the Applied Activity at the end of this section titled "A New Identity." Choose a disability for your identity transformation.*

Think "People First"

Language is a reflection of how people see each other. That's why the words we use can hurt. It's also why responsible communicators are now choosing language which reflects the dignity of people with disabilities— words that put the person first, rather than the disability. Read on for a short course on using language that empowers.

1. Think "people first." Say "a woman who has mental retardation," rather than "a mentally retarded woman."
2. Avoid words like "unfortunate," "afflicted," and "victim." Also, try to avoid casting a person with a disability as a superhuman model of courage. People with disabilities are just people, not tragic figures or demigods.
3. A developmental disability is not a disease. Do not mention "symptoms," "patients" or "treatment," unless the person you're writing about has an illness as well as a disability.
4. Use common sense. Avoid terms with obvious negative or judgmental connotations, such as "crippled," "deaf and dumb," "lame" and "defective." If you aren't sure how to refer to a person's condition, ask. And, if the disability is not relevant to your story or conversation, why mention it at all?
5. Never refer to a person as "confined to a wheelchair." Wheelchairs enable people to escape confinement. A person with a mobility impairment "uses" a wheelchair.
6. Try to describe people without disabilities as "typical" rather than "normal."

Note: From Ohio Public Images/Public Images Network

Don't Look Too Closely

Nels Goud

Almost everyone I know feels that a job is out there which is just right. It offers everything we desire—challenge, money, recognition, use of capacities, and the feeling of looking forward to going to work. We know these jobs exist because other people have them.

Since high school I've always dreamed of being a big band lead trumpeter. Now *there* is a perfect job. Playing gigs all around the country, screaming off high ones to the applause of an appreciative audience, and of course the inevitable groupies. I have talked to many professional trumpeters. When I was 17, I chatted with a trumpeter of the Jimmy Dorsey band. He didn't want to talk too much about trumpeting, except for telling me he did not like what he had to play. He was lonely for his children, about my age, he said. The traveling for ten months each year was now too much for him. "But what else can I do at my age?" Twenty years later I was talking with the lead trumpeter of the Buddy Rich band. This guy had been hitting notes a few minutes earlier that must now be soaring past Saturn. I asked him how he liked playing. "I'm getting tired of this lead trumpet stuff." He was all of 25 years old. As with the trumpeter I met two decades earlier, I figured he was having a bad night. He couldn't really mean that. I mean, he could hit double high C! What more could any human want?

Then at another time I met a famous psychologist who had left the university life and started a center for human growth. Having myself reached a point where classes were a bit repetitive, and feeling restricted by the publishing game, I felt this guy had it made. We spent a day talking about our lives and jobs. His main advice was "Stay with the university. I often wish I had. It is a real hassle to keep a center like this going. I'm more of an administrator than anything." Well, must have been one of those days.

One of my favorite places is a large nature preserve owned by the university. I was taking a leisurely stroll along a trail bounded by tall oaks and stopped at an outlook over a large lake. Every time I take this walk I envy the staff out here who get to run outdoor education programs in surroundings like these. The Associate Director happened by and we talked for a few minutes. I asked him what it was like working here. He looked up at the trees and said "You know this is the first chance I've had to notice the new leaves on the oaks this spring. It seems I'm always in the office answering the phone, writing memos, or trouble shooting a maintenance or personnel problem. I'd rather just be a student or visitor out here. Then maybe I would get to see the trees." Obviously I had caught him at a low moment.

I don't give up easily. While I was taking a break on a spring biking expedition in Florida, an old, dust-covered Buick pulled off the road and parked next to me. The driver, the only occupant, leaned over and rolled down the passenger window.

"Hey, I'm curious. What kind of biking group are you with? I've been seeing groups of bikers with orange flags like yours all day." I explained that we were just a bunch of

Hoosiers who think that biking a couple hundred miles along the Florida Atlantic coast is the proper way to spend a relaxing spring vacation. Noticing his out-of-state license, I asked him what he was doing here. He handed me a business card that said Vern C— Acrobat, Juggler, Unicyclist. This was not your usual Florida tourist.

"I go around to schools and do my act. Been doing it for 31 years now."

I looked a little closer. He had wavy hair, mainly gray with intermittent black strands. His face resembled what Errol Flynn would have looked like at 66. He was dressed in all black, slacks and a long sleeved turtleneck. Only a small paunch showed on an otherwise athletic frame. I was wondering how crowds of high school students reacted to a late middle-aged man juggling bowling pins while riding a unicycle. Then I realized ol' Vern had tapped another of my job fantasies. I had long considered putting together a dynamite program for public schools on human relations. Besides saving the youth of America, I would get the chance to travel and live the free life on the road. Shades of Kerouac. Here was a chance to get some ideas on how to do it.

"Vern, tell me a little bit what it's like going around to schools all year giving programs."

"Well, first of all, I'm going to quit next year. I'm tired. I'm tired of the motels. The one I'm staying in tonight doesn't even have a telephone or cable TV. The one in Daytona Beach cost five dollars less and had a TV and telephone."

"Un, yeah, sounds like a bummer. But tell me more about your career, like how do you get these school assembly jobs?"

"First of all you have to get an agent. There's all sort of circuits in this business, you know. You need to get the publicity and a name for yourself. I come down here during the winter months. Do the midwest in the fall.

I do about ten schools a week. Man, I'm tired. Gave three shows today and no time for lunch or anything. Just give the program, pack up, and rush over to the next school. Tonight all I'm going to do is watch some TV and drink beer. Then two more shows tomorrow. Do you know of any good motels in Titusville?"

"Not really, Vern. We throw down sleeping bags in school gyms or churches. No cable TV there either. How did you get started in this?"

"My old man was a circus acrobat. I learned the trade from him. He and Uncle Sam—I was in the Army once—have been my only bosses. I'm an independent contractor." He was proud of that.

"I have been married three times," he added without prompting. He needed to talk. But then again, so did I. We were barroom buddies on the berm of state road A1A. "My first wife ran off with my brother. Guess I wasn't around home enough. The second one got cancer and died. I got a regular job then for a few years. Got married again and the third wife got cancer too. She is still alive but, you know, didn't want to see anyone so I just went out on the circuit again. I call her every once in a while to see how she's doing." He paused for a minute and stared ahead. "I bought a home in Virginia last year. Planning to retire there. Just sit around and enjoy life and no more motels and three shows a day. But this has been my life. I don't know if I could just sit around. I am so tired, though."

We both had to go. I invited him to visit us where we were staying that night. Vern never showed up. Probably downed a few beers and went to sleep in that motel room without a cable TV. I had a lot of sympathy for Vern. But it would be different for me giving those school programs. I know it would.

Talking with people who have perfect jobs has taught me one thing—make sure I catch them on a good day next time.

Follow-Up

1. *For many, an occupation is a central component of their identity. They believe it is important to find just the right work to express themselves and find fulfillment. What are the characteristics of a "perfect job" for you? Is there such a thing?*
2. *The author, a persevering malcontent, kept encountering people who did not like their "perfect jobs." Interview people who have what you consider to be an ideal job. See if this ideal work is what you expected.*
3. *If you're interested in reading about ways to find a balance between personal and work lives, you may want to check out* Down-Shifting: Reinventing Success on a Slower Track *by Amy Saltzman, 1991, HarperCollins.*

Occupational Exploration

When I first entered college as an undergrad, I was a product of my parents' wishes—they wanted me to become a physician, so that's what I worked toward. But the courses were mind numbingly boring, and I realized that the course they had set for me was not what I wanted. The problem was, I didn't know what I wanted either.

After dropping out of school, finding a job and supporting myself for several years, I decided that being a blue collar worker (a shipping dock worker at a meat packing plant in Chicago) wasn't really me either. I enjoyed the money and the independence, but felt I was not fulfilling my potential, that I could do better and find a fulfilling career. So I decided to go back to school and get a very practical business degree (this after several other part-time "false starts"). While pursuing my business degree, I took a required computer course and decided—Ah, this is something I enjoy, that I want to do. This was a key turning point in my life—it was the first time I discovered something I really wanted to do and pursued it.

After graduation, I got a position in the computer field and enjoyed the challenge of my new responsibilities and the prestige of my own office. I now felt much closer to "Me," but there was still something missing, something within me still unfulfilled. I had always enjoyed helping others, and found the most enjoyable aspect of my new job was the time I spent training and teaching them. This was a life thread that felt like "Me." So in need of some extra money anyway, I decided to look for a part-time teaching job. To do this, I had to cope with a lifelong fear of public speaking. It wasn't easy, but the reward was worth the risk. I feel I have finally found a direction for myself that's "with the grain."

—Christopher A. Schaefer

Follow-Up

1. *Sometimes it takes some actual experience to find out what you like and dislike in a job. This person kept trying on jobs and taking courses until he found a position that matched his strengths and identity. What has been your job history and level of satisfaction? Do you think you will be in a continual search to find or create a job that matches your identity?*

2. *James A. Michener, the novelist, discusses his experience in career exploration in "Wasting Time," a short essay in the last section of this book.*

To a Body, With Love

Abe Arkoff

At midnight on October 22, 1780, Benjamin Franklin was in agony with the gout. He decided to have a written conversation with this old enemy, and this is how the interchange began:

> **Franklin:** *Eh! Oh! Eh! What have I done to merit these cruel sufferings?*
>
> **Gout:** *Many things; you have ate and drank too freely, and too much indulged those legs of yours in their indolence.*
>
> **Franklin:** *Who is it that accuses me?*
>
> **Gout:** *It is I, even I, the Gout.*
>
> **Franklin:** *What! My enemy in person?*
>
> **Gout:** *No, not your enemy.*[1]

The gout is quite eloquent and goes on to make its case that it is not the enemy, but a friend trying to get Franklin to abandon his dissolute habits. Franklin promises to mend his ways, but the gout takes its leave with the uneasy feeling that prudence would not long prevail.

To some observers, it appears that many of us treat our bodies as the enemy. A tidal wave of recent books and articles suggests that we are not at home or at ease with our bodies. Although as a nation we are healthier than ever, we worry more about our health. Furthermore, the body is to us an unknown continent—we scarcely know our esophagus from our elbow. To make matters worse, we don't like what we see in our mirrors. Surveys show that a lot of us aren't content with the way we look.

A lack of knowledge about the body can be a serious matter. This lack can cause us to neglect needed medical attention and to waste time and money on attention that either is not needed or can even harm us. Similarly, a lack of satisfaction concerning the body must be taken seriously. Body-image researcher Thomas Cash[2] writes, "Obviously, if one dislikes the body one 'lives in,' it's difficult to be satisfied with 'the self who lives therein' " (p. 61). Research shows that body satisfaction and self-esteem are strongly related to each other.[3–6] More is said about this later in this reading.

Actually—after 3 million years of evolution—the human body is quite remarkable. It has developed its own considerable defenses against disease, as well as powerful mechanisms for regeneration and healing. How sad that, like Rodney Dangerfield, our bodies frequently seem to "get no respect." Following are some simple suggestions on how we can take responsibility for and come to know, care for, and even love them.

OWN YOUR BODY

Your body belongs to you. It doesn't belong to any disease process. It doesn't belong to your doctor. It doesn't belong to the advertising or fashion industries. It is not the property of the state or national government. Your body is yours, but have you taken ownership of it and accepted full responsibility for it?

Each of us is a psychobiological unit integrated with the external environment, and a disturbance in any part of this system affects all of it. Much of this system is or can be brought under our own control. Speaking of an illness, we say, "I got sick." But often it might be as accurate to say, "I made myself sick; I've eaten/drunk/smoked too much." Or "I've driven myself too hard." Or "I've done nothing to deal with my physical/emotional/

spiritual/vocational/etc. problems that are grinding me down."

Some of us ignore the condition of our bodies until we are laid low in some way. Then, accepting little responsibility for our bodies' disrepair and not much for their rehabilitation, we deliver them into the hands of physicians. "My body is sick; make it well," is what our actions say.

The notion that we need take no responsibility for our health or our illnesses increasingly has come under attack. A related and equally changeworthy notion is that we need take no responsibility for our lives, for frequently, the pain and suffering we ask our physicians to relieve or to tranquilize out of existence are integral parts of living that call for some courage and effort rather than medication.[7]

Norman Cousins is a classic example of a person who took responsibility for his own body and health. Suffering from a crippling collagen (connective tissue) disorder which physicians believed to be irreversible, he personally devised, with the support of his doctor, a new regimen, which included large doses of vitamin C and laughter (the latter provided by such things as *Candid Camera* video classics and humor books). He returned himself to health and in his account of his experience wrote, "I have learned never to underestimate the capacity of the human mind and body to regenerate—even when the prospects seem so wretched."[8]

In response to his article, Cousins received some 3,000 letters from physicians. Many of these letters reflected the view that no medication a doctor prescribes is as potent as the state of mind in which the patients address their own illness. These doctors felt that their most valuable service was to help each patient mobilize her or his own physical and psychological recuperative powers.[9]

When we take ownership of our bodies, we put ourselves in charge of their welfare. That doesn't mean we should not seek professional advice and assistance. But it does mean that whether we are in the pink or near the pale, we take full responsibility for what we do to our bodies and what we allow others to do to them.

KNOW YOUR BODY

Most of us know very little about our bodies. Seymour Fisher[10] writes that although our bodies are our dearest possessions and confront us everywhere, they remain a mystery. Why should this be so?

One reason suggested by Fisher is that our bodies are frequently concealed from sight by clothing. Even with our clothes off, it would be difficult to get a view of many bodily parts without some ingenious arrangement of mirrors. Then too, our bodies are constantly changing, and there may be a considerable time lag before we bring our body images up to date.

Even when we seek to scrutinize our bodies, we may have trouble in doing so. Fisher writes that when we look at our bodies, we do so through "an elaborate set of selective filters and screens." We may feel shamed by the appearance of certain parts and worried by the fragility of others. We see only what we want to see or what we will allow ourselves to see.

Sometimes we see what we are afraid we'll see. Of a group of nearly 500 children, more than half the girls considered themselves overweight although only 15% were.[11] In a survey of college students, it was found that of those who were actually normal in weight, 58% of the women and 20% of the men classified themselves as overweight.[12] Misbeliefs about weight can have an important bearing on eating habits and disturbances, as well as on general well-being.

When we feel sick, often it is not because our bodies aren't right, it's because our lives aren't right, and we somaticize our problems. It's easier to blame our bodies and seek a potion than to evaluate our lives and work to make them better. Barsky points out that how we feel about our bodies may symbolize how we feel about ourselves and our lives. If we don't like our bodies or if we feel they are weak, inadequate or sick, it can be a comment on our larger self. We may not need a better body, we may need to get ourselves a life. Barsky writes that no amount of medication or surgery can cure a person who "needs to be sick." Illness may be a way of asking for help or attention, or of seeking a way out of a difficult life situation. Illness can confer power by entitling the person to special consideration.

Paradoxically, we expect both too much of our bodies and too little. We expect to be symptom free and to have all our sufferings remedied. At the same time, we give too little credit to our bodies' ability to protect and repair themselves. Barsky writes, "The human body is actually a remarkably rugged and hardy biological system, one that is extraordinarily resistant to disease and injury" (p. 17). In his book, *Lives of a Cell*, Lewis Thomas[13] writes, "The great secret . . . is that most things get better by themselves. Most things, in fact, are better by morning" (p. 100).

We need information about bodies in general and our own bodies in particular. For those of us who lack this information, some excellent books are available at almost every bookstore. An example is *Core Concepts in Health* (brief sixth edition) by Paul Insel et al.,[14] which is used as a text in the "Modern Health" course at my university. One of the authors' goals is to instill in the reader a sense of personal power in health matters. They write, "Everyone has the ability to monitor, understand, and affect his or her own health."

Each body, of course, is like no other body and has its own special requirement, aversions, and eccentricities—its own way of making itself known. By paying attention to our bodily signs, signals, and symptoms, we can learn a lot about ourselves.

One of the most important sets of symptoms relates to anxiety. *Anxiety* is a state of arousal caused by threat or challenge, but in a particular situation, we may be aware only of a subjective feeling of dread and/or physical upset but not of the causes. With medical assurance that our symptoms are those of anxiety, we gain some important information about ourselves that we can put to use in future situations. We learn that sudden difficulty in breathing, heart palpitations, overwhelming weariness, or other idiosyncratic symptoms or patternings represent signs of threat or challenge. We then can pursue and deal with these threats or challenges (if we resist the urge to run from the situation or to deaden ourselves with tranquilizers).

One rather fascinating and ingenious way of getting to know your body better involves opening a new channel of communication. Ira Progoff[15] recommends that you have a dialogue with your body. (Benjamin Franklin's conversation with his gout is an example of this approach.) You can start by writing down all the salient memories you have of your body, such as the time you broke your leg, learned to swim, were first aware of your sexual feelings, and so on. Next, drawing upon these memories, write a brief summary of your relationship to your body. Then relax, sense the presence of your body as though it were a person, speak to it, allow it to speak to you, and write down your dialogue.

A similar but somewhat simpler method is one called "Body Letters." You simply sit down and without stopping to think, write a letter to your body, saying everything you wish to say to it. Then you become your body (you are anyway, of course) and without pausing, write a reply.

Here, as an example for those who don't mind reading the mail of others, is an exchange of letters:

Dear Body,

Well, I've resisted writing to you, just as I've sometimes resisted living in you these past many years. I haven't thought too much of you as a body (at least, what met the eye below the neck)—you were too short, too unmuscled, too nearsighted, too allergy-prone, too this, too that. I've put you down and largely abandoned you to take up residence in my (or is it "your" or "our") head. Now, I'm back in some surprise to say: I think I like you, and what was all the fuss about?

I stand in front of the mirror and look at you. There you are—a bit dilapidated after many years of wear, tear and deferred maintenance—but still all in one piece and functioning well enough for my purposes. You have passion. You almost never catch a cold or get the flu. You don't need much sleep. You only bulge a little despite our sweet tooth. You're content with long walks and hardly cast an envious glance at the joggers and runners zipping by.

Sometimes I wonder what I would have become had you developed in accordance with my boyhood dream. Instead, I spent my adolescence in the library and a lot of the rest of my life as well. My life has worked out well for me: I have a family that's dear, good friends, and enjoyable work in a beautiful place. We've been companions on an increasingly pleasant journey.

So this is an apology, thank-you, and let's-get-better-acquainted letter. I know I've made you promises, and I hereby promise to come down out of my head and start keeping them. Now that I think you're okay—well, even better than okay—I'm looking forward to a happier and happier association.

With love,
Abe

Dear Abe,

After all these years, it was good to get your letter showing (if you will permit a body metaphor) some change of heart. You know, having you for an inhabitant hasn't been the easiest thing in the world for me. There are moments and even days when you seem to care, but you are (oops, here comes another one) something of a backslider.

But give credit where it's due, I always say. You're a faithful walker. You watch your diet (except for, ah yes, that tooth and midnight raids on the refrigerator). You don't smoke, and there's only an occasional vodka martini (well, make that a double). The results of our last physical were okay, considering the mileage. It's only that we could be so much more to each other (notice how I'm trying to put this in a positive and cooperative way). Remember that series of massages so long ago—how good they felt? Why did we stop? Let's get some more. The "chi" class was nice, but you said it might be followed by some more. What happened? And, since we're walkers, how about some serious hiking and even backpacking (notice that no mention has been made of the north face of Mount Everest).

I think there is more in me than you suspect. You seem so concerned these days with your spiritual growth, and you proceed almost as if you want to rise above your body—me, that is. But don't forget that body, mind, and spirit proceed together, and body discipline can be an avenue to what's above.

Now that we have some communication started, let's try to (brace yourself) stay in touch. We've got some good years ahead, and I'll be with you every step of the way.

Faithfully,
Your Body

References

1. Franklin, B. (1945). *A Benjamin Franklin reader* (N. G. Goodman, Ed.). New York: Thomas Y. Crowell Company.
2. Cash, T. F. (1990). The psychology of physical appearance: Aesthetics, attributes, and image. In T. F. Cash & T. Pruzinsky (Eds.), *Body images: Development, deviance, and change* (pp. 51–79). New York: Guilford Press.
3. Berscheid, E., & Walster, E. (1974). Physical attractiveness. In L. Berkowitz (Ed.), *Advances in experimental social psychology* (Vol. 7, pp. 158–216). New York: Academic Press.

4. Cash, T. F., Winstead, B. W., & Janda, L. H. (1986, April). The great American shape up: Body image survey report. *Psychology Today,* pp. 30–37.

5. Franzoi, S. L., & Shields, S. A. (1984). The body esteem scale: Multidimensional structure and sex differences in a college population. *Journal of Personality Assessment, 48,* 173–178.

6. Striegel-Moore, R. H., Silberstein, L. R., & Rodin, J. (1986). Toward an understanding of risk factors for bulimia. *American Psychologist, 41,* 246–263.

7. Paton, A. (1974, December 7). "Medicalization" of health. *British Medical Journal,* 573–574.

8. Cousins, N. (1977, May 28). Anatomy of an illness (as perceived by the patient). *Saturday Review,* pp. 4–6, 48–51.

9. Cousins, N. (1978, February 18). What I learned from 3,000 doctors. *Saturday Review,* pp. 12–16.

10. Fisher, S. (1973). *Body consciousness: You are what you feel.* Englewood Cliffs, NJ: Prentice-Hall.

11. Seligman, J., Joseph, N., Donovan, J., & Gosnell, M. (1987, July). The littlest dieters. *Newsweek,* p. 48.

12. Klesges, R. C. (1993). An analysis of body-image distortions in a non-patient population. *International Journal of Eating Disorders, 2,* 35–41.

13. Thomas, L. (1975). *The lives of a cell.* New York: Bantam Books.

14. Insel, P., Roth, W. T., Collins, L. M., Petersen, R. A., & Stone, T. (1990). *Core concepts in health* (brief 6th ed.). Palo Alto, CA: Mayfield.

15. Progoff, I. (1975). *At a journal workshop: The basic text and guide for using the Intensive Journal.* New York: Dialogue House.

Follow-Up

1. *Do you own your body? To answer this question, discuss how responsible you have made yourself for what you and others do to your body.*

2. *Do you accept your body? What relationship do you see between your acceptance or rejection of your body and your overall self-esteem?*

3. *How much do you love your body? To answer this question, write a love letter to your body. Then, as your body, write a reply.*

Applied Activities for Section One

ARE YOU AN ADULT?

Most people offer psychological reasons rather than legal ones when describing how they knew they were an adult. Richard Cohen, for example, discovered he was an adult when he paid a restaurant tab. Here are some other events that trigger the adulthood realization (as obtained from interviews): the first day on a full-time job; buying a house; filling out income tax returns; attending the funeral of a friend or a parent; being referred to as *lady* by a patient; being asked to leave home by parents and pursuing a dream (such as playing rock music for a living) that others consider impractical. One 23-year-old, a married college grad and a health professional, still does *not* feel like an adult "because my husband now does everything for me that my father used to do." Try to complete one of the following items:

1. I became an adult when:

I took responsibility of myself, pay my own bills, clothes, credit cards, make decisions for myself.

2. I do *not* believe I am an adult yet because:

fully I don't believe because I still live w/ my parents. I don't have the full responsibility of paying rent & a car payment,

Suggested Follow-Up Activities
1. Ask others outside of class if they think they are adults.
2. Ask older family members when they considered themselves adults. Are you considered an adult by the people in your family?
3. Analyze the responses to the adulthood question for underlying themes (responsibility, independence, etc.).
4. Discuss (or write about) your findings.

A NEW IDENTITY

It was a good night's sleep, but as you start to awake you sense something is different, even strange. Crawling out of bed, you pass a mirror—you stop and stare.

Somehow, overnight you've changed to a person of the opposite gender. Take a few minutes to ponder this change and answer these questions:

1. How do you *feel* about this change?
2. What are you going to *do* in the immediate future concerning this identity?
3. In what ways would you have to *change* how you live?

Discuss (or write about) your reactions to this new identity.

Variations—Other identity transformations you could try to imagine include: different race, different age, and from physically abled to disabled or the reverse.

GENDER ROLE: POSITIVE AND NEGATIVE

Directions: Complete steps 1 and 2 individually. Form groups (2–6 members of the *same* gender) and discuss your results. Attempt one or more of the Follow-Up activities.

1. List two advantages and two disadvantages of being a *male* today:

Advantages _____

_____

Disadvantages _____

_____

2. List two advantages and two disadvantages of being a *female* today:

Advantages _____

_____

Disadvantages _____

_____

Follow-Up

Compare and discuss* your results in one or more of the following ways:

1. In *mixed* gender groups (2–6 members)

2. Post all the lists on the wall. Have all participants read them. Conduct a whole class discussion on the perceptions and questions from these lists.

3. Discuss the following question in either mixed gender groups and/or with the whole class: What can be done to maximize the advantages and minimize the disadvantages for each gender?

4. Write about what you've learned after completing one or more of the above activities.

*Note: Listening skills are essential with any of the above activities.

SECTION
two

HUMAN COMMUNICATION

O ne of the things you can do that a squirrel cannot is talk. Another is to wonder why you are being compared to a squirrel. You can talk and wonder because of a part of the human brain called the cerebral cortex. Talking does not necessarily make us any wiser than the squirrel or other animals that do not have a cerebral cortex. We just do it a lot. We spend a good amount of our time hearing and watching others in person, in print, on TV, on the radio, and on all kinds of electronic technology. We tell about our experiences and listen to others' stories. We even talk to ourselves.

Humans seemingly have a need to put into words almost anything they experience. Communication research has shown that humans devote approximately 70% of their waking time in verbal communication. We communicate for instrumental reasons—our messages are a means to get information, objects, attention, affection, influence, or to explain. We also communicate for expressive reasons. Our messages are valued for their own sake—we just enjoy the process of communicating. Being human means to communicate.

Underlying all the reasons to communicate is the need to make a connection with another person (or even with yourself). We all have a basic need to express what is going on in our life and have someone hear it in the way we intended. If this connection is appropriately made, we have genuine communication. If this connection is not consistently achieved, humans often become angry, lonely, alienated, or even sick. The articles in this section feature some of the more significant concepts and techniques for making communication connections.

- In "Interpersonal Communication" Warner Burke provides a basic model of communication. He explains effective and ineffective approaches for sending and receiving messages.
- Psychologist Carl Rogers offers a personalized account of his experiences as a listener in "To Hear and To Be Heard." Rogers says that true listening is a source of deep joy and satisfaction.
- In "Self-Disclosure" Nelson Goud discusses the dynamics of how to make disclosures to others, examining under- and over-disclosure as well as appropriate disclosure. He offers guidelines for becoming an effective self-discloser. This article introduces the concept of fusion communication.
- The seemingly different wavelengths for men and women and their communication behavior are the theme of Deborah Tannen's "You Just Don't Understand." Six ways men and women differ are described in a highly practical fashion.
- Arthur J. Lange and Patricia Jakubowski distinguish three forms of expressing needs and rights in "Assertive, Nonassertive, and Aggressive Behavior." Applied suggestions for engaging in assertive communication is the focus of this article.
- In "King of the Purple Tree" author Nels Goud essentially tells a story of his failures in communication. Interactions with a club musician lead Goud and some of his students to new understandings.

Interpersonal Communication

Warner Burke

Communication, by definition, involves at least two individuals, the sender and the receiver. Consider yourself, first of all, as the sender of some message. There are certain filters or barriers (internal) which determine whether or not the message is actually transmitted. These barriers may be categorized as follows: (1) Assumptions about yourself—Do I really have something to offer? Am I safe to offer suggestions? Do I really want to share the information? Will others really understand? How will the communication affect my self-esteem? (2) Attitudes about the message itself—Is the information valuable? Do I see the information correctly, or understand it well enough to describe it to others? (3) Sensing the receiver's reaction—Do I become aware of whether or not the receiver is actually understanding? Or in other words, can I "sense" from certain cues or reactions by the receiver whether or not we are communicating?

Now consider yourself as the receiver. As a receiver you may filter or not hear certain aspects (or any aspect for that matter) of a message. Why? Because the message may seem unimportant or too difficult. Moreover, you may be selective in your attention. For example, you may feel that the sender is being redundant, so you quit listening after the first few words. You may be preoccupied with something else. Or your filtering or lack of attention may be due to your past experience with the sender. You may feel that "this guy has never made a point in his life and never will!"

Many times the receiver never makes use of his "third ear." That is, trying to be sensitive to nonverbal communication. The sender's eyes, gestures, and sometimes his overall posture communicate messages that the insensitive listener never receives.

There may be barriers that exist between the sender and the receiver, e.g., cultural differences. Environmental conditions may also cause barriers, e.g., poor acoustics. More common, however, are the differences in frames of reference. For example, there may not be a common understanding of purpose in a certain communication. You may ask me how I'm feeling today. To you the phrase, "How ya doing?" is nothing more than a greeting. However, I may think that you really want to know and I may tell you—possibly at length.

Now that some of the problems in interpersonal communication have been mentioned, let us delve somewhat deeper into this process of transferring a message from the brain and emotion of one person to the brain and emotion of another human being.

SENDING THE MESSAGE

In communicating a message effectively to another person, there are several obvious factors which are beneficial. Such things as correct pronunciation, lack of distracting brogue, dialect, or accent, or a pleasant resonance in one's voice usually facilitate the sending of a message.

Assuming the sender of a message really has a desire to be heard and understood and not just speak for the sake of speaking, he wants some assurance that he has communicated. The key to effective communication on the part of the speaker, then, is to obtain some feedback, of one form or another, from his listener(s). Some bright persons who really have something to say are ineffective speakers, be it lecturing or speaking to someone at a cocktail party, because they are unable to tell or care whether their listener(s) is understanding, or they do not make any effort to check on their effectiveness as a communicator. For example, many lecturers in a classroom situation are often unaware of when a listener is sound asleep. Unless there is interaction of some type between the speaker and his listener, the speaker is susceptible to "losing" his listener. Often the speaker must take the initiative in order to receive any feedback regarding the effectiveness of his communication. When speaking before a large group, I often resort to the simple act of requesting my audience to shake their head "yes" if they understand what I have just said, or "no" if they did not understand. Even though this technique is simple, I usually get considerable feedback quickly and I know immediately what I must do at that point to make my speech more effective or whether to continue on with my next point.

Even when talking to just one other person the speaker must often take the initiative, in an interactive sense, to determine whether his message is being understood. Even though I sometimes take the risk of "bugging" my listener, I often stop and ask him if he understands what I mean, or I occasionally ask him to tell me what he thinks I meant in my message.

There is a fairly small percentage of people who speak articulately and clearly enough to be understood most of the time. Most of us have to work at it, especially when we are attempting to communicate a message which is fairly abstract or when we want to tell something which is quite personal or highly emotional. In sending the message effectively, we must do two things simultaneously: (1) work at finding the appropriate words and emotion to express what we want to say, and (2) continually look for cues from the listener to get

some feedback even if we must ask our listener for some.

RECEIVING THE MESSAGE

In considering interpersonal communication, we might, at first thought, think that listening is the easier of the two functions in the process. If we assume, however, that the listener really wants to understand what the speaker is saying, then the process is not all that easy. The basic problem that the listener faces is that he is capable of thinking faster than the speaker can talk. In their *Harvard Business Review* article, Nichols and Stevens state that the average rate of speech for most Americans is about 125 words per minute. Most of our thinking processes involve words, and our brains can handle many more words per minute than 125. As Nichols and Stevens point out, what this means is that, when we listen, our brains receive words at a very slow rate compared with the brain's capabilities.

As you have experienced many times, you know that you can listen to what someone is saying and think about something else at the same time. As the "cocktail party" phenomenon illustrates, the human brain is truly remarkable in its ability to process a considerable amount of input simultaneously. Sometimes, at a cocktail party, I want to hear not only what the person in my small gathering is saying, but also what that lovely creature is talking about in the group about six feet away. If the overall noise level is not too loud, I can hear and understand both conversations.

The problem with listening, then, is that we have "spare" time in our thinking processes. How we use that spare time determines the extent of our listening effectiveness. It is easy for us to be distracted in listening, especially if the speaker talks slowly or haltingly or if he says something that stimulates another thought. For example, suppose you are listening to a friend who is telling you about a problem he is having in his department. In the process of describing the problem, he mentions a person whom you know, whereupon you start thinking about the person at length. Later, when your friend asks you what you would do about his problem, you're apt to respond, "what problem?"

Thus, a fundamental problem the listener must consider in the communicative process is the fact that his brain is capable of responding to a speaker at several different levels simultaneously. Naturally, this can be an asset to the listener rather than a problem. For example the listener can attend to nonverbal cues the speaker gives, e.g., facial expression, gesture, or tone of voice, as well as listen to the words themselves.

Besides a highly active brain, an effective listener has another factor to consider in the communicative process. This factor involves the process of trying to perceive what the speaker is saying from his point of view.

A BARRIER AND A GATEWAY

According to Carl Rogers, a leading psychotherapist and psychotherapy researcher, the major barrier to effective communication is the tendency to evaluate. That is, the barrier to mutual interpersonal communication is our very natural tendency to judge, to evaluate, to approve or disapprove the statement or opinion of the other person or group. Suppose someone says to you, "I didn't like what the lecturer had to say." Your typical response will be either agreement or disagreement. In other words, your primary reaction is to evaluate the statement from your point of view, from your own frame of reference.

Although the inclination to make evaluations is common, it is usually heightened in those situations where feelings and emotions are deeply involved. Thus, the stronger our feelings, the more likely it is that there will be no mutual element in the communication.

There will be only two ideas, two feelings, two judgments, missing each other in the heat of the psychological battle.

If having a tendency to evaluate is the major barrier to communication, then the logical gateway to communication is to become an active listener, to listen with understanding. Don't let this simple statement fool you. Listening with understanding means to see the expressed idea and attitude from the other person's point of view, to see how it feels to him, to achieve his frame of reference concerning his subject. One word that summarizes this process of listening with understanding is "empathy."

In psychotherapy, for example, Carl Rogers and his associates have found from research that empathetic understanding—understanding with a person not about him—is such an effective approach that it can bring about major changes in personality.

Suppose that in your next committee meeting you were to conduct an experiment which would test the quality of each committee member's understanding. Institute this rule: "Each person can speak up for himself only after he has first related the ideas and feelings of the previous speaker accurately and to that speaker's satisfaction." This would mean that before presenting your own point of view, it would be necessary for you to achieve the other speaker's frame of reference—to understand his thoughts and feelings so well that you could summarize them for him.

Can you imagine what this kind of approach might mean if it were projected into larger areas, such as congressional debates or labor-management disputes? What would happen if labor, without necessarily agreeing, could accurately state management's point of view in a way that management could accept; and management, without necessarily approving labor's stand, could state labor's case in a way that labor agreed was accurate? It would mean that real communication was es-

unconditional positive regard

tablished, and conditions would be more conducive for reaching a workable solution.

TOWARD MORE EFFECTIVE LISTENING

Some steps the listener can take to improve interpersonal communication have been stated. To summarize and be more explicit, let us consider these steps.

1. Effective listening must be an active process. To make certain that you are understanding what the speaker is saying, you, as the listener must interact with him. One way to do this is to paraphrase or summarize for the speaker what you think he has said.
2. Attending to nonverbal behavior that the speaker is communicating along with his verbal expression usually helps to understand the oral message more clearly. Often a facial expression or gesture will "tell" you that the speaker feels more strongly about his subject than his words would communicate.
3. The effective listener does not try to memorize every word or fact the speaker communicates, but, rather, he listens for the main thought or idea. Since your brain is such a highly effective processor of information, spending your listening time in more than just hearing the words of the speaker can lead to more effective listening. That is, while listening to the words, you can also be searching for the main idea of the message. Furthermore, you can attempt to find the frame of reference for the speaker's message as well as look at what he is saying from his perspective. This empathetic process also includes your attempting to experience the same feeling about the subject as the speaker.

These three steps toward more effective listening seem fairly simple and obvious. But the fact remains that we don't practice these steps very often. Why don't we?

According to Carl Rogers, it takes courage. If you really understand another person in this way, if you are willing to enter his private world and see the way life appears to him without any attempt to make evaluative judgments, you run the risk of being changed yourself. This risk of being changed is one of the most frightening prospects many of us face.

Moreover, when we need to utilize these steps the most, we are likely to use them the least, that is, when the situation involves a considerable amount of emotion. For example, when we listen to a message that contradicts our most deeply held prejudices, opinions, or convictions, our brain becomes stimulated by many factors other than what the speaker is telling us. When we are arguing with someone, especially about something that is "near and dear" to us, what are we typically doing when the other person is making his point? It's certainly not listening empathetically! We're probably planning a rebuttal to what he is saying, or we're formulating a question which will embarrass the speaker. We may, of course, simply be "tuning him out." How often have you been arguing with someone for 30 minutes or so, and you make what you consider to be a major point for your point of view, and your "opponent" responds by saying, "But that's what I said 30 minutes ago!"

When emotions are strongest, then, it is most difficult to achieve the frame of reference of the other person or group. Yet it is then that empathy is most needed if communication is to be established. A third party, for example, who is able to lay aside his own feelings and evaluation, can assist greatly by listening with understanding to each person or group and clarifying the views and attitudes each holds.

When the parties to a dispute realize that they are being understood, that someone sees how the situation seems to them, the statements grow less exaggerated and less defensive, and it is no longer necessary to maintain the attitude, "I am 100% right and you are 100% wrong."

SUMMARY

Effective communication, at least among human beings, is not a one-way street. It involves an interaction between the speaker and the listener. The responsibility for this interaction is assumed by both parties. You as the speaker can solicit feedback and adjust your message accordingly. As a listener, you can summarize for the speaker what you think he has said and continually practice the empathetic process.

One of the joys of life, at least for me, is to know that I have been heard and understood correctly and to know that someone cares enough to try to understand what I have said. I also get a great deal of satisfaction from seeing this same enjoyment on the face of a speaker when he knows I have understood him.

Follow-Up

1. *Choose one statement from this reading that describes one of your strengths as a communicator. Choose one statement that describes an area where you need improvement as a communicator.*
2. *Burke says that he sometimes initiates getting feedback from a listener to be sure he was understood. Consider trying this idea for times when you are not sure your message is understood.*
3. *Burke states that human thought is much faster than human speech. This fact often results in distracted thoughts and ineffective listening. Does this often happen to you? Try to focus on your listener more if it does.*
4. *Empathy is the ability to perceive another person's world as they do. Another option is to perceive a statement only from your own point of view. Try to understand what other people say from their point of view before you offer your viewpoint. What differences do you notice in the way you relate to one another? See the Applied Activity "Point of View" at the end of this section for a way to develop this skill.*
5. *Burke mentions that it takes courage to be an empathic listener because you run the risk of being changed yourself. You may hear something contrary to your existing beliefs that makes sense. Then you have to reexamine your beliefs and possibly make major changes, and this is threatening. Has this ever happened to you? Can you recognize when this is happening?*
6. *Burke states that when emotions are intense, true listening is especially important. But, of course, this is the time when listening is the most difficult. Experiment a few times with being a good listener during times when you can sense "hot" emotions. If this is done correctly, the defensiveness should decrease.*
7. *The Applied Activities at the end of this section allow you to apply most of the ideas mentioned in this article.*

John Steinbeck on Listening

We had had many discussions at the galley table and there had been many honest attempts to understand each other's thinking. There are several kinds of reception possible. There is the mind which lies in wait with traps for flaws, so set that it may miss, through not grasping it, a soundness. There is a second which is not reception at all, but blind flight because of laziness, or because some pattern is disturbed by the processes of the discussion. The best reception of all is that, which is easy and relaxed, which says in effect, "Let me absorb this thing. Let me try to understand it without private barriers. When I have understood what you are saying, only then will I subject it to my own scrutiny and my own criticism." This is the finest of all critical approaches and the rarest.

The smallest and meanest of all is that which, being frightened or outraged by thinking outside or beyond its pattern, revenges itself senselessly; leaps on a misspelled word or a mispronunciation, drags tricky definition in by the scruff of the neck, and, ranging like a small unpleasant dog, rags and tears the structure to shreds. We have known a critic to base a vicious criticism on a misplaced letter in a word, when actually he was venting rage on an idea he hated. These are the suspicious ones, the self-protective ones, living lives of difficult defense, insuring themselves against folly with folly—stubbornly self-protective at too high a cost.

Note: From *Log from the Sea of Cortez* by J. Steinbeck, 1976, New York: Penguin Books.

To Hear and to Be Heard

Carl Rogers — Humanist

The first simple feeling I want to share with you is my enjoyment when I can really *hear* someone. I think perhaps this has been a long standing characteristic of mine. I can remember this in my early grammar school days. A child would ask the teacher a question and the teacher would give a perfectly good answer to a completely different question. A feeling of pain and distress would always strike me. My reaction was, "But you didn't *hear* him!" I felt a sort of childish despair at the lack of communication which was (and is) so common.

I believe I know why it is satisfying to me to hear someone. When I can really hear someone it puts me in touch with him. It enriches my life. It is through hearing people that I have learned all that I know about individuals, about personality, about psychotherapy, and about interpersonal relationships. There is another peculiar satisfaction in it. When I really hear someone it is like listening to the music of the spheres, because beyond the immediate message of the person, no matter what that might be, there is the universal, the general. Hidden in all of the personal communications which I really hear there seem to be orderly psychological laws, aspects of the awesome order which we find in the universe as a whole. So there is both the satisfaction of hearing this particular person and also the satisfaction of feeling oneself in some sort of touch with what is universally true.

When I say that I enjoy hearing someone I mean, of course, hearing deeply. I mean that I hear the words, the thoughts, the feeling tones, the personal meaning, even the meaning that is below the conscious intent of the speaker. Sometimes, too, in a message which superficially is not very important, I hear a deep human cry, a "silent scream," that lies buried and unknown far below the surface of the person.

So I have learned to ask myself, can I hear the sounds and sense the shape of this other person's inner world? Can I resonate to what he is saying, can I let it echo back and forth in me, so deeply that I sense the meanings he is afraid of yet would like to communicate, as well as those meanings he knows?

I think, for example, of an interview I had with an adolescent boy, the recording of which I listened to only a short time ago. Like many an adolescent today he was saying at the outset of the interview that he had no goals. When I questioned him on this he made it even stronger that he had no goals whatsoever, not even one. I said, "There isn't anything you want to do?" "*Nothing* . . . Well, yeah, I want to keep on living." I remember very distinctly my feeling at that moment. I resonated very deeply to this phrase. He might simply be telling me that, like everyone else, he wanted to live. On the other hand he might be telling me, and this seemed to be a distinct possibility, that at some point the question of whether or not to live had been a real issue with him. So I tried to resonate to him at all levels. I didn't know for certain what the message was. I simply wanted to be open to any of the meanings that this statement might have, including the possible meaning that he might have at one time considered suicide. I didn't respond verbally at this level.

That would have frightened him. But I think that my being willing and able to listen to him at all levels is perhaps one of the things that made it possible for him to tell me, before the end of the interview, that not long before he had been on the point of blowing his brains out. This little episode constitutes an example of what I mean by wanting to really hear someone at all the levels at which he is endeavoring to communicate.

I find, in therapeutic interviews, and in the intensive group experiences which have come to mean a great deal to me in recent years, that hearing has consequences. When I do truly hear a person and the meanings that are important to him at that moment, hearing not simply his words, but *him*, and when I let him know that I have heard his own private personal meanings, many things happen. There is first of all a grateful look. He feels released. He wants to tell me more about his world. He surges forth in a new sense of freedom. I think he becomes more open to the process of change.

I have often noticed, both in therapy and in groups, that the more deeply I can hear the meanings of this person the more there is that happens. One thing I have come to look upon as almost universal is that when a person realizes he has been deeply heard, there is a moistness in his eyes. I think in some real sense he is weeping for joy. It is as though he were saying, "Thank God, *somebody* heard me. Someone knows what it's like to be me." In such moments I have had the fantasy of a prisoner in a dungeon, tapping out day after day a Morse code message, "Does anybody hear me? Is there anybody there? Can anyone hear me?" And finally one day he hears some faint tappings which spell out "Yes." By that one simple response he is released from his loneliness, he has become a human being again. There are many, many people living in private dungeons today, people who give no evidence of it whatever on the outside, where you have to listen very sharply to hear the faint messages from the dungeon.

I LIKE TO BE HEARD

Let me move on to a second learning, which I would like to share with you. I like to *be heard.* A number of times in my life I have felt myself bursting with insoluble problems, or going round and round in tormented circles or, during one period, overcome by feelings of worthlessness and despair, sure I was sinking into psychosis. I think I have been more lucky than most in finding at these times individuals who have been able to hear me and thus to rescue me from the chaos of my feelings. I have been fortunate in finding individuals who have been able to hear my meanings a little more deeply than I have known them. These individuals have heard me without judging me, diagnosing me, appraising me, evaluating me. They have just listened and clarified and responded to me at all the levels at which I was communicating, I can testify that when you are in psychological distress and someone really hears you without passing judgment on you, without trying to take responsibility for you, without trying to mold you, it feels *damn good.* At these times, it has relaxed the tension in me. It has permitted me to bring out the frightening feelings, the guilts, the despair, the confusions that have been a part of my experience. When I have been listened to and when I have been heard, I am able to reperceive my world in a new way and to go on. It is amazing that feelings which were completely awful, become bearable when someone listens. It is astonishing, how elements which seem insoluble become soluble when someone hears; how confusions which seem irremediable turn into relatively clear flowing streams when one is understood. I have deeply appreciated the times that I have experienced this sensitive, empathic, concentrated listening.

I have been very grateful that by the time I quite desperately needed this kind of help, I had trained and developed therapists, persons in their own right, independent and unafraid of me, who were able to go with me through a dark and troubled period in which I underwent a great deal of inner growth. It has also made me sharply aware that in developing my style of therapy for others, I was without doubt, at some unconscious level, developing the kind of help I wanted and could use myself.

WHEN I CANNOT HEAR

Let me turn to some of my dissatisfactions in this realm. I dislike it in myself when I can't hear another, when I do not understand him. If it is only a simple failure of comprehension or a failure to focus my attention on what he is saying, or a difficulty in understanding his words, then I feel only a very mild dissatisfaction with myself,

But what I really dislike in myself is when I cannot hear the other person because I am so sure in advance of what he is about to say that I don't listen. It is only afterward that I realize that I have only heard what I have already decided he is saying. I have failed really to listen. Or even worse are those times when I can't hear because what he is saying is too threatening, might even make me change my views or my behavior. Still worse are those times when I catch myself trying to twist his message to make it say what I want him to say, and then only hearing that. This can be a very subtle thing and it is surprising how skillful I can be in doing it. Just by twisting his words a small amount, by distorting his meaning just a little, I can make it appear that he is not only saying the thing I want to hear, but that he is the person I want him to be. It is only when I realize through his protest or through my own gradual recognition that I am subtly manipulating him that I become disgusted with myself. I know too from being on the receiving end of this how frustrating it is to be received for what you are not, to be heard as saying something which you have not said and do not mean. This creates anger and bafflement and disillusion.

WHEN OTHERS DO NOT UNDERSTAND

The next learning I want to share with you is that I am terribly frustrated and shut into myself when I try to express something which is deeply me, which is a part of my own private, inner world, and the other person does not understand. When I take the gamble, the risk, of trying to share something that is very personal with another individual and it is not received and not understood, this is a very deflating and a very lonely experience. I have come to believe that it is that experience which makes some individuals psychotic. They have given up hoping that anyone can understand them and once they have lost that hope then their own inner world, which becomes more and more bizarre, is the only place where they can live. They can no longer live in any shared human experience. I can sympathize with them because I know that when I try to share some feeling aspect of myself which is private, precious, and tentative, and when this communication is met by evaluation, by reassurance, by denial, by distortion of my meaning I have very strongly the reaction, "Oh, what's the use!" At such a time one knows what it is to be *alone*.

So, as you can see, a creative, active, sensitive, accurate, empathic, non-judgmental listening, is for me terribly important in a relationship. It is important for me to provide it. It has been extremely important especially at certain times in my life to receive it. I feel that I have grown within myself when I have provided it. I am very sure that I have grown and been released and enhanced when I have received this kind of listening.

1. *Try to think of a time when you, like Carl Rogers, felt a sense of enjoyment and satisfaction from really hearing someone.*
2. *Rogers claims that when you are really heard there is an inner release, a feeling of freedom, and a desire to share more of yourself. Has this been true for you? Has there been, in your life, a listener who hears you deeply?*
3. *Rogers is a highly influential therapist and theorist. However, even he dislikes himself "when I cannot hear the other person because I am so sure in advance of what he is about to say that I don't listen." And "still worse are those times when I catch myself trying to twist his message to make it say what I want him to say, and then only hearing that." Most of us engage in one or both of these non-listening behaviors. Monitor your listening behavior; attempt to catch yourself listening poorly. See if you can change your approach and just listen without imposing your thoughts.*
4. *Select any other point that Rogers makes in this article and offer your view on its validity.*
5. *Develop your listening skills by attempting one or more of the Applied Activities at the end of this section.*

A Teacher Hears

Listening, and hearing deeply, I feel, is the most important skill I must constantly strive to improve. Listening to my students tells me what they understand as opposed to what they can regurgitate. It tells me how they feel about the subject, about me, and about themselves.

Sometimes what I hear is silence. My classes are very active. No one goes quietly through the period. In the beginning of the year this surprises some students and even makes some uncomfortable. But soon they become accustomed to it. William was one of my new seventh-grade students this year. Early in the year I called on him. "So what law allows us to say that 3 + 7 is the same as 7 + 3? William? William? . . ." Nothing. No sound. No eye contact. Nothing. I approached him. My normal reaction was to tease. "Is there anybody in there?" Something in me said "not this time." I had never seen a reaction like this. I was to find out later that William was a victim of abuse. He was terrified of being hurt—of being wrong. Gradually as the year progressed, William has learned to trust me. Although it has not been easy for either of us, I now can call on him, and he will look at me and softly, very softly, tell me what he knows.

Sometimes what I hear is non-verbal. Meghan is a bubbly, bright, tiny little girl in the same class as William. Meghan works very hard on a consistent basis to keep herself at the top of this class. In early June she took her final and completely fell apart. I recognized a full-blown case of test anxiety. The following day, the last day the class would meet, there was time left at the end of the period and the class visited among themselves. I approached Meghan's desk. As I began to ask her about how she felt taking the final, I saw eyes filling with tears, and a strong little girl trying very hard not to cry. We talked about what had happened, about her competitive drive, about how important her math *grade* had become in her mind, and about how we could attempt to conquer the problem next year. The entire time she sank lower in her chair, trying to answer my questions, but without much success. What a painful chord we had struck. As I left school later that day, I noticed a note attached to my windshield wipers. "Mrs. R., This year has been really great. I can't wait till next year. Meghan." It seems both of us had listened.

Sometimes I hear boredom. One day last year I looked up at my seventh grade class and not one single student was "in attendance." Furthermore they weren't even being disruptive. It was like they had run into a really bad TV program! They were slouching and looking down or out the window. Total boredom had invaded that room. I was still in shock as I headed home that day. What I had heard in that room that period could not have been more clear if they, as a class, had gotten up and left!

Sometimes I hear confusion, frustration. Dara is an outstanding math student. She learns easily and well. Very often, however, when I am teaching a new concept, I often hear Dara say that "This is stupid" or "I don't like this." It was after a number of times of hearing this from her that I realized what I was really hearing was "I don't quite understand" or "I haven't completely processed what you are saying." In fact, she doesn't think it is stupid at all but rather is openly expressing a moment of confusion that she is experiencing.

And sometimes I fail to hear at all. Josh had done a beautiful job in math for three quarters. I'd had his older brother in past years, so he came to me already motivated. Suddenly in the fourth quarter he quit—missing or lost or half-done assignments, inattention in class. My response was annoyance, almost anger. After about three weeks of this, his mother called. Josh, it seemed, had had some bouts with depression and self-doubt in the past. Again it had flared up. He felt he had disappointed me and that I didn't "like" him. How could I have interpreted his behavior so wrongly? How could I have failed to hear what he was saying to me?

There are all kinds of hearing skills to be cultivated in teaching. It is the main link to the student-teacher chain, and perhaps is the most underrated of all the communication skills.

—A middle school teacher

Self-Disclosure

Nelson Goud

No man can come to know himself except as
an outcome of disclosing himself to another
person. . . . if we want to be loved, we must
disclose ourselves.

—Sidney Jourard

*I am afraid to tell you who I am, because, if I
tell you who I am, you may not like who I am,
and it's all that I have.*

—John Powell

Self-disclosure is what we reveal about ourselves to others. As the above quotes illustrate,
self-disclosure has the potential for great gains
but also contains significant risks. We are continually faced with the choice of revealing or
concealing ourselves to others.

Growth psychologists contend that the
quality of authenticity is one of the marks of a
mature, healthy person. In contrast is the
person who primarily acts in the form of false
fronts or facades. With an authentic person we
do not have to always wonder "What is she or
he *really* like?" Authenticity contains a good
dose of naturalness and reality. The ability to
self-disclose is one component of authenticity.
Rogers (1994, 1961) believes that a movement
away from facades to genuineness is a key
sign of personal growth. Pearson (1985) sum-
marized several studies that demonstrated a
close relationship between self-disclosure
and a person's level of self-esteem and self-
actualization.

Learning to appropriately self-disclose is
essential for establishing intimate relationships, avoiding social alienation, and knowing
oneself. Some of the major dimensions of effective self-disclosure will be examined in the
following discussion.

DISCLOSURE BREADTH AND DEPTH

Self-disclosure can be classified according to
both breadth and depth. Breadth refers to the
range of topics disclosed. Depth refers to the
degree of intimacy and completeness (feelings and ideas) of a disclosure. In general, the
more the depth, the more the risk and vulnerability. For example, casual relationships usually have breadth but little depth. Or, it is
possible to have a relationship characterized
by intense depth in one domain but little
depth or breadth in other domains (a brief love
affair would be an example).

What is considered low, moderate, and
high disclosure varies greatly among individuals. You may feel very comfortable discussing your feelings about your age, but
another may find this deeply personal and of
a high disclosure nature. A person must be
aware of these individual disclosure preferences if effective communication is to occur.
Additionally, there are wide cultural differences in the appropriateness of disclosure
levels (this article will emphasize general
American norms). You may even experience
variations in your willingness to disclose on
the same topic to different people, or under
different circumstances. Even with these individual variations, there are some common
findings which relate to most people.

Several studies of self-disclosure have
found that positive mental health is characterized by high disclosure to a few significant
others; poorly adjusted persons tend to over-
disclose or under-disclose to almost everyone
(Cozby, 1973; Chaikin & Derlega, 1975; Johnson, 1993). Optimum disclosure depends on

many factors: the purpose of disclosing, the nature of the relationship, the context of the disclosure, and the possible consequences. Most negative consequences result from either under- or over-disclosing.

UNDER-DISCLOSURE

There are many reasons why people may not reveal themselves. Derlega and Chaikin (1975) state that low revealers may not trust in the good will of others and may be "afraid of ridicule, rejection, or the possibility that the listener will reveal the information to others" (p. 14). Sometimes the low revealer is perceived to be a person of little emotion and having few major problems. That person's uniqueness also is masked. If concealment becomes the predominant way of relating to others, there may be a number of detrimental consequences: loneliness, mistrust from others because they do not know how this person thinks or feels, little shared intimacy, loss of a major source of self-knowledge, and a higher than normal amount of psychological energy expended to maintain a persona.

Sidney Jourard (1971) contends that how people choose to fulfill their life roles can influence disclosure levels. Life roles refer to the expected behaviors for a man or a woman, occupation, age. A healthy person can perform these roles and also express other dimensions of personhood. However, some people define themselves entirely by the roles they perform and are unaware of their interior life. Self-disclosure depends on an awareness of this interior life. Role conformity can lead to a "normal existence" but, as Jourard says, "it is possible to be a normal personality and be absolutely miserable" (p. 28).

Low self-revelation may be purposeful for some but not for others. Verbal self-disclosure depends on the ability to first recognize what you are feeling and thinking, and second, to place these interior states into words. Some people have deficiencies in one or both of these capabilities. In many ways, self-disclosure is a learned skill. Without experience in recognizing emotions and how to verbalize them, it is not possible to disclose them. Ask a young child to express emotions and the majority fall into the "sad, bad, glad" categories. Many persons do not develop beyond this level because they are not taught or encouraged to do so. Even today, conventional socialization still tends to favor females over males in these abilities. Pearson (1985) cites many studies that demonstrate the greater facility of females in verbal and non-verbal emotional expression (and recognizing the same).

OVER-DISCLOSURE

> There's this girl on my floor in the dormitory who's really weird. She tells people she's just met about really personal things, like all these guys she's sleeping with. Everyone tries to avoid her. I think she really needs help (A college coed, as quoted in Derlega & Chaikin, p. 10).

In one of my first graduate counseling courses we formed a group and the instructor told us to share how we felt about ourselves. A man on my right was the first to volunteer. He said, "My name is John and for the past year I have been in a psychiatric hospital. For quite awhile I had been hallucinating about cadavers and talking with them. I decided to get help. It worked. I do not have my hallucinations very much anymore." No one knew how to react to John's revelation. His openness was respected, but we felt uneasy. His disclosure was introduced before most of us were really capable of hearing him. We did not know enough about each other to place his deeply revealing comment in context. Instead of creating a closeness, I felt more distanced from John—Was he really OK now? If he reveals at this level so readily, will he be able to keep our in-class disclosures confidential?

These instances are examples of what most would consider over-disclosing. Over-disclosing is characterized by immediate revelations of high intimacy without considering the context or others' readiness to hear. Instead of encouraging closeness, over-disclosing tends to produce avoidance behaviors. Many over-disclosers are perceived as strange or deviant. Being so open about their own private lives, over-disclosers may not be trusted with reciprocal disclosures from others. Over-disclosers may initially solicit some sympathy, but if they continue, others will begin to ignore them or become annoyed.

To engage in effective disclosure, a person must observe many cues. A good deal of sensitivity is required to accurately judge the changing conditions of trust, vulnerability, and context. Some guidelines to consider on the topic of self-disclosure are offered next.

GUIDELINES FOR EFFECTIVE SELF-DISCLOSURE

Interpersonal Relationships

The degree of intimacy in a relationship closely parallels the level of mutual self-disclosure. The more that you know of another, the deeper the foundation for trust (or in some cases, mistrust, as with some over-disclosers). Self-disclosure is a primary path to discovering shared interests, values, and life perceptions—all major components of intimacy (both romantic and non-romantic). Some basic findings are listed below.

1. For early stages of a relationship, the preferred pattern is to initially share a lot of information at low disclosure levels. Higher degrees of disclosure follow at a gradual rate. Each disclosure level change is generally reciprocated by each partner if the relationship is to deepen. Changing levels of disclosure requires one of the parties to take a risk. If the other party is willing to strengthen the relationship at that moment, a reciprocating disclosure will usually occur. The reciprocity of disclosure may not be as significant in advanced, established stages of intimacy. Here trust has already been developed and attention can be focused on the topic being divulged by one of the parties (Jourard, 1971; Pearson, 1985; Johnson, 1993).

2. Should I conceal or reveal? Some disclosures are so powerful that they can cause major shifts, positive or negative, in a relationship. You love her but you do not know if she "likes or loves" you. One night she says "I love you." This propels the relationship to a new dimension. A few months later you want to share your whole life because of this deep intimacy but it includes (choose at least one): sexual fantasies with others, shameful past experiences, a disliked aspect of your partner. Will it be dishonest if you do not share yourself completely, or are some things best left unsaid?

Even the experts vary in their guidance on these issues. Harry Browne in Arkoff (1993) says that if you strive to be an honest person then "the only way to demonstrate your honesty is by simply responding honestly to everything (and to everyone)." Morton Hunt in Arkoff (1993) believes that people should be selective in what they reveal to intimates because often they release their own pain only to transfer it unnecessarily to the partner. "There are limits to intimacy," says Hunt, "not only for our own good, but for the good of those we love."

Carl Rogers, one of the most influential psychologists of this century, offers this example and guideline. He described a wife who was becoming increasingly sullen, angry, guilty and expressing these feelings in ways that were damaging her marriage. She realized that some unresolved issues from affairs with married men prior to her marriage were part of the problem, but felt that she could not express these to her husband. He might change his mind about what kind of person she was to him (which was as a loving, "nice girl"). Deciding that concealing was doing as much or more harm, she revealed her feelings. She did not go into details, but focused on the effects of those affairs. In her case it was heard and understood, and cleared the way for a deeper relationship with her husband. She believed that her desire for a good marriage was worth the risk of disclosure.

Rogers offers a helpful guideline on whether to disclose or not in an intimate relationship: ". . . in any continuing relationship any persistent feeling had better be expressed. Suppressing it can only damage the relationship. The first sentence is not stated casually. Only if it is a significant continuing relationship, and only if it is a recurring or persistent feeling, is it necessary to bring the feeling into the open in the relationship. If this is not done, what is unexpressed gradually poisons the relationship" (Rogers, 1972, pp. 20–21).

Jennifer and Scott have gradually developed a close, intimate relationship. They find it exhilarating to be able to trust each other with deep disclosures. They both believe that they want a relationship based on total honesty. However, Jennifer still finds herself attracted to other men, though she does not act on these feelings. She wonders if she should share this with Scott (in order to be totally honest). She also knows that Scott is somewhat insecure about losing her. In this instance it would probably be premature for Jennifer to disclose her feelings of attraction to other men. The relationship would be unnecessarily threatened by feelings that are quite common and not strong enough to warrant a major negative shift in their developing relationship. If these feelings persist and influence her relationship with Scott, then disclosure should be considered.

There are many other instances where non-disclosure is the appropriate choice given the multiple circumstances surrounding a relationship. What good does it do to mention a flaw of a friend, lover, parent when it is not significant to a continuing relationship? There are many times when a leader, parent, or others in an authority position must *not* disclose their fears in order to keep a problem situation manageable for others. I remember how my own parents were somehow strong and lively during the whole period that I had a mild case of polio. If they had shared their fears with me as a ten year old, I would have been frightened for the duration of the illness. Through their actions I remained relatively confident and positive during my hospitalization and recovery.

Purposes of Self-Disclosure

As a sender and receiver it is important to realize the intent of a self-revelation. Knowing another's motive helps to determine the kind of response to offer. Here are selected motives of self-disclosure, both negative and positive:

1. A genuine desire to establish more closeness or intimacy.
2. A catharsis or release of burdensome emotions. It is crucial here to consider the effects of this release on the receiver. Imagine that Carol has been suffering intense shame and hurt from abusive childhood experiences. She needs to express this to someone. Carol should consider talking to someone who can offer sound guidance, such as a counselor, spiritual advisor, or family doctor. In general, for disclosures that are primarily cathartic and confessional in nature, it is usually wise to share them initially with non-involved third parties.
3. Sometimes a person self-discloses to avoid responsibility. Instead of taking responsibility to right a wrong or to solve a problem, a person may intentionally tell

someone, hoping that person will shoulder the load.

4. Knowing that self-disclosure often creates affection and closeness, some persons take advantage of this knowledge in a self-serving manner, in what might be called manipulative intimacy. People may reveal just the right amount of information to be trusted, but the trust is used for their gain only (sexual, financial, or status). They have no intent of establishing a genuine relationship through this kind of self-disclosure.

Multiple Receivers

It is helpful to have several persons to whom you can disclose on different topics and intimacy levels. It is almost impossible for one person, even a spouse or close friend, to be an appropriate receiver for all your feelings and experiences. For example, you may need to talk *about* your spouse/friend, and this requires someone else you can trust. Most often a single receiver does not have all the needed background to understand everything you want to share. Think of a time when you tried to share an intense experience from your job, hobby, or school major but your receiver had no relevant experience. You undoubtedly found yourself explaining background information rather than the experience you wanted to share. I find there are some aspects of university life that are inaccessible to those outside of the university. Here I seek a university friend if I have a need to communicate. The same holds true for my trumpet-playing.

Context

For effective self-disclosure to occur, the circumstances must be considered. Some of the major circumstances include the following.

Emotional and Physical Readiness. It is difficult to send or receive high levels of disclosure when you are tired, rushed, anxious, in the midst of problem solving, and so on. While a person does not always have to be in a perfect mental or physical condition, make sure that at least minimal readiness levels are met.

Time Framework. Is there sufficient time to comprehend and discuss the disclosure (especially high level ones)? Try to avoid the last minute disclosure. In this approach a person delays a disclosure until the last possible moment to avoid possible further discussion or consequences. For example, counselors often hear the most important revelations in the last five minutes of a counseling session. Or imagine an ongoing couple at the end of a regular date. While about to leave, Rodolfo turns and says, "Oh, by the way, I think it might be good if we spent a little time apart—G'night."

Physical Setting. Attempt to be aware of the effects of the physical environment, such as temperature, noise level, and the presence of other people. Susie may be very comfortable disclosing in a crowded restaurant but Jake is not. Sometimes movement is a factor. I know of many people, including myself, who prefer to self-disclose while going on a walk, during breaks on a long bike ride, or driving in a car. My son and I have our best disclosure times during these kinds of activities. My daughter and I have our mutual disclosures while sitting out on the patio.

Dyad Effect. A two-person group (dyad) has been found to be the preferred number for self-disclosure (Pearson, 1985). Trust and confidentiality seem to occur more readily in dyads. Effective disclosure is possible in larger groups but there is more initial resistance.

Some Exceptions. There are two contextual circumstances where high disclosure occurs faster than normal. One is during crisis situations such as disasters, accidents, serious illness or death of a loved one, or being trapped in an enclosed space. In these situations, participants share a common and intense bond of danger or loss. The normal rules of disclosure are often shelved in order to restore a sense of safety and support.

The second instance is the stranger phenomenon first mentioned by the German sociologist Georg Simmel in the late 1800s. Here a person discusses intimate topics to a complete stranger at a bar, on a plane, in a hotel restaurant, on a park bench, and so on. Another and more recent version is to reveal oneself to strangers in cyberspace on the Internet. There are several reasons why a stranger may be the recipient of high self-disclosures. A stranger has little likelihood of using the information against the sender—in short, there is little threat. An Internet user does not have to worry about following up a disclosure or getting further involved. Sometimes a stranger may offer an outsider's point of view of your situation. Disclosures to strangers may be helpful, but only if not used as regular substitutes for genuine and consistent intimate relationships.

Fusion Communication

Usually the sender and receiver of a message are different people. It is possible for a person to be both the sender and receiver. I call this fusion communication. There are times when there are no appropriate receivers available to hear your disclosure. Or you cannot adequately verbalize certain feelings or experiences to others in a way they could understand, but you must express yourself. In this instance you may appoint yourself as the receiver. Some forms of fusion communication are discussed below.

Internal Dialogues. Internal dialogues include talking to yourself (silently or out loud); writing interpretive diaries or journals; or expressing your inner world through art forms —poetry, song, or dance. Anne Frank used

fusion communication during her confinement by keeping a diary "in order to bring out all kinds of things that lie buried deep in my heart. . . . The reason for my starting a diary . . . is that I have no . . . real friend."

Boomerang Dialogues. In boomerang dialogues, individuals seem to be disclosing to something else, but they are really communicating to themselves. You may, for example, speak to a pet about a current life dilemma or problem. Your message is bounced off the pet to you. Almost any external object can be a target of boomerang dialogue—plants, trees, a car, hello walls, the sky or the ocean. Young children often disclose to real or stuffed animals or to invisible friends. Some forms of prayer function as fusion communication.

Deceased loved ones can also be recipients of self-disclosures. In *The Winter of Our Discontent,* John Steinbeck explains the essence of this form of fusion communication: "Much of my talk is addressed to people who are dead . . . Nothing mysterious or mystic about that. It's asking for advice or an excuse from the inner part of you that is formed and certain" (p. 57).

Kempler (1987) discusses how some inner experiences have stages of maturity. To disclose them prematurely may damage their full expression. This is particularly true for new inspirations, emotional self-insights, intuitive illuminations. Forms of fusion communication should be considered in these instances.

Fusion communication is one valuable self-disclosure strategy under the conditions described above. If it is the only form of self-disclosure, that indicates something is amiss. Interpersonal and fusion communication are both essential for a balanced life.

Self-Disclosure and Self-Knowledge

We gain knowledge of ourselves through several means. Two major sources are feedback from others and knowledge gained from our experiences. Talking about our inner reactions to experiences is also a primary path to self-awareness. Johnson (1983) says, "When you explain your feelings, perceptions, reactions, and experiences in words, they become clearer, better organized, and take on new meanings" (p. 35).

While disclosing some confused feelings or intuitions with someone you trust, you may suddenly stumble over an insight, or discover "I didn't know I felt this way." Jourard (1971) contends that without sufficient self-disclosure individuals may learn to conceal their own identities from themselves. One path to deep inner knowledge, he continues, is this: "When a person has been able to disclose himself utterly to another person, he learns how to increase his contact with his real self, and he may then be better able to direct his destiny on the basis of this knowledge" (p. 6).

Gender and Self-Disclosure

There are some gender differences on self-disclosure behavior. Below are selected findings as reported by Pearson (1985). These are group tendencies and do not automatically apply for every male or female:

- Women self-disclose more easily and more often than men.
- Women self-disclose more negative information.
- Women self-disclose more on intimate topics; both men and women self-disclose at similar levels on non-intimate topics.
- Increased eye contact and a closer personal space encourage self-disclosure for women, but decrease it for men.
- Positively interpreted touch increases self-disclosure for both men and women.
- Both men and women tend to disclose more as they get older; females disclose at higher levels at all age stages.

A sign points to the spot where campers can cast their rubbish. Campers leave the dumping station with lighter backs and more room in their tents.

Our minds could use a dumping station. A mind, too, functions better if it is lighter and has more room. It means that one must try to jettison unnecessary guilt, prolonged worry, immobilizing fear, or chronic mourning. It may mean talking it out with someone, doing more or doing less, or getting help. But cleaning out emotional debris is essential if life is to be lived as intended. Cleaning the mind starts with first knowing what to throw away. What would make your mind lighter?

"Dumping Station" by Nelson Goud. Copyright © 1996.

CONCLUSION

One requirement of an individual identity is boundaries. Without boundaries it is difficult to perceive where one person begins and another ends. Sometime it feels nice to merge identities for awhile (such as the infant-mother bond or the initial stages of intense intimacy). Continuing these merged identities for too long, however, will eventually stunt full development. Our growth depends on realizing unique and individual potentialities.

Self-disclosure is closely tied to identity boundaries. Becoming close to another can be described as allowing another to enter—to pass through a boundary gate and see what is there. The further along another is allowed to pass boundary gates, the deeper the intimacy. In the most intimate of relationships there still may be some boundary gates that remain closed. We may have parts of ourselves that we wish not to reveal, or it may be that we just cannot explain some knowings of our interior life. Some of our unconscious stirrings are unknown to anyone, including us. Finally, we may purposely choose to have a hideaway which needs privacy in order to produce a sense of uniqueness, mystery, and constructive surprise.

The choice is ours. We can let everyone pass through our boundary gates at the costs of indistinct identities and interpersonal sameness. We can let no one in at the expense of loneliness, mistrust, and the loss of a major source of understanding oneself. Keeping our gates locked also means we cannot venture out; we, too, are locked out of others' lives. Or we can learn selectivity. We experiment and observe and even "goof." Eventually we will create and discover the art of knowing when to open and when to close our boundary gates, when to embrace the world and when to seek some privacy.

References

Arkoff, A. (1993). *Psychology and personal growth* (4th ed.). Boston: Allyn & Bacon.

Cozby, P. C. (1973). Self-disclosure: A literature review. *Psychological Bulletin, 79,* 73–91.

Derlega, V. & Chaikin, A. (1975). *Sharing intimacy.* Englewood Cliffs, NJ: Prentice-Hall.

Johnson, D. (1993). *Reaching out.* Boston: Allyn & Bacon.

Jourard, S. (1971). *The transparent self.* New York: Van Nostrand Reinhold Co.

Kempler, B. (1987). The shadow side of self-disclosure. *Journal of Humanistic Psychology, 27,* 109–117.

Pearson, J. (1985). *Gender and communication.* Dubuque, IA: Wm. C. Brown.

Rogers, C. (1961). *On becoming a person.* Boston: Houghton Mifflin.

Rogers, C. (1972). *Becoming partners: Marriage and its alternatives.* New York: Delacorte Press.

Rogers, C. & Freiberg, H. (1994). *Freedom to learn* (3rd ed.). New York: Merrill/Macmillan.

Follow-Up

1. *Select two statements from the article that have relevance for your life.*
2. *Describe a time when you self-disclosed but wish you had not. What happened to make you feel this way? What did you learn about disclosure from*

this experience? (You do not have to reveal private details here, just general situations.)

3. *Try to remember a time when you took a risk and self-disclosed and it turned out well. What did you learn about disclosure from this experience?*
4. *Overall, are you an under-discloser, over-discloser, or an appropriate discloser? Explain why you see yourself this way.*
5. *Try to describe any experience or preference in fusion communication strategies. Under what conditions, if any, do you find them helpful?*
6. *Select one or more Guidelines for Effective Self-Disclosure and apply them in your current situation.*

You Just Don't Understand

Deborah Tannen

A married couple was in a car when the wife turned to her husband and asked, "Would you like to stop for a drink?"

"No, thanks," he answered truthfully. So they didn't stop.

The result? The wife—who had indeed wanted to stop—became annoyed because she felt her preference had not been considered. The husband, seeing his wife was angry, became frustrated. *Why didn't she just say what she wanted?*

Unfortunately, he failed to see that his wife was asking the question not to get an instant decision, but to begin a negotiation. And the woman didn't realize that when her husband said no, he was just expressing his preference, not making a ruling. When a man and woman interpret the same interchange in such conflicting ways, it's no wonder they can find themselves leveling angry charges of selfishness and obstinacy at each other.

As a specialist in linguistics, I have studied how the conversational styles of men and women differ. We cannot, of course, lump "all men" or "all women" into fixed categories—individuals vary greatly. But research shows that the seemingly senseless misunderstandings that haunt our relationships can at least in part be explained by the different conversational rules by which men and women often play.

Whenever I write or speak about this subject, people tell me how relieved they are to learn that what they had previously ascribed to personal failings is, in fact, very common. Learning about the different (though equally valid) conversational frequencies men and women are tuned to can help banish blame and help us truly talk to one another. Here are some of the most common areas of conflict.

STATUS VS. SUPPORT

Men grow up in a world in which a conversation is often a contest—either to achieve the upper hand or to prevent other people from pushing them around. For many women, however, talking is typically a way to exchange confirmation and support. I saw this firsthand when my husband and I had jobs in different cities. When people made comments like "That must be rough" and "How do you stand it?" I accepted their sympathy.

But my husband would react with irritation. Our situation had advantages, he would explain. As academics, we had long weekends and vacations together.

Everything he said was true, but I didn't understand why he chose to say it. He told me that he felt some of the comments implied: "Yours is not a real marriage. I am superior to you because my wife and I have avoided your misfortune." It had not occurred to me there might be an element of one-upmanship, though I recognized it when it was pointed out.

I now see that my husband was simply approaching the world as many men do: as a place where people try to achieve and maintain status. I, on the other hand, was approaching the world as many women do: as a network of connections, in which people seek consensus.

INDEPENDENCE VS. INTIMACY

Since women often think in terms of closeness and support, they struggle to preserve intimacy. Men, concerned with status, tend to focus on establishing independence. These traits can lead women and men to starkly different views of the same situation.

When Josh's old high-school friend called him at work to say he'd be in town, Josh invited him to stay for the weekend. That evening he told Linda.

Linda was upset. How could Josh make these plans without discussing them with her beforehand? She would never do that to him. "Why don't you tell your friend you have to check with your wife?" she asked.

Josh replied, "I can't say I have to ask my wife for permission!"

To Josh, checking with his wife would mean he was not free to act on his own. It would make him feel like a child or an underling. But Linda actually enjoys telling people, "I have to check with Josh." It makes her feel good to show her life is entwined with her husband's.

ADVICE VS. UNDERSTANDING

Eve had a benign lump removed from her breast. When she confided to her husband, Mark, that she was distressed because the stitches changed the contour of her breast, he answered, "You can always have plastic surgery."

This comment bothered her. "I'm sorry you don't like the way it looks," she protested, "but I am not having any more surgery!"

Mark was hurt and puzzled. "I don't care about a scar," he replied. "It doesn't bother me at all."

"Then why are you telling me to have plastic surgery?" she asked.

"Because *you* were upset about the way it looks."

Eve felt like a heel Mark had been wonderfully supportive throughout her surgery. How could she snap at him now? The problem stemmed from a difference in approach. To many men, a complaint is a challenge to come up with a solution. Mark thought he was reassuring Eve by telling her there was something she could *do* about her scar. But often women are looking for emotional support, not solutions.

INFORMATION VS. FEELINGS

A cartoon I once saw shows a husband opening a newspaper and asking his wife, "Is there anything you'd like to say before I start reading?" We know there isn't—but that as soon as the man begins reading, his wife will think of something.

The cartoon is funny because people recognize their own experience in it. What's not funny is that many women are hurt when men don't talk to them at home, and many men are frustrated when they disappoint their partners without knowing why.

Rebecca, who is happily married, told me this is a source of dissatisfaction with her husband, Stuart. When she tells him what she is thinking, he listens silently. When she asks him what is on his mind, he says, "Nothing."

All Rebecca's life she has had practice verbalizing her feelings with friends and relatives. To her, this shows involvement and caring. But to Stuart, like most men, talk is for information. All his life he has had practice in keeping his innermost thoughts to himself.

Yet many such men hold center stage in a social setting, telling jokes and stories. They use conversation to claim attention and to entertain. Women can wind up hurt that their husbands tell relative strangers things they have not told them.

To avoid this kind of misunderstanding, both men and women can make adjustments.

A woman may observe a man's desire to read the paper, for example, without seeing it as rejection. And a man can understand a woman's desire to talk without feeling it an intrusion.

ORDERS VS. PROPOSALS

Diana often begins statements with "Let's." She might say, "Let's park over there" or "Let's clean up before lunch." This makes Nathan angry. He has deciphered Diana's "Let's" as a command. Like most men, he resists being told what to do. But to Diana, she is making suggestions, not demands, Like most women, she wants to avoid confrontation and formulates requests as proposals rather than orders. Her style of talking *is* a way of getting others to do what she wants—but by winning agreement first.

With certain men, like Nathan, this tactic backfires. If they perceive someone is trying to get them to do something indirectly, they feel manipulated and respond more resentfully than they would to a straightforward request.

CONFLICT VS. COMPROMISE

In trying to prevent fights, some women refuse to openly oppose the will of others. But at times it's far more effective for a woman to assert herself, even at the risk of conflict.

Dora was frustrated by a series of used automobiles she drove. It was she who commuted to work, but her husband, Hank, who chose the cars. Hank always went for automobiles that were "interesting," but in continual need of repair. After Dora was nearly killed when her brakes failed, they were in the market for yet another car.

Dora wanted to buy a late-model sedan from a friend. Hank fixed his sights on a 15-year-old sports car. Previously, she would have acceded to his wishes. But this time Dora bought the boring but dependable car and steeled herself for Hank's anger. To her amazement, he spoke not a word of remonstrance. When she later told him what she had expected, he scoffed at her fears and said she should have done what she wanted from the start if she felt that strongly about it.

As Dora discovered, a little conflict won't kill you. At the same time, men who habitually oppose others can adjust their style to opt for less confrontation.

When we don't see style differences for what they are, we sometimes draw unfair conclusions ("You're illogical," "You're self-centered," "You don't care about me"). But once we grasp the two characteristic approaches, we stand a better chance of preventing disagreements from spiraling out of control. Learning the other's ways of talking is a leap across the communication gap between men and women, and a giant step toward genuine understanding.

Follow-Up

1. *Describe an instance when you and someone of the opposite gender seemed to communicate on different wavelengths (or from distinctly separate frames of reference). Can you understand the other's framework?*
2. *Tannen shows how different gender mindsets result in different interpretations of the same situation. She gives examples from six conflicting patterns.*

Do you act in accordance with your gender in each of these six patterns? Explain why or why not.

3. *Which of the six gender communication patterns were practiced by your parents or guardians in the way Tannen describes? How has this influenced your communication preferences?*
4. *Observe men–women conversations to see if Tannen's ideas hold true.*
5. *Attempt the He Said, She Said Applied Activity at the end of this section.*

Assertive, Nonassertive, and Aggressive Behavior

*Arthur J. Lange
and Patricia Jakubowski*

Assertion involves standing up for personal rights and expressing thoughts, feelings, and beliefs in *direct, honest,* and *appropriate* ways which do not violate another person's rights.[1] The basic message in assertion is: This is what I think. This is what I feel. This is how I see the situation. This message expresses "who the person is" and is said without dominating, humiliating, or degrading the other person.

Assertion involves respect—not deference. Deference is acting in a subservient manner as though the other person is right, or better, simply because the other person is older, more powerful, experienced, or knowledgeable or is of a different sex or race. Deference is present when people express themselves in ways that are self-effacing, appeasing, or overly apologetic.

Two types of respect are involved in assertion: respect for oneself, that is, expressing one's needs and defending one's rights, as well as respect for the other person's needs and rights. An example will help clarify the kind of respect involved in assertive behavior.

A woman was desperately trying to get a flight to Kansas City to see her mother who was sick in the hospital. Weather conditions were bad and the lines were long. Having been rejected from three standby flights, she again found herself in the middle of a long line for the fourth and last flight to Kansas City. This time she approached a man who was standing near the beginning of the line and said, pointing to her place, "Would you mind exchang-

ing places with me? I ordinarily wouldn't ask, but it's extremely important that I get to Kansas City tonight." The man nodded yes, and as it turned out, both of them were able to get on the flight.

When asked what her reaction would have been if the man had refused, she replied, "It would have been OK. I hoped he would say yes, but after all he was there first."[1]

In this example the woman showed self-respect for her own needs by asking whether the man would be willing to help her. Also, she respected the man's right to refuse her request and not fulfill her need.

How is respect shown when refusing another's request? It depends on how that request is refused. A request may be refused aggressively: "What do you mean you want to borrow my car! I don't know where you get your nerve!" Such aggressive refusals involve only one-way respect; that is, respect for one's right to refuse but not for the other person's right to ask. A request may also be refused nonassertively: "What can I say . . . I feel just awful saying this, really bad . . . I can't loan you my car. Oh gee, what a terrible thing to say!" Here the person refused the request, but did it in a way that showed lack of self-respect: It suggested that the refuser was a bad person who should not have denied the request. In addition, the nonassertive refusal did not respect the other person's right to be treated as a capable person who can handle a disappointment. In contrast, an assertive refusal would be: "I'd like to help you out, but I feel uncomfortable loaning my car." The assertive refusal shows the two-fold respect: self-respect in the self-confident way the request is refused and respect for the other person's right to ask.

In our view, the goal of assertion is communication and "mutuality"; that is, to get and give respect, to ask for fair play, and to leave room for compromise when the needs and rights of two people conflict. In such compromises neither person sacrifices basic integrity and both get some of their needs satisfied. The compromise may be one in which one person gets her needs taken care of immediately while the other party gets taken care of a little later. For example, one weekend the friends see a movie and the next weekend they bowl. Or the compromise may involve both parties giving up a little. They attend *part* of an outdoor concert and then take a short walk and talk. When personal integrity is at stake, a compromise is inappropriate and nonassertive.

We are opposed to viewing assertion as simply a way "to get what one wants" for three reasons. First, this view emphasizes success in attaining goals. Thus it can cause people to become passive when they believe that acting assertively will not get them what they want. Second, this view concentrates only on the asserter's right and not on the personal rights of both parties. Such an attitude increases the chances of people using aggressive or manipulative methods to get what they want. Third, it may lead to irresponsible behavior in which assertion is used to take advantage of other people. We have frequently heard people say that they can assertively ask for favors and it's just too bad that the other person is not strong enough to refuse their requests. In contrast, we advocate *responsible* asserting which involves mutuality, asking for fair play, and using one's greater assertive power to help others become more able to stand up for themselves. Interestingly, a by-

product of responsible assertion is that people often do get what they want. Why? Because most people become cooperative when they are approached in a way which is both respectful of self and respectful of others.

Nonassertion involves violating one's own rights by failing to express honest feelings, thoughts, and beliefs and consequently permitting others to violate oneself, or expressing one's thoughts and feelings in such an apologetic, diffident, self-effacing manner that others can easily disregard them.[1] In the latter type of nonassertion, the total message which is communicated is: I don't count—you can take advantage of me. My feelings don't matter—only yours do. My thoughts aren't important—yours are the only ones worth listening to. I'm nothing—you are superior.

Nonassertion shows a lack of respect for one's own needs. It also sometimes shows a subtle lack of respect for the other person's ability to take disappointments, to shoulder some responsibility, to handle his own problems, etc. The goal of nonassertion is to appease others and to avoid conflict at any cost.

Aggression involves directly standing up for personal rights and expressing thoughts, feelings, and beliefs in a way which is often dishonest, usually inappropriate, and always violates the rights of the other person. An example of "emotionally dishonest" aggression is a situation where individuals who feel saddened by another person's mourning for the death of a loved one sarcastically degrade the mourner ("That's just what I like to see—a grown person sniveling like a two-year-old brat"), instead of revealing their own sad and helpless feelings.

The usual goal of aggression is domination and winning, forcing the other person to lose. Winning is insured by humiliating, degrading, belittling, or overpowering other people so that they become weaker and less able to express and defend their needs and rights. The basic message is: That is what I think—you're stupid for believing differently. This is what I want—what you want isn't important. This is what I feel—your feelings don't count.

NONVERBAL COMPONENTS OF ASSERTIVE, NONASSERTIVE, AND AGGRESSIVE BEHAVIOR

So far we've discussed the verbal components of assertive, nonassertive, and aggressive behavior. The nonverbal components of these behaviors are equally important, if not more so. Research has shown that the vast majority of our communication is carried out nonverbally.[2] Take a moment to consider how the statement "I like you" can be said as a sincere statement, a question, or a sarcastic remark, by simply changing voice inflection, facial expression, and hand gestures. Likewise, an otherwise verbal assertive statement can become nonassertive or aggressive depending on the nonverbal behaviors which accompany the verbal statement.

Eisler, Miller, and Hersen[3] have pinpointed some of the nonverbal behaviors which may be important in assertion: duration of looking at the other person, duration of speech, loudness of speech, and affect in speech. Research has generally supported the importance of these nonverbal behaviors[3] with the exception of the length of time it takes the person to respond to the other individual.[4] Other nonverbal behaviors which may be important in assertion, nonassertion, and aggression are described below.

In assertive behavior, the nonverbals are congruent with the verbal messages and add support, strength, and emphasis to what is being said verbally. The voice is appropriately loud to the situation; eye contact is firm but not a staredown; body gestures which denote strength are used; and the speech pattern is fluent—without awkward hesitancies—expressive, clear, and emphasizes key words.

In nonassertive behavior, the nonverbal behaviors include evasive eye contact, body gestures such as hand wringing, clutching the other person, stepping back from the other person as the assertive remark is made, hunching the shoulders, covering the mouth with the hand, nervous gestures which distract the listener from what the speaker is saying, and wooden body posture. The voice tone may be singsong or overly soft. The speech pattern is hesitant and filled with pauses and the throat may be cleared frequently. Facial gestures may include raising the eyebrows, laughs, and winks when expressing anger.

In general, the nonassertive gestures are ones which convey weakness, anxiety, pleading, or self-effacement They reduce the impact of what is being said verbally, which is precisely why people who are scared of acting assertively use them. Their goal is to "soften" what they're saying so that the other person will not be offended.

In aggressive behavior, the nonverbal behaviors are ones which dominate or demean the other person. These include eye contact that tries to stare down and dominate the other person, a strident voice that does not fit the situation, sarcastic or condescending tone of voice, and parental body gestures such as excessive finger pointing.

EXAMPLES OF ASSERTIVE, NONASSERTIVE, AND AGGRESSIVE BEHAVIOR

In each example, the first response is aggressive, the second, nonassertive, and the third is assertive.

Confronting a Professor Who Gives Inappropriate and Excessive Amounts of Work—

1. Dr. Jones, you have some nerve giving me this kind of work. I know you have control

over me, but I don't have to take this stuff. You professors think you can use grad students for anything you please—Well not this time!

2. OK, Dr. Jones, I'll do it. I guess you must have a reason for asking me to do this stuff . . . even if it isn't related to my assistantship. I don't suppose you'd consider letting me off the hook this time? Huh?

3. Dr. Jones, when you give me work that's not related to your class, I'd have to put in extra hours beyond what's appropriate for my assistantship. For those reasons I need to say no on this extra work.

Talking with Someone Who Has Just Made a Sexist Remark—

1. Who the hell do you think you are? God's gift to women?
2. Oh come on (ha ha). You know how much that irritates me when you say things like that (ha ha).
3. Frankly, I think that remark demeans both of us.

Refusing an Extra Helping of Food at a Dinner Party—

1. You'd just love me to put on a few pounds of fat!
2. Gee . . . ah . . . Well, since you insist . . . I'll change my mind. Yeah, give me another piece.
3. That food does look good but I don't want any more.

Trying to Get a Group on the Subject After They've Wandered into Tangential Areas—

1. Can't you people get back to work and stop this goofing off?
2. I guess it's just my hang-up. Do you think it'd be OK if we got back to the original subject? I've forgotten it myself (ha ha).

3. What we're talking about is interesting; however, I'm feeling the need to get back to the original subject.

TYPES OF ASSERTION

Basic Assertion

Basic assertion refers to a simple expression of standing up for personal rights, beliefs, feelings, or opinions. It does not involve other social skills, such as empathy, confrontation, persuasion, etc. Examples of basic assertions are:

When being interrupted—
Excuse me, I'd like to finish what I'm saying.

When being asked an important question for which you are unprepared—
I'd like to have a few minutes to think that over.

When returning an item to a store—
I'd like my money back on this saw.

When refusing a request—
No, this afternoon is not a good time for me to visit with you.

When telling a parent you don't want advice—
I don't want any more advice.

Basic assertion also involves expressing affection and appreciation toward other people:

I like you.
I care for you a lot.
Having a friend like you makes me feel happy.
You're someone special to me.

The following is a particularly touching example of assertively expressing affection:

A father overheard his five-year-old child saying to a playmate: "Are you having a good time?" When the playmate replied "Yes," the child continued, "I am too. I'm so glad that I invited you to come over and play!"

Empathic Assertion

Often people want to do more than simply express their feelings or needs. They may also want to convey some sensitivity to the other person. When this is the goal, the empathic assertion can be used. This type of assertion involves making a statement that conveys recognition of the other person's situation or feelings and is followed by another statement which stands up for the speaker's rights.[1] Examples of empathic assertions are:

> When two people are chatting loudly while a meeting is going on—
>
> You may not realize it, but your talking is starting to make it hard for me to hear what's going on in the meeting. Would you keep it down?
>
> When having some furniture delivered—
>
> I know it's hard to say exactly when the truck will come, but I'd like a ball park estimate of the arrival time.
>
> When telling a parent that you don't want advice—
>
> I know that you give me advice because you don't want me to get hurt by mistakes I might make. At this point in my life, I need to learn how to make my own decisions and rely on myself, even if I do make some mistakes. I appreciate the help you've given me in the past and you can help me now by not giving me advice.[1]

There is considerable personal power in the empathic assertion because other people more easily respond to assertion when they have been recognized first. This power, however, should not be used as a manipulation to merely gain one's own ends, without genuine respect for the other person. Repeatedly saying, "I understand how you feel but . . . " can be just "mouthing" understanding and conning other people into believing that their feelings are being taken into account when in fact their feelings are really being discounted. Such behavior does not involve empathic assertion.

Another important benefit of the empathic assertion is that it causes the speaker to take a moment to try to understand the other person's feelings before the speaker reacts. This can help the speaker keep perspective on the situation and thus reduces the likelihood of the speaker's aggressively overreacting when irritated.

Escalating Assertion

According to Rimm and Masters,[5] escalating assertion involves starting with a "minimal" assertive response that can usually accomplish the speaker's goal with a minimum of effort and negative emotion and a small possibility of negative consequences. When the other person fails to respond to the minimal assertion and continues to violate one's rights, the speaker gradually escalates the assertion and becomes increasingly firm. We have observed that often it is not necessary to go beyond the initial minimal assertion; but if it is necessary, the person can become increasingly firm without becoming aggressive. The escalating assertion can occur from a request to a demand, from a preference to an outright refusal, or, as the following example illustrates, from an empathic assertion to a firm basic assertion.

> The speaker is in a bar with a woman friend, and a man repeatedly offers to buy them drinks—
>
> That's very nice of you to offer, but we came here to catch up on some news. Thanks, anyway!
>
> No, thank you. We really would rather talk just to each other.
>
> This is the third and last time I am going to tell you that we don't want your company. Please leave![6]

In this example, the final blunt refusal was appropriate because the earlier escalating assertions were ignored. If the woman had started with the highly escalated assertion the first time the man had approached, her response would have been inappropriate. Since assertion involves direct, honest, and *appropriate* expressions of thoughts and feelings, her reaction would be aggressive, rather than assertive. Likewise when a person has not objected to taking the minutes of a meeting, but one day suddenly says, "I'm getting sick and tired of being the secretary just because I'm the only woman in the group," her response would be aggressive, rather than assertive. Only if her comment had been preceded by successively escalated assertions which had been ignored would her comment be appropriate and assertive.

A final point about the escalating assertion is that just before making the final escalated assertion, we suggest that one consider offering a "contract option," in which the other person is informed what the final assertion will be and is given a chance to change behavior before it occurs. For example, when a repair shop repeatedly refuses to settle an unreasonable bill, one may say, "I'm being left with no other alternative than to complain to the Better Business Bureau and your distributor. I'd prefer not to do that but I will if this is the only alternative I'm left with." Often people only recognize that one means business at the contract option point.

Whether the contract option is simply a threat depends on how it is said. If it is said in a menacing tone of voice which relies on emotionality to carry the argument, it is a threat. When the contract option is carried out assertively, it is said in a matter-of-fact tone of voice which simply gives information about the consequences which will occur if the situation is not equitably resolved.

Confrontive Assertion

Confrontive assertion is used when the other person's words contradict his deeds. This type of assertion involves objectively describing what the other person said would be done and what the other actually did do, after which the speaker expresses what he wants.[1] The entire assertion is said in a matter-of-fact, nonevaluative way, as the examples below show:

I was supposed to be consulted before the final proposal was typed. But I see the secretary is typing it right now. Before he finishes it, I want to review the proposal and make whatever corrections I think are needed. In the future, I want to get a chance to review any proposals before they're sent to the secretary.

I thought we'd agreed that you were going to be more considerate towards students. Yet I noticed today that when two students asked for some information you said that you had better things to do than babysit for kids. As we discussed earlier, I see showing more consideration as an important part of your job. I'd like to figure out what seems to be the problem.

I said it was OK to borrow my records as long as you checked with me first. Now you're playing my classical records without asking. I'd like to know why you did that.

The above are examples of initial confrontive assertive statements. In most cases the ensuing conversation would be an extended interaction between the two people. This is particularly true in the last two examples in which the speaker wanted additional information and the resulting discussions would be problem-solving ones.

In contrast to assertive confrontation, aggressive confrontation involves judging other people — rather than describing their behavior—and trying to make others feel guilty. For example:

Hey, those are my records! Evidently your word means absolutely nothing to you! Just for that I want my records right now and in the future you're going to find them locked up. Then you'll have to ask me first.

SUMMARY

Assertion involves standing up for personal rights and expressing thoughts, feelings, and beliefs in direct, honest, and appropriate ways which respect the rights of other people. In contrast, aggression involves self-expression which is characterized by violating others' rights and demeaning others in an attempt to achieve one's own objectives. Nonassertion involves behavior which violates one's own self by failing to express honest feelings or thoughts. It may also involve diffident, overly apologetic, or effacing expression of personal rights and preferences.

It is important that assertive skills be used responsibly, that is, used in ways which treat others fairly and help facilitate others becoming more assertive.

Losing others' approval is a major fear which prompts many individuals to act nonassertively. For those who are frequently aggressive, a typical fear concerns their losing control and power over other people. A major reason for acting assertively rather than unassertively is that assertion increases one's own sense of self-respect and personal control.

References

1. Jakubowski, P. (1977). Assertive behavior and clinical problems of women. In E. Rawlings & D. Carter (Eds.), *Psychotherapy for women: Treatment towards equality.* Springfield, IL: Charles C. Thomas.
2. Mehrabian, A. (1972). *Nonverbal communication.* Chicago: Aldine/Atherton.
3. Eisler, R. M., Miller, P. M., & Hersen, M. (1973). Components of assertive behavior. *Journal of Clinical Psychology, 29,* 295–299.
4. Galassi, J. P., Galassi, M. D., & Litz, M. C. (1974). Assertive training in groups using video feedback. *Journal of Counseling Psychology, 21,* 390–394.
5. Rimm, D. C., & Masters, J. C. (1974). *Behavior therapy: Techniques and empirical findings.* New York: Academic Press.
6. Jakubowski, P. (1977). Self-assertion training procedures for women. In E. Rawlings & D. Carter (Eds.), *Psychotherapy for women: Treatment towards equality.* Springfield, IL: Charles C. Thomas.

Follow-Up

1. *Give examples when you acted in these ways: nonassertively, assertively, aggressively (as explained in the article). What is your predominant style in expressing your rights and beliefs? Give a brief explanation supporting your answer.*
2. *While there is a difference between assertive and aggressive behavior, some see both as pushy. Is this true for you? Explain your response.*
3. *If you have been aggressive in expressing your rights and beliefs, what have been the consequences?*

4. *Choose one or more of the following types of assertion and attempt to be more skillful expressing them: basic assertion, empathic assertion, escalating assertion, confrontive assertion.*

5. *Assertive behavior is closely related to self-esteem. One approach to enhancing your own esteem level is to become more appropriately assertive. Try some gradual and appropriate risks in assertiveness to see if this is true for you.*

6. *For further reading on this topic go to almost any major bookstore and browse the Self-help or Psychology sections. One highly recommended practical book on assertiveness is the most recent edition of* Your Perfect Right *by Alberti and Emmons.*

King of the Purple Tree

Nels Goud

"Why don't we go out and get something to eat and talk about it more there?"

The others liked the idea and grabbed their notebooks and started to leave the classroom. One turned to me and asked "How about joining us? Maybe we'll see what you are really like outside of the prof role," she smiled.

Well, that would be true, but then they weren't around to see everything that happened later. I don't know if a prof should have acted as I did, but it was what I was "really like."

We went to a lounge called The Purple Tree. It was a large room with tables arranged in lop-sided circles around a huge purple tree like the kind you see in Japanese paintings. Most of the tables were filled. Some people were singing under the direction of the performer of the month, Rey Morada. *Rey* means king in Spanish, a student told me. The King sat on a stool in a far corner and was surrounded by speakers, consoles, microphones, guitar amplifier, synthesizer, and lines of cords. The King could also hook up an amplified harmonica around his neck if he wanted. The King had built an electronic castle.

The King was a performer who tried to excite his audience and get them to participate. If a tune triggered a few shouts or singing, he would turn up the volume and urge the patrons to sing louder. If a few more tables joined in, then the speakers would be turned up even higher. Four tables crowded with conventioneers were right in front of the King, and they sang almost every song. There is a strange kind of loneliness at conventions.

You run out of things to talk about. The loneliness starts coming, and singing chases it away for awhile. The conventioneers were singing loudly.

We wanted to talk and found a table in the opposite corner from the King. The waitress brought a couple of pitchers of beer and took the food orders. We listened to the King for a few minutes. The King stopped to adjust his electronic empire. A student leaned over and continued the class discussion—"How can you really be honest most of the time without hurting another's feelings?" She was serious and wanted some guidance.

"But if you aren't honest then you are a phony and that is worse," said another student. "I'm tired of just trying to please everybody," he added.

"Are these the only choices?" I asked.

"What did you say?" asked another. The King had found a crowd pleaser. "Cuando? Cuando? Cuando?" shouted the conventioneers. The King paused a moment to turn several knobs on his console.

"What are other choices besides being honest or a phony?" continued the student.

"You could choose to be true to another value besides honesty," I said.

"I don't get it," said one of the students.

"Suppose a friend starts dating a new guy but does not tell her current boyfriend this. The boyfriend asks you if your friend is dating anyone else. Will you be true to loyalty, or honesty?"

"Are you saying then you have to choose what truth to be honest to?"

"Yes."

"Yeah, but . . ." a student started to add. He could not be heard because the King had turned up the speakers and all you could hear was the amplified clangor of "Cuando? Cuando? Cuando?"

A student shouted across the table "I wish he would turn it down!" Everybody nodded. It was a common reaction in the other tables too. A few people were gesturing to the King to tone it down. The King smiled and pulled the mike closer to him and in grand fortissimo sang "Cuando? Cuando? Cuando?" The conventioneers responded in kind. The King called the tune at The Purple Tree.

"Why don't you ask him to quiet it some, Nels?" Mary asked. I was still the authority and could change things.

"Mary, what is your class project?"

"Assertiveness," she said.

"Well," I said, "Here's a chance to try it. What would an assertive person say?"

"OK, OK, I get your point. But what if he doesn't turn it down?"

"Hey," said another student, "All you can do is try and be honest."

"I guess you're right." Mary got up and walked over to the King. We could see her talk and smile and the King smiled and strummed his guitar. Mary returned, all excited, and said, "I did it! I was assertive!" We applauded her and the King shouted "Cuando? Cuando? Cuando?" and the whole song was repeated. The Purple Tree shivered from the tweeters and woofers of the large speakers.

"It's all right, Mary. You gave it a try," said someone. We tried to continue our conversation by shouting. You could not hear anyone more than two seats away. Except for the conventioneers in front of the King, all the other patrons were leaning forward and shouting their conversations, and all this did was increase the sound level. I became irritated and got up.

"Guess I'll give it a try," I said.

"Let's see how a pro does it," shouted a student.

"Say, Rey," I said as the King was adjusting his console, "How about playing those nice tunes a bit softer so we can talk. It is really hard to hear." The King sat up and stared at me. I continued, "You have some fine equipment, but it's overwhelming even back there." I pointed to our table.

"I'm paid to provide entertainment," the King said.

"You *are* entertaining, but we would like to talk, too."

"Too bad," the King said. He was smirking now.

"A real musician could entertain without blasting, Rey," I said and walked back to the table. Well, that was a notch beyond assertiveness, I thought. It was an honest statement, though. Honest to my anger.

"Cuando? Cuando? Cuando?" rang out as I sat down. I was beginning to dislike this song that I had liked before coming to The Purple Tree. I gestured to our group that it was hopeless. "Assertiveness and honesty aren't in tonight, gang. At least for us."

The King finally took a break and we could talk for a few minutes on being honest and authentic. The King was returning for another set and someone said, "I'm going home. It's going to get noisy again." The whole group agreed. We left our tip and walked by the purple tree on our way out. Someone called out, "Hey Nels, come on over." A couple of former students were at a table with a large group. They had just arrived.

"Hi, Steve. What's the occasion?"

"We just finished our crisis hotline training and are celebrating a bit. Come join us."

"OK."

The crisis people were in the second layer of tables from the King's electronic empire. It was going to be very loud sitting there, but they didn't know this yet. I sat at the end of the table with the King at my back. We talked for a minute or so about their training sessions and when they would be starting on the phone lines.

"Nels," Steve said with a worried, puzzled look, "The musician guy behind you is talking about you."

I turned around and the King was perched on his stool with his guitar, glaring at me. I looked at him, then turned back to Steve and asked, "What did he say, Steve?"

"He told everyone he won't play with you here."

I turned around again and the King was still staring. He bent over to his mike and said, "I will not play if this guy stays here." He pointed at me.

The lounge was as quiet as it was going to get. Several tables of patrons were looking at the King and me and asking each other what was going on. I turned back. The crisis people sat looking at me, not knowing what to do, either. Hey, crisis counselors, I thought, here's a chance to use your training. Well, they aren't on duty yet.

The King repeated his command and I turned and said, "I'm not leaving, Rey. What is your problem?" The King looked out to the crowd and said "He has got to go." He was angry now and pointing with a clenched fist.

"I am not leaving, Rey." Something was going to happen soon. The King was pushing the point. I could feel my heart slamming my chest and adrenaline had kicked in. Why stay? To not stay would be wrong and cowardly. I had done nothing but ask him to quiet down, as many had that evening. He responded smartly and so did I, so we were even. Until now. I sat still and sipped my drink and waited. It was his move.

The King glowered and the lounge crowd was getting uneasy, not knowing what was going on or what to do. The crisis people were silent and wide eyed. I was alone and knew I had to stay. It was the right thing to do. Too bad my students had left. We could have had a good discussion on being honest and true after this thing was over. I was hoping for it to be over soon, but this would have to wait, too.

The King was hoping I would pack and leave and I could not show any sign that I was.

Someone in the back shouted, "Rey, sing something."

"Not with this guy here," said the King.

"Aw come on, Rey, how about 'Cuando? Cuando? Cuando?' "

The King shuffled on the stool and said "All right. I'll do it for you but not for him." I sat still. You will not make me leave acting like that, Rey. I sat through three more songs. The crowd was singing along and it was back to the normal din. I explained to Steve what had happened earlier and got up to leave. It was all right to leave now. It was my choice and not the King's.

I walked slowly past the table and the large purple tree. Now that the fear and the confrontation were settled a strong sense of indignation surfaced. The King had insulted a customer. If I were true and honest, the management should hear about this. Truth and honesty were taking a beating so far, but that would change now. I was right. So right that I was feeling righteous. If you feel right you may or may not act. If you feel righteous, then you act—and this is not always the right thing to do.

"Where's the manager?" I asked of a waitress behind the bar.

"He's not here. What do you need?" she asked.

"I want to talk about the way your musician treats customers."

The waitress motioned to the bartender and said, "He's the guy who caused all the trouble."

"What are you saying?" I asked.

"You are the one who caused the commotion," she repeated in a righteous and loud voice.

"Yeah, sure." I walked out.

In the parking lot it was turning cool and dark enough to see the moon and a few stars. I could hear "Cuando? Cuando? Cuando?" through the walls of the Purple Tree.

Follow-Up

1. *Offer your views on the author's thoughts and actions after being challenged by the singer to leave.*
2. *Much to the author's surprise, he was told by the management that* he, *not the singer, was the problem. Describe an instance and how you reacted when you thought you were obviously "in the right" but found out that others differed.*
3. *Offer your views and give examples for one or more of the following statements:*
   - *If you feel right you may or may not act. If you feel righteous, then you act—and this is not always the right thing to do.*
   - *But if you aren't honest then you are a phony.*
   - *Sometimes you have to choose between competing truths (e.g., loyalty vs. honesty).*
4. *Choose any other statement or idea in the article and provide your reaction.*

Applied Activities for Section Two

EFFECTIVE COMMUNICATOR CHECKLIST

Sending and listening skills are listed below. Rate your skill at each one, using the code provided. (If you prefer, ask someone else to rate you.)

1 = Very Poor   2 = Poor   3 = Adequate

4 = Good   5 = Excellent

Sending Skills

___ Have something useful to say

___ Have necessary knowledge of the topic

___ Attempt to detect how the message is understood by the receiver(s)

___ If possible, use multiple methods (such as writing, talking, nonverbal expressions)

___ Be aware of the *context* (the time factor, noise level, distractions, and emotional state of the situation)

___ Make your verbal and non-verbal messages match (for example, do not smile when angry, and look concerned if you say you are)

Listening Skills

___ Can understand (or attempt to) the speaker from his or her point of view

___ Can focus on the speaker without getting caught up in distracting thoughts or your own ideas

___ Can understand another even when emotions or beliefs are at a high intensity level (especially if you differ)

___ Give verbal and nonverbal feedback to the speaker on how they are being received

___ Can pick out the main idea or feeling without getting distracted by secondary points.

Consider choosing at least one sending and one listening skill to further develop.

THE WORLD OF _____

One of the most basic skills in relating and communicating is empathy—the ability to sense how another perceives the world. The World Of _____ activity is a direct attempt to experience empathy. Here are the directions.

1. Describe in writing how someone or something other than yourself might perceive the world. You may choose a living or non-living subject.
2. You may have to observe your subject for a period of time in order to get a feel for its world. Place yourself in the position of your subject and attempt to describe how it feels and responds. The time perspective can range from a few minutes to years.
3. Complete your description on one side of a sheet of paper. Place the name of your subject on the back (do not name the subject in your description).
4. When all descriptions are completed, form groups of 3–5 members. Members read their descriptions. The others try to guess the correct answer.
5. Discuss or write about what you learned from this experience.
6. Discuss or write about one or two situations where it would be beneficial to practice more empathy.

Examples of The World Of _____ Descriptions Are Seen Below

(a) My mate and I have been here about two years. It is incredible the things we hear and encounter. Most people take us for granted. They use us for their own convenience with little or no regard for us. Sometimes the rough treatment, the wrath, the scorn, and the abusive language are unbearable. We have also heard the sorrow, suffering, and anguish of many. It's enough to break one's heart. But then, there are the loving caresses, sweet words, and kisses that make it all bearable and worthwhile. In spite of everything we are content to be what we are. We are here to serve mankind.

(b) My day often starts very early in the morning and sometimes I don't get to sleep until way past midnight. I see people when they awake and at bedtime. Usually my location is stationary, but things around me are always moving. I guess I feel important because almost always when someone passes by they give me a look. Their look is longer than a mere glance, but they really aren't looking at *me*! Some people make funny faces at me. I see people as they are, but they see only what they want to see. My life is sad because I never can see myself. But I often bring superficial pleasure to each individual who passes by. Some of my relatives are usually in motion but they are handicapped because they can only view what has already passed by—never able to see ahead. Most of us can see only one side of any circumstance. Although I am very fragile, people can never fake their true emotions with me.

Answers:
(a) Pair of pay telephones
(b) mirror

POINT OF VIEW

1. Choose a topic about which you have strong beliefs and feelings; for example, the death penalty, prayer in schools, Republicans, Democrats, assisted suicide, a current crime trial, a current world/national/local issue, a controversial person, movie, or book.
2. Interview others on this topic until you find two persons who essentially have the same views as yours and two persons who have opposing views. Your interview should last at least 4–5 minutes to gather sufficient information.
3. During each interview you are to remain as nonjudgmental as possible. The other person should not know your stance on the topic as you converse. Your sole mission is to find out the other person's thoughts and feelings on the topic. You may ask questions, but only those that are necessary to clarify the other person's views. You could consider yourself a news reporter who is interviewing people for their views on a story. You may have to explain your role to others prior to the interview.

Complete the above actions before continuing to the next steps.

4. Describe your thoughts and feelings while interviewing those who disagreed with you. Do the same for those who agreed.
   • Did you have any interfering listening reactions during the interviews (e.g., strong urges to present your ideas, thinking of other arguments while listening, impatience, and so on)? If yes, how did this influence your understanding of the other person?
   • How did the others respond when you showed that you understood their positions without a challenge?
   • What have you learned, if anything, from this experience that can be used elsewhere?

(If this activity was difficult to accomplish, consider trying it several times until you have mastered this skill.)

SENDER-RECEIVER EXCHANGE

This activity combines self-disclosure, listening, and self-knowledge. It has the most value when participants have some beginning acquaintance and are willing to disclose new dimensions of themselves. The procedure is as follows:

1. Read the articles on self-disclosure and listening in this book or other resources.
2. Choose a partner (there might be one three-member group).

3. Find a location with a minimum of distractions. It is recommended that 60 minutes be given to this activity (with a minimum of 30 minutes).
4. The basic task is for each participant to finish the sentences below. Each person is to complete an item before going on to the next. If you are in the sender role, complete the sentence in the most genuine manner possible (which can be the choice of *not* talking). If you are in the receiver role, your mission is to understand but not to offer reactions or interpretations.
5. It is more important to take quality time per item than to race through the list. If you cannot think of an adequate response to an item, skip it and go on to the next (you can always return to the skipped item if you choose).

Sender-Receiver Items

1. The name I'm to be called is _____ .

2. One of the best experiences I had during the past year was _____ _____ .

3. Two traits or qualities others say I have are _____ and _____ .

4. One of my favorite free-time activities or hobbies is _____ .

5. One impression I seem to give to others that isn't totally true is _____ _____ .

6. If, for some reason, I could only keep three possessions (excluding houses, vehicles, properties), they would be _____ , _____ and _____ .

7. If given *one* of the following at this time in my life, it would be _____ _____ because _____ .
   (a) a week alone in a favorite spot
   (b) an activity with excitement, adventure
   (c) a new friend to share experiences with
   (d) an answer to what I should be in life
   (e) an intimate, loving relationship
   (f) accepting myself as I am
   (g) a chance to help make a positive change in another's life
   (h) to be recognized as being an expert in some field
   (i) a deep spiritual/religious experience

8. Given some time with any person of my choice (current or historical), it would be _____ because _____ .

9. One thing I would like to change about myself is _____ .

10. My age is _____ and how I feel about it is _____ .

11. (a) I *like* being a male/female because _____ .

    (b) I *dislike* being a male/female because _____ .

    (c) One way I interact differently with the opposite sex is _____

    _____ .

12. The degree of satisfaction and fulfillment with my occupation or major is

    _____ .

13. I am fully accepted for who I am (no conditions) by _____ .

14. Compared to age 15, how are you different? _____

    _____ .

    The same? _____ .

15. A way I am the *same* as one or both of my parents (guardians) is _____

    _____ .

16. For at least two of the following emotional states, explain what normally causes them and how you react:

    Worried-anxious-nervous   Wonder-awe-amazement
    Lonely-not belonging-alienated   Joy-ecstasy
    Angry-frustrated   Loved-intimate-belonging
    Inadequate-inferior-failure   Confident-self respect
    Confused-uncertain-lost   Sense of purpose and direction

17. My spiritual beliefs emphasize _____ .

18. A potential or ability that I have not fully developed, and want to, is _____

    _____ .

19. Describe two activities that tend to produce for you a sense of well-being, centeredness, or harmony with life. How often do you experience these activities?

20. Within the next year it will be very important for me to _____

    _____ .

Follow-Up

1. Discuss in small groups and/or the whole class the following: What ideas in the article on self-disclosure applied to this experience (for example, trust, over/under-discloser, appropriate discloser)?
2. Write a brief reaction paper on what you learned from this activity.
3. Try this activity with someone outside class (if they agree to the conditions).
4. Estimate how one of your significant others would respond to some or all of these items (check it out with their permission).
5. Select one item from the Sender-Receiver list to explore in more depth (either through writing, talking, or reflection).
6. Complete this activity one year from now.

HE SAID, SHE SAID

Below are selected findings from research on differences between men and women on how they communicate. These are group averages, which means that there will be individual exceptions. Observe several men and women as they communicate. Observe in a variety of formal and informal situations and from several age categories. You might consider pairing with a partner of the opposite gender for a couple of observation sessions. You can include your own interactions as part of this activity. According to the scale, circle the number that most closely matches your observations.

SCALE

1 = Mainly untrue   2 = Somewhat untrue   3 = Somewhat true
4 = Mainly true   5 = Cannot determine

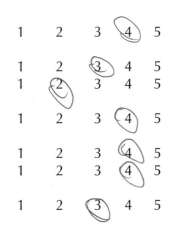

1. Men talk mostly about events, issues, and things; women talk about people and themselves.   1   2   3   4   5
2. Men prefer to interact face to face; women prefer to interact side-by-side.   1   2   3   4   5
3. Men touch others more than women do.   1   2   3   4   5
4. Women establish more eye contact and engage in more facial mirroring than men.   1   2   3   4   5
5. Women are more emotionally expressive than men.   1   2   3   4   5
6. Women self-disclose more than men.   1   2   3   4   5
7. Women are the preferred receivers of disclosures for both men and women.   1   2   3   4   5

8. Women use fewer gestures than men; women use more gestures with other women than with men.   1   2   3   (4)   5

9. Women smile more than men and are more likely to return smiles.   1   2   3   (4)   5

10. Men interrupt women more often than women interrupt men.   1   2   3   (4)   5

11. Men use hostile words and profanity more often than women do.   1   2   3   (4)   5

12. Women use more tentative and qualifying language ("I guess," "Maybe," "If you don't mind," "I hope that you don't think").   1   2   3   (4)   5

Follow-Up Ideas

- Discuss your findings with classmates and compare your observations.
- Discuss or write how these gender communication differences reflect cultural norms for men and women.
- What happens if a man or woman deviates from one or more of the above communication patterns?
- Rate yourself on the above items and provide a brief interpretation.
- Consider adding more items from your observations of men and women as they communicate.

References for "He Said, She Said"

Brehm, S. S. (1992). *Intimate relationships.* New York: McGraw-Hill.

Lindsey, L. L. (1990). *Gender roles: A sociological perspective.* Englewood Cliffs, NJ: Prentice-Hall.

Pearson, J. C. (1985). *Gender and communication.* Dubuque, IA: Wm. C. Brown Publishers.

Wilson, G. L., Hantz, A. M., Hanna, M. S. (1992). *Interpersonal growth through communication.* Dubuque, IA: Wm. C. Brown Publishers.

A COMMUNICATION MEDLEY

Try one or more of these communication experiences to enhance your sending or listening skills:

1. Watch a few TV talk shows with the intent of observing communication skills, particularly listening. Observe the effects of good and poor sending

and listening behaviors (the Effective Communicator Checklist located in this section may be of help here).

2. Watch a TV drama or rented video *without* sound. Attempt to understand what is happening by observing only nonverbal actions (gestures, facial expressions, and movement). If the show is recorded, rerun the tape with audio to check your accuracy.

3. Some hints that indicate you need work on sending skills: others often ask you to clarify something you said; you notice others get that glazed look after several minutes of listening to you; others nod politely but find an excuse to leave before you have finished.

4. Approximately two-thirds of our emotions are sent and received through nonverbal channels. If you are experiencing difficulty in having others understand your emotions, try experimenting with nonverbal behaviors. For example, warmth and caring is expressed with a genuine smile, consistent but nonpiercing eye contact, and closer proximity. Enthusiasm is generally expressed with active gestures, vocal variety, and facial vitality. It is also helpful to observe others who are good at showing the particular emotion you want to convey and watch their nonverbal communication.

GROWTH
DYNAMICS

C hange is inherent in growth. In the accompanying magnolia photo we
see this change in the stages of bloom—full, partial, and buds repre-
senting potential flowering. Similarly, human potentialities exist in
various stages of maturity. Growth psychologists contend that there is
a basic underlying force directing growth.

Whether one calls it a growth tendency, a drive toward self-
actualization, or a forward-moving directional tendency, it is the
mainspring of life. . . . It is the urge which is evident in all organic
and human life—to expand, extend, become autonomous, develop, mature—the tendency to express and activate all the capacities of the organism [and] [t]he actualizing tendency can be
thwarted or warped, but it cannot be destroyed without destroying the organism (Rogers, 1980, p. 118; 1961, p. 35).

We have, each one of us, an essential inner nature which is in-
stinctoid, intrinsic, given, "natural". . . and which tends strongly
to persist. . . . Each person's inner nature has some characteristics
which all other selves have (species-wide) and some which are
unique to the person (idiosyncratic). . . . This inner core or self
grows into adulthood only partly by (objective or subjective) discovery . . . Partly it is also a creation of the person himself. . . . If
this essential core is frustrated, denied or suppressed, sickness results (or one becomes) a "diminished or stunted person" (Maslow,
1968, pp. 190–93).

113

"Magnolia" by Nelson Goud. Copyright © 1996.

Barry Stevens (1971) refers to this growth tendency as her "built-in pathfinder" which, if listened to, helps a person to see clearly even in times of turmoil. This growth tendency can be inhibited or enhanced by interactions with the outside world (especially other people), and by individual decisions. A person's growth status is the outcome of the continual interaction of this actualizing tendency and demands from the outside world.

Carl Rogers (1994, 1971, 1961) describes some valued directions of persons moving toward greater growth and maturity.

- A movement away from facades, pretense, defensiveness, and putting up a front.
- A movement away from pleasing others as a goal in itself.
- Being real and genuine is positively valued. A person tends to move toward his or her real self and real feelings.
- Self-direction is positively valued. A person discovers an increasing pride and confidence in making choices and guiding his or her life.
- A person becomes more open to experience, becomes increasingly able to sense inner experience and external reality *as it is,* rather than distorting it to fit a preconceived pattern. The person can react more readily to new people and situations and tolerate more ambiguity, with this kind of perception.

- Being a process is positively valued. A person accepts himself or herself as a stream of becoming, not a finished product. A person prefers the process, both fascinating and uncertain, of being in the midst of constantly developing potentialities.
- Others are increasingly appreciated for what they are, just as the person has come to appreciate his or her being. The person seeks to achieve close and real relationships, including the deeply intimate.

Abraham Maslow (1970, 1968) also found the qualities listed above in his studies of self-actualizing persons. He added the following items to the list of self-actualizing characteristics.

- A problem-centered versus an ego-centered orientation. A person devotes much energy to a life mission, a cause, or a task beyond his or her own existence.
- An ability to appreciate, again and again, basic life experiences with awe, pleasure, and wonder.
- A special kind of creativity evident in a person's attitude and unique ways of doing even everyday things.
- There is a framework of values, a philosophy to live by.

For Further Reading

Maslow, A. H. (1970). *Motivation and personality.* New York: Harper & Row.
Maslow, A. H. (1968). *Toward a psychology of being.* New York: Van Nostrand Reinhold.
Rogers, C. R. (1980). *A way of being.* Boston: Houghton Mifflin.
Rogers, C. R. (1961). *On becoming a person.* Boston: Houghton Mifflin.
Rogers, C. R. & Stevens, B. (1971). *Person to person: The problem.* New York: Pocket Books.

READINGS OVERVIEW

Factors that impede or promote growth are the central topics of the readings in this section.

- Nels Goud engages in a one-person dialogue on the question of "Uniqueness." He offers arguments both pro and con on whether an individual human is truly unique.
- In "The Meaning of Personal Growth," Abe Arkoff discusses the multiple dimensions of growth. The propensity to grow, as well as the burdens of growth, are highlighted.
- Scott Peck explores one of the core themes of growth in his article on "Responsibility." Peck shows how avoiding personal responsibility leads to losing personal freedoms.

- Tom Keating introduces a common man, "Herbie." We are asked at the end of the article whether Herbie fulfills the criteria of healthy growth.
- Gail Sheehy contends that we now have three adulthoods and that age expectations have shifted considerably. The new choices and uncertainties are examined in "New Passages."
- In "The Lesson of the Cliff," Morton Hunt provides a guide for facing fears that can block our growth. He discusses how this idea enabled him to face his growth fears in a variety of circumstances.
- Amy Gross demonstrates how daily encounters can have the same qualities as heroic adventures. She explains how common challenges produce "Small Terrors, Secret Heroics."
- In "Using Our Flaws and Faults," Marsha Sinetar explains how a negative trait can become an ally in our growth.
- Harold Bloomfield and Robert Kory present many practical ideas for overcoming feelings of stagnation and powerlessness in "Getting Unstuck: Joyfully Recreating Your Life."

You are invited to attempt one or more of the Applied Activities at the end of this section. These exercises are designed to apply the concepts of this section to your life. The questions posed at the end of each article also aim at personalizing the selections.

Uniqueness

Nels Goud

As a kid I spent many hours daydreaming what I would be when I grew up. I had this intuition that I had some kind of specialness. The intuition was a faint but persistent voice, somewhat like sensing the dim signals sent by a distant star.

I grew up. I look about me for evidence of what I was destined to uniquely accomplish. Maybe I need help—please let me know if you have spotted it. I am even finding out that my special destiny fantasy is quite common, perhaps you have experienced it also. Even my daydreams aren't original.

Sometimes this special destiny illusion persists and lingers until just the right circumstances arise to release it. Then "if only's" get in the way —"I could be great if only I had more time; if only I had the resources and opportunity; if only others didn't make so many demands; if only the sun wasn't in my eyes; if only the world would adjust itself solely to me." Most of us, though, gradually learn that only a rare few invent a cure for a major disease, create pieces of art and music that express the human soul for millions, or develop a theory that completely changes how people view the world and themselves. How humbling to know whatever your accomplishments, only a few will have intimate knowledge of them. Most of what we do in life has either been done before or is, at best, a new variation of themes others have created. Surprisingly I remain unconvinced by my own arguments. The faint inner voice still says, "You are a unique person." So the dialogue must continue.

One comment that makes us feel unique is "You're one in a million." Then we read that the current U.S. population is around 275 million. This means that there are 275 Americans just like you. If extended to the world population, there are 6,000 people just like you. You could form a small town made up of persons exactly like you. You would never need a mirror or snivel that "no one understands me." If we buy the estimate that there are 100 billion planets in our galaxy alone that are capable of supporting life forms, then what are our chances of being special or significant?

I still feel unique. OK, let's try another angle. We can examine our significance and specialness over time. In *The Dragons of Eden*, Carl Sagan condensed the 15 billion year lifetime of the universe into a single calendar year. Here are a few events in the history of the universe, including your life, if they had occurred in twelve months.

- Big Bang—
  January 1
- Origin of the Milky Way Galaxy—
  May 1
- Our solar system—
  September 9
- Earth appears—
  September 14
- First life on Earth—
  September 25
- Invention of sex (by microorganisms)—
  November 1
- Oldest photosynthetic plants—
  November 12
- First humans—
  December 31 (10:30 p.m.)
- Invention of agriculture—
  December 31 (11:59:20 p.m.)
- European Renaissance—
  December 31 (11:59:59 p.m.)

What we studied in history took place in less than a second. Our current lives would not even merit a rapid eye-blink. We are not even cosmic trifles. We make no difference at all. In a way, after some initial chin dragging, this could be welcome news. No longer do we have to despair at a low grade, or get upset by an unfair supervisor, or losing a lover—what difference do they make anyway?

It seems, you may say, that the arguments here are one-sided. You would be correct. There are some unresolved questions concerning human uniqueness. Why is it, for example, that one of life's most fundamental impulses is to produce such astounding variety? Why are there over 1,000,000 species of bugs? At least 175,000 species of trees? Even the green stuff we see on ponds and the seas, algae, has 25,000 forms. Experts won't even venture a guess at how many species of fish there are. There are so many kinds of living organisms that some scientists devote whole careers trying to classify them. My personal favorite, the one-celled Euglena, is so unique that experts cannot determine whether it is a plant or animal—now that's originality!

We are part of a universal life force that presses toward variation and individuality. It is our first affirmation that we have the potential for uniqueness.

Our bodies show uniqueness. With some exceptions for identical twins, each of us has distinctive cell protein makeup; scents; blood antigen combinations; teeth surface patterns; and, naturally, fingerprints. Differences become even more pronounced between individual humans when we examine the psychological, social, and various mental behaviors. Even identical twins can show wide variations in the latter areas.

Each minute of existence is a changing combination of sensory inputs, other people, and your inner world of thoughts and feelings. How you make sense of these demands minute-by-minute is a distinctive act. No one experiences the world exactly like you, nor can your experience be duplicated. "Every new mind is a new classification . . . and is new in nature," exclaims Emerson (Edman, ed., 1926). This continuing process of unique experiencing is a fundamental source of original ideas and behavior, and of being in the world.

Pulitzer Prize-winning author Annie Dillard claims that our creative uniqueness helps keep the universe together. According to the law of entropy, things eventually disintegrate. Citing Buckminster Fuller, she says that "by creating things, by thinking up new combinations, we counteract this flow of entropy. We make new structures, new wholenesses, so the universe comes out even. A shepherd on a hilltop who looks at a mess of stars and thinks, 'There's a hunter, a plow, a fish,' is making mental connections that have as much real force in the universe as the very fires in those stars themselves."

This whole discussion is starting to get a bit confusing and contradictory. First we see that attaining cosmic uniqueness and significance is futile. We are told that anything we do is not truly original, but a variation on existing themes. Our "special destiny" is but an illusion. Then we are presented with the view that a basic life force compels variety and individuality in all living organisms, even in a one-celled Euglena. In humans this variation is demonstrated in both bodily and psycho-social traits. How we experience life in each moment is offered as a kind of uniqueness.

There is more. . . . The least discussed kind of uniqueness is our *way of being*. The distinctive manner in which we carry out life's activities, the way we do things—this can be a source of true uniqueness. It is not unique to be a teacher, secretary, executive, friend, lover, or parent. But we have a choice on how to perform these and other major life roles. We can perform them in a standard, conventional manner, or we can choose to have them be mediums of our own individual personality.

Sometimes style is substance. Imagine two of your favorite singers singing the same song. It is the style of each performer which makes the performances unique. John Steinbeck describes a woman who was valued for her unique style of human interaction. "She had a way of laughing appreciatively at everything anyone said, and, to merit this applause, people tried to say funny things when she was about. . . . She made people feel good. No one could ever remember that she said anything, but months after hearing it, they could recall the exact tones of her laughter." We know a person has developed an individuality of style when it is said, "I don't know quite how to explain it, but he has a way about him."

Role models can help us develop a way of being. There comes a point, though, when we have to say that we have learned all we could from them and then venture out to find our own voice. Miles Davis, the pioneering jazz trumpeter, is known for his special tone and phrasing. When asked how he learned this style, Davis said that he did not play in this manner at first. Instead, he started by playing like other jazz trumpeters. Eventually he decided to blend techniques from them with his own "feel" of the music. He concluded that "it takes a long time to play like yourself." Thanks, Miles, for taking that time. It will take some time, some experimenting, but we too can learn to "play like ourselves."

Earlier it was contended that only the "greats" create the ideas and products of the first magnitude, the grand themes. This does not mean that there is no room left for originality in our creations—they are just of another magnitude. As the naturalist John Audubon pointed out, "The fields would be

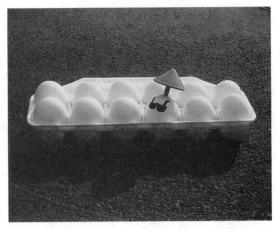

"Unique" by Nelson Goud. Copyright © 1996.

very silent if no birds sang there except those who sang best." What a loss if only the best chirpers sang and they were all in a distant village. What a loss if only the greatest could perform life's tasks—could we exist for long this way? All our voices, especially those which show our special way of being, are needed if life is to function as it is intended.

I've always been a bit puzzled by the philosopher Martin Buber's idea that if there were other persons just like us, then there would be no need for us to be in the world. It is now starting to make sense. Life is *asking us* to share our specialness. This is not a selfish or oddball act. Choosing to share our uniqueness is a profound way to follow a primary life directive and to form a connection with the world. We can contribute a dimension of required newness. It is our choice though.

So, how are you expressing your specialness?

Follow-Up

1. *Did you, like the author, have a "special destiny intuition" as a child? What has happened to it? If it still persists, what direction is it pointing toward?*

2. It is stated that "Most of what we do in life has either been done before or is, at best, a new variation of themes others have created." Do you agree with this? Explain your answer.

3. Relate one or more of the following statements to your life:
   - "The distinctive manner in which we carry out life's activities, the way we do things—this can be a source of true uniqueness."
   - "It takes a long time to play like yourself." (Miles Davis)
   - Choose any other statement which evoked a reaction in you.

4. In what ways are you unique without doing anything but just existing? In what ways do you have to make a conscious choice and effort to develop your uniqueness?

The Meaning of Personal Growth

Abe Arkoff

Imagine yourself in this situation: You are an illegitimate, six-year-old child. Your mother is a deaf-mute. You have spent most of your life with your mother in a dark room separated from the rest of your mother's family. What kind of person would you be and become?

Isabelle (a pseudonym) actually spent the first part of her life in the condition just noted. When she was discovered at the age of six, she appeared to be half infant and half wild animal. The professionals who examined her concluded she was feeble-minded and uneducable. Fortunately, they decided to try. A year and a half later Isabelle had blossomed into a "very bright, cheerful, and energetic little girl" At the time of the last report, she was fourteen, doing well, and had just passed the sixth grade (Davis, 1940, 1947).

There appears to be a strong impulse to grow in every person (as indeed there was in Isabelle). We desire to be more than we are. Each of us will have our own idea of what we wish to become. Perhaps more informed and knowledgeable, or more understanding and loving, or more capable and creative, or more joyful and serene.

On the path of growth, sometimes we trudge and sometimes we leap ahead. We occasionally have a growth spurt when we make rapid progress and we have an exhilarating sense of being more than we were. It may be a particular summer or year when everything seems to be going just right or it may involve a particular relationship in which we find an enlarged sense of ourselves.

Just as there is a strong impulse to grow, there are strong impediments to growth. Rarely are they as complete and obvious as in the case of Isabelle. But there are growth blocks or impasses in which we are frustrated and seem unable to progress at all. There are even growth reversals—times when we appear to regress and give up hard-earned gains.

Personal growth, as it is defined here, is simply change in a desired or valued direction. Values, of course, vary from person to person. I may feel I have grown when I have freed myself from dependence on my parents. You may experience personal growth when you change your conception of yourself and begin to respond to the world in a new and freer way. My parents, however, may not agree that my new-found autonomy is growth, and your spouse may be threatened by your new self-definition and put pressure on you to revert to the person you were.

Potentiality refers to inherent capacity for growth. What's possible for us? What can we become? What can keep us from becoming all we wish to become? How can we find a path of growth that's right for us? These are some of the questions we will consider in the material that follows.

THE POTENTIAL FOR GROWTH

A Russian scientist has estimated that with our brain working at only half capacity, we could learn 40 languages with no difficulty (Otto, 1972). Many of us, however, find it something of a struggle to learn more than 1. From this perspective, we certainly seem to be less than we could be.

What has come to be called the "human potential movement" began during the 1960s and was dedicated to helping people make the most of their capacities. An underlying assumption—sometimes called "the human potential hypothesis"—was that most people function at only a small fraction of their potential. A further assumption was that by proceeding in certain ways much more of this potential could be realized.

Nearly a century ago William James, one of the earliest American psychologists, estimated that humans, on the average, functioned at about 10% of their capacity. Later, anthropologist Margaret Mead put this figure at 6%. Human potentialist Herbert Otto's original estimate of average fulfillment was a modest 5%, which he later reduced to 4%. He writes that the estimated percentage has been decreasing because "we are discovering that every human being has more powers, resources, and abilities than we suspected ten years ago, five years ago" (1972, p. 14).

A trio of psychologists—Arthur Combs, Donald Avila, and William Purkey (1978)— maintain that human beings are "overbuilt." They write, "One of the most exciting discoveries of this generation is the idea that human capacity is far greater than anything ever thought possible. The fascinating thing about human beings is not their limitations, but their immense capabilities. . . . From everything we can observe, it seems clear that few of us ever remotely approach the potentialities for effective behavior that lie within us. Most of us use but a small fraction of our capabilities" (pp. 69–70, 71).

Norman Cousins administered his own recovery from a supposedly incurable illness. In looking back on this experience, he wrote that what he had learned was to "never underestimate the capacity of the human mind and body to regenerate—even when the prospects seem most wretched" (1977, p. 5). Later, in looking back on his entire life, he wrote,

> What, then, have I learned? The most important thing I think I have learned is that human capacity is infinite, that no challenge is beyond comprehension and useful response. I have

learned that the uniqueness of human beings is represented by the absence of any ceiling over intellectual or moral development. In this sense, the greatest gains achieved by the species are not connected to the discovery of nuclear fission or the means by which humans can be liberated from earth gravity. The greatest gains are related to expanding knowledge about the human brain itself. (1980, p. 10)

One of the most optimistic of the human potentialists is Will Schutz (1979). "As human beings," he writes, "we are without limit" (p. 25). In his opinion, the limits we experience are "limits of belief" but not "limits of the human organism." He points out that there are pragmatic advantages to assuming that one is limitless: "If indeed I am truly limitless, and I assume I am, then I may discover that limitlessness. On the other hand, every limit I assume I have prevents me from discovering whether that limit is in fact real" (p. 26). Claim a limit, Richard Bach says, and it's yours.

Despite these enthusiastic voices, optimism about human potentiality is not widespread. Psychiatrist Cornelis Bakker (1975) has observed a deep sense of pessimism in some quarters concerning basic personality change. Bakker calls this "the myth of unchangeability." It is a myth to which some persons in mental health subscribe when they see dramatic improvements that somehow do not last. It is a myth held by parents who look at their adult child and see what appears to be almost the same personality that was present at age seven or eight. It is a myth any one of us might tend to embrace as we see ourselves wrestling with seemingly the same basic problems year after year or decade after decade.

Bakker has found "a good deal of evidence" to support the thesis that "people are extremely changeable" (p. 164). He feels there are two reasons why the myth of unchangeability persists. One reason is the long-standing hypothesis in Western culture that each person has a basic essence or soul or personality or character which biases the observer against perceiving change. The second reason is there are a number of stabilizing factors that can keep people the same if they allow this to happen. Some of these stabilizing factors are considered later in the section concerning obstacles to growth.

Support for Bakker's thesis is provided by George Vaillant's study (1977) of a group of Harvard students. Vaillant followed this group from college age to about age 50 and found their lives were "full of surprises" and even "startling change and evolutions" (p. 372). Quite notable was a subset of men in the study who had very serious psychological problems, which they dealt with by themselves to arrive at quite satisfactory patterns of adjustment.

Not all students of human nature are convinced that the myth of unchangeability is fully a myth. One of the most eloquent of these is psychologist Bernie Zilbergeld (1983). From his examination of the evidence, he arrives at conclusions far different from Bakker. Summing up, he writes that "people are very difficult to change" and "there are limits to how much each of us can change." In his opinion, "the limits of human malleability are much closer to the ground than they are to the sky" (p. 247). He adds that we may have to question utopian notions and give up our ideas about what is possible for humans.

However, there is a silver lining to Zilbergeld's dark cloud. Although he believes that human beings are difficult to change, he also concludes that there is not as much need for change as is commonly thought. He makes a strong case that many of the most creative and productive persons—Charles Darwin, Abraham Lincoln, Goethe, William James, August Strindberg, Virginia Woolf, Van Gogh, Einstein, etc.—were laden with personal problems and far from "normal." Zilbergeld believes that people don't need fixing as much as they need to change their unrealistic notions of what life can be. He writes, "Much of what we think of as problems —things that ought to be altered and for which there are so-lutions—are not so much problems as inescapable limits and predicaments of life" (p. 251).

The Burden of Growth

Is the impulse to grow a blessing or a burden? Little Linus in a *Peanuts* comic strip once lamented his own situation, saying "there is no heavier burden than a great potential." Maslow (1972) cautioned his own students: "If you deliberately plan to be less than you are capable of being, then I warn you that you'll be deeply unhappy the rest of your life" (p. 36).

In one of her books, Eda LeShan (1976) eloquently describes her own feelings of guilt for not having made more of her own childhood opportunities for growth:

> Many years ago my husband [psychologist Lawrence LeShan] explained to me the meaning of "ontological guilt." He told me it was the very worst kind. It means feeling guilty because one is not living one's own life, fulfilling one's own potentials. As the years have passed I have come to understand this more deeply, and it accounts for my awful sensitivity about examining my own adolescence; I have too much ontological guilt.
>
> The problem is that no matter how much one learns about human fallibility, compassion and acceptance are still hard to come by. When I became deeply depressed at the prospect of having to write this chapter, I said to Larry, "I can't forgive myself for the fact that I was a coward; that I didn't have the guts to fight harder to become free, when that's what I should have been doing." His answer was, "You have nothing to forgive yourself for. You were a nice person—decent and brave—and you couldn't bear to hurt your parents when you knew how much they loved you. You made a sacrifice which you later discovered had cost you too much—but it was done out of tenderness, and you have had the courage to fight for your own growth ever since." (p. 128)

In her notebook, Jungian analyst Florida Scott-Maxwell (1968) writes of our need to "live our strengths." She recalls that a client once told her: "I don't mind your telling me my faults, they're stale, but don't tell me my virtues. When you tell me what I could be, it terrifies me" (p. 22).

In her book *Smart Girls, Gifted Women*, Barbara Kerr (1987) takes gifted women to task for not achieving their full potentiality. She maintains that women "are too well adjusted for their own good. They are great at adjusting resourcefully and congenially to whatever situation is handed to them" (p. 5). Kerr herself was criticized for not accepting the women's own choices, but she stuck to her guns suggesting that self-actualization is more than right—it is a responsibility.

The human potentialists and, indeed, the entire field of psychotherapy have been criticized for tending to make people dissatisfied with themselves. Like some other industries that sell their products by convincing people they are not all they should be or can be—that they don't look right or smell right or are not always free of aches and anxieties—potentialists may create or exacerbate the very conditions or dissatisfactions they seek to correct.

Schutz (1979) takes a view contrary to those who see potential as a burden. He understands his own assumption of "human limitlessness" is frequently resisted since there is an implied demand that one live up to one's potential. He maintains there is no obligation to be everything of which one is capable. "If I wish," he writes, "I can choose to feel inadequate because I have not realized myself fully. But it is not inherent in the assumption of limitlessness that failure to achieve all that is possible must lead to feelings of guilt and depression" (p. 26).

Those who have been stuck on life's path—at impasses, up blind alleys, forever marking time, caught up in maintenance, low-level enterprises, getting by perhaps but not getting anywhere—will know the burden that the potentialists write about. Those who have gotten themselves "unstuck" and suddenly able to make more, maybe much more of their lives will know the exhilaration that comes when one is becoming more and more who one can be.

SUCCESS AND FAILURE IN GROWTH

Not long ago, one of my friends was telling me about an old acquaintance who was going to visit him soon. It was someone with whom he had gone to college but who afterward never seemed to make very much of his life. This acquaintance had never married and had moved from job to job in the same industry but none very much different or better from the other. From the outside, at least, it looked like not very much of a life.

A character in Anne Tyler's novel *Breathing Lessons* is rather taken aback when her daughter asks her, "Mom? Was there a certain conscious point in your life when you decided to settle for being ordinary?" Do any of us prepare ourselves for an "ordinary" life? What would you have answered if someone at your high-school graduation asked if you would be willing "to settle for being ordinary"?

Thinking it over, I wonder how my friend's acquaintance regarded his life. Did he see it as disappointingly ordinary, comfortably ordinary, or not ordinary at all—which is the way Tyler's character responded as she recalled the incident with a friend: "It got to me," she said. . . . "I mean, to *me* I'm not ordinary."

I have never been to a high school or college reunion, but more faithful alumni have told me one of the attractions is learning what one's classmates have done with their lives. How high have they climbed on the ladder of success? What have they accomplished? Who have they married? How much have they changed? (One woman told me she went to see how much hair had gone from the heads of her ex-beaus and how much flesh had gathered on the hips of her old rivals.)

Two better alumni than I, Michael Medved and David Wallechinsky (1976) made a study of their high school class 10 years after graduation. They published it as *What Really Happened to the Class of '65?* The class happened to be the one *Time* magazine featured in its cover story "Today's Teenagers," who were said to be then "on the fringe of a golden era." Instead, the 10 years proved to be a sad and turbulent decade that included the second Kennedy assassination, drugs, the draft, and the Vietnam War.

During the decade, some alumni continued to blossom, some were transformed, and others met with tragedy. The alumna who had been voted "the most outstanding woman" of the class got her doctorate and a professorship at Princeton. The young man voted "most reserved" earned a degree in engineering and became a Krishna devotee. The quarterback of the football team, "an athletic ladies' man," became a Hollywood masseur. "The grind" went on to graduate from Stanford, drop out of graduate school at UCLA, and then was under intensive care at a state psychiatric institution. The member of the class voted "most popular"—an all-Western League End and baseball team captain—committed suicide.

Ten years later, Wallechinsky did a second survey on the class of '65, but this time not just his own high school. He traveled all over the country and surveyed a varied sample of his generation of age peers. Out of this came a book, *Midterm Report*, which includes a report card on his generation midway in life. How do you judge a whole generation? Wallechinsky's criterion: "Did they leave the world in a better condition than they found it?" After considering what the generation had done for culture, education, freedom, peace and security, technology, environment, and standard of living, he awarded it the midterm grade of B. But as he pointed out, the final grade—which was still to be determined—is the more important one.

Continuing the matter of prefinal grades, Gail Sheehy (1981) reviewed the lives of some of history's greats and found they often seemed to be and thought themselves to be failures at some time in their lives. The career of British statesman and author Benjamin Disraeli was described as "failure, failure, partial success, renewed failure, ultimate and complete triumph" (Sheehy, p. 386). Robert Rhodes James titled his biography of Winston Churchill *Churchill: A Study in Failure* because Churchill's career appeared to have ended in complete failure before it renewed and outdid itself. Golda Meir failed as a wife and was far from a model mother but became the mother figure of Israel.

Meir was a failure as a homebody but a success as a public person, and many of society's or history's greats were notable failures in one or more aspects of their personal lives. Charles Darwin, Lord Byron, Shelley, and Tennyson were all hypochondriacs. Ernest Hemingway, Jack London, Edgar Allan Poe, F. Scott Fitzgerald, John O'Hara, William Faulkner, Edwin Arlington Robinson, Eugene O'Neill, James Joyce, Sinclair Lewis, Jack Kerouac, Raymond Chandler, and Thomas Wolfe were alcoholics. Virginia Woolf, Sylvia Plath, George Eastman, Van Gogh, and also Hemingway and London took their own lives (Zilbergeld, 1983).

The memory of Martin Luther King, Jr., has been said by some to have been tarnished by posthumous revelations of promiscuity and plagiarism, but King was highly critical of himself. In one sermon, he said, "You don't need to go out this morning saying that Martin Luther King is a saint. I want you to know this morning that I am a sinner like all of God's children, but I want to be a good man and I want to hear a voice saying to me one day, 'I take you in and I bless you because you tried.'" Neither we nor those who inspire us will be without failure and flaws, but the weeds in our gardens need not choke out the flowers. Speaking of King, Ellen Goodman (1990) writes, "Here was a man, an ordinary man, with human strengths and weaknesses. But when the time came and much was demanded of him, he found the greatness within himself . . . and he changed the world we live in" (p. A-16).

Obstacles to Growth

Why don't we make more of ourselves and our lives? Why don't we realize more of our potential? These are important questions— and ones many philosophers and psychologists and stuck, bewildered souls have pondered.

A Diminished Conception of Ourselves. One reason we don't make more of ourselves is that we may have a diminished view of who we are and what we can become. To some extent, we are who we *think* we are, and some of us may not think we're much. Although research suggests we are more likely to overestimate than underestimate ourselves, two psychologists, Ellen Langer and Carol Dweck (1973) write, "We maintain that there are few, if any, of us who have a truly satisfying self-concept. People occasionally put on a good show and seem to others to be on top of it all, but these very same people often think: 'if they only knew the real me'" (p. 29).

The basic goal of many personal growth programs and psychotherapies is to get the individuals concerned to enhance their self-concept and to accept, love, and prize themselves more. A basic goal of some transpersonal approaches is to inspire persons with awe or reverence for themselves and their place in the universe. As such individuals come to see more in themselves, they attempt and accomplish more, and accomplishing more they further enhance their conception of themselves.

The following true story (recalled by a woman psychologist from her prepsychology days) indicates how important an obstacle a negative self-concept can be, and how a positive self-concept can both instigate and stem from growth:

I was living out in San Francisco at the time. While coming home from work one day I got involved in an accident and required the attention of a doctor. A friend of mine mentioned the accident to his friend, an eager, but not yet established, young lawyer. The lawyer contacted me, and then proceeded to persuade me that I had a case and that he was the one to handle it.

That was the way I met Hank. The impression I got of him after talking over the phone for the next week or so was that he was enthusiastic, good humored, and sort of charming. When he came over to my house to discuss the case further, I had to add unattractive to the list of adjectives.

After we concluded our discussion of business matters, we got involved in a friendly and rather personal conversation. Hank had recently come to San Francisco from New York. He was divorced and was eager to tell me about the marvelous changes in his life. It seemed that his ex-wife had constantly told him how ugly he was. I thought that that was both cruel and accurate—but kept the latter thought to myself. Hank explained how inhibited this made him with other people. "I had little confidence in myself and was enormously shy." I said I couldn't believe that he was very shy. He recounted some experiences he had had at parties and with clients to convince me. He was successful in gaining my sympathy.

Then he told me how different he was now. He had traveled across the country with the thought that he just might not be as homely looking as she said—so he took some risks. He gradually improved his opinion of himself. He put this a little differently though: "I slowly started to recognize how wrong she was. Now I know I'm good looking. When I walk into a room people take notice of me and believe it or not (I didn't) the girls are all over me at parties." We talked some more, and then a horn started honking outside. He said it was his new girlfriend picking him up. We went over to the terrace to see if it were she—it was, and she was simply beautiful. For a moment I couldn't believe the whole episode. What was even more bewildering was that I started finding him attractive.

Although Hank's somewhat dramatic tale is not unique, most people with negative self-concepts never bother to test out other hypotheses about themselves, as he did. While at first he accepted his wife's opinion as indisputable truth, he later formulated an alternative positive view, "I am *not* ugly," and set out to confirm it. Now Hank tells people how to respond to him. His new manner has an air of confidence, and the subtle and not so subtle cues are effective. It is not surprising that most people listen. (Langer and Dweck, 1973, pp. 40–42)

A Fixed Conception of Ourselves. A second reason we don't grow as much as we might is that we fix our conception of ourself. We begin to think, "Well, I've always been this way." We each begin to think of ourself as a person who can do this but can't do that. In this situation, growth concedes to "destiny."

To find out where our "I've always been this way" originated, Bloomfield and Kory (1980) recommend that we quiz the significant others of our childhood days. How did they see us? What labels did they apply to us? We may hear from their lips the same labels we have come to apply to ourselves. If we announce we're going to change, how do they respond? Does their response seem to say: "Lots of luck and you'll need it because 'you've always been this way.' " For illustration, here is a case presented by Bloomfield and Kory:

John, a college student, complains, "I can count the number of dates I've had on one hand and not run out of fingers." He's obviously got a sense of humor, but he is afraid to be himself around women. "I'm shy," he says. "That's my nature." John recalls his mother telling people that he was "the shy one." He never realized that his mother had an emotional investment in keeping him tied to her apron strings. John spent his childhood and adolescence living up to the family label of "the shy one." No doubt he had a tendency to be shy as a little boy, but with their labeling, his parents helped him develop that tendency into a full-blown personality characteristic. The question is whether John

is going to continue justifying his fears of women with the rationale: "Shyness is my nature." (p. 167)

A fixed notion of who we are can easily result when we continue to move around in the same old sub-environments that call forth the same old response. We can develop a kind of comfort in leading our familiar life and in being our familiar self. To change and grow might bring welcome hope and pleasurable excitement, but it might also bring unwelcome anxiety. More about this in the material that follows.

The Need for Safety. A third obstacle to growth concerns an unwillingness to leave safe places. Maslow (1968) hypothesized that in addition to growth forces, each person also has safety forces and these two sets work in opposition to each other. Maslow noted that the conflict between these forces could block the individual. He diagrammed this process as follows:

Safety ←PERSON →Growth

Elaborating on these opposing forces, Maslow wrote,

Every human being has *both* sets of forces within him. One set clings to safety and defensiveness out of fear, tending to regress backward, hanging on to the past *afraid* to grow away from the primitive communication with the mother's uterus and breast, *afraid* to take chances, *afraid* to jeopardize what he already has, *afraid* of independence, freedom and separateness. The other set of forces impels him forward toward wholeness of Self and uniqueness of Self, toward full functioning of all his capacities, toward confidence in the face of the external world at the same time that he can accept his deepest, real, unconscious Self. (p. 46)

Maslow noted that both safety and growth have drawbacks and attractions for the individual. The person grows when the drawbacks of safety and the attractions of growth are greater than the attractions of safety and the drawbacks of growth. Parents, teachers, and therapists sometimes are able to step in to change the weight of safety and growth vectors. As our conception of ourselves is enhanced, safety becomes less attractive and necessary and growth becomes more attractive and even irresistible.

When I consider the lives of my mother and father, it is easier for me to think of my mother's life as a success. Both my parents were immigrants, my mother from Latvia, my father from Russia. Both were looking for better lives in a new land, and both made their way to a small Midwestern city where they found each other, married, and raised five children.

Success in life, according to Freud's barebones set of criteria, requires success in loving and working but I never felt my father found his true work or calling. He was a brilliant and spiritual man who would have been fulfilled as a rabbi or teacher. Instead, for almost all of his adult life, he spent six-and-one-half long days a week in a little store, an occupation for which he exhibited little zest or talent. In his late-middle years, he became for awhile quite depressed—his response, I believe, to his inability to move his life along.

Some years ago, I went back to my home town just to wander again around old boyhood places. My parents were long since dead, and no relatives or close friends remained, but I found a man who had known my father quite well. We had coffee together and talked about the old days. He remembered how my father had been a force in the usually rabbi-less Jewish community and one who took it upon himself to round up 10 mostly reluctant men so that a Friday night sabbath prayer meeting could be held. "But," he added, "one thing about your father, he wasn't willing to take a chance."

I wondered about that: my father, a man who went AWOL from the Czar's army and came to a far-away land whose language and culture was completely strange to him, who fell in love, married, started a business, had five children, became a pillar of his religious community. He had taken chances, made commitments, achieved. What had happened to him along the way? How had he gotten so mired, so stuck?

In her book *Pathfinders,* Gail Sheehy describes a group of "people of high well being"—those who successfully negotiate the crises of life. She concludes that the "master quality" possessed by pathfinders is their willingness to take risks. In her study of lives she found that a continuing sense of well-being generally required a continual willingness to risk change. Similar findings came out of a longitudinal study of men and women by social scientists at the University of California at San Francisco (Lowenthal, 1980). Although the researcher expected those adults who showed a strong sense of continuity in values and goals would show the greatest sense of well-being instead it was those who demonstrated change.

The Fear of Growth. A fourth obstacle to growth concerns fear of what growth may bring. A number of students of human nature have noted an absolute fear of growth in some individuals. Why should some of us fear to grow? One reason may be that we fear the unknown. Even if we do not like or are not comfortable with who we are, at least, we are accustomed to ourselves. We hesitate to risk what we have (even though it's not all we want) to get something that may be less or worse.

A second reason we fear growth is that we may see growth as bringing responsibilities we doubt we will be able to meet. If we succeed, more will be expected of us and we may doubt our ability to continually meet these expectations. "The higher you climb, the harder you fall," we tell ourselves, "so maybe it's better not to reach too high."

There is a third fear of growth that Maslow (1971) called "the Jonah Complex." This complex (named after Jonah who wound up in the whale when he ran from a mission he had been given from on high) refers to our fear of our own greatness. Maslow hypothesized that in the presence of very special individuals (saintly persons, geniuses, beauties, etc.) we may tend to feel uneasy, envious, or inferior and therefore countervalue (or depreciate) them or their qualities. Maslow suggests that if we could bring ourselves "to love more purely the highest values in others," we would become better able to discover and love and make the most of these qualities in ourselves.

PATHWAYS TO GROWTH

All of life is concerned with growth, as is all of this book. It would be impossible and unnecessary here to review every pathway to growth that has been proposed or pursued. But it may be helpful to distinguish between two main paths that have aroused some controversy.

One path to growth is an individual way. Its emphasis is on oneself and involves developing one's own potentiality and making the most of one's life and spirit. It is an essentially inner path, although it may move out like a widening spiral to encompass more than oneself.

A second path is an outer and collective path—one of social activism and change. It involves finding ways to change the institutions of society—for example, the home and school and marriage—to enhance the lives of all people. It involves taking responsibility for the betterment of everyone everywhere and especially those less fortunate than oneself.

Some advocates of the second path have called the first a "narcissistic" one because they view it as a selfish pursuit. To them, it is a kind of self-absorption when the times call for social change and the reconstruction of social agencies. They fear that in frustration, people are "searching within" when they should be "reaching out."

Proponents of the first path vigorously disagree. They feel that personal growth or enhancement is a necessary first step—that one cannot reach out if one's center is hollow. If one wants a better world, the way to begin is to make oneself a better or fuller person. They ask how those who do not and cannot respect and love and help themselves hope to relate to and help others.

Roberts Samples (1977) calls the first path "self*ness*." This is "the state in which self is celebrated in a nonexploitative mode." It is distinct from self*fish*, the exploitation of others for the benefit of oneself and also distinct from self*less*, the exploitation of oneself for the benefit of others. He writes,

> The search for self, alone and in the quiet of one's own skills of introspection, is never done at the expense of the whole. A person who looks inward is no more a deviant from the whole than is a cloud from rivers and seas when one contemplates the water cycle. When one looks inward, it is difficult to avoid coming back more whole, more intact. Of course, here I exclude that small fringe group who look inward and stay there. When those who come back choose to enter a relationship, a community or a culture, they seldom bring a more despotic, more deficient human back into the action. Such people, with a fuller knowledge of their own strengths and limitations, are richer and closer to being psychically balanced and complete.
>
> It is these balanced humans who can be counted on to exercise the most basic kind of morality. I call it *selfness*. From this point, growth and being become a celebration of one's own person and the purity of all that is called humanness is then extended outward to the whole community of humankind. The extension of this process one day will hopefully eliminate the social and cultural inequities that currently exist—inequities nourished by leaders and followers whose psychic selves are empty. (p. 2)

There is, it seems, nothing essentially incompatible in the two paths. Service to others is a time-honored avenue to transcendence and so is the deep inner pursuit of oneself. One can grow from the inside out or from the outside in or both ways at once. There are many kinds of growth and many routes—each of us can find our own way.

References

Astin, A. W. (1977). *Four critical years.* San Francisco: Jossey-Bass.

Bakker, C. B. (1975). Why people don't change. *Psychotherapy: Theory, Research and Practice, 12*(2), 164–172.

Bloomfield, H. H., & Kory, R. B. (1980). *Inner joy.* New York: Wyden.

Combs, A. W., Avila, D. L., & Purkey, W. W. (1978). *Helping relationships: Basic concepts for the helping professions* (2nd ed.). Boston: Allyn & Bacon.

Cousins, N. (1977, May 28). Anatomy of an illness (as perceived by the patient). *Saturday Review,* pp. 4–6, 48–51.

Davis, K. (1940). Extreme social isolation of a child. *American Journal of Sociology, 46,* 554–565.

Davis, K. (1947). Final note on a case of extreme isolation. *American Journal of Sociology, 52,* 432–437.

Kerr, B. (1986). *Smart girls, gifted women.* Columbus: Ohio Psychology Publishing.

Langer, E. J., & Dweck, C. S. (1973). *Personal politics: The psychology of making it.* Englewood Cliffs, NJ: Prentice-Hall.

LeShan, E. J. (1976). *In search of myself and other children.* New York: M. Evans.

Maslow, A. H. (1968). *Toward a psychology of being* (2nd ed.). New York: Van Nostrand Reinhold.

Maslow, A. H. (1970). *Motivation and personality* (2nd ed.). New York: Harper & Row.

Maslow, A. H. (1972). *The farther reaches of human nature.* New York: Viking.

Medved, M., & Wallechinsky, D. (1976). *What really happened to the Class of '65?* New York: Random House.

Otto, H. A. (1972). New light on human potential. In College of Home Economics, Iowa State University (Ed.), *Families of the future* (pp. 14–25). Ames: Iowa State University Press.

Samples, B. (1977, May). Selfness: Seeds of a transformation. *AHP Newsletter,* pp. 1–2.

Schutz, W. (1979). *Profound simplicity.* New York: Bantam.

Scott-Maxwell, F. (1968). *The measure of my days.* New York: Knopf.

Sheehy, G. (1981). *Pathfinders.* New York: William Morrow.

Szent-Gyoergyi, A. (1974). Drive in living matter to perfect itself. *Synthesis, 1,* 14–26.

Vaillant, G. E. (1977). *Adaptation to life.* Boston: Little, Brown.

Wallechinsky, D. (1986). *Midterm report: The class of '65—Chronicles of an American generation.* New York: Viking.

Zilbergeld, B. (1983). *The shrinking of America: Myths of psychological change.* Boston: Little, Brown.

Follow-Up

1. *Do you now believe, or have you ever believed, "the myth of unchangeability"? If so, give your reasons, and indicate the effect of this myth on you.*
2. *Do you have any sense of a drive within yourself toward growth, enhancement, or perfection? Discuss this aspect of yourself.*
3. *Have you felt any guilt because of your failure to make more of yourself or a nostalgia for the person you might have become? Discuss this aspect of yourself.*
4. *Would you be willing to settle for an "ordinary life"? Why or why not? If not, what would it take to make your life acceptably "extraordinary"?*
5. *Are you a risk-taker or a security-seeker? What are the relative strengths of safety and growth forces in your life? Discuss this aspect of yourself.*

Responsibility

M. Scott Peck

We cannot solve life's problems except by solving them. This statement may seem idiotically tautological or self-evident, yet it is seemingly beyond the comprehension of much of the human race. This is because we must accept responsibility for a problem before we can solve it. We cannot solve a problem by saying, "It's not my problem." We cannot solve a problem by hoping that someone else will solve it for us. I can solve a problem only when I say "This is *my* problem and it's up to me to solve it." But many, so many, seek to avoid the pain of their problems by saying to themselves: "This problem was caused me by other people, or by social circumstances beyond my control, and therefore it is up to other people or society to solve this problem for me. It is not really my personal problem."

The extent to which people will go psychologically to avoid assuming responsibility for personal problems, while always sad, is sometimes almost ludicrous. A career sergeant in the army, stationed in Okinawa and in serious trouble because of his excessive drinking, was referred for psychiatric evaluation and, if possible, assistance. He denied that he was an alcoholic, or even that his use of alcohol was a personal problem, saying, "There's nothing else to do in the evenings in Okinawa except drink."

"Do you like to read?" I asked.

"Oh yes, I like to read, sure."

"Then why don't you read in the evening instead of drinking?"

"It's too noisy to read in the barracks."

"Well, then, why don't you go to the library?"

"The library is too far away."

"Is the library farther away than the bar you go to?"

"Well, I'm not much of a reader. That's not where my interests lie."

"Do you like to fish?" I then inquired.

"Sure, I love to fish."

"Why not go fishing instead of drinking?"

"Because I have to work all day long."

"Can't you go fishing at night?"

"No, there isn't any night fishing in Okinawa."

"But there is," I said. "I know several organizations that fish at night here. Would you like me to put you in touch with them?"

"Well, I really don't like to fish."

"What I hear you saying," I clarified, "is that there are other things to do in Okinawa except drink, but the thing you like to do most in Okinawa is drink."

"Yeah, I guess so."

"But your drinking is getting you in trouble, so you're faced with a real problem, aren't you?"

"This damn island would drive anyone to drink."

I kept trying for a while, but the sergeant was not the least bit interested in seeing his drinking as a personal problem which he could solve either with or without help, and I regretfully told his commander that he was not amenable to assistance. His drinking continued, and he was separated from the service in mid-career.

A young wife, also in Okinawa, cut her wrist lightly with a razor blade and was brought to the emergency room, where I saw her. I asked her why she had done this to herself.

"To kill myself, of course."

"Why do you want to kill yourself?"

"Because I can't stand it on this dumb island. You have to send me back to the States. I'm going to kill myself if I have to stay here any longer."

"What's is it about living on Okinawa that's so painful for you?" I asked.

She began to cry in a whining sort of way. "I don't have any friends here, and I'm alone all the time."

"That's too bad. How come you haven't been able to make any friends?"

"Because I have to live in a stupid Okinawan housing area, and none of my neighbors speak English."

"Why don't you drive over to the American housing area or to the wives' club during the day so you can make some friends?"

"Because my husband has to drive the car to work."

"Can't you drive him to work, since you're alone and bored all day?" I asked.

"No. It's a stick-shift car, and I don't know how to drive a stick-shift car, only an automatic."

"Why don't you learn how to drive a stick-shift car?"

She glared at me. "On these roads? You must be crazy."

Most people who come to see a psychiatrist are suffering from what is called either a neurosis or a character disorder. Put most simply, these two conditions are disorders of responsibility, and as such they are opposite styles of relating to the world and its problems. The neurotic assumes too much responsibility; the person with a character disorder not enough. When neurotics are in conflict with the world they automatically assume that they are at fault. When those with character disorders are in conflict with the world they automatically assume that the world is at fault. The two individuals just described had character disorders: the sergeant felt that his drinking was Okinawa's fault, not his, and the wife also saw herself as playing no role whatsoever in her own isolation. Almost all of us from time to time seek to avoid—in ways that can be quite subtle—the pain of assuming responsibility for our own problems. For the cure of my own subtle character disorder at the age of thirty I am indebted to Mac Badgely. At the time Mac was the director of the outpatient psychiatric clinic where I was completing my psychiatry residency training. In this clinic my fellow residents and I were assigned new patients on rotation. Perhaps because I was more dedicated to my patients and my own education than most of my fellow residents, I found myself working much longer hours than they. They ordinarily saw patients only once a week. I often saw my patients two or three times a week. As a result I would watch my fellow residents leaving the clinic at four-thirty each afternoon for their homes, while I was scheduled with appointments up to eight or nine o'clock at night, and my heart was filled with resentment. As I became more and more resentful and more and more exhausted I realized that something had to be done. So I went to Dr. Badgely and explained the situation to him. I wondered whether I might be exempted from the rotation of accepting new patients for a few weeks so that I might have time to catch up. Did he think that was feasible? Or could he think of some other solution to the problem? Mac listened to me very intently and receptively, not interrupting once. When I was finished, after a moment's silence, he said to me very sympathetically, "Well, I can see that you do have a problem."

I beamed, feeling understood. "Thank you," I said. "What do you think should be done about it?"

To this Mac replied, "I told you, Scott, you do have a problem."

This was hardly the response I expected. "Yes," I said, slightly annoyed, "I know I have a problem. That's why I came to see you. What do you think I ought to do about it?"

Mac responded: "Scott, apparently you haven't listened to what I said. I have heard you, and I am agreeing with you. You do have a problem."

"Goddammit," I said, "I know I have a problem. I knew that when I came in here. The question is, what am I going to do about it?"

"Scott," Mac replied, "I want you to listen. Listen closely and I will say it again. I agree with you. You do have a problem. Specifically, you have a problem with time. *Your* time. Not *my* time. It's not my problem. It's *your* problem with *your* time. You, Scott Peck, have a problem with your time. That's all I'm going to say about it."

I turned and strode out of Mac's office, furious. And I stayed furious. I hated Mac Badgely. For three months I hated him. I felt that he had a severe character disorder. How else could he be so callous? Here I had gone to him humbly asking for just a little bit of help, a little bit of advice, and the bastard wasn't even willing to assume enough responsibility even to try to help me, even to do his job as director of the clinic. If he wasn't supposed to help manage such problems as director of the clinic, what the hell was he supposed to do?

But after three months I somehow came to see that Mac was right, that it was I, not he, who had the character disorder. My time *was* my responsibility. It was up to me and me alone to decide how I wanted to use and order my time. If I wanted to invest my time more heavily than my fellow residents in my work, then that was my choice, and the consequences of that choice were my responsibility. It might be painful for me to watch my fellow residents leave their offices two or three hours before me, and it might be painful to listen to my wife's complaints that I was not devoting myself sufficiently to the family, but these pains were the consequence of a choice that I had made. If I did not want to suffer them, then I was free to choose not to work so hard and to structure my time differently. My working hard was not a burden cast upon me by

hardhearted fate or a hardhearted clinic director; it was the way I had chosen to live my life and order my priorities. As it happened, I chose not to change my life style. But with my change in attitude, my resentment of my fellow residents vanished. It simply no longer made any sense to resent them for having chosen a life style different from mine when I was completely free to choose to be like them if I wanted to. To resent them was to resent my own choice to be different from them, a choice that I was happy with.

The difficulty we have in accepting responsibility for our behavior lies in the desire to avoid the pain of the consequences of that behavior. By requesting Mac Badgely to assume responsibility for the structure of my time I was attempting to avoid the pain of working long hours, even though working long hours was an inevitable consequence of my choice to be dedicated to my patients and my training. Yet in so doing I was also unwittingly seeking to increase Mac's authority over me. I was giving him my power, my freedom. I was saying in effect, "Take charge of me. You be the boss!" Whenever we seek to avoid the responsibility for our own behavior, we do so by attempting to give that responsibility to some other individual or organization or entity. But this means we then give away our power to that entity, be it "fate" or "society" or the government or the corporation or our boss. It is for this reason that Erich Fromm so aptly titled his study of Nazism and authoritarianism *Escape from Freedom*. In attempting to avoid the pain of responsibility, millions and even billions daily attempt to escape from freedom.

I have a brilliant but morose acquaintance who, when I allow him to, will speak unceasingly and eloquently of the oppressive forces in our society: racism, sexism, the military–industrial establishment, and the country police who pick on him and his friends because of their long hair. Again and again I have tried to point out to him that he is not a child. As children, by virtue of our real and extensive

"let's see...who's fault is it?
who can i blame?"

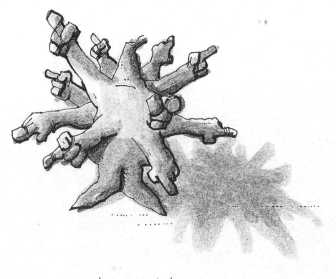

tom mcCain 11/23/80

"Responsibility" by Tom McCain. Copyright © 1996.

dependency, our parents have real and extensive power over us. They are, in fact, largely responsible for our well-being, and we are, in fact, largely at their mercy. When parents are oppressive, as so often they are, we as children are largely powerless to do anything about it; our choices are limited. But as adults, when we are physically healthy, our choices are almost unlimited. That does not mean they are not painful. Frequently our choices lie between the lesser of two evils, but it is still within our power to make these choices. Yes, I agree with my acquaintance, there are indeed oppressive forces at work within the world. We have, however, the freedom to choose every step of the way the manner in which we are going to respond to and deal with these forces. It is his choice to live in an area of the country where the police don't like "long-haired types" and still grow his hair long. He has the freedom to move to the city, or to cut his hair, or even to wage a campaign for the office of police commissioner. But despite his brilliance, he does not acknowledge these freedoms. He chooses to lament his lack of political power instead of accepting and exulting in his immense personal power. He speaks of his love of freedom and of the oppressive forces that thwart it, but every time he speaks of how he is victimized by these forces he actually is giving away his freedom. I hope that some day soon he will stop resenting life simply because some of its choices are painful.

Dr. Hilde Bruch, in the preface to her book *Learning Psychotherapy,* states that basically all patients come to psychiatrists with "one common problem: the sense of helplessness, the fear and inner conviction of being unable to 'cope' and to change things." One of the roots of this "sense of impotence" in the majority of patients is some desire to partially or totally escape the pain of freedom, and, therefore, some failure, partial or total, to accept responsibility for their problems and their lives. They feel impotent because they have, in fact, given their power away. Sooner or later, if they are to be healed, they must learn that the entirety of one's adult life is a series of personal choices, decisions. If they can accept this totally, then they become free people. To the extent that they do not accept this they will forever feel themselves victims.

Follow-Up

1. *Describe an instance from your life for each of the following situations:*
   - *Assumed responsibility for a life problem even though it was difficult (and tempting not to do so).*
   - *Avoided responsibility for a life problem and gave it to someone or something else.*
2. *Peck argues that by not taking personal responsibility we give away part of our freedom to live. Discuss this idea and provide some examples.*
3. *Choose another idea or statement from this reading and provide a reaction.*

Herbie

Tom Keating

If you have lived between 16th Street and Broad Ripple in the last 25 years you probably have seen him a dozen times and likely bought his goods.

He is a little old fellow, slightly stooped. He walks with a shuffle and always carries two shopping bags. And he always smiles.

His name is Herbert Wirth. Most people call him Herbie. He is 72 and has made his living since 1944 selling dishrags and wash cloths door to door.

He has never owned a car. He calculates he has walked more than 50,000 miles since he began his selling career at the age of 57 after losing his job at a dry goods company.

He works 9 a.m. to 6 p.m. six days a week and doesn't stop for lunch.

But, he doesn't just pick a street at random and start selling.

"Everything I do has been worked out systematically over the years through trial and error," he explained.

"I start at 46th Street and Winthrop Avenue and in one day will work up the east side of Winthrop to the canal in Broad Ripple. Then the next day I'll work the west side of Winthrop all the way to the canal again. After that I just keep moving over a street every day working from 46th to the canal until I reach Boulevard Place.

"After that I start again at 46th and Winthrop and this time work down to Fall Creek. Again I work one street at a time until I get to Pennsylvania Street. Every day I cover at least one whole side of a street, catching the side streets as I go along.

"It takes me about four months to complete the whole circuit. Then I start all over again. This way I get around to my customers three times a year.

"The reason I don't bother with lunch is because I found out that it takes me almost exactly nine hours to cover one street, and if I stop to eat it throws my schedule off. I do stop for a glass of water several times during the day. People are real nice about that."

Wirth starts each day with two large shopping bags filled to the brim with the six items he sells—dishrags, wash cloths, pot scrapers, large red handkerchiefs, two sizes of ladies hankies and black, brown and white shoelaces.

"I sometimes think the weight of the bags (25 pounds each at the start) acts as an incentive for me to sell.

"My feet never bother me. I guess once you get used to walking a lot. your feet get tough. It varies how much I sell each day. I usually average around 40 dishrags, 35 wash cloths and 25 pot scrapers. They all sell for a quarter."

"I use psychology in my work. There is a great art to selling. I try not to make a pest of myself. If people want my products, fine. If not, I thank them and be on my way. I don't try to play on people's sympathy. I don't want them to buy anything they can't use just because they feel sorry for me.

"I know many housewives are afraid of door-to-door salesmen, but by now most everyone knows me so I have somewhat of an advantage in this respect. I even have people who call me at home now to order articles.

"The Northside has changed a lot in the last 25 years, but the people have stayed about the same. Most are basically good. I get a door slammed in my face once in a while, but only once or twice a year.

"And regardless of what a lot of people say about youngsters, they are every bit as nice today as they were in the 1940s and 1950s.

"I get along with kids and dogs real well. I've always heard that postmen have trouble with dogs. I've never been able to figure that out. I guess some people just don't understand dogs."

Born in Lake Forest, Ill., Wirth moved here at the age of 13. He lives in a small house almost in the middle of his territory.

"When you get to be 72 you find yourself looking back and wondering what would have happened to your life if you had done this or that at a certain time. But, it's too late at my age to do anything but wonder. I guess that is the worst thing about growing old.

"I don't see any reason I can't keep working for many years. I feel great and I think I'd go out of my mind if I had to sit around and loaf every day.

"I've always taken life very seriously— probably too seriously. I've never had the time for many hobbies. In my free time about all I do is watch TV and read. I made the mistake of never getting married when I was young and now I don't have any close family. I live by myself and it's not too much fun.

"I know that selling dishrags is not the most important job in the world. I sometimes have envied men who are doing exciting and glamorous things.

"There won't be much of a dent in the world when I die, but at least I can say I made an honest to God try to do what I did as a nice man."

[One year later.] Despite the fact he was well known, he had no relatives so he lived alone for the last 20 years or so and worked at his job with few complaints and few fears.

But, he was afraid of one thing—that he wouldn't have anyone at his funeral.

He explained two years ago that he didn't mind living alone, except maybe at Christmas, but he didn't like the idea of dying without someone taking the time to say a few prayers for him and remember that he had "tried to be a good man."

Saturday, Herbert Wirth died of a heart attack in a Northside supermarket. There was some concern for a while because no relatives could be found to handle the funeral arrangements.

But Herbie had known that this would be the case and on March 5, 1968, he had paid cash to the Flanner and Buchanan Mortuaries for a complete funeral and burial.

He requested that there be no service in the funeral home nor in a church. All he wanted was a graveside service.

And that some people be there.

Something kind of strange and warm and you might even say wonderful happened in Indianapolis yesterday.

More than 1,000 persons showed up for the funeral of a 73-year-old man who sold dishrags door to door.

Not a tycoon nor a big politician nor a sports idol—just a little old fellow who lived alone and peddled odds and ends on the Northside for 25 years and never did anything special except be himself.

His name was Herbie Wirth and he said a couple of years ago that he didn't want to be buried without someone there to say a prayer or two for him.

A newspaper story Tuesday mentioned this wish and everyone thought maybe 10 or 20 or even 30 people might show up for the graveside services at Crown Hill Cemetery.

But shortly before 10 a.m. a huge bell in the cemetery gate tower began ringing for the first time in more than 40 years and when the services started there were more people present than have attended a graveside funeral in this city in possibly 20 years, according to cemetery officials.

The people who were there were white and black, old and young, rich and poor.

They were soldiers in uniform, flower children with long flowing hair, businessmen in suits and overcoats, women carrying babies, truck drivers, elderly people who had to be helped up the icy hill to the grave, and teenagers cutting school.

Wives and husbands who hadn't told each other of their plans, met unexpectedly at the grave.

Many of these people said they didn't even know Herbie. Many others did. For whatever reason they came, not one stood to gain a thing, not even gratitude.

Coming to this funeral was not a casual stop. Many had to park their cars at least a mile from the grave and walk over hills in a snowstorm in 20-degree weather.

Why did so many come?,

Well, you think it might have something to do with the almost universal fear of being alone, of having no one. You think it might also be because Herbie was well-liked and the simplicity of his life was what was being honored.

But when a thousand people stand in freezing weather to pay homage to a little man who was neither rich nor famous, you have to think above all that it is simply because a lot of people do care about others.

Someone brought a large guest book to the grave and most of the people present signed it before leaving.

Because Herbie had no relatives, the book was placed in the casket with him.

It was a very full book.

Follow-Up

1. *What are your feelings and thoughts about Herbie's story?*
2. *Tom Keating gave his conclusions on why so many people attended Herbie's funeral at the end of the article. Comment on his interpretations and possibly add your own if different from Keating's.*
3. *Did Herbie live a life in a healthy, responsible manner according to the concepts mentioned in the earlier articles by Goud, Arkoff, Peck, and the psychologists cited in the introduction?*

Just a Regular Kid

I teach fifth grade. The children are 10 years old. I would venture to say 99% of them think, learn and act like they are 10. It doesn't seem to be enough. Administrators, teachers, parents and members of the community seem to always want a 10 year old (or whatever age) *to be better than 10.*

Don't misunderstand, I am in favor of excellence or striving for it. I am for the gifted child. I am for intellectual and physical achievement. What I am against is the thought that there must be something wrong if a child thinks, acts, or feels his age.

Adults become ecstatic if at grade level 5.0 a child tests 8.2. If at 10, a child pitches a ball like a 12 year old, adults are impressed. How many accomplish these feats? I would venture to say one out of 100. What happens to the other 99? They have their moments, I'm sure, but seldom are parents or teachers satisfied. The world today is agog with achievements. I grant it would be a thrill to parent or teach a president, a Nobel Prize winner, an Olympic champion. Yet, why is it not enough to have been influential in the life of an intelligent, moral, healthy, productive human being?

Immaturity is often used as an excuse for the errors of the young. I don't think so. I think most youngsters are maturing through their successes *and* errors. Adults expect so much so soon. Yet, how many adults are error-free?

I should like a little more calm in the business of helping children grow. I should like a little less push. I should like us to all be more content with each individual child. When 10 year olds act or learn like they're 10, let's say hurrah! What a blessing! They'll only be 10 once. How great to flub and win, to fail and pass, to laugh and be hurt on a 10-year-old level when you're 10. Why must we expect children "to take it like a man" or "act like a lady"?

As a parent and teacher I have been caught up in this push for the young to "grow up." As my own children grow and leave childhood behind I realize perhaps we pushed too soon. We took their young lives and expected adult behavior and thinking from children. I see other parents do the same. Parents and teachers seem to forget a child's best has to be good enough. They want their child to be the best.

Children are children. Thank goodness! If I do nothing else as a teacher I hope I remember this fact. They will falter. They will be mischievous. They may even be bad. They will achieve. They will laugh. And they will learn. I'm hopeful I can help the children, their parents, and myself to understand that it is quite acceptable to do all these things in a childlike way.

—A fifth grade teacher and graduate student

Follow-Up

1. *Do you agree with the main idea expressed in this essay?*
2. *Were you expected to be more than a child when you were young?*

New Passages

Gail Sheehy

In the space of one short generation, the whole shape of the life cycle has been fundamentally altered. Since the publication of my book *Passages* in 1976, age norms have shifted and are no longer normative.

Consider: Nine-year-old girls are developing breasts and pubic hair; 9-year-old boys carry guns to school; 16-year-olds can "divorce" a parent; 30-year-old men still live at home with Mom; 40-year-old women are just getting around to pregnancy; 50-year-old men are forced into early retirement; 55-year-old women can have egg donor babies; 60-year-old women start first professional degrees; 70-year-old men reverse aging by 20 years with human growth hormone; 80-year-olds run marathons; 85-year-olds remarry and still enjoy good sex; and every day, the "Today" show's Willard Scott says "Happy Birthday!" to more 100-year-old women.

What's going on? There is a revolution in the adult life cycle. People today are leaving childhood sooner, but they are taking longer to grow up and much longer to die. That is shifting all the stages of adulthood ahead—by 10 years. Adolescence is now prolonged for the middle class until the end of the 20s. Today, our First Adulthood only begins at 30. Most baby boomers don't feel fully "grown up" until they are into their 40s. When our parents turned 50, we thought they were old! But today, women and men I've interviewed routinely feel they are five to 10 years younger than the age on their birth certificates. Fifty is what 40 used to be; 60 is what 50 used to be. Middle age has already been pushed far into the 50s—in fact, if you listen to boomers, there is no more middle age. So what's next?

Welcome to Middlescence. It's adolescence the second time around.

The territory of the 50s, 60s and beyond is changing so radically that it now opens up whole new passages leading to stages of life that are nothing like what our parents experienced. An American woman who today reaches age 50 free of cancer and heart disease can expect to see her 92nd birthday. The aver-

"Happy 100th Birthday Mother" by Nelson Goud. Copyright © 1996.

age man who is 65 today—an age now reached by more than 70 percent of the U.S. population—can expect to live until 81. That amounts to a second adult lifetime.

Stop and recalculate. Imagine the day you turn 45 as the old age of your First Adulthood. Fifty then becomes the youth of your Second Adulthood. First Adulthood just happens to you. Second Adulthood, you can custom-design. It's a potential rebirth that offers exhilarating new possibilities. But only for those who are aware and who prepare.

For those who are approaching 50, the question increasingly becomes. "How shall we live the rest of our lives?" And the tantalizing dynamic that has emerged in our era is that the second half of adult life is not the stagnant, depressing downward slide we have always assumed it to be.

In the hundreds of interviews I have done with men and women in middle life, especially pacesetters in the educated middle class, I have discovered that people are beginning to see there is the exciting potential of a new life to live: one in which they can concentrate on becoming better, stronger, deeper, wiser, funnier, freer, sexier and more attentive to living the privileged moments—even as they are getting older, lumpier, bumpier, slower and closer to the end. Instead of being a dreary tale of decline, our middle life is a progress story, a series of little victories over little deaths.

We now have not one but three adult lives to anticipate: Provisional Adulthood from age 18 to 30, First Adulthood from 30 to 45 and Second Adulthood from 45 to 85 and beyond. The most exciting development is that Second Adulthood contains two new territories—an Age of Mastery from 45 to 65 and an Age of Integrity from 65 to 85 and beyond. The startling life changes awaiting all of us are now being charted by path breakers from the World War II generation and the "silent" generation of those who came of age in the 1950s, who are writing new maps for everyone else to follow.

THE FLOURISHING FORTIES

The two generations of baby boomers—the Vietnam generation of the 1960s and the "me" generation of the 1970s—are set to become the the longest-living humans in American history. The first of them will officially turn 50 in 1996. A million of them, the Census Bureau predicts, will live past 100. Having indulged themselves in the longest adolescence in history, they betray a collective terror and disgust of aging.

Early in life, baby boomers got used to having two things: choice and control. That means that when life's storm clouds threaten, people in their 40s today are likely to feel more out of control than ever. Wally Scott, a participant in one of many "Midlife Passages" group discussions I've attended in recent years, put it this way: "All of a sudden, you have to listening to the little voices inside: What do I really want to invest my life in? How can I construct a life that fits the me of today as opposed to the me of 15 years ago?"

The Flourishing Forties can be complicated for women by the storms of perimenopause and menopause. Men may face their own version of biological meltdown. Although it is not strictly a male menopause, many men in middle or later life do experience a lapse in virility and vitality and a decline in well-being. About half of American men over 40 have experienced middle-life impotence to varying degrees. This decline can definitely be delayed. It can even be corrected. In the near future, it may even become preventable. But first a man must understand it.

The social arena contains its own challenges as women in their 40s continue to explore new roles, struggle with late child rearing or mourn their lack of children. As couples are forced to renegotiate traditional relationships and medical crises intrude on well-laid plans, men and women in this age group begin to feel their mortality.

Today, smart men and women will use their early 40s as preparation for a custom-designed Second Adulthood. What do you need to learn to maximize your ability to respond quickly to a fluid marketplace? A single, fixed identity is a liability today. Recent research also suggests that developing multiple identities is one of the best buffers against mental and physical illness. When a marriage blows up or the company shuts down or the whole nature of a profession is changed by technology, people with more than one identity can draw upon other sources of self-esteem while they regroup. Such resilience is essential.

SECOND ADULTHOOD

John Guare has been doing what he most loves since he was 9 years old—writing plays. But even the brilliant creator of *Six Degrees of Separation* and *House of Blue Leaves* knows he cannot rest on his laurels. He was 56 when I mentioned to him that I was exploring our Second Adulthood. "I was just saying to my wife, 'I've got to reinvent my life, right now!'" he exploded. "Or we'll be dead. Worse than dead—the walking dead."

That is the challenge of making the passage to Second Adulthood. This new life must be precipitated by a moment of of change—the "Aha!" moment. It forces us to look upon our lives differently and to make a transition from survival to mastery. In young adulthood we survive by figuring out how best to please or perform for the powerful ones who will protect and reward us—parents, teachers, lovers, mates, bosses, mentors. It is all about proving ourselves. The transformation of middle life is to move into a more stable psychological state of mastery, where we control much of what happens in our life and can often act on the world rather than react to whatever the world throws at us. Reaching this state of mastery is also one of the best predictors of good mental and psychological functioning in old age.

Second Adulthood takes us beyond the preoccupation with self. We are compelled to search for a greater significance in our engagement in the world. "We are all hungry for connection." said James Sniechowski, a 51-year-old men's group leader in Santa Monica, Calif. *Connection* was a word that came up again and again in my discussions with groups of middle-aged men.

Increasingly, women who have mastered the silent passage through menopause feel a power surge—post-menopausal zest. As family obligations fade away, many become motivated to stretch their independence, learn new skills, return to school, plunge into new careers, rediscover the creativity and adventurousness of their youth and, at last, find their own voices.

THE FLAMING FIFTIES

By the time they reach their Flaming Fifties, most educated women have acquired the skills and self-knowledge to master complex environments and change the conditions around them. Over and over, women who have crossed into their 50s tell me with conviction, "I would not go back to being young again." They remember vividly what it was like to wake up not knowing exactly who they were, to be torn between demands of family and commands of career, to be constantly changing hats (and hairstyles) in the attempt to fit many roles and often losing focus in the blur of it all.

In three major national opinion surveys I have done in the past seven years, I have learned that by Second Adulthood, the dominant influence on a woman's well-being is not income level or social class or marital status. The most decisive factor is age. Older is happier.

"Fifty for me was a time when I really, for the first time, owned my body." said Ginny Ford, a Rochester, N.Y., businesswoman, whose blond hair and dimpled smile evoke Doris Day movies. "I had been very ashamed of my body, and now I love it. Now, there's all this inner stuff going on. I'm probably 10 pounds heavier, my thighs are a little rumply, my arms have flab. Fifteen years ago I would have starved myself. But now I'm enjoying my husband's pasta. I exercise every day. I enjoy myself sexually and I'm proud of this body. It really works!"

For men entering their 50s today, there is no script. It has traditionally been assumed that aging is kinder to men, but a different truth comes out in personal interviews. I found far more uncertainty among men in middle life than among women: indeed, they often appear to be going in opposite directions. Overall, the over-50 men in my surveys don't experience the great transformation from First to Second Adulthood that women do. Most appear to be more resigned to accepting life as it is: Two thirds are not anticipating any major change, and one third feel more concerned about just getting by. Half of these men feel tired and like they're "running out of gas." Their greatest worry is that they can no longer take their health for granted.

Intimate Attachments
But among those men I have studied who are were educated, particularly those with an entrepreneurial temperament, a good many are enjoying a sense of mastery. They say the best things about being over 45 are being able to rely on their experience and being clearer about what is truly important in life. Still others find new richness in forging closer, more intimate attachments with their wives or in becoming start-over dads.

How can we make this passage more positively? Find your passion, and pursue it. How do you know where to look? You can start by seeing if it passes the time-flies test. What activity do you do in which time goes by without your even knowing it? What did you most

love to do when you were 12 years old? Somewhere in that activity there is a hook to be found that might pull up your dormant self.

Men and women who emerge psychologically healthiest at 50 are those who, as their expectations and goals change with age, "shape a 'new self' that calls upon qualities that were dominant earlier." This was the principal finding of longitudinal studies at the University of California at Berkeley. Men have always been able to start over, and not once but more than once. What is really new is that women now have the option of starting second lives in their mid-40s or 50s and increasingly they are doing so.

For some that will lead to intellectual pursuits. A remarkable surge is already occurring in higher education among older women. Only 3.2 percent of the women in the World War II generation went back to post-high-school education between the ages of 40 and 54. But fully 11 percent of the "silent" generation of the 1950s went back for some college education in those middle years. In 1991, nearly 1 million women over 40 were enrolled in college nationwide.

This stage brings with it much greater emotional and social license, and a majority of these women have claimed it, becoming more outspoken and less self-conscious. After interviewing 14 women from my national survey who emerged in their 50s with optimum well-being, I learned that they see themselves as survivors. That is not the same as seeing themselves as former victims of terrible physical or emotional abuse, although some do describe overcoming such situations in their lives. What they have "survived" are the economic biases and stereotypical sex roles that threatened to inhibit their development as fully independent adults. They are so strong that they do not expect to feel "old" until they are about 70.

One striking finding among researchers is that men over 50 are becoming somewhat more dependent on their wives, emotionally and financially, and less certain about their future goals. The special stresses of an economy in transition, with its punishing wage declines for non-college-educated workers and corporate downswing that now robs many college-educated men of identity and meaning, have been added to classic biological stresses, especially the decline of men's physical prowess and, for many, the sagging of their sexual performance. Given this new set of conditions, men at middle life probably face the roughest patch of all in mapping the new adult life across time.

"Men over 45 are becoming the new at-risk population for significant problems with anxiety and depression." says Ellen McGrath, a psychologist and author *When Feeling Bad Is Good*. "And for the first time ever, some of them are acknowledging it and reaching out for help. This is a brand-new trend."

Making a passage to the Age of Mastery often means men are giving up being the master. Alan Alhadeff, a Seattle lawyer of 45, described his "Aha!" moment on a basketball court: "This 20-year-old kid was checking me real hard in the back court. I'm then about 20 pounds heavier than people my height should be. So I pushed him away, somewhat aggressively. I said, 'C'mon. I'm old enough to be your dad.'" The young man looked the older man straight in the eye: "Then get off the court."

"After that day on the basketball court, I mellowed. I realized I don't have to prove myself in physical contests anymore. I don't see that as a negative at all." Indeed, this freed Alhadeff to try other forms of expression he had never entertained before: art, music, gardening, gourmet cooking. "And they're all a lot easier on the knees!"

The real winners among men in middle life do make this shift. Nearly all have developed passions or hobbies that happily occupy and challenge them outside their workaday routines. Such occupations are crucial in off-setting the disenchantment with their profession that polls show is now felt by large numbers of doctors, or the boredom of the accountant defending yet another tax audit of a rich client or the weariness of the dentist who cannot expect to be wildly stimulated by drilling his billionth bicuspid.

THE SERENE SIXTIES

The 60s have changed just as dramatically as the earlier stages of middle life. What with beta blockers and hip replacements, you're as likely to run into a man of 65 rollerblading in the park as to see him biking with his youngest child, enjoying the adolescent boy in himself as well as the recycled father. Only 10 percent of Americans 65 and over have a chronic health problem that restricts them from carrying on a major physical activity.

Clearly the vast majority of American women and men now in their 60s have reached the stage where maximum freedom coexists with a minimum of physical limitations. And another passage looms: the one from mastery to integrity. Experts in gerontology make a clear distinction between passive aging and successful aging. To engage in successful aging is actually a career choice—a conscious commitment to continuing self-education and the development of a whole set of strategies.

Resilience is probably the most important protection one can have entering the Age of Integrity. An impressive study of the sources of well-being in men at 65 found that the harbinger of emotional health was not a stable childhood or a highflying career. Rather, it was much more important to have developed an ability to handle life's accidents and conflicts without passivity, blaming or bitterness. "It's having the capacity to hold a conflict or impulse in consciousness without acting on it," concludes George Vaillant, a psychiatrist now at Harvard Medical School, who has been scrutinizing—in the Grant Study—the same

173 Harvard men at five-year intervals since they graduated in the early 1940s.

A related finding in the Grant Study: Time does heal. The research shows that even the most traumatic events in childhood had virtually no effect on the well-being of these men by their mid-60s, although severe depression earlier in life did predispose them to continuing problems. Traits that turned out to contribute to happiness in the golden years were not the same ones that had influenced people back in their college days: spontaneity, creative flair and easy sociability. Instead, the traits important to smooth functioning as we get older are being dependable, well organized and pragmatic.

The major predictable passage in this period for most people is retirement, though many consider part-time work to help pay for their longer lives and perhaps to handle other family cares like aged parents or the needs of grandchildren. Forty-one percent of retirees surveyed in New York City in 1993 said the adjustment to retirement was difficult. The younger the retiree, the harder the transition. And the higher the status one's work conferred, the steeper the slide to anonymity.

The comfort of mature love is the single most important determinant of older men's outlook on life. Continued excitement about life is the other factor in high well-being for men at this stage. My research with members of the Harvard Business School class of 1949 shows that those who enjoy the highest well-being had reached out for new adventures in half a dozen new directions *before* retiring. They see semi- or full retirement as an enticing opportunity to add richness to their lives.

Grandparenthood can jump-start the transition to the Age of Integrity. For women or men who had to learn, painfully, in First Adulthood how to compartmentalize their nurturing selves and achieving selves, grandparenthood is a particularly welcome second chance to bring all the parts of their lives in harmony.

THE SAGE SEVENTIES

Those who thrive into their 70s and beyond "live very much in the present, but they always have plans for the future," argues Cecelia Hurwich in her doctoral thesis at the Center for Psychological Studies in Albany, Calif. The seventysomethings Hurwich studied had mastered the art of "letting go" of their egos gracefully, so they could focus their attention on a few fine-tuned priorities. These zestful women were not in unusually good physical shape, but believing they still had living to do, they concentrated on what they could do rather than on what they had lost. Every one acknowledged the need for some form of physical intimacy. They found love through sharing a variety of pleasures: music, gardening, hiking, traveling. Several spoke enthusiastically of active and satisfying sex lives.

After that life stage, the most successful octogenarians I have come across seem to share a quality of directness. Robust and unaffected, often hilariously uninhibited in expressing what they really think, they are liable to live with a partner rather than get married or to pick up an old sweetheart and marry despite their kids' disapproval. They have nothing left to lose.

The Age of Integrity is primarily a stage of spiritual growth. Instead of focusing on time running out, we should, make it a daily exercise to mark the moment. The present never ages. And instead of trying to maximize our control over our environment, a goal that was perfectly appropriate to the earlier Age of Mastery, now we must cultivate greater appreciation and acceptance of that which we cannot control. Some of the losses of Second Adulthood are inconsolable losses. To accept them without bitterness usually requires making a greater effort to discern the highest spiritual truths that shape the changes and losses of the last passage of life.

Follow-Up

1. *Sheehy claims that adult stages have shifted 10 years forward. Provisional Adulthood extends from 18–29; a First Adulthood starts at 30; a Second Adulthood at 45. From the people you know, including yourself, are her main points accurate?*

2. *In her interviews, men seem to have more difficulty in the Second Adulthood stage (45 and older). Do you agree with her analysis of this finding? Explain your answer.*

3. *Interview some people of both genders in each of the decades that Sheehy mentions. See if they agree with her points. Sheehy's findings are based on middle-class people. Try to see if non-middle class people fit her findings.*

4. *If you are in your "Provisional Adulthood" (18–30), how does your future look to you if Sheehy's ideas are accurate? Is there anything you can do now to help make the necessary transitions as you age?*

5. *Discuss or write about any other idea mentioned in this article.*

The Lesson of the Cliff

Morton Hunt

It was a sweltering July day in Philadelphia—I can feel it still, 56 years later. The five boys I was with had grown tired of playing marbles and burning holes in dry leaves with a lens and were casting about for something else.

"Hey!" said freckle-faced little Ned. "I got an idea. We haven't climbed the cliff for a long while."

"Let's go!" said someone else. And off they went, trotting and panting like a pack of stray dogs.

I hesitated. I longed to be brave and active, like them, but I'd been a sickly child most of my eight years and had taken to heart my mother's admonitions to remember that I wasn't as strong as other boys and not to take chances.

"Come on!" called Jerry, my best friend. "Just because you've been sick is no reason to be a sissy." "I'm *coming!*" I yelled, and ran along after them.

Through the park and into the woods we went, finally emerging in a clearing. At the far side, 40 to 50 feet away, loomed the cliff, a bristling, near-vertical wall of jutting rocks, earth slides, scraggly bushes and ailanthus saplings. From the tumbled rocks at its base to the fringe of sod at its top, it was only about 60 feet high, but to me it looked like the very embodiment of the Forbidden and Impossible.

One by one, the other boys scrabbled upward, finding handholds and toeholds on rocky outcrops and earthen ledges. I hung back until the others were partway up; then, trembling and sweating, I began to climb. A hand here, a foot there, my heart thumping in my skinny chest, I made my way up and up.

At some point, I looked back—and was horrified. The ground at the base of the cliff seemed very far below; one slip and I would fall, bouncing off the cliff face and ending on the rocks. There, shattered and strangling on my own blood, I would gurgle, twitch a few times, and then expire, like the cat I had seen run over a few days earlier.

But the boys were chattering above me on an earthen ledge two-thirds of the way to the top. It was 5 to 6 feet deep and some 15 feet long. I clawed my way up to them; then I crawled as far back on the ledge as I could, huddling against the rock face. The other boys stood close to the edge and boldly urinated into space; the sight made me so queasy that I surreptitiously clutched at the rocks behind me.

In a few minutes, they started up to the top.

"Hey, wait," I croaked.

"So long! See you in the funny papers," one of them said, and the others laughed.

"But I can't . . . I . . . " That spurred them on: jeering and catcalling back to me, they wriggled their way to the top, from where they would walk home by a roundabout route. Before they left, they peered down at me.

"You can stay if you want to," mocked Ned. "It's all yours." Jerry looked concerned, but he went with the others.

I looked down and was overcome by dizziness; a nameless force seemed to be impelling me to fall off. I lay clinging to a rock as the world spun around. I could never climb back down. It was much too far to go, too hazardous; partway, I would grow feeble or faint, lose my grip, fall and die. But the way up to the top was even worse—higher, steeper, more treacherous; I would never make it. I heard someone sobbing and moaning; I wondered who it was and realized that it was I.

Time passed. The shadows gradually lengthened, the sun disappeared from the treetops beyond the clearing below, dusk began to gather. Silent now, I lay on my stomach as if in a trance, stupefied by fear and fatigue, unable to move or even to think of how to get back down to safety and home.

January 1945, Watton Air Base, East Anglia. This morning I found my name posted on the blackboard: Tomorrow I fly another weather reconnaissance mission over enemy territory. All day my mind was whirling; at dinner I felt as if I might throw up at any moment.

I knew that I needed a good night's sleep, so I took a pill and went to bed early, but I could not make myself stop imagining the endless flight in which I, as pilot, and my navigator would venture in our unarmed twin-engine Mosquito far into German-held territory.

Hour after hour I thrashed around in bed; from time to time I would drift off, only to wake with a dreadful start, gasping for breath, my heart flopping like a beached fish as I imagined the shellburst in the cockpit, the blood and the sickening white-hot pain, the fire, smoke and spurting oil, the Mozzie winging over into a spin while I, shattered and half-conscious, am too weak either to fight the controls or pull myself up and out the escape hatch as the plane screams down and down.

Next morning, in the locker room, as I get into my flight outfit, it is clear to me that I simply can't do it. The mission is a 1000-mile trip, three hours of it over German-held territory and Germany itself—too deep in to go unnoticed. I can't possibly strap myself into that defenseless little plane and, with my own hands and feet, make it climb 5 miles high, guide it out over the winter sea and into a Europe bristling with Nazi anti-aircraft batteries, radar stations and fighter planes, and finally make it back to safety.

Even as I zip up my boots and pull on my helmet, I know I can't. I will get in the plane, warm up and check out the engines, but at the runway my hands will freeze on the controls, and I will be unable to make the plane move.

January 1957, New York. I'm delirious with joy.

I've always felt that if I didn't write a book by the time I was 40, I'd never do so. With only three years to go, I've been offered a book contract—by the most distinguished of American publishers. Alfred Knopf himself, after reading an article of mine, had written to invite me to submit a proposal. After months of hard work, I had turned in an outline and sample chapter. Now Knopf and his editors have said yes.

But, later in the day, I begin to fear that I have made a terrible mistake. I've suggested a history of love, tracing its evolution from the time of the early Greeks to the present—a vast project, but fun to think about and to sketch in outline form. Yet now that the moment of truth has come, I see how rash I've been. Having spent months researching and writing the sample chapter, I can look ahead—and what I see is frightening.

How could I have imagined I'd ever be able to learn what love meant to the ancient Greeks, to the imperial Romans, to the ascetic early Christians, to the knights and ladies of the Middle Ages, to—? Enough! It's hopeless, impossible, more than any one person can do.

COMING TO A ROADBLOCK

"Coming to a Roadblock" by Tom McCain. Copyright © 1996.

Or, at least, more than I can do. Even if I found everything I needed in the library and took reams of notes, how could I ever make sense of it all? Or organize it? Or write about it entertainingly, sentence after sentence, page after page, chapter after chapter? Only now, when a contract is being offered me, can I see clearly what I will have to do—and realize that I cannot.

June 1963, New York. I am lying in bed, sleepless, although it is 2 a.m.; I suspect that she, quiet in the dark next to me, is awake too. Tonight we agreed that it was useless to go on and that I should move out as soon as I can.

But I feel as if the ground is giving way beneath me, as if I am falling through space. How can we ever decide how to divide our possessions and our savings? How will we work out my rights as an absentee father? Will I be able to find a place for myself and, without help, make it homelike? I have never lived alone, how will I feel when I close the door at night and am imprisoned in my solitude?

What will I tell my family, and how will they take it? Will my married friends shun me? What can I say to my 8-year-old son, and what will happen to his feelings about me? Where will I meet single friends? Whom will I talk to, eat with, share my life with? I haven't the least idea how to start; I haven't been single since my 20s.

Yet what if, somehow, after a while, I were to meet the right woman and feel desire stirring in me? But here my mind goes blank. I haven't been to bed with another woman in over 17 years; how should I behave, what should I do? What if my hesitant actions are scorned? What if I seem clumsy, gross, nervous, foolish?

And even if all goes well, how will I know whether what I feel is love or only lust? Can I trust myself to love again—or trust anyone else to love me? Will anyone, could anyone, ever do so? Will I ever want to marry again? There is so much to be said, learned, worked out first; so many hints, allusions, promises, bargains, plans; so many beliefs and tastes to be exchanged and harmonized—no, it is too hard a road to travel, too remote a goal. I can't do it.

Twilight, a first star in the sky, the ground below the cliff growing dim. But now in the woods the beam of a flashlight dances about and I hear the voices of Jerry and my father. My father! But what can he do? Middle-aged and portly, he cannot climb up here. Even if he could, what good would that do?

Staying well back from the foot of the cliff so that he can see me, he points the beam up and calls to me. "Come on down, now," he says in a perfectly normal, comforting tone. "Dinner's ready."

"I can't!" I wail. "I'll fall, I'll die!"

"You got up," he says. "You can get down the same way. I'll light the way."

"No, I can't!" I howl. "It's too far, it's too hard, I can't do it."

"Listen to me," my father says. "Don't think about how far it is, how hard it is. All you have to think about is taking one little step. You can do that. Look where I'm shining the light. Do you see that rock?" The beam bounces around on a jutting outcrop just below the ledge. "See it?" he calls up.

I inch over. "Yes," I say.

"Good," he says. "Now just turn around so you can put your left foot on that rock. That's all you have to do. It's just a little way below you. You can do that. Don't worry about what comes next, and don't look down any farther than that first step. Trust me."

It seems possible. I inch backward, gingerly feel for the rock with my left foot and find it. "That's good," my father calls. "Now, a little bit to the right and a few inches lower, there's another foothold. Move your right foot down there very slowly—that's all you have to do. Just think about that next step, nothing else." I do so. "Good," he says. "Now let go of whatever you're holding onto with your left hand and reach back and grab that skinny tree just at the edge, where my light is. That's all you have to do." Again, I do so.

That's how it goes. One step at a time, one handhold at a time, he talks me down the cliff, stressing that I have only to make one simple move each time, never letting me stop to think of the long way down, always telling me that the next thing I have to do is something I *can* do.

Suddenly I take the last step down onto the tumbled rocks at the bottom and into my father's strong arms, sobbing a little, and then, surprisingly, feeling a sense of immense accomplishment and something like pride.

January 1945. I taxi out onto the runway and firmly shove the throttles forward. I remember at last that I *know* how to do what I must. All I have to do is take off and climb to 25,000 feet, heading eastward over East Anglia; that's all I need think about right now. I can do that.

Later: The North Sea is just ahead. All I have to do, I tell myself, is stay on this heading for about 20 minutes, until we have crossed over Schouwen Island in the Netherlands. That's all; I can do it.

Over Schouwen Island, my navigator tells me to turn to a heading of 125 degrees and hold it for 10 minutes, until we reach our next checkpoint. Good; that's not so hard; I can do that.

That's how it goes. I drive the roaring little plane across Holland and Germany, high over fields and woods, cities, rivers and mountain ranges, never envisioning the whole trip but only the leg we are flying, never thinking of the hours ahead but concentrating on getting through each brief segment of time, each measured span of miles, until at last sunlight dazzles off the wrinkled sea ahead of us and in a few minutes we are out of enemy territory, safe and still alive.

January 1957. After tossing about much of the night, thinking about the impossibly ambitious book I had said I could write, I remember the old lesson once again: Though I know what the goal is, I can avoid panic and vertigo if I look only at the next step.

I'll keep my gaze on the first chapter. All I have to do is read whatever I can find in the library about love among the Greeks; that isn't impossibly hard. Then I'll tell myself that all I have to do is sort out my notes, dividing the chapter into a number of sections; I can do that. Then I'll make myself look no further ahead than writing the first section. And with that thought, I heave a great sigh and fall asleep.

And that's the way I spend more than two and a half years. Then, one exhilarating afternoon, the last of 653 pages emerges from my typewriter and, like a boy, I turn somersaults on the living room floor in sheer joy. Some months later, I hold in my hands the first copy of my book, *The Natural History of Love*—already chosen by the Book of the Month Club—and a few weeks after that I read my first major review, praising the book, in the *New York Times Book Review.* For a while, I occasionally leaf through the book, marveling that I could ever have done all this—and knowing that I learned how, long ago, in the dusk on the face of a small cliff.

September 1963. I unlock the door of my tiny apartment, carry my bags in and close the door behind me. I have taken one step; it wasn't so hard. I had remembered the lesson that I have applied again and again throughout my life; one step at a time, one step that I can manage.

The first was to find an apartment; I looked no further into the future until I had done that. Then I went about furnishing my two rooms, I looked no further ahead until that was done. Today, I am moving in; I have made my own little nest, and it looks pleasant. I unpack, make a few phone calls, fix lunch, feel at home. Good; I've taken that step.

By the next year, I have constructed a new life, gotten my final divorce decree, acquired the social and emotional skills that I need as a middle-aged single man (I would remain one for five years), and even have become a passable bachelor cook. And discovered once more, to my surprise, that I do know how to make my way toward a distant, difficult goal.

I have realized with the same surprise, time and again throughout my life, that, having looked at a far and frightening prospect and been dismayed, I can cope with it after all by remembering the simple lesson I learned so long ago. I remind myself to look not at the rocks far below but at the first small and relatively easy step and, having taken it, to take the next one, feeling a sense of accomplishment with each move, until I have done what I wanted to do, gotten where I wanted to be, and can look back, amazed and proud of the distance I have come.

Follow-Up

1. *Describe a problem that overwhelmed you, but which you might have dealt with successfully by working on it one step at a time.*

2. *Describe a problem that you dealt with successfully by working on it one step at a time.*

3. *Describe a formidable problem or task that you now face in your life. What is the first step that you might take toward its mastery?*

Small Terrors, Secret Heroics

Amy Gross

People think adventure is to be found outside the usual course of life. They set aside vacations for the pursuit of danger, they travel to it, buy equipment for it, and after their wrestle with the elements, or the rapids, or the mountain side, they return to hohum life. And they regard as heroes those who have made danger their way of life. It's not hard to understand the call of that sort of heroism, the seduction of the big dare. Entering that space between life and death, you taste perfect freedom.

People theorize that modern life is so tame, the opportunities for raw bravery and aggression so rare, that only through vigorous sports and dangerous play can we detonate our pent-up energies and remember our animalhood. That physical putting-to-the-test is the great escape from the predominantly mental lives we live. For many, work is an abstraction and its reward, money, is another abstraction, an essentially arbitrary gauge of achievement except for a gambler whose work is collecting money. The bodily tests of one's powers—win or lose, survive or not—is nothing if not concrete.

But it seems to me that these sports, these physical challenges are really only exercises. When you think of the adventures, the terrors, the possible leaps, the opportunities in every-day life to choose between heroism and cowardice, you know that you don't have to travel to danger. In fact, the stakes are higher at home. It is easier to risk death scaling a mountain than to risk being old and alone, or unloved and unneeded, or being thought stupid or insane. It is easier to die than to live as a failure. And so, every day, there are risks we refuse, possible terrors we avoid. We do what other people expect from us, so they'll love and want us; we perform according to the rules of success and sanity; we remain silent when we should speak up and speak though we have nothing to say; and our lives stay small. We don't recognize as adventures the challenges that come to us, and we shrink from designing our own. Only in a somewhat extraneous experiment like riding the rapids or skydiving do we dash out of the tameness enforced on us by our own fears. I'm not saying that someone who lives courageously every day wouldn't want or need to spend a week in the wilderness; only that attention should be paid to the opportunities for wildness at home.

These more subtle heroics are seemingly small acts. The fact that they require enormous courage is usually known only to the protagonist. For one man, speaking in public is so terrifying he gratefully allows others in his work-group to talk for him. It would be a very small act if he were once to present his own work, a very private victory. For him, afraid of appearing afraid, certain he was about to make a fool of himself, the experience would be a free-fall. He would be risking everything. In anyone else's eyes, he would only have stopped being silly. These small acts have to do, often, with overcoming the terrors other people tell you are silly. The reason to overcome is not to please these other people. The reason is the one offered by the man who climbs the mountain—because it's there. The at-home fears block one's way more resolutely than any mountain.

For many people, silly as it sounds, going to a party is a small act of courage. Initiating a conversation with that stranger across the room, for some people, can be an act no less noble than facing a bull in a ring. I'm not being facetious here. I've stood at a party a step away from an author whose work awes me, mentally testing and rejecting opening lines, choking when one or another began to rise out of my throat. Getting back on a horse after you've been thrown is simple (and practical—how else are you going to get back to the stables?). To venture a conversation with a superior stranger is to risk everything—being seen as an ant. Your specialness is at stake. Will the superior being recognize your own superiority? Will you come off as just another face? Are you just another face? Dragons test only your strength. Strangers test your wit, or your face, or whatever it is you rely on to barter your way through the open market. If I ever approach that author and survive, I'll feel as though I'd vanquished dragons.

Daring to make a soufflé, to argue a grade, to tell the truth, to say yes or to say no, to admit "I want," or "I deserve," these can all be moments of heroism, invisible leaps that free you, if only from the fear of accepting the dare. I read that someone is going to motorcycle-jump a string of 17 trucks, a large and remarkably useless act. A woman who has been painting for years, who one day picks herself up and brings her work to a gallery, is leaping further than that. Risking being told she's no good, risking her hope that she is saying something unique with her paints, that *she* is unique—that's a very great risk. If she avoids the gallery judge's criticism, she can continue to cherish what are possibly fantasies of talent and success. To bring in her work is to subject her fantasies to the test of reality. There are all kinds of ways to deal with the rejection that might be her reward. Would she have the wisdom to apply those ways? Should she protect herself from such a challenge to her wisdom? Sure. Why not? It's not noticeable cowardice to

play life safe, it's the way we all play it, one way or another. But to risk, to leap, to throw one's fantasies into the ring is to pursue danger. Mighty exciting. The truth, we've been told, will set us free, one way or another.

There's a woman I know, a social worker who has to commute an hour and a half every day to the hospital where she's on staff. She hears about a job opening at a better hospital, only ten minutes from home; the job is bigger than hers and so is the salary. This is terribly upsetting news. She asks everyone what she should do, apply or not. Of course, everyone tells her to apply. But, she argues, what if she got the job and then couldn't do the work? A challenge like hers, when unmet, is obsessing. She talks and talks about applying. Finally, the decision is made for her—she hears the job is taken.

When people asked her, "What do you have to lose?" she thought they didn't understand what was at stake. Her definition of herself, her "ego" as she put it. She has a bank of negative judgments and if she were to apply and not get the job, or get the job and then be fired, all those judgments would be confirmed. Once and for all she would know herself—and the world would know her—to be a failure. The underlying premise is that her success to date is due to luck and the gullibility of her supervisors. By not applying for the bigger job, she protects herself from the confirmation of that premise, and retains the right to think she might have been able to do the job. It's a common bargain, but a bad one. Not risking defeat is always defeat. The fact is, she did have nothing to lose—by not applying she's already lost. Once a dare, the opportunity to leap presents itself, you can't escape a sense of failure until or unless you abandon yourself to the leap. And the defeat following a risk taken must be, at the least, a peaceful one. The defeat of not even trying is acidified by the anger of impotence.

Another woman has been living with a man for several months. The basis of her attachment is in its alterative—being alone, having to look for a new man. Now, nothing is ever so clear-cut that rationalization is impossible. She argues that she has some feeling for the man, she has not met anyone better, the man is easy, undemanding. In her mind, leaving him would be like cutting herself off from an anchor. She would be adrift. She doesn't see how she could take care of herself, what would happen to her . . . she might be alone forever. Her fear is the expectation of total catastrophe. Ignoring all the laws of probability, she is positing only one alternative and that one is unacceptable.

For her to break out would be a feat more astonishing, if less flamboyant, than any escape performed by a Houdini. She would be setting off on an adventure comparable to Robinson Crusoe's, as true a test of individual resources as his. No ferreting for berries, but could she nourish herself?

Her refusal to try—to leap into the fear—is not blatant cowardice. Her dread of aloneness is ubiquitous and natural. How many of us ever leave a bad setup without the towrope of The Other Man or The Other Woman? I never have. If she were to let go of her man—cleanly and crisply—it would be an ostensibly small act. In my eyes, at least, it would be heroic.

I remember a friend of mine telling a man who had just swallowed his first tab of LSD (remember LSD?), "If you see anything frightening, walk towards it." Afterwards, the man described what happened when he hallucinated grotesque faces. At first, he had shuddered and pulled back, and the faces continued to menace. Then he tried staring them down, moving towards them. The faces turned into fantastic Thai dancers, costumed in spangles, and apparently arranged just for his delight. It meant something to the man that he could defend himself against his own monsters. You could shrug off his adventure by saying that his fears were only hallucinations, but so are most fears hallucinations.

Staring down monsters is the essence of adventure, and the monster is never the mountain or the bull or the string of 17 trucks or the stranger. The monster is always your own self-doubts. And whether you're daring to explore a dark cave or daring to dial a certain telephone number, the aftereffects are the same. You've called on your own power and it's been there for you; you've learned, once again, that you have nothing to fear from yourself and so it seems there's really nothing at all to fear, and, for a while, anyway, you know you are larger than your fears. And when you feel the snap of that fear-band breaking—when you submit the piece of work, or close the oven door on the soufflé, that moment of letting go, falling free, taking your chances—what a rush that is. I don't know what residue is left by adrenaline after its surge has powered you through a crisis. But whatever the residue is, someone ought to bottle it. The high doesn't last long, but it's what makes the pursuit of danger so addictive.

I got hooked on fear four years ago. I was spending a week at Big Sur, taking a seminar at Esalen, a so-called "growth center," famous primarily for its hot-springs baths where men and women bathed in the nude. The place was on a cliff above the Pacific and the bathhouse was pronged into the side of the cliff, cantilevered out over the ocean. Idyllic setting. Tainted only by the fact that I was there with a man and between us, something had gone very wrong. Some poisonous combination of fear and rage had made us each other's enemies. So there we were, in this paradise, on teeth-edge with each other, and the second day, he said he was going to the baths and was I coming? I was not, in no way. He was impatient—no, disgusted is more accurate—with my uprightness. Okay, he said, and slapped a towel over his shoulder and walked away, down the thin rocky path to the bathhouse.

The grounds were deserted. I figured everyone was at the baths, or resting between seminars, and I started towards our room.

And then I thought about never having been in a hot-springs bath, and from what I'd read, it must be luxurious, and my friend's sneer kept stabbing at me, and I knew that the only reason I wasn't going to the baths, and was instead going to spend a gorgeous afternoon hiding away in a dark room, was that I was afraid to take off my clothes in front of strangers. All the rage I'd been secretly storing suddenly turned itself on me. Coward. Idiot.

I remember clearly what it felt like to turn my body back towards the baths. Like an unoiled robot, commanded by a distant brain. It is not an exaggeration to say I was trembling. My throat felt strangled, my stomach was clamped in a spasm, and various loud throbbings in my body distracted me from seeing or hearing as I went down that path. At the bathhouse, there were a few stone steps and two signs, "Men" and "Women." I turned left towards "Women" and immediately knew the signs were vestigial. Half the bodies were male. There were four square cement tubs—shallow, about three feet deep—and one was empty of people. That's all I was looking for and all I saw. Mechanically, I ripped off my clothes and aimed the body towards my tub. I sank into a corner, immobile, and stared and saw nothing.

When I came to, sometime later, I noted that the bathhouse was three-sided, and I was facing the fourth side, open onto the sky and the ocean. Between the railing and the tubs were massage tables. On one was a naked young woman sitting in lotus position and playing a recorder. On the next, was a young man in an inverted lotus—head and shoulders on the mat, legs folded in air, also very naked. They were beautiful, those two, with their background of sky, and the music was perfect, and I decided I would come to Esalen and live, I would be a waitress.

Later I found my friend sitting on the steps of the lodge with his towel. Where were you? he asked.

I was at the baths.

He looked surprised, pleased. Oh, you must have been on the other side. I thought you weren't going.

I started to explain and then I started to cry, and then I noticed that my eyes were focusing peculiarly. Objects—trees, rocks, a porch railing—were startlingly three dimensional. I was seeing their spaces and the depth

A seed drops to the earth. Slowly the seed emerges, only to find itself surrounded by a hard, round wall. It grows the only way it can. Each year its spindly branches broaden and stretch a few more inches to the sky. This year it is showing off its first leaves of spring. It is becoming a tree. A tree that will one day outgrow its wall.

Some people are like this tree. A few, through no design of their own, have hard walls placed around them. Others seem to build hard walls around them, knowingly or not. But it takes only a few spurts of life to show that it is possible. That it is possible a life can still happen.

"One for the Tree" by Nelson Goud. Copyright © 1996.

of space between them, and there seemed to be a fresh space in my own head. And looking at him, I saw just my old friend. Not the monster I'd been living with. I could see his kindness and his concern. He was just my friend. My usual eyes had slipped an evil mask over his face.

We had a good time together for the next few days. We had fun, I was light and playful. No self-consciousness, no need for it. Who was watching me? Whose judgment could I fear? What did a judgment have to do with me? I, anyone, was as impossible to judge as a stone. One can, of course, judge a stone, but does that judgment worry the stone?

In those few days, I was fearless. Fearless, as I remember it, feels like innocence. As though I didn't know what it was to be hurt, or to inflict hurt. No second thoughts. That automatic and unconscious rating of myself against other people was unnecessary—every person was my peer. Laughter was different too, sweeter.

The fog came down again, but those few days of superclarity were a taste of a possible state, a place I want to return to. The price of passage there was self-defiance, overruling powerful habits of defense. And the only route there was through the fear. There's always the chance now that another fear walked into might take me back.

It's pretty funny to talk about stripping as the way to Nirvana, but silly as it sounds, taking off my clothes was as much a plunge into terror, and the unknown, and freedom, as skydiving would be for me. My point is not to denigrate skydiving. It is, rather, to say that you don't have to rent a plane to fall free. Life is so playfully arranged, we can trust it to supply us with endless opportunities to turn our bodies around, and walk into terror. Why we are, most of us anyway, so afraid, I don't know. Maybe we're trained in fear, by people who are fortunate enough to have a lot to lose. But hoarding security, like hoarding money, leaves us nothing to show. A miser lives in destitution. Risking it all, pursuing danger, whether in the air or in the living room, seems to be the better way to play this game. The alternative is flight, constant flight.

Follow-Up

1. *Amy Gross writes, "When you think of the adventures, the terrors, the possible leaps, the opportunities in everyday life to choose between heroism and cowardice, you know that you don't have to travel to danger." Discuss and/or write a brief paper describing the challenges you find in your own everyday life, along with your heroic or cowardly responses.*
2. *Discuss and/or write a brief paper about the "secret heroics" you have shown in the face of one of your "small terrors."*
3. *Discuss and/or write a brief paper about the "blatant cowardice" you have shown in the face of one of your "small terrors."*
4. *Discuss and/or write a brief paper about some current "small terror" or fear in your life, indicating what it is, how it affects you, and how you deal with it.*

Using Our Flaws and Faults

Marsha Sinetar

People who function effectively in their work know their limits. They use them in the service of their lives, managing to integrate these limitations into the way they work best. Rightly, they have discovered that somehow they must attend to their own physical and psychological makeup, emotional tendencies and concentration patterns, and that these are good helpmates in getting a job done. In fact, a person's combined limitations form a complex of attributes that has meaning beyond anyone's current understanding—even the individual's. This complex is the essence of one's expressive life.

A client of mine is a hall wanderer. By nature restless, he thinks best when strolling around. Because he has come to accept this about himself, others have too. After many years of working with him, colleagues now expect him to walk the halls. Of course, his superior thinking has made millions of dollars for his company, and he has earned the "right" to stroll as much as he wishes.

Another person, a scientist, prefers to work in isolation in a company that values an open door policy. She regularly closes her door at work, even though at first she was soundly criticized for doing so. Stubbornly aware of how she needed to work in order to produce quality results, she stuck to her favored workstyle. Others eventually came to accept it.

All of these people have adopted a way of working that harmonizes antagonistic tendencies: the desire to concentrate with the need to walk around, and the desire to fit into a corporation with the need to act out a personal working style.

"Use your faults" was the motto of French songstress Edith Piaf. Perhaps this matter of understanding and using our limitations revolves around just such a slogan. I'm not sure whether the traits I'm discussing here are "limitations," but certainly they can seem to be when measured against the behavior stereotype that others have for our way of being.

For instance, a writer friend of mine and I often discuss our "laziness." Each of us realized years ago that part of our creative process encompassed a period of complete torpor, a sort of resting or idea-incubation. This seems unattractive, even "bad," when looked at on the surface, when compared with how we have been taught to work. The Puritan work ethic of my own upbringing strongly opposes resting during the day. Yet after some creative projects I find that this is what I must do in order to go on to the next project.

My friend laughingly tells of staying in bed all day, watching soap operas on television, while she unconsciously builds up a new storehouse of images and ideas for her next books. "I used to hate seeing myself lie there. It went against all my pictures of what I 'should' be doing and how I 'should' look. In my mind's eye, I felt that I was supposed to be a starched and immaculate vision in white all day, a Betty Crocker of the typewriter, constructively producing neat and clean copy twenty-four hours a day, like perfect cookies from the oven." She gradually realized that if she didn't give herself time out when she needed it, her next project was contrived, forced, never truly original.

I take long drives into the rural countryside where I live, listening to music as I drive. I have always loved barn and church architecture. A couple of days of looking at old, weather-beaten buildings of this type, traveling up and down dusty roads or along the Pacific Coast's rugged Highway One, is for me both a rest, and a symbolic visual journey. It mirrors the subjective, spiritual route that my creative side needs to take as I summon up energy to produce yet another chapter or article.

No other part of our personality reveals our basic temperament, our fundamental way of working, more than does our dark side—the part of ourselves which illogically unfolds at its own time and which has its own requirements. I'm referring to our uncontrollable impulses, the habits we simply can't break; the unacceptable, contradictory tendencies moving us in opposition to the way we intended to go. These are the opposing thrusts that give our life richness and mystery. These impulses, habits and contradictions even supply the dynamic energy that gives our lives distinction and drive. Jung described it this way:

> Conscious and unconscious do not make a whole when one of them is suppressed and injured by the other. If they must contend, let it at least be a fair fight with equal rights on both sides. Both are aspects of life . . . and the chaotic life of the unconscious should be given the chance of having its way too—as much of it as we can stand. This means open conflict and open collaboration at once. That, evidently, is the way human life should be. It is the old game of hammer and anvil: Between them the patient iron is forged into an indestructible whole, an "individual."

This attitude does not mean that we continue to harm ourselves, or that we ignore or escalate addictive, self-limiting behaviors. It means that we stop warring against ourselves.

We try to take an objective, aerial view of what each behavior is saying about us, what it means in the big-picture of our self's journey unto itself. Here are some helpful questions to use in spotting the potential value of our "bad habits."

- Do you have work-habits which you may have rigidly suppressed in an attempt to conform and be more like others?
- Do you have personality traits which you, like my writer friend and myself, initially struggled against, thought were wrong and tried to change or hide?
- Have you stopped trying to achieve something in some "nonsignificant" areas of life because you were once told these weren't important enough to warrant attention?
- Is there a "time-out" activity (like sleeping, watching TV, fishing, listening to music, daydreaming, etc.) that gives your work efforts renewed vigor, but which you feel you shouldn't do?

If we can examine ourselves as constructed to express a total creative statement with our life, then our habits, daydreams, fantasy life, values, the dualities of our personality can all be understood and used in the service of this statement. It is not only our words, works and relationships which say something about us as individuals. It is what we are that makes a statement. As such, the controversial aspects of our personality may be adding a needed color, tone or impetus that energizes our movement toward selfhood and the life/creative statement of our very selves.

Follow-Up

1. *Try to think of one of your traits that is labeled a flaw or fault, but also has some constructive qualities.*
2. *Choose one of the questions Sinetar poses at the end of her article and relate it to your life.*

3. *Sinetar follows Carl Jung in saying that a person must recognize and learn from negative and unliked impulses instead of denying them. They can be a source of vitality and provide more color and richness in our lives. By integrating them along with our more desired impulses a person will become more balanced. Examine your life to see if you can think of an area where the positive and negative energies have been combined to produce a more dynamic and balanced person. Are there other areas where this could be helpful?*

No One's Perfect

No one's perfect . . . they say
Well I disagree!
I happen to be a perfect example of a perfect person
I'm perfectly good in my goodness
Perfect at being angry when I'm mad
I'm perfectly disagreeable when I argue
And make perfect mistakes in my errors
I develop a perfectly negative attitude when moody
I'm perfectly happy in my happiness
And will cry perfectly when sad
I'm perfectly calm in my coolness
Fall perfectly short in my shortcomings
And when I make a mess . . . it's a perfect wreck
I pout . . . shout . . . and strike out perfectly
In the insanity of living in this perfectly imperfect world.
So no one's perfect?
WELL!! PERFECTLY, I DISAGREE!

—Daphne Haygood-Benyard

Note. From *The Doors Are Always Open,* by D. Haygood-Benyard, 1994, East Orange, NJ: Daphne's Creations. Copyright © 1994 by Daphne's Creations. Reprinted with permission.

Getting Unstuck:
Joyfully Recreating Your Life

Harold H. Bloomfield
and Robert B. Kory

I feel trapped. I spend my days wiping runny noses, preparing meals that get cold before they get eaten, doing dishes, clipping supermarket coupons, cleaning house. No matter how hard Jim works, we always seem to be scrimping to get by. This isn't what I had in mind when I said "to have and to hold till death do us part." Some days I get the urge to pack up and leave. Other days I feel depressed, sort of sorry for myself. Most of the time I'm just bored.

These are the words of a young mother, married to a young aerospace engineer. They live in a quiet residential area, have a small house, two cars, and a future that promises them all the comforts of the suburban American lifestyle.

Jim and Barbara love each other, and their marriage has been stable. Neither raves about their sex life, but neither has sought extramarital sexual contact. Casually appraised, they are beneficiaries of the American dream, both college-educated, both products of middle-class families. Nevertheless, Barbara feels she is suffocating; Jim feels too pressured by his work to be of help. Both feel stuck . . . good and stuck.

The "I'm stuck" syndrome, an anhedonic* emotional trap if ever there was one, is reaching epidemic proportions. It's wide-

*Anhedonic is a word derived from the Greek *an-* (not) and *hedone* (pleasure) and refers to the inability to experience pleasure. *Anhedonic* means inhibiting pleasure or interfering with pleasure. For more about anhedonia and anhedonic things, see their book *Inner Joy* from which this reading was condensed.—THE EDITOR

spread among young marrieds, but the same feelings of depression and resignation are showing up among adults at every stage of life. Perhaps you're feeling stuck in your job. If you're older, you may feel cornered by inflation or illness. Many a mother going back to work soon feels stifled by the limited opportunities. Having played out the singles scene, you may be pessimistic about your chances of finding a lasting relationship that will work. Or you may be twenty years into a bad marriage and unable to get out. The common denominator is the feeling of being caught by a situation beyond your control, it leaves you depressed about the present and resigned to the future.

If you've been bitten hard by the "I'm stuck" bug, you can marshal any number of reasons to justify your frustrations. You may get angry at the company that doesn't recognize your ability and give you the promotion you feel you deserve. You may complain about the government, which mishandles the economy and allows inflation and taxes to keep rising through the roof. If you're a woman, a black, a Chicano, or a member of any other group that has suffered discrimination, you can blame the system that denied you your opportunities. Spouses make excellent targets to blame for your distress.

The frustrations of the "I'm stuck" syndrome may be more or less legitimate: you are facing a very difficult and perhaps oppressive situation. But that insight doesn't accomplish very much other than to justify indulging in self-pity. The important questions are: Why do you let difficult situations make you feel powerless? What can you do to start molding your life to suit your desires?

PUTTING IT OFF

Some people get themselves stuck with what may seem to be the best of intentions. They don't want to make trouble for others, or don't want to risk losing what they have in order to create something better. Rather than take control of their lives and accept the risks of growth, they choose to put up with stifling jobs, lingering health problems, collapsing marriages, or destructive habits. It's an anhedonic trap. The longer they procrastinate, the more difficult change becomes, and the more desperate they are likely to feel.

John, a college student, complains, "I can count the number of dates I've had on one hand and not run out of fingers." He's obviously got a sense of humor, but he is afraid to be himself around women. "I'm shy," he says. "That's my nature." John recalls his mother telling people that he was "the shy one." He never realized that his mother had an emotional investment in keeping him tied to her apron strings. John spent his childhood and adolescence living up to the family label of "the shy one." No doubt he had a tendency to be shy as a little boy, but with their labeling, his parents helped him develop that tendency into a full-blown personality characteristic. The question is whether John is going to continue justifying his fears of women with the rationale: "Shyness is my nature." Whenever you resort to a label to explain a negative personality characteristic, you're only making excuses for avoiding the challenge of growth.

Gloria is twenty-six and overweight. She has tried every imaginable diet, managed on several occasions to lose over thirty pounds, but always put the weight back on. She says she wants to shed her excess poundage forever, but in the same breath she

reveals why she has always been unsuccessful in her attempts up to now. "I've always had a weight problem, ever since I was a little girl. I must have too many fat cells or a low metabolism or something." Gloria keeps herself stuck with the classic recall to her physiology. What she doesn't see is the hidden payoff. As long as she is fat she has a built-in excuse for feeling lonely and unattractive. Terrified by the prospect of rejection, she avoids it by rejecting herself, then hiding her self-rejection ("I've always been that way"). You may be tall, short, fat, thin, big-bosomed or small-breasted, bushy-headed or bald as a snowball. None of these physiological characteristics is justification for keeping yourself stuck and unhappy. They just aren't that important. Far more significant is your vitality, your friendliness, your self-confidence, your inner joy. These are the qualities you can choose to make outstanding in your life.

Vanessa at twenty-eight has been offered a major promotion at work. A vice-president has asked her to become his administrative assistant. The new job requires that Vanessa polish up on her basic math. Vanessa wants the job, but she is afraid to take it because she has always had difficulty with math. "I barely passed math in high school," she says. "Numbers make me nervous. I can't even balance my checkbook." For sixteen years Vanessa used this "I've always been" to avoid the extra effort required for her to become proficient in basic math. Now she has a choice. She can continue to use her "I've always been that way" as an excuse, or she can decide to focus whatever energy it takes for her to develop her math skills. The first choice is guaranteed to keep her stuck; the second opens broad new possibilities for success. Who knows why she has had difficulty with math in the past? It really doesn't matter, because she has the intelligence to acquire the skills the new job demands. All she needs now is the courage to challenge her "I've always been."

Tim is known for a short temper and frequent angry outbursts. His boss has told him that if he wants to make any kind of progress with the company he will have to learn to control his temper and develop his interpersonal skills. Tim's response has been consistent, "Sure, I have a short temper! I'm Irish." Ever since Tim got into fights on the school playground, his parents indulged his temper with this excuse. Now Tim sits at his desk in a sullen rage; his boss has told him that due to economic pressures on the company, Tim will be out of a job. His boss did not hide the fact that Tim, of all the junior executives, was dismissed because senior management found him hard to work with. This blow was finally enough for Tim to realize he had to make some changes. The alternative was to get stuck not only emotionally, but also economically. Having put all his excuses aside, Tim is now working on developing the emotional skills he needs to be a better manager.

SOME STEPS TOWARD SELF-DIRECTION

Once you have decided to take control, you *have* the power to create your own life according to your personal vision. You *can* establish your own values based on your own experience. To get unstuck, you need to seize this power to break free from your past and transform your intuitions into realities. The decision to take control of your life is a first step. Transforming that decision into action is the real test. Here are some suggestions that you may find useful:

Stop thinking of yourself as fragile.

Behind every anhedonic choice that keeps you stuck is the belief that you (or your life) will fall apart if you challenge the rules. This is a powerful myth! It can keep you absolutely paralyzed! The only way to rid yourself of it is to put your psychological strengths to the test. Few people realize how strong they really are until they stop putting up with the problems in their lives and take some steps toward change. It won't be easy. You may get knocked down a few times, but you won't fall apart. On the contrary, the more you assert your ability to take control over your life, the stronger you'll become. Developing psychological strengths is just like developing physical abilities. The more you exercise, the stronger you become.

Once and for all, you must eliminate the words wish, hope, and maybe from your vocabulary.

These are sedatives you administer to yourself to numb your sensitivity to your emotional realities. Like any narcotic, wishing and hoping weaken your power to take control of your life. In place of wishing and hoping, you have to substitute a new confidence in your willpower.

Substitute *"I will make it happen"* for "I hope things get better."

Substitute *"I am going to do x, y, z, so I'll feel better"* for "I wish things were better."

Substitute *"I will make my marriage work"* for "Maybe my marriage will still work out."

Start considering yourself too important to put up with anxiety about the obstacles in you life.

The best antidote for anxiety is action. Instead of bemoaning your problems or worrying about the long way to a major goal, take the first step. If your job is suffocating you, stop complaining and put together your résumé. Get any assistance you need to make certain it's the best résumé you can possibly write. If you're in a relationship that is faltering, gather up the courage to have a long talk about your future with your lover. Don't put it off until tomorrow. Do it today! Action, even one small step, breaks the illusion that makes personal problems seem insurmountable. You can only solve your problems one step at a time. Taking the first step has the amazing effect of reducing any problem to life size.

Choose one of your bigger dreams and start making it a reality.

One of my clients had always dreamed of exploring the Inca ruins in Peru. She had never been out of the United States and, as a secretary, didn't earn a large income. Nevertheless, this was the dream she chose. I suggested she contact travel agencies, museums, and local universities to explore all possibilities for her trip. The cost of a commercial tour was out of her reach, but she did discover that she could for a modest cost join an archaeological expedition from a local museum. She paid for some of her expenses and joined in the work as a volunteer. The result was the most rewarding vacation of her life. More: by actualizing just one of her dreams, she broke the cycle of defeatism that was keeping her stuck. Now at twenty-seven she is back at school to study archaeology. Fulfilling a dream is an exercise in discovering personal power. It can turn your life around.

Stop feeling you always have to have a plan.

Plans have their place, but planning involves only half of your brain, the verbal, analytic hemisphere. There is a huge silent dimension of your personality, the intuitive dimension, and you're probably not using it. Scientific research on creativity shows indisputably that the creative process depends just as much on the right brain functions (intuition) as on the left brain operations (analysis and language). If you insist on always having a plan, you cut yourself off from your intuitive self and the inner joy it provides. To break planning addiction, indulge in one freedom. Decide to spend a day exploring a park or a neighborhood with curiosity as your sole guide. Enroll in a local university and take a course that strikes your interest. You never know, it may lead you into a new occupation. The next time you feel attracted to someone you don't know, and want to introduce yourself, go ahead. You're likely to make a new friend. By giving yourself freedom to follow your hunches, even in small ways, you develop your sensitivity to your inner voice. You learn to hear the quiet messages that can make your life an adventure.

CREATE AN INTEGRATED SUCCESS PROFILE

Here are some techniques to help you reshape your success profile.

Begin by giving yourself full permission to succeed.

Most people are held back by the fear that they don't have what it takes. While they may pay lip service to believing in themselves, they turn right around and complain about all the obstacles that stand in the way: the boss, the company, too much work, too little work, too many "bad breaks." The fact is that many successful people do not have exceptional ability and many have limited education. They didn't score at the top in IQ tests, nor did they go to the best schools or get the best grades. Many come from humble backgrounds and have had bad breaks. The common denominator among all successful and happy people is desire, determination, and confidence. Your chance of success and fulfillment is just as good as anyone else's, and probably much better than you think. Only when you understand this key fact can you plunge ahead with enthusiasm and start functioning at your full potential.

Think of success as a process, not a final destination.

Highly successful people don't set out to achieve one grand goal and, on achieving it, pronounce themselves successful. They view their lives as an adventure and themselves as the heroic players. Perhaps this seems a little grandiose to you, but it's far better to think of yourself as a hero and play life to the fullest than to minimize your abilities and never give yourself a chance to exercise all your talents. You are the creator of your life; why not create it heroically? It doesn't matter how old you are or where you may be on the success ladder. You have the power to create a life that will exceed your highest expectations. All you have to do is learn how to use it.

Beware of any lingering fears of success.

It may surprise you to hear that many people block their success by fear, but the facts are there to be examined. Success implies change—in responsibility, life-style, relationships, and many other aspects of life—and for most people change is frightening. They're reluctant to surrender the safety of the routine and the familiar. Except in rare individuals, the instinct to resist change, do nothing, and accept the mediocre is measurably stronger than the desire to succeed.

People undermine their success in subtle ways. They choose wrong jobs, submit to employers who use them, behave in ways that undermine their chances of promotion, rely on weakness out of habit, and ignore strengths out of ignorance. To create a success profile of maximum opportunity you have to put an end to any lingering fears of success. You must be determined to discover your strengths and cultivate your talents; you must learn to relish your own growth.

Set attainable goals and learn to enjoy each small step of progress.

One of the most common ways people sabotage themselves is by trying to achieve too much too fast. There is a Wall Street saying that warns against this folly: "Bulls make money, bears make money, hogs never make money." While learning to take risks is important, foolish risks are nothing other than foolish.

Don't overschedule.

Most people have a tendency to assume they can accomplish more in a given period than they actually can. The problem arises from planning a project without allowing enough extra time for things to go wrong (as they always do). Deadlines are valuable, because most people are more efficient and creative when they accomplish a task within a given period. However, you would be wise in setting your deadlines to allow an extra 20 percent for things to go wrong. When deadlines are so short that they cause anxiety and a last-minute rush, you and your work suffer unnecessarily.

Insulate yourself as much as possible from interruption.

Nothing is more jarring to the nervous system than repeated interruptions when you're in the midst of concentrating on an important problem. One of the worst mistakes is to get into the habit of taking every phone call no matter what you're doing. A good way to handle the telephone is to concentrate your calls in one time segment, say between nine and ten in the morning or four and five in the afternoon. During that time you take all calls, and call people back who called you. You aren't being rude to refuse a call because you are busy. You are being wise. If you are a victim of the telephone, telephone screening can change your work life.

Consciously project ease and enjoyment.

For example, when you're at a meeting, sit back and relax. This is far more effective for listening than sitting on the edge of your chair. When you wish to speak, your movement forward will draw attention and quiet the group. Above all, don't hurry your speech. When you have something important to contribute, there is no rush! Your *words* are going to have an impact on your listeners. Take your time, be brief, and speak clearly. Intersperse pauses after key points. The value of silence is too often ignored. Be sure to enjoy yourself. That way you project maximum power and make others feel most comfortable. It's always a pleasure to listen to someone who is calm, speaks clearly, and projects a natural enthusiasm.

Become aware of your natural optimum work/play cycles.

Just as you have a unique personality, you have an optimum work cycle that is likely to be different than anyone else's. Some people do their best work in the morning, others have an intense burst of concentration toward the end of the day. There are also people who have concentration bursts for brief intervals throughout the day. We call these periods of maximum alertness "prime time." Once you understand your prime time, you can schedule your activities so that you'll tackle the important and challenging ones at your peak creative periods and relegate mundane activities to your low points. Substantial evidence indicates that your prime time and optimum work cycle are biologically or even genetically determined. Trying to force yourself into in unnatural pattern (such as doing your most difficult work in the morning when you concentrate best in the afternoon) is a big mistake. You will cause needless tension, your work will suffer, and you will cheat yourself out of the most important thing of all—enjoying what you're doing.

Identify the conditions that help you get into a "state of flow."

Almost everyone has had the experience of starting work on a project and getting so immersed that they completely forget time, fatigue, even where they are. Many hours later, when the task is complete, they become aware that they've been functioning at a unique, high level where creative energies pour out effortlessly. Psychologists call this a state of flow. This wonderful and productive state is not arbitrary. You can learn how to create it and then use it at will to accomplish a great deal of work in the shortest time. The key is learning what conditions trigger the inner shift from ordinary functioning to flow. For some people, quiet is necessary. Most people must be well rested. Time of day is almost always a key factor. Flow is much more likely during your prime time than during a low period. Perhaps you need to be working at a particular desk or computer for flow to happen. There could be any number of critical conditions. Once you have learned what they are, you have made a major discovery. Flow is one of the basic means of "doing less and accomplishing more." It is also a natural state of inner joy, even ecstasy.

Follow-Up

1. *Describe a "stuck" time in your life, indicating how you got stuck and how you got yourself unstuck (or are trying).*
2. *Review "Some Steps Toward Self-Direction." Choose one or more to apply to your life if you are stuck in your growth.*
3. *Select and apply one or more of the ideas mentioned in the section "Create An Integrated Success Profile."*

The Pace of Growth

Below are excerpts from two novelists and an undergraduate student.

INDIAN SUMMER

His goal was simply to be a full human man, making the best of himself. He was disgusted and fearful of what failure to do that had done to many people, to most people he knew. He did not want to be . . . twisted by subservience . . . ground down by poverty . . . slowly poisoned by contempt for (him)self. . . . Most of all, he did not want to be defeated as most people in the world were, that is, simply by not really living, eaten by the termites of a half life semilived.

All the same there was one wonderfully encouraging fact, which he kept the firmest possible grip on at all times. He actually knew one or two people who had broken past all these blocks and became real, true, full human beings.

Very soon now he was going to have to put a stop to this downward path he had let himself be persuaded to set out upon; he was going to have to halt this descent very soon or else, he sensed, it would be too late because he would have lost the power to escape. . . . If he took one gram too much of humiliation here, then the fuel of self-liking necessary to carry him away might be gone, and like so many . . . he would turn from a venturer into a clinger, caution would move one degree higher on the scale than ambition and so dominate it and finally crush it, doubt would inch ahead of certainty, fear would crowd out confidence, and his life would in all essentials be finished and its great issue lost.

We're out of phase with life; we live our lives out of season . . . [we] begin to fall behind too, like everybody else, into an Indian summer of brief, too late, doomed flowering.

—John Knowles

LEARNING THE WRONG THINGS

"I'm confused and frustrated. Humans are very adaptable to situations. We do learn from everything we do. What happens when you learn what you don't want to learn, but as a result of that exposure it becomes a part of you anyway? You should be very aware of the learning environments you find yourself in. If you're not, then in subtle ways you are going to become what you do. If you're in an environment you disagree with, you'd better do something before it changes you."

—An undergraduate student

THE BUTTERFLY

I remembered one morning when I discovered a cocoon in the bark of a tree, just as the butterfly was making a hole in its case and preparing to come out. I waited a while, but it was too long appearing and I was impatient. I bent over it and breathed on it to warm it. I warmed it as quickly as I could and the miracle began to happen before my eyes, faster than life. The case opened, the butterfly started slowly crawling out and I shall never forget my horror when I saw how its wings were folded back and crumpled; the wretched butterfly tried with its whole trembling body to unfold them. Bending over it, I tried to help it with my breath. In vain. It needed to be hatched out patiently and the unfolding of the wings should be a gradual process in the sun. Now it was too late. My breath had forced the butterfly to appear, all crumpled, before its time. It struggled desperately and, a few seconds later, died in the palm of my hand.

That little body is, I do believe, the greatest weight I have on my conscience. For I realize today that it is a mortal sin to violate the great laws of nature. We should not hurry, we should not be impatient, but we should confidently obey the eternal rhythm. . . . Ah, if only that little butterfly could always flutter before me to show me the way.

—Nikos Kazantzakis

Follow-Up

1. *The first two authors warn against staying too long in an environment that stunts their growth. Can you think of an example where this happened to you or someone you know? Is it happening now to you?*
2. *Kazantzakis's excerpt provides a warning for pushing growth too quickly—forcing something before its time. Has this ever happened to you in some aspect of your life? How about now?*

3. *Do you tend to err in lingering too long or pushing too hard in your own personal growth? What are some specific steps you could take to create the best pace or tempo for your growth?*

4. *John Knowles's character mentions that he knew one or two people who were "real, true, full human beings." How many do you know (if any)? If you do, what makes them this way?*

5. *Discuss and/or write a reaction paper to one or more of these questions.*

Applied Activities for Section Three

FIRST TIMES

One way to chart your life journey is to remember "first times." Each first time becomes a small or even a major threshold of your personal development. Try to list as many first times as you can. Here are some examples taken from several adults.

I'll never forget the first time I . . .

Rode a bike on my own
Drew an original picture
Went to school
Could read something
Flunked a test
Saw my baby sister
Bought a new baseball glove
Played a song on my trumpet
Kissed a boy
Played in a recital
Had a child

Had a period
Flew on an airplane
Went to a prom
Got my driver's license
Voted
Got drunk
Made a stand
Was totally out of line
Went to a funeral
Visited a foreign country

Now it's your turn. Write as many as you can on a separate piece of paper.

I'll never forget the first time I . . .

Follow-Up Ideas:

1. Discuss one or more first times with someone.
2. Write a reaction paper on what these first times meant to you.
3. For further reading on this topic, see Robert Fulghum's *From Beginning To End: The Rituals of Our Lives* (1995).

EVOLUTION OF A PERSON #1

1. **Lifeline.** List the major events and people that have significantly influenced your life development. These are the events and people that have made a difference in determining your self-image, interests, and skills; how you relate to other people; career and school choices; and values. As you examine your life, past and present, what have been some turning points? A path you did not take but wonder about now? A decision which turned out right? What are some untried dreams or goals? Place these persons and events along a line starting with your birth and ending with the current date.

2. **Symbolic drawing.** On a single piece of paper draw a shape that symboli-
cally represents your life from birth to the present. This drawing does not
have to look artistic. Use shapes, lines, or even shadings and colors. Sometimes you have to think about your whole life in a gentle, reflective manner
for a few minutes and wait for an image to appear. If an image does not immediately appear, do not force it. Wait a few hours or a day or two and probably one will emerge. A single drawing will be easier to remember and will
tend to capture the emotional tones better than words.

3. In your lifeline and symbolic drawing, make sure to include all major influences, whether positive or negative. If you do not want anyone to see your
work, disguise an event by using your own symbols (for example, you could
use a number to represent a particular traumatic event).

4. Discuss what you have learned with classmates or write a reaction paper. Remember that you need only share what you are comfortable in disclosing.

5. An extension of this activity will be explored later in an Applied Activity
called, appropriately, *Evolution of A Person #2*. (See the last section, A Quality Life.)

STRENGTHS RECOGNITION

A healthy self-perception depends in part on an awareness of personal strengths.
In general, the more genuine strengths a person recognizes and values, the
higher the level of self-esteem. It is not a common experience, though, to talk
about your strengths without it being classified as bragging. However, it is socially acceptable to have someone else recognize and mention your strengths. It
is important to talk about strengths, because this is a major way to maintain
strength awareness. The following activities are two methods for recognizing
strengths in others. You may be surprised how others react to these acknowl-
edgments.

1. A strength is excellence in any skill, knowledge, or personal quality. In a
proper time and context, directly tell three or more people what you believe
to be one of their strengths. It is also helpful to provide an example of this
strength. Note the immediate verbal and nonverbal reactions of those being
acknowledged. Did they accept the recognition, or tend to sidestep or downplay it? Did they feel compelled to say something complimentary back to
you?

2. If you have been part of an ongoing small group, in or outside of class, consider this activity. Tape a blank sheet of paper on the back of each group
member. Distribute packets of Post-it notes. Then each person thinks of two
strengths of every other group member. These are written on separate Post-it
notes. After everyone has had time to complete writing, meander around and
place your strengths notes on the back of the appropriate person. You may

want to share your impressions and thoughts with the group after viewing your strengths notes.

3. Discuss or write about what you learned from one or both of these strengths recognition activities.

TRAIT EXAGGERATION

If you desire to strengthen a quality in your natural repertoire, you may have to *over*practice it for awhile (like learning an athletic or musical technique). For example, let's say you want to become a better listener. For two weeks saturate yourself in learning and practicing listening—watch good listeners, read about listening, purposely emphasize listening in your normal interactions. This same approach can be used for almost any interpersonal or emotional quality. Describe your activities, results, and what you learned.

STRETCHING LIMITS

Knowing personal limits is necessary for making wise life choices. Often, however, a person constructs internal boundaries that are too constricting. Certain qualities are not expressed because opportunities to draw them out are not taken. Fears, a few failures, or plain inexperience restrain what we think we can do. Only when individuals do something they "are not capable of" are the internal boundaries challenged and usually expanded. When boundaries are extended, life is experienced more fully.

There are two ways to check whether your inner limits are too restrictive: (1) attempt to take a current strength to higher or deeper levels, (2) attempt a task which taps an undeveloped capacity, one you believe you have but have given little chance to develop.

The key is to design activities that challenge you to think and act at higher levels. In short, you are to set up realistic, but challenging, goals. For example, let's say that you have always wanted to try a few original ideas in your work but have not done so. You would then select the "best chance" new idea and design an action plan to try it out. You might consider telling a trusted other of your plan in order to develop a support person. Report what you learned about stretching your limits.

SECTION
four

EMOTIONS AND FEELINGS

From the list below, place a check by the five feeling states that you most like to experience:

1. Excited	16. Angry
2. Afraid	17. Proud
3. Confident	18. Embarrassed
4. Ashamed	19. Brave
5. Tranquil	20. Hurt
6. Despairing	21. Marveling
7. Joyous	22. Rejected
8. Lonely	23. Trusting
9. Loving	24. Nervous
10. Jealous	25. Inspired
11. Surprised	26. Hopeless
12. Guilty	27. Spontaneous
13. Friendly	28. Resentful
14. Disgusted	29. Admiring
15. Reflective	30. Confused

Review your choices—there is a high probability that the majority are odd-numbered items. These are some of the positive emotions we experience. The even-numbered feeling states are those that most humans do not desire to experience. The listed feeling states are only a small sample of what a human is capable of experiencing. Like colors, emotions can blend to form an almost infinite range of feeling tones. For example, if you are happy, you may be either pleased, cheerful or ecstatic. If you are angry, your range of anger can extend from annoyance to rage.

To be human means to experience a rich and complex world of emotions. Almost everyone has an approach–avoidance relationship with emotions. We welcome some emotions, resist or even deny others. We easily reveal some emotions, but we have trouble expressing others. Sometimes we even try to conceal how we feel, only to be betrayed by a tapping foot or quivering lips. Occasionally, humans use one emotion to mask another (e.g., we feel rejected but we show anger, or we feel attracted to another but we look unconcerned, aloof). We know that many of our "disliked" emotions, such as anxiety, are sending us helpful warnings, but often we don't like the message and "blame the messenger."

If our thoughts are like books on library shelves, then our emotions are like wildlife creatures wandering through the library—some playful and curious, some quiet and timid, some sitting sullenly in corners, and some snarling and prowling about when the lights are out.

Sometimes, to fully experience a life event, emotions are *required*. Victoria Lincoln explains why in a passage from a short story she wrote over 50 years ago in *The New Yorker* (Sept. 28, 1946):

Why are we never prepared, why do all the books and all the wisdom of our friends avail us nothing in the final event? How many deathbed scenes we have read, how many stories of young love, or marital infidelity, of cherished ambition, fulfilled or defeated. There is nothing that can happen to us that has not happened again and again, that we have not read over a thousand times, closely, carefully, accurately recorded; before we are fully launched on life, the story of the human heart has been opened for us again and again with all the patience and skill of the human mind. But the event, when it comes, is never anything like the description; it is strange, infinitely strange and new, and we stand helpless before it and realize that the words of another convey nothing, nothing.

What good are emotions? Probably the best way to answer this query is to imagine a life without them. Do you love someone and are you loved? Do you anticipate with great joy an upcoming concert or athletic event? Have you found that anxiety, guilt, anger, or envy have actually helped you to function better at times? Think of any event or time that is a milestone in your life. Would it be a milestone without emotion? "Nothing great was ever achieved without enthusiasm," said Emerson. It's the emotions that provide our lives with a sense of aliveness and mystery. Emotions alone would lead to a chaotic existence. But thoughts alone would lead to an arid, stale existence. The best balance we can hope for is a good thought propelled by sound emotion.

Selections in this section include:

- Willard Gaylin writes about seven kinds of pleasure in "Feeling Good."
- In "Emotional Intelligence," Daniel Goleman explains how emotional qualities are a major component of a successful life.
- Overwhelming anxiety is almost always detrimental. In "The Positive Face of Anxiety," Daniel Sugarman and Lucy Freeman show how less intense forms of anxiety are helpful and necessary for growth.
- Carol Tavris discusses the nuances and consequences of expressing "Anger: The Misunderstood Emotion."
- Five dimensions of loneliness are discussed and examined by William A. Sadler, Jr., in "The Causes of Loneliness."
- Tom Peyton reveals how he self-imposed a feeling of aloneness in "My Tyrant."
- In "You Never Know," Nels Goud highlights the power of the need to belong in a story of a high school student.
- Abe Arkoff introduces a powerful and simple way to experience happiness in "Little Joys."
- The nature and effects of "Jealousy and Envy: The Demons Within Us" are examined by Jon Queijo.
- "Sarcasm and Apathy" are the theme of an essay written by a mother and teacher (anonymous).
- A personalized account of reacting to the death of a parent is expressed by Sanford Colley in "On the Death of a Father."
- "Loss and Mourning" phases are explained and illustrated by Judith Viorst.
- Sometimes a person's emotional life can make one "loopy." A sanity test is offered by Nelson Goud in "The Madness Personality Inventory."

Practical applications involving emotions are found in the Follow-Up questions and in the Applied Activities.

Feeling Good

Willard Gaylin, M.D.

"Feeling good" is generic and vague. Whenever questioned, any individual will find "reasons" why he feels good, but the emotion itself eludes specific cause and specific description. Lightness, buoyancy, aliveness, enthusiasm, optimism, peace, relaxation, hope, involvement—all are words that have been used to amplify the specific feeling of feeling good. All of us know that feeling good can be independent of a right to feel so, and can irrationally occur in the midst of problems. A day dawns like any other and we wake up "feeling good."

If there is a common ingredient to the various sources and forms of pleasure, the only one that I can identify is that they all seem to contribute to an enhanced sense of self. Pleasurable events either intensify our sense of ourselves or enlarge our view of ourselves. We tend to stretch to our limits, and satiation and easy gratification ultimately destroy pleasure. Samuel Johnson recognized this when he said:

. . . [The Pyramid] seems to have been erected only in compliance with that hunger of imagination which preys incessantly upon life. . . . *Those who have already all that they can enjoy, must enlarge their desires. He that has built for use, till use is supplied, must begin to build for vanity. . . . I* consider this mighty structure as a monument to the insufficiency of human enjoyments.

A second category of pleasures—beyond particularly physical sensation, invoking our total self as person—is discovery. I have already discussed the sheer joy of the child on finding something new; observe his pleasure even in the pursuit of the unknown—in poking, examining, and exploring. Discovery takes us beyond mere stimulation. It allows us by using our distance perceptors, combined with our intelligence, to produce a form of pleasure that fuses the sensate with the intellectual.

Discovery can even abandon sensation and still produce pleasure. There is the form of pure discovery in the intellectual world. To those who have not experienced the pleasure of immersion in the world of knowledge and ideas, the phenomenon will be as impossible to communicate as to explain music to the deaf. There are people who have never developed intellectual pleasure. Obviously, an author is reasonably secure in the knowledge that the mere fact someone is reading his book means that whether the reader is getting pleasure in this specific book or not, he has an awareness of intellectual pleasure. There is something in the learning experience, independent of usefulness, that seems to give us joy. And it is again the concept of the enlargement of self. Our intellect extends our horizons. It frees us from the limits of our own experience. It allows us to transcend our own world, our own time, and our own identity.

The whole book of Canticles used to be pleasant to me, and I used to be much into reading it . . . and found, from time to time, an inward sweetness that would carry me away in my contemplations. This I know not how to express otherwise than by a calm, sweet abstraction of soul from all the concerns of this world. . . . The sense I had of divine things would often of a sudden kindle up, as it were, a sweet burning in my heart; an ardor of soul, that I know not how to express.

All individuals originally have joy in discovery. It is part of the common developmental experience. Discovery is an essential ingredient in the separation process which leads a child away from the protection of the maternal environment into the large world. The two-year-old is a bundle of intellectual curiosity. He is explorer, adventurer, philosopher, and scientist. What in heaven's name happens to this questing creature? How is it that as our sensate pleasures expand through adolescence, so many of us lose this other source of joy? Surely they need not be alternative sources. Is there a natural attrition of pleasure in discovery—particularly intellectual discovery—with aging, or is it some dreadful artifact of our educational and cultural system? I suspect that the latter must play some part. To have delivered to an educational system such an incredibly curious creature as the average five-year-old, and to have delivered back to us, after twelve years of education, the average seventeen-year-old, seems to imply certain complicity in the educational process. Even allowing that there may be a natural attrition in delight in life (necessitated by our eventual need to abandon existence), seventeen seems too early an age for the processes to have started!

I do believe that the capacity for all pleasure diminishes with age, and that diminution serves a purpose. The acceptance of death, intolerable as it now is, would be too unbearable if we carried into our seventies the intensity and passion of sixteen or seventeen. It would be too much to ask that we give up a food so nourishing. But later, when much of the experience of life is tinged with pain, when we are left with the dry residue of unfulfilled hopes and the remembrance of powers that are lost, friends that are gone, and sensations that are no longer—an end can at least be contemplated if not accepted.

A third category of pleasure, closely related to discovery, is the concept of expansion and mastery. We enjoy the sense of growth, of improvement. There is incredible pleasure in the smooth, unhurried, perfectly timed backhand passing shot, when it is executed. There is an elation in any athletic endeavor when one has the sense of one's body having done well. A thrill can be experienced merely by the sense of our own muscles, sinew and tendon perfectly timed and perfectly executing an action. The fact that it comes so rarely to most of us only enlarges the pleasure of mastery.

Mastery also occurs with mental processes. Mastery is the capacity to say, "I did it," with pride. The intellectual aspects of pleasure then go well beyond just discovery. Think of the joy of using your mind, independent of any useful purposes or accretion of knowledge. Think of problem solving. There is a delight for many in mathematics, in logical reasoning, or in the efforts of the kind of thinking associated with solving puzzles. It is a mental exercise. What we enjoy is the nimbleness of our mind. It is the pleasure of sensing our minds in operation. It is in every way an enhancement of the sense of self, if only the intellectual self.

Obviously, we do many things perfectly which we do not comment about. We are all master breathers, and the mechanics of breathing is intricate and magnificent. The moving of the diaphragm, which creates a negative vacuum, which allows for the influx of air; the stretching of the intercostal muscles between the ribs, which allows for the expansion of the rib cage and the dilatation of the lungs and the biological and chemical transactions across the lung membrane—all exercised so beautifully many times a minute, yet producing no pride or pleasure. Pleasure comes with the *sense* of enlargement or enrichment, and it must involve awareness of change from other conditions.

One of the real confusions about pleasure is the assumption that it is the opposite of pain. This confusion can be best resolved by considering mastery. In this category we can readily see that most things that involve great pleasure also involve pain. Here, without the pain, there would be no pleasure. The "I did it" phenomenon is significant only when there is the sense that what was done was difficult to do. Otherwise, where is the achievement? There is pleasure in attending a beautiful play. There has to be infinitely greater pleasure in having written one. The pleasure of seeing a superbly executed piece of cabinetry is far exceeded by the creativity of having made it. Part of the joy to the woodworker involves the hundreds of hours of painstaking, boring, painful sanding and finishing necessary to produce the perfection of fit and finish that goes into a beautiful cabinet. It is only because of the awareness of the sweat, toil, perseverance, and agony involved that the words "I did it!" have so rewarding a quality. The implication is: "It was not easy; and having done it, I have proved something about myself and my nature."

The cabinetmaking is, in fact, an example of a fourth category of pleasure that follows closely on mastery—and is simply an extension of it. That is creativity. The fact of having done something well is expanded in joy when it is more than a graceful turn on the ski slope, but actually a production of something of worth.

To make something, to be a maker of things, is a worthy pursuit. In that pursuit we often experience a fifth form of pleasure—immersion. To be totally immersed in something, to have lost the sense of time, perception, and seemingly sense of self, is obviously a joyous experience. This at first may seem contrary to the principle of expansion of self. I think not. The immersion of ourselves in an activity allows us to transcend our awareness of bodily needs, pain, trivial sensate pleasure. Immer-

sion is profound involvement of thing with self. It allows us to sense ourselves in a new environment like floating in water; the environment of the activity allows for a new awareness of ourselves through a new surrounding medium.

Closely related to the idea of immersion in things is the idea of fusion with people—our sixth category. What does one make of the pleasure that is achieved by playing in an ensemble or orchestra, singing in a choir, being a part of team activity? Here the individual's effort is not isolatable from the effect of the total group. This is the distinction between the soloist with the choir and the choir singer. Surely this, then, beyond immersion may be seen as a denial of self. But here again I think not. Rather than disappearing into the crowd, we are allowed by the pleasure of fusion to enlarge ourselves in identifying with the larger body. That we—knowing the limitations of our own voice—are part of that glorious sound emerging from the chorus is awesome and thrilling. We have found a form of enlargement through joining with our fellows. We are not lost in the group, intimidated by the mass, as when we are part of an inchoate crowd. That mighty sound of the chorus is *our* voice. We are the group. This is the thrill one gets in all cooperative effort. It is the excitement of sitting in a scull, pulling together, where your own backbreaking effort is indistinguishable from those fore and aft of you. The sense of power and motion is compounded by the fact that you are pulling all together, and at times the whole scull seems to be moving by your own individual effort. Fusion activities of all sorts are profound delights.

Fusion is a bridge in helping us understand our seventh category of pleasurable experience. For want of a better word, I will call it the transcendental experience. The transcendental experience is that sense of feeling lifted out of oneself. In the same way that immersion in an activity or fusion with a group allows us to expand the limits of self by including the activity or the others in our sense of self, the transcendent feeling allows for an even larger attachment beyond groups, things, people, world. When we are moved by some transcendental experience, we are reminded that we are a part of something even larger than the course and activities of our life. It is our sense of continuity beyond existence. To be a part of the cosmos, to affirm our place in the larger order of things, excites us. It is for this reason that confrontation with nature is the most common source of this experience.

My categories of pleasure are undoubtedly incomplete. Each individual may have unique sources of pleasure unto himself, and each will dictate different sets of categorization. In every list will be discovered, however, that enlargement of self which goes into feeling good. Was it chance that I uncovered seven? Or was it the magic of the number intruding on the unconscious of a hedonist and an optimist? It is nice to balance the seven deadly sins and the seven cardinal virtues with seven sources of pleasure.

There are specific qualities of feeling good, however, that are unrelated to pleasure. There is a form of feeling good related to the alleviation of distress. There is the feeling good that follows reassurance. In this sense, the feeling of goodness is related not to pleasure but to the removal of a threat. We feel good, independent of what pleasure there may be in our life, when we are told that the sickness from which we are still suffering is not the cancer we suspected. This is feeling good even while in a state of misery.

All feeling good, therefore, does not necessarily tie to pleasure—even in its broadest sense. The term is too vague. A sense of well-being may come into play with a removal of pain or a revival of hope.

Then, beyond all rationality, there is the pure and existential feeling good simply related to being alive. Considering the impact of existentialism on our society, and the amount of thought devoted to existential anxiety, it is incredible how little thinking has been devoted to existential pleasure. Directly analyzing existential pleasure is uncommon, because we usually believe that despair is close to an antithesis of feeling good. All feeling is a reminder that we exist, and all good is defined in the existence of ourselves and our species.

When we "feel good," we carry the feeling so tightly to our senses that we are often unaware of its existence. Like the fluid movements of a healthy body, we most often accept the value of feeling good without acknowledging its existence. But that sense of good feeling, whether exploited for other purposes or enjoyed directly, is the sole support of the value of living in this world. It is, at any rate, good "to feel good."

Follow-Up

1. *Gaylin's seven kinds of pleasure are: physical sensation, discovery, mastery, creativity, immersion, fusion with people, transcendental experience. From your experience, give an example of each kind of pleasure. Are there one or two pleasure categories that are "shouting" to be recognized at this time?*
2. *Gaylin says that a person can "feel good" even during times of misery or distress. Has this ever happened to you or someone you know? What does this say about a human being's balancing mechanisms?*

3. Sometimes we may feel anxious but do not know what is causing it—anxiety simply floats in. Gaylin says that we can also experience "existential pleasure"—a pure and joyous state related to being alive. Try to provide examples of both "floating" anxiety and pleasure.
4. Choose any other idea or statement in this article to write about or to discuss.

What's Your Emotional IQ?

Daniel Goleman

It was a steamy afternoon in New York City, the kind of day that makes people sullen with discomfort. I was heading to my hotel, and as I stepped onto a bus, I was greeted by the driver, a middle-aged man with an enthusiastic smile.

"Hi! How're you doing?" he said. He greeted each rider in the same way.

As the bus crawled uptown through gridlocked traffic, the driver gave a lively commentary: there was a terrific sale at that store . . . a wonderful exhibit at this museum . . . had we heard about the movie that just opened down the block? By the time people got off, they had shaken off their sullen shells. When the driver called out, "So long, have a great day!" each of us gave a smiling response.

That memory has stayed with me for close to 20 years. I consider the bus driver a man who was truly successful at what he did.

Contrast him with Jason, a straight-A student at a Florida high school who was fixated on getting into Harvard Medical School. When a physics teacher gave Jason an 80 on a quiz, the boy believed his dream was in jeopardy. He took a butcher knife to school, and in a struggle the teacher was stabbed in the collarbone.

How could someone of obvious intelligence do something so irrational? The answer is that high I.Q. does not necessarily predict who will succeed in life. Psychologists agree that I.Q. contributes only about 20 percent of the factors that determine success. A full 80 percent comes from other factors, including what I call *emotional intelligence.*

Following are some of the major qualities that make up emotional intelligence, and how they can be developed:

1. Self-awareness. The ability to recognize a feeling as it happens is the keystone of emotional intelligence. People with greater certainty about their emotions are better pilots of their lives.

Developing self-awareness requires tuning in to what neurologist Antonio Damasio, in his book *Descartes' Error,* calls "somatic markers"–literally, gut feelings. Gut feelings can occur without a person being consciously aware of them. For example, when people who fear snakes are shown a picture of a snake, sensors on their skin will detect sweat, a sign of anxiety, even though the people say they do not feel fear. The sweat shows up even when a picture is presented so rapidly that the subject has no conscious awareness of seeing it.

Through deliberate effort we can become more aware of our gut feelings. Take someone who is annoyed by a rude encounter for hours after it occurred. He may be oblivious to his irritability and surprised when someone calls attention to it. But if he evaluates his feelings, he can change them.

Emotional self-awareness is the building block of the next fundamental of emotional intelligence: being able to shake off a bad mood.

2. Mood Management. Bad as well as good moods spice life and build character. The key is balance.

We often have little control over *when* we are swept by emotion. But we can have some say in *how long* that emotion will last. Psychologist Dianne Tice of Case Western Reserve University asked more than 400 men and women about their strategies for escaping foul moods. Her research, along with that of other psychologists, provides valuable information on how to change a bad mood.

Of all the moods that people want to escape, rage seems to be the hardest to deal with. When someone in another car cuts you off on the highway, your reflexive thought may be, *That jerk! He could have hit me! I can't let him get away with that!* The more you stew, the angrier you get. Such is the stuff of hypertension and reckless driving.

What should you do to relieve rage? One myth is that ventilating will make you feel better. In fact, researchers have found that's one of the worst strategies. Outbursts of rage pump up the brain's arousal system, leaving you more angry, not less.

A more effective technique is "refraining," which means consciously reinterpreting a situation in a more positive light. In the case of the driver who cuts you off, you might tell yourself: *Maybe he had some emergency.* This is one of the most potent ways, Tice found, to put anger to rest.

Going off alone to cool down is also an effective way to defuse anger, especially if you can't think clearly. Tice found that a large proportion of men cool down by going for a drive—a finding that inspired her to drive more defensively. A safer alternative is exercise, such as taking a long walk. Whatever you do, don't waste the time pursuing your train of angry thoughts. Your aim should be to distract yourself.

The techniques of refraining and distraction can alleviate depression and anxiety as well as anger. Add to them such relaxation techniques as deep breathing and meditation and you have an arsenal of weapons against bad moods. "Praying," Dianne Tice also says, "works for all moods."

3. Self-motivation. Positive motivation—the marshaling of feelings of enthusiasm, zeal and confidence—is paramount for achievement. Studies of Olympic athletes, world-class musicians and chess grandmasters show that their common trait is the ability to motivate themselves to pursue relentless training routines.

To motivate yourself for any achievement requires clear goals and an optimistic, can-do attitude. Psychologist Martin Seligman of the University of Pennsylvania advised the MetLife insurance company to hire a special group of job applicants who tested high on optimism, although they had failed the normal aptitude test. Compared with salesmen who passed the aptitude test but scored high in pessimism, this group made 21 percent more sales in their first year and 57 percent more in their second.

A pessimist is likely to interpret rejection as meaning *I'm a failure, I'll never make a sale.* Optimists tell themselves, *I'm using the wrong approach,* or *That customer was in a bad mood.* By blaming failure on the situation, not themselves, optimists are motivated to make that next call.

Your predisposition to a positive or negative outlook may be inborn, but with effort and practice, pessimists can learn to think more hopefully. Psychologists have documented that if you can catch negative, self-defeating thoughts as they occur, you can reframe the situation in less catastrophic terms.

4. Impulse Control. The essence of emotional self-regulation is the ability to delay impulse in the service of a goal. The importance of this trait to success was shown in an experiment begun in the 1960s by psychologist Walter Mischel at a preschool on the Stanford University campus.

Children were told that they could have a single treat, such as a marshmallow, right now. However, if they would wait while the experimenter ran an errand, they could have two marshmallows. Some preschoolers grabbed the marshmallow immediately, but others were able to wait what, for them, must have seemed an endless 20 minutes. To sustain themselves in their struggle, they covered their eyes so they wouldn't see the temptation, rested their heads on their arms, talked to themselves, sang, even tried to sleep. These plucky kids got the two-marshmallow reward.

The interesting part of this experiment came in the follow-up. The children who as four-year-olds had been able to wait for the two marshmallows were, as adolescents, still able to delay gratification in pursuing their goals. They were more socially competent and self-assertive, and better able to cope with life's frustrations. In contrast, the kids who grabbed the one marshmallow were, as adolescents, more likely to be stubborn, indecisive and stressed.

The ability to resist impulse can be developed through practice. When you're faced with an immediate temptation, remind yourself of your long-term goals—whether they be losing weight or getting a medical degree. You'll find it easier, then, to keep from settling for the single marshmallow.

5. People Skills. The capacity to know how another feels is important on the job, in romance and friendship, and in the family. We transmit and catch moods from each other on a subtle, almost imperceptible level. The way someone says thank you, for instance, can leave us feeling dismissed, patronized or genuinely appreciated. The more adroit we are at discerning the feelings behind other people's signals, the better we control the signals we send.

The importance of good interpersonal skills was demonstrated by psychologists Robert Kelley of Carnegie-Mellon University and Janet Caplan in a study at Bell Labs in Naperville, Ill. The labs are staffed by engineers and scientists who are all at the apex of academic I.Q. tests. But some still emerged as stars, while others languished.

What accounted for the difference? The standout performers had a network with a wide range of people. When a non-star encountered a technical problem, Kelley observed, "he called various technical gurus and then waited, wasting time while his calls went unreturned. Star performers rarely faced such situations because they built reliable networks *before* they needed them. So when the stars called someone, they almost always got a faster answer."

No matter what their I.Q., once again it was emotional intelligence that separated the stars from the average performers.

Follow-Up

1. *Rate yourself, or have someone you know well rate you, on the five major qualities of "emotional intelligence."*

1 = *Very low*   2 = *Low*   3 = *Average*
4 = *High*   5 = *Exceptionally high*

1. *Self-awareness*	1	2	3	4	**5**
2. *Mood Management*	1	2	3	**4**	5
3. *Self-motivation*	1	2	**3**	4	5
4. *Impulse Control*	1	2	3	4	**5**
5. *People Skills*	1	2	3	**4**	5

2. *Choose one or more of the five factors of emotional intelligence to further develop in yourself and report your actions.*

3. *Observe persons who are very skillful in one or more of the five areas of emotional intelligence and report what you learned.*

4. *One of the more powerful techniques for managing moods is "reframing"—how to reinterpret a situation. Try this idea in your life and report on the results.*

5. *Discuss or write about your reactions to Goleman's contention "that IQ contributes only about 20% of the factors that determine success."*

The Positive Face of Anxiety

*Daniel A. Sugarman
and Lucy Freeman*

Anxiety is the most painful of all emotions, and many people will do anything to avoid direct confrontation with it. Like a child terrified of going to the dentist, they permit anxiety to fester and cause psychic decay. They refuse to submit to the direct confrontation which removes the decay and the chronic pain. Some use so much energy defending themselves against anxiety that there is little left for the enjoyment of living.

We are learning that it is not anxiety itself, but the way we handle anxiety, that makes the difference between emotional sickness and health. A refusal to acknowledge the anxiety within us prevents the possibility of greater personality growth.

The widespread use of tranquilizers has helped—and hindered. On one hand, millions have obtained sufficient relief from anxiety to cope with daily difficulties; but the indiscriminate use of these powerful medications has prevented many from coming to terms with their conflicts. If they were just a little more desperate, they might seek psychological help and get at the source of the anxiety.

THE GIFT OF ANXIETY

In our hedonistic society, it is difficult for many to believe that anything which stings a bit can be of value. Nevertheless, in spite of our love of the sun, rainy days are important in the total scheme of things. Without any anxiety, we would become like vegetables, unable to sense the passing danger that threatens us from every side. The hyper-vigilance anxiety brings makes it easier for us to detect danger and take appropriate measures against it.

One mother described to me how, in putting her eight-month-old baby to bed one night, she felt suddenly anxious about his health. It seemed he did not look healthy, as though he were coming down with a cold; nor did she like the way he sounded when he cried. With these thoughts in mind, when she went to bed, she had difficulty sleeping. About two in the morning, she became aware of wheezing noises from the child's bedroom. Dashing to his side, she found him in the midst of a severe attack of the croup. Hardly breathing, the child was rushed to the emergency room of a hospital where his life was saved. In this case, as in others, without anxiety on the part of the mother, there might have been a tragedy.

A patient of mine, made anxious one evening by a television program warning against breast cancer, decided to examine her breasts. To her horror, she noted a small lump. Prompt biopsy, performed forty-eight hours later, revealed the lump to be malignant. Although she lost a breast, she is now, five years later, very much alive and well. Without her anxiety, the outcome probably would have been different.

Too often we are ashamed to admit anxiety. Nourished by an emotional diet of heroes, we inflict unreasonable expectations upon ourselves. A deer or rabbit, unencumbered by the pretense of courage, will take to its heels at the first sign of danger and, by doing so, ensure its survival.

An adolescent patient told me that several other teenagers had tried to tempt him into I drag race on a busy highway. When he refused to take part because he felt that to race on that particular highway was too dangerous, the others called him chicken. He replied, "I'd rather be a chicken than a dead duck."

Often those willing to acknowledge their anxiety turn out to be stronger than those who equate anxiety with cowardice. I have seen patients delay treatment because they were "going to work it out by myself," only to crack under the burden of unbearable anxiety.

One woman developed a severe anxiety condition during the early 1940s. Sent to a state mental hospital she was given shock treatments, insulin therapy, and medication. In spite of all attempts to help her, her anxiety remained at a painfully high level. After five years of unsuccessful attempts to cure her, her family signed a permission form for a lobotomy (an experimental operation in which certain sections of the brain are destroyed, causing the person to become unable to experience anxiety in any depth).

After the lobotomy, she seemed considerably improved. She began to sleep and gained over fifty pounds. She no longer was agitated or anxious, and it was decided she could be sent home. Once home, however, she had to be cared for almost constantly by her family because she had lost all sense of possible danger. She could not emotionally comprehend that cars traveling at a rapid speed could pose a threat, and she would cross the street on a red light. One day, while no one was watching, she blindly walked into a speeding car. Although she survived the accident, she paid a terrible price for her lack of fear.

The more psychologists learn about the child, the more they learn about the role anxiety plays in helping us to grow into human beings. Some feel that without anxiety the child would never learn the social skills required to live among other people. It is probably the anxiety over losing the approval and love of parents that propels us to higher marks in school and control of our aggressive and sexual impulses.

Anxiety is the force behind much learning. A student under the pressure of a final examination in physics may be motivated to pick up the book, burn the midnight oil, and cram. As a result, he may find that, not only has he passed the test, but learned a bit of physics. His more carefree classmate, not anxious enough to study, may find his academic career prematurely terminated as a result of flunking the exam.

In many ways, anxiety can force us to learn something that will increase our security. Psychoanalysts point out that one of the greatest motivations for a child to learn to walk is that once he learns, he can overcome to some extent the anxiety he feels when separated from his mother. Being able to walk permits him to reach his mother more readily, and he no longer feels so helpless.

Anxiety can also be a sign that we have violated some moral code. One woman, although in love with her husband, started an affair in a childish attempt to get revenge because she felt he had neglected her. As the affair progressed, she developed many symptoms of anxiety. She felt shaky and lightheaded and very depressed. During the course of psychotherapy, she became aware of the underlying motives for her affair and gave up the destructive relationship with her lover. She was able to tell her husband how she felt about him. Although there was a period of strife, their problems were out in the open, and her anxiety diminished. In this case, as in others, anxiety had mounted to the point that the person finally did something about an unhappy life.

Anxiety may also prepare us for a stressful future situation. A man who has to give an important speech can be goaded by anxiety to rehearse not only his speech but the fear he may feel on the podium. As he faces this fear in anticipation of the event, there is a better chance that on the day of the speech he will be less afraid.

Dr. Irving Janis, a psychologist, studied the relationship between anxiety in patients about to undergo surgery and their recovery. He reported that those patients completely without anxiety before an impending major surgical operation had a more difficult postoperative period. He concluded that patients who expressed reasonable anxiety before surgery had fewer reactions of fear and anger after surgery.[1]

THE SIGN OF GROWTH

One young man in his middle twenties came to me for psychological consultation and testing. He drank excessively and was separated from his wife, whom he had beaten rather cruelly on several occasions. He had a severe psychosomatic skin condition which had persisted for seven years. Repeated consultations with dermatologists produced little change, and every dermatologist he saw suggested that he receive psychotherapy. Although not painful, the skin condition was disfiguring and marred what otherwise would have been a handsome appearance.

After looking over his psychological test and the interview material, I felt the prognosis for the change in this man was dim. In both his interview and the projective testing, it seemed that he rarely experienced even a twinge of overt anxiety. It was evident his symptom was bound up with whatever anxiety he felt and that he had little conscious awareness of being anxious.

The appearance of anxiety in psychological testing or clinical interview is a favorable prognostic sign. Psychotherapists know that when a patient complains of anxiety and tension and anxiety-related symptoms, his chances of recovery are usually good; but when a patient has an his anxiety bound up in a particular symptom and feels little overt discomfort, the path of therapy is likely to be extremely difficult. The more anxious a patient, the greater his motivation to change and to explore his unconscious conflicts. As he be-

comes more comfortable, this motivation may diminish, so that he loses interest in further exploration.

When I was interning in clinical psychology, I worked at a large Veterans Administration neuro-psychiatric hospital, which held several thousand patients. At that time, the hospital was divided into two units. One was an acute intensive treatment unit for recent admissions and patients readmitted after having made a good adjustment for a time outside the hospital. In general, the treatment facilities were aimed at this particular group, thought to have the best prognosis for recovery and discharge. The second unit was for continued care. On this service were placed patients who had either been hospitalized for many years or whose prognosis was poor.

I was impressed with the fact that, for the most part, those patients in the second unit made the best hospital adjustment and were relatively free from anxiety. Many, having lived in the hospital for years, were allowed grounds privileges, went home weekends, and in general were model patients. They slept well, ate well, and required little tranquilizing. The staff referred to them as burnt out. This meant there was little evidence of anxiety or conflict, that they had adjusted to a marginal level of existence.

On the acute intensive treatment unit, however, the situation was very different. These patients were agitated, anxious, fearful, and confused. When you walked into one of these wards you could sense the suffering and turmoil, signs that the patients were still fighting to resolve their conflicts rather than giving in to the regressive illness.

THE PRICE OF GROWTH

As we move through life, the stability of our personality is not always the same. There are times our defenses work well and life proceeds with little anxiety; but there are other times when defenses fail and we feel less stable or more anxious. Sometimes we experience anxiety when underlying growth is taking place. There has been little awareness that hardly any personality growth occurs without some anxiety.

Even the ancients recognized that anxiety and growth were associated. In the Bible a state of fear and anxiety is closely connected with impending revelation. When Moses came down from the mountain after his encounter with God, he frightened the people of Israel; it is written that, "When Aaron and all the people of Israel saw Moses, behold, the skin of his face shone, and they were afraid to come near him."[2]

The study of history and social psychology suggests that, in many situations, a state of national panic is the prelude to increased awareness of national goals and to legislation that may create a period of greater calm and stability.

Many positive steps in our life are accompanied by anxiety. Each time we extend ourselves further, accept new responsibility, or affirm our independence, we may also feel a measure of anxiety.

Once while traveling on a train in September, I sat next to a young girl who, pale and tense, sat with her teeth clenched, obviously very anxious. We began to talk; she told me she was on her way to college and that this was the first time she had ever been away from her family. As she spoke of leaving home, she plainly revealed both the anxiety she felt and her determination to become independent.

She described how she had always been overprotected by her mother and three older brothers and said that although it was hard for her to do, she had decided it would be the best thing for her to go to college in a distant city.

After she got off at her destination, I thought about her and the fact that she would have been relatively free of anxiety had she decided to remain at home. She was not going to let a little anxiety stop her from developing into an independent young woman. Some others, afraid of the anxiety of separation, have remained home, tied to mother and hearth forever.

In children the relationship between anxiety and growth is emphasized. I observed my son at the local swimming pool. Barely knowing how to swim at the beginning of the summer, he made tremendous advances under the tutelage of a good instructor. Towards the middle of the summer, he was able to navigate anyplace in the pool. Not content with this, he began to eye the diving board. With some trepidation, he first dived from the side of the pool. He then tried the low board. After a time, he looked up at the high board. After some encouragement, he mounted to the top of the high board, a pathetic sight to see. He was pale, tense, and very anxious. Finally, he jumped. When he emerged from the depths, he had on his face that smile of pure joy that comes from having conquered anxiety.

Observation of children shows that they will attack again and again a fear situation until it no longer causes anxiety. Once they have mastered it, they are ready to move on to the next fearful situation. Almost every sign of growth and independence contains some seeds of anxiety. The first day at kindergarten, the first night of sleeping at a friend's house, the first time on a bicycle—all produce anxiety. The child who has learned early not to shrink in the face of anxiety, but to move through it, will have that sense of increasing mastery which sets the foundation for a healthy personality.

Adults, too, may experience anxiety when they are about to grow or undertake some new responsibility. One man described the anxiety he felt at his house-closing. He had always had difficulty in accepting responsibility or long-term commitments. He had been living in a small overcrowded apartment with his wife and two children. Although wanting to own a house, he had previously rejected this idea as bearing with it too much responsibility. Intellectually, he knew that living in a house was the only sensible thing to do, but his emotional difficulties prevented him from taking the step. After some therapy which helped him gain confidence in himself, he bought a house. His anxiety at the closing could be seen only as a prelude to growth and a rejection of his old neurotic patterns of behavior. After a short spell of discomfort, he began to feel good about what he had done.

Often we feel anxiety when we violate some childish, no longer appropriate, taboo. I worked with a young lady who was in acute conflict over her wish to remain home with her aged father and her love for a young man who wanted to marry her. She had been raised in a home where she had been controlled by a guilt-inducing father. After her mother had died, five years prior to treatment, her father in subtle, and not-so-subtle, ways had made it clear that he "probably couldn't live if she left him." After work, she would come home to care for this tyrant. She felt chronically depressed, but did not realize the cause of the depression.

The situation came to a crisis when she fell in love. When the young man proposed, she was thrown into acute anxiety, and sought help. After a short period of treatment, she decided she would accept the proposal of marriage, but still became anxious each time her father made her feel guilt for leaving him. Shortly after the wedding, however, she felt happier than she had been in her entire life. Her father, now thrown on his own, became more active socially and even resumed working. She reported he was faring better than at any time since his wife had died.

Almost every milestone in our life may be a source of anxiety—the first day of school, graduation, the first job, marriage, the birth of a child, the sending of a child to camp. Sometimes, too, anxiety will arise when we assert ourselves to others, going against the dreams they may have for us. A young adolescent I saw was rather introverted, preferring to spend time either by herself or with one or two close friends. She had literary ability and in one afternoon might produce a poem or short story, many of which were published by the school magazine. Her English teacher, recognizing her talent, encouraged her to send her work to other magazines. When writing or with one or two of her friends, she felt at peace with herself and the world.

Her mother, however, had different ideas about the proper activities for her daughter. When she sat down to write, her mother would disparage her efforts, asking why she was not out with the group.

After a period of therapy, armed with a greater sense of self-respect and self-understanding this girl was able to take a stronger stand against her mother's demands. As she did so, she began to experience anxiety. Although more uncomfortable, she was now accepting a sense of her own identity.

Sometimes anxiety will flash to warn us that something is amiss. One man, a patient of mine, for several years had held a particular job that was well below his potential. This man was bright, sensitive, and alert, but because he had a low sense of self-esteem, his level of aspiration was far below his ability. In treatment, it became evident he was bored by his job—the boredom that comes from doing something for which one is highly unsuited. After a while, he resolved to give up the job and go back to school. Not unexpectedly, his anxiety decreased. Boredom is a way of denying anxious feelings.

In essence, anxiety warns us that our relationship with ourselves is not all it should be. Seen in this light, anxiety no longer is a frightening enemy which must be tranquilized out of sight.

AT TIMES OF CRISIS

At the time of a psychic crisis, anxiety mounts just the way our temperature rises as our body defenses rally to fight an infection.

Anxiety, viewed correctly, can be seen as an indicator of a possible threat to our integrity and personality. If we can affirm ourselves by moving through rather than fleeing from anxiety, healthy growth can be the result.

Once I served as head counselor in a girls' camp situated in a rural secluded area. The counselors were young and insecure, hardly much older than the girls they were hired to supervise. Most of the young counselors felt homesick during the week of orientation that preceded thearrival of the campers. Observation of two preceding years in this camp had taught me that if the counselors could endure the first week of indoctrination, their homesickness would end as soon as they became busy with responsibilities. Life in camp would then settle down into pleasant routine.

One morning, about three days before the girls were to arrive, two tearful seventeen-year-old junior counselors came to see me and said they were so homesick that they wanted to leave. I allowed them to express their feelings, gave them Kleenex to wipe away the tears, and pointed out that for them to remain in camp and follow through on a commitment they had made would be a sign of growth. I suggested that before they made any decision about leaving, they wait and see how they felt when camp swung into full operation in a few days.

One of the young counselors, unable to tolerate her separation anxiety for one more day, decided she wanted to leave immediately, and arrangements were made for her to depart the next morning. The other one clenched her teeth and said she would give it a try for one week more. When the campers arrived and a full program went into operation, she became involved in camp activities and was visibly more content. There was no more talk of going home. One day towards the end of the summer, she spontaneously came over to me and said, "I want to thank you! I feel more grown-up than ever before."

Although hardly a controlled experiment, this illustrates the point that whenever we feel in conflict, with heightened anxiety, the way is open either to growth or regression. If we can learn to use anxiety as a mandate to growth, we will be far happier.

It is precisely at times of crisis and acute anxiety that old patterns begin to break down and there comes the chance to build new ones. During heightened anxiety, we become inordinately suggestible and seek new solutions to problems. This is why someone in a crisis very often needs prompt, understanding, professional help.

When a patient is in therapy, one often sees an increase in his anxiety as the herald of improvement. Sometimes a patient finds this alarming. At such times, it is necessary for him to be aware that the anxiety indicates something within is stirring and does not necessarily mean he is getting worse.

Dr. Karen Horney wrote: "Any anxiety that does arise during analytic therapy is usually alarming to the patient because he tends to regard it as impairment. But more often than not this is not so . . . emerging anxiety may also have an eminently positive meaning. For it may indicate that the patient now feels strong enough to take the risk of facing his problems more squarely. . . ."[3]

When a patient begins to *feel* his suffering for the first time in his life, anxiety may result. I worked with a young, unmarried, professional woman who, at the beginning of therapy, had many symptoms of, although she experienced little, overt anxiety. As she began to get more in touch with her feelings, her anxiety increased, for she confronted her own emptiness, yearnings, and unfulfilled desires.

During this difficult time in her therapy, I received a letter in which she said that she could not sleep, that she had a million conflicting thoughts, that she felt depressed and lonely, and that anything could start her crying. She said that she was ashamed of her feelings and almost wished she had never gone into therapy because before it, she had felt that she could never love anyone or anything and could accept not getting married or having anybody, but that now she felt capable of loving deeply and wanted a family.

In many ways she *was* more comfortable before therapy. Although she had symptoms, she was protected behind the barricade of not feeling. As her feelings were released, she felt at first as if she would be swept away by their intensity. But after a short while, she was able to live more comfortably with herself in a manner she never before believed possible.

Sometimes patients avoid anxiety in the early stages of therapy by blaming all their difficulties upon their mother or father or society. After a while, if therapy is successful, the patient realizes that while all these may have contributed to his emotional distress, his own strong desires and imagination were partially responsible. He also knows that what he does about his life now is solely up to him. This may create new anxiety for a time.

Dr. Thayer A. Greene wrote:

How much easier and less anxiety-producing it is to perceive the problem as social and collective rather than individual and personal. Yet whatever social forces operate upon our lives, it is we who must make an individual response. No single lesson makes itself more clear to those who have gone through extensive psychotherapy than that to blame it all on God, society, mother and father, rarely if ever brings healing and change. When all the accounts have been added up, the individual must still pay the bill if he is to be freed from the negative and confining power of the past—not only his own but that of his family and culture. Whether or not the particular dilemma in which an individual finds himself is his "fault" is usually quite beside the point. The handicap, the crippling anxiety, the behavioral compulsion, may not be his fault at all and yet be his *fact*, i.e, the reality of his life situation. He must engage himself personally with this fact in order to grow.[4]

With patients who do well in psychotherapy, I have noted that although in the early part of treatment, they handle severe anxiety by saying, "Isn't it awful?" or "Aren't I terrible?", they gradually accept anxiety as an *opportunity* to learn more about themselves. When anxiety can be regarded as a teacher, the patient often becomes an apt pupil. To use anxiety constructively, as a valuable tool in learning about ourselves and what threatens us, is not an easy task. But if we can learn to do this, we will be rewarded with the prize of increased self-knowledge.

Sometimes psychotherapy allows a patient to become *too* comfortable; his anxiety has been tranquilized. Then the job of the therapist is to mobilize a bit of anxiety so that the healing process may once again take place.

THE WILLINGNESS TO BE HUMAN

To some extent I have stressed the anxiety that results from conflict and from crisis. There is, however, the anxiety that comes from being alive, for, to be human is to be finite and limited, and to be finite and limited is to be anxious.

In some dark, deep recess of our minds, in spite of the din of music and noise and friends and work and travel and sports and food, we never lose the awareness that some day we will die. When we feel alive, we are using our full potential and the thought of death drifts into the shadows.

The knowledge of our finiteness can help us to savor the moments we live, to help us use our limited time in a useful, enjoyable manner. That knowledge can also help keep us appropriately humble in the face of the forces of nature, can make us give pause and consider our little vanities. The knowledge that we are temporary visitors on this planet can put petty quarrels into proper perspective. Temporary frustrations can be seen as part of reality. We can live more in the present and stop pursuing a vain, relentless search for security. Once we accept a certain basic anxiety, we can begin to live more fully.

The willingness to recognize the reality of anxiety indicates an ability to recognize all of reality. Most of us are all too eager to deny that we are anxious. When we do, we gain momentary relief, but pay a high price. We keep out of touch with our real feelings. Our chances of facing our conflicts and easing our anxiety are lessened. We find that we are more alienated than ever, both from our feelings and other people.

If one is able to acknowledge anxiety and battle it, healing forces are frequently set in motion. Dr. Paul Tillich once spoke of the necessity of having the "courage to be," which includes the acceptance and facing of anxiety.

Paradoxically, true courage seems to begin with the admission of anxiety, just as the possibility of true living begins when we do not deny the possibility of death.

THE FEAR OF FEAR

In our society which, sometimes subtly, sometimes not so subtly, suggests that we should be happy all the time, anxiety is too often hidden; unhappiness, uncertainty, conflict, and doubt are all denied. I have seen a large number of patients who practically considered it un-American to be anxious. They feel guilty because they have moments of panic in spite of having accumulated all the necessary material possessions they wish. Often the first step with such patients is to help them feel less guilty about the fact that they *are* anxious.

Anxiety is as normal a part of the life process as teething. Like teething, it can be unpleasant and, if severe, cause pain. Too often, the fear of anxiety makes the anxious person avoid anything that might possibly cause it. Then a growing fear of anxiety results which may create more discomfort than the original fear.

If you ski, you know that the ability to ski increases by taking the risk of feeling frightened on the new high slope that looks possible but difficult. As soon as you master this slope, skiing down it without anxiety, you are ready to move to the next mountain, one that offers still more challenge.

If someone looks on anxiety as an enemy, a "disease," the therapeutic way is likely to be rougher and longer. But if he views anxiety as an opportunity to look within, as a mandate for further development, not only will the psychic way be easier, but his anxiety will also lessen that more swiftly. Anxiety is a feeling to become aware of, to be faced, to be understood, and then, almost automatically, it is present only when we realistically need it.

References
1. Janis, I. L. (1958). *Psychological stress.* New York: Wiley.
2. Exodus 34:30
3. Horney, K. (1950). *Neurosis and human growth* (p. 340). New York: W. W. Norton.
4. Greene, T. (1967). *Modern man in search of manhood* (p. 12). New York: Association Press.

Follow-Up

1. *Respond to the authors' argument that anxiety is a gift. Provide examples from your life.*

2. *How has anxiety presented itself during periods in your life? Discuss the ways you handled it.*
3. *The authors propose that by accepting and trying to understand anxiety, we can learn what is needed and the anxiety will decrease. Explain an instance where this has happened to you, or possibly apply this idea to your current situation.*
4. *Choose any other idea from the article to write about or discuss.*

Anger: The Misunderstood Emotion

Carol Tavris

Woman A: *You'll feel better if you get your anger out.*

Woman B: *Anger? Why should I be angry?*

Woman A: *Because your father left you. Underneath, you're blaming him for not keeping his obligation to protect you forever.*

Woman B: *Left me? What are you talking about? He died. I don't feel angry I feel sad.*

Woman A: *Why are you denying your true feelings?*

Woman B: *Margaret, you're going to drive me crazy. I don't feel angry, damn it!*

Woman A (smiling): *So why are you shouting?*

That exchange, overheard in a New York City restaurant, illustrates one of today's most accepted myths of popular psychology: that expressing anger is crucial to health and happiness. Social psychologist Leonard Berkowitz of the University of Wisconsin calls advocates of this view "ventilationists," because they believe it's unhealthy to bottle up feelings. "Many go further," he writes, "and argue that by showing our emotions we eliminate tensions, conquer aches and pains, and promote 'more meaningful' relationships with others."

"There is a widespread belief that to discharge one's feelings is beneficial," writes psychiatrist John R. Marshall of the University of Wisconsin department of psychiatry. "People feel that there's some value in hitting, throwing or breaking something when frustrated."

But is there? In the aftermath of the abrupt transition from Puritan restraint to liberated self-expression, many people are uncertain how to behave: some overreact angrily at every thwarted wish; others suffer injustice in silence. Who's right?

In one experiment, psychologist Jack Hokanson of Florida State University found that aggression was cathartic: the blood pressure of angry male students would return to baseline more quickly when they could retaliate against the man who had angered them. But this was true only when the man who angered them was a fellow student; when he was a teacher, retaliation had no cathartic effect. Expressing anger to a superior is *itself* an arousing anxiety-producing action. Far from reducing anger, it complicates it.

Then Hokanson noticed that women were not behaving the same as men. When insulted, women didn't get belligerent; instead, they said something friendly to try to calm the woman who angered them. For women, any aggression, even toward a classmate, was as arousing and upsetting as aggression toward authority was for men.

Further research gave Hokanson the idea that aggressive catharsis is a learned reaction to anger, not an instinctive one. The learned aspect of catharsis works like this: someone irritates you and provokes you over the edge of self-control. Now you do something—you swear, or hit, or pound out Stravinsky on the piano. All these reactions lessen your physiological arousal and its corresponding sensation that your blood is boiling. At the same time, you're acquiring a cathartic habit.

This habit doesn't mean you'll be less angry in the future. It means that when you *are* angry, you're apt to do whatever worked for you before, whether it was swearing, writing a

"Anger" by Tom McCain. Copyright © 1996.

letter, having a drink, or hitting the person who aroused you.

Thus most ventilationist theories today concentrate on what a person should do to bring down anger. But *any* emotional arousal will eventually simmer down if you just wait long enough. This is why the classic advice for anger control—count to ten—has survived for centuries.

Berkowitz, who has studied the social causes of aggression, finds that ventilation-by-yelling does not reduce anger. "Frequently, when we tell someone off, we stimulate ourselves to continued aggression," he observed. This is why a minor annoyance, when expressed in hostile language or behavior, can flare into a major argument.

Anger and its expression do not exist in a vacuum. In all areas of our lives we make choices about how to behave, when to speak, whether to reveal anger. Suppressed anger can be "bad" if, because we do not reveal our feelings, a stressful situation continues; expressed anger can likewise be "bad" if, in revealing our feelings, we make the stressful situation worse.

Actress Lynn Fontanne once said that the secret of her successful marriage and acting partnership with Alfred Lunt was that they were never impolite to each other. Civility is not, mind you, the same as silence. Couples who aren't defeated by rage know two things: when to keep quiet about trivial angers, for the sake of civility, and how to discuss important ones, for the sake of personal autonomy and change. As the catharsis studies show, sometimes the best thing you can do about anger is nothing. Let it go, and it will often turn out to be unimportant and quickly forgotten. Keeping quiet also gives you time to cool down and decide if the matter is worth discussing.

The most successful therapeutic methods for helping people who are quick to rage take mind and body into consideration. Practitioners of yoga learn techniques to calm distracting or infuriating thoughts. Western psychologists are catching on. Ray Novaco of the University of California at Irvine, for example, works with people who have problems with chronic anger, teaching them three things: how to think about their anger; how to control arousal; how to behave constructively. Anger is often inflamed by the statements we make when we are provoked: "Who does he think he is to treat me like that?" "What a vile and thoughtless woman she is!" Novaco teaches people to empathize with the provocateur's behavior, trying to find justification for it and ways to deal with it: "Maybe he's having a rough day" or "She must be very unhappy if she would do such a thing."

On the ground that you can't laugh and frown at the same time, some psychologists use "humor therapy" with clients who have anger problems. When I was a child, my father often used this tactic on me. Once, when I was enjoying an angry mood, he insisted I accompany him to an afternoon of Charlie Chaplin movies. There I learned that you cannot maintain a sullen mood when you are laughing out loud.

Many believe that talking out anger gets rid of it—or at least makes you feel less angry. But several studies show that talking out an emotion often doesn't reduce it and may, in fact, merely *rehearse* it. As you recite your grievances, your emotional arousal builds again, making you feel as angry as you did when the infuriating event first happened. Anger only feeds on itself. And, sure as the sunrise, it makes for a grumpy life.

Now, none of this is to make a case for *always* keeping quiet when you're angry. The point is to understand what happens when you *do* decide to express anger. Each of us must find his own compromise between expressing every little thing that irritates, and passively accepting the injustices we feel. Discussing anger can lead to practical solutions; it can also become obsessive and useless.

Thus the decision about whether or not to express anger rests on what you want to communicate and what you hope to accomplish. If you want your anger to dissipate and the association in question to remain congenial, keep quiet. But if you want to *stay* angry, if you want to use your anger, keep talking.

The moral use of anger requires an awareness of choice and an embrace of reason. For the small indignities of life, the best remedy is almost always a Charlie Chaplin movie. For the larger ones, fight back. And, most important, learn the difference.

Follow-Up

1. *Describe a situation in which you* suppressed *your anger with unfortunate results.*
2. *Describe a situation in which you* suppressed *your anger with fortunate results.*
3. *Describe a situation in which you* expressed *your anger with unfortunate results.*
4. *Describe a situation in which you* expressed *your anger with fortunate results.*
5. *How do you typically deal with your anger? What effect has this had on you and your relationships?*

The Causes of Loneliness

William A. Sadler, Jr.

About a year ago, I had an interview with a reporter that illustrates one of the paradoxes associated with loneliness. She called to ask about my work on the subject, hoping to get help with an article. After giving her some information, I suggested she get in touch with the department of urban studies at a university in the city where she worked. I felt certain that its in-depth, long-range study of a large urban area would yield some insights into loneliness that would be relevant to her article and her newspaper's readers.

Several weeks later, the reporter called back to say that she had been turned away at the university. She was told by the department's assistant director that loneliness was not a social problem worth studying, that no data on loneliness were available, and that none was expected from their study program. Yet during the reporter's visits to mental health clinics and counselors in that area she was told that breakdowns, divorces, alcohol and drug addiction, and suicide were markedly increasing, and that problems such as these were related to chronic loneliness.

That's the paradox. Loneliness is so often dismissed by experts studying modern life, while at the same time it is reported to be an increasingly significant problem in individual and social being.

How can we account for the fact that loneliness, which I find to be a serious problem for many persons in modern America, is virtually ignored by the social sciences? I think there are two basic reasons. The first is theoretical. Until recently we lacked the clear concepts that would allow investigators and counselors to define loneliness and to understand it in a re-

liable way. The second reason is personal and has to do with the general attitude of the public toward loneliness, which sees it merely as a symptom of a weak character. The result is that one tends to downplay the impact it has in one's life, or even to deny that it has any significance at all. A common response given to persons who admit being lonely is: "Well, what's wrong with you? You don't need to be lonely. Go out and get busy. Join a club. Do something." Frequently through workshops, interviews, and articles I have found the response to be even more negative than this.

Investigations done in the last few years have permitted us to be more precise in defining loneliness. The conceptual understanding of loneliness, which will be presented in this article, shows why the accusatory response misses the mark. Many people in our society are lonely, not because of personality defects, but because there are factors "out there" that cause them to be lonely. Hopefully, this attitude will do more than resolve the paradox. It will help us all understand loneliness more intelligently and sympathetically, and provide a few realistic ideas about how to cope with it productively.

What is meant by *loneliness?* People use the term in different ways. Often loneliness is confused with merely being alone or with isolation. Your own experience should tell you that these are not identical. You can be alone and not lonely. People locked in solitary confinement do not always experience loneliness, at least not to any severe degree. To concentrate on isolation as much as social science has done when it has tried to get at loneliness is to miss the obvious. Some of the most painful, lonely feelings arise in the midst of a relationship or a group. Dr. Carl Jung suggested that "loneliness does not come from having no people about one, but from holding certain views that others find inadmissible." Adolescents, for example, frequently complain of the loneliness they experience in their homes, when they sense a generation gap. Adults they love simply do not understand them.

For this reason I suggest that loneliness is not just a physical condition. It is primarily an *experience*. Furthermore, it is probably unique to mankind. In his study on "the biology of loneliness" the late Dr. Ralph Audy Ph.D., M.D., of the U.C.L.A. Medical Center in San Francisco came to the conclusion that although there are analogies to it in the animal world, only human beings really know loneliness. Animals certainly manifest discomfort from prolonged separation. Ethologists and animal psychologists suggest that there is a basic animal need for attachment and that problems arise when that need is frustrated. It seems likely that humans have a similar need. But the kind of loneliness that I think is particularly troublesome in modern society is more complicated than mere frustration of this need for attachment.

In studying countless expressions of loneliness, both of modern Americans and from other times and places, I have found some common elements. The first and most outstanding feature of loneliness is a painful feeling, sometimes experienced as a sharp ache, as in moments of grief or separation; but it can also be a dull lingering form of stress that seems to tear a person down. Sometimes lonely feelings produce the "blues" of depression; but again, there is a difference between loneliness and depression. In the latter case, when a person is really "feeling down," he does not want to do anything. Depression corrodes motivational resources. Loneliness, by contrast, has a driving power. It sets people in motion—to go out, turn on TV, write a letter, make a phone call, or even get married.

There is another important aspect to this feeling. It is a significant signal coming from within ourselves that something is missing from our lives. Isolation does not imply any special type of awareness; loneliness does. A chief element of loneliness is a painful feeling that tells us something unpleasantly important about ourselves. All types of loneliness that I have studied have this element of painful self-awareness.

Loneliness also speaks of relationship, or rather, the absence or weakness of relationship. There are many different forms of relationship that can produce loneliness. One can be lonely for another person, a group, a home, a homeland, a tradition, a type of activity, and even a sense of meaning, or God.

A notable factor in much modern American loneliness is the quality of surprise. Loneliness so often strikes us unexpectedly. If you plan a trip by yourself, you prepare for lonely moments along the way. When they occur, you can handle them. When loneliness happens where you least expect it, such as in the home, at work, or among friends, it has a tremendous impact. We often do not know how to cope. It can make us confused, distraught, depressed, frightened, and even outraged.

Loneliness that frustrates our expectations is particularly hard to manage. It is this kind that so frequently disturbs people today. In nomadic and hunting societies persons were reared to expect long periods of aloneness. Facing loneliness was once a mark of manhood in American civilization. In an earlier era, Americans were reared to face life on their own in the struggle to achieve success through work. In that sense, being alone was part of the definition of successful living.

In this century the emphasis has been different. "Making it" has come to include "getting along with others." Learning to "fit in" is stressed at home, in school, in churches, and even in sports. Growing up in America often means developing expectations of involvement, popularity, and numerous attachments.

Today, as we tend to evaluate our personal success in terms of being liked, loneliness strikes with a force that is hard to handle. It suggests failure or at least a frightening vulnerability.

One reason loneliness hangs on is because people are either not fully aware of it or not prepared for it. They push it out of their consciousness. They try to find some remedy in drugs, in "busyness," in overly dependent relationships, or by increasing their memberships. I am convinced that much of the fear associated with loneliness, as well as many behavioral problems that arise from too much of it, are unnecessary. We will continue to misunderstand the pain and the problem associated with loneliness until we recognize how complex its multiple causes or sources can be.

I have chosen to refer to these different sources and types of loneliness in terms of *dimensions*. After studying a variety of expressions of lonely people in different contexts, I now classify these expressions according to the object that a person feels is missing or from which he or she feels separated. The dimension aspect refers to the area of relationship a person perceives to be the source of his suffering. There seem to be *five* fairly distinct dimensions. I have labeled them: *interpersonal, social, cultural, cosmic,* and *psychological.* The term dimension suggests that the loneliness has a particular source and also constitutes a distinct type. However, there are few pure types. Sometimes people may experience several of these dimensions at once, often without being fully aware of it. More importantly, they indicate the extent of distress that lonely people may experience. For example, when individuals experience loneliness in four or five dimensions simultaneously and over a long period of time, they can find the stress intolerable and eventually break down.

Of the five the *interpersonal dimension* is generally the most familiar type. In this situation one person misses another. Often it is most intense when a very special person is missed. For example, one English study done by the Women's Group on Public Welfare, a social action organization, suggested that in this context the worst loneliness is a communication gap, such as one preceding the dissolution of a marriage:

"Perhaps there is no greater loneliness than that suffered when a marriage breaks down, particularly in a situation where partnership has so far foundered that communications between the two have become impossible," the study stated. "The divorced and widowed are often more lonely than those who have never been married. This deeper loneliness could be due not only to the loss of a close companion but also where, having married young they have never learned to live with or face up to loneliness in earlier life."

The *social dimension* of loneliness is another familiar type. Here the individual feels cut off from a group that he or she considers important. Here it is a social relationship rather than an interpersonal one that is felt to be ruptured or lacking. Terms such as *ostracism, exile, rejection, blackballed, fired, discrimination,* and *expelled,* to mention only a few, resonate with the sense of this particular kind of loneliness. Often one gets an important sense of self-worth through membership and participation in a particular social environment. Once that membership is denied and participation is no longer possible, a person feels not just cut off but lacking in self-esteem. Not surprisingly a person who feels this social isolation often develops a low self-image and feels impotent to change this unsatisfactory relationship. Literature of minority groups, deviants, and more recently both the youth and the elderly is filled with lamentation and outrage at this kind of loneliness that is unwittingly imposed by society.

When these two forms of loneliness occur in the same individual simultaneously over a prolonged period of time, the result can be unfortunate in growth as well as behavior. Dr. Gisela Konopka, professor of social work at the University of Minnesota, found, for example, that complex, chronic loneliness was a primary factor contributing to the delinquency of adolescent girls. They were unwanted at home, often had no close friends, and were rejected at school and by clubs. Without any meaningful social role in which to demonstrate their worth and have it approved, as well as being without intimate communication, they acted out their feelings of lonely worthlessness in destructive acts of crime. The same applies to boys. The black Puerto Rican author, Piri Thomas, in his autobiography *Down These Mean Streets,* traces back the violent behavior, which led to his imprisonment, to an agonizing loneliness that stemmed from two sources: a lack of communication in his family, and ostracism by a white society because of his dark skin.

Retired persons may also experience an unexpected frustration associated with job severance. These people feel cut off, not merely from work, but from a network of relationships that had provided them with companionship and meaningful support. Housewives, too, have complained of similar combinations of lonely feelings, especially after several moves which leave them cut off from old friends, neighborhoods, and favorite groups.

My own research suggests that there may be a connection between rage and unmitigated complex loneliness. I have found that as you press people with questions on their loneliness they get very violent. In one group I had there was a divorced woman who felt extremely hostile toward her husband. She had lost her father at an early age and looked to her husband as a kind of father figure. He was a failure in every conceivable way and as a result she had bottled up this frustrated rage toward him. One day I threw a pillow down on the floor and said "There's your husband. Do to it what you would do to him." She killed him. Stomped him to death.

I believe that further investigation will bear out this tentative conclusion: very lonely people, who get angry rather than get depressed, will be prone to express their lonely frustration in destructive ways. I do not think it is mere coincidence that we are witnessing an unequalled rise in violence at the same time loneliness is so pervasive and intense. Personal accounts like that of Piri Thomas and studies of the Watts riots have shown that loneliness can be linked with violence when it is combined with a deep sense of frustration, especially in the economic and political realms.

The *cultural dimension* of loneliness refers to an experience some people have who feel themselves separated from a traditional system of meanings and a way of life. Immigrants and people who are continually mobile often experience this in the form of homesickness. People in America can sense this kind of loneliness if they feel the American heritage to be disintegrating. The term alienation may point to this form of loneliness, when it refers to a particular perception. Alienated people often feel that they are strangers in their own land. Members of American minority groups are particularly prone to this kind of loneliness. Even with close family relations they sometimes suffer from lingering loneliness, of being unable to identify with the American cultural heritage.

The feelings linked with cultural dislocation and culture shock likewise indicate a distinct form of loneliness, a sense of being uprooted and out of place. The nostalgia for those "good old days" when there was predictable order and cohesiveness also suggests this form of loneliness. In some cases loneliness may merely be a part of alienation; but in others, where there is a definite awareness of being separated from a meaningful tradition, I think the term loneliness is more accurate.

The *cosmic dimension* of loneliness may take a variety of forms, but essentially it refers to an experience in which a person feels out of touch with an ultimate source of life and meaning. Often it takes a religious form. Religious persons sometimes lament a felt absence of God. The Bible is filled with expressions of lonely persons longing for God. Much contemporary religion also answers to this need of loneliness, promising people a sense of presence and communion in their condition of existential estrangement or loneliness.

In workshops I have had persons express this cosmic loneliness in various ways. One middle-aged man confessed that a constant source of frustration came in the form of "missing God." Earlier he had been a strong believer, but now was an agnostic. He missed the sense of relatedness his youthful faith had given him. Religious persons who have been divorced have found themselves excluded from their religious community and they too have felt the anguish of this kind of loneliness. Some people have expressed a cosmic loneliness in their perception of the apparent absurdity of life. Erich Fromm suggested in *Escape from Freedom* that the experience of being morally and cosmically lonely is characteristic of persons who have realized the implications of autonomy in the modern world. Flight into conformity, becoming overly dependent on others, obsessive concern with others, a compulsive drive for achievement and recognition are some of the unproductive attempts of people to escape this dimension of loneliness.

The *psychological dimension* refers both to the experience a person has of being separate from himself as well as to the personal impact of the other four causes. A student who was in one of my courses made an observation that I have found many respond to: "I am loneliest when I am out of touch with myself." William James and C. J. Jung suggested the experience of a divided self is the root of modern man's search for a deeply personal religion or self-actualization or both. Much success of the Human Potential movement is related to the resolving of loneliness within one's self as well as that which comes from the lack of any intimate relationships with others. The perception of one's self as divided is a distinct form of "suffering self-recognition of separateness." Here again one usually stumbles into this perception unawares so that this loneliness is aggravated by a clash of expectations.

The psychological dimension indicates a distinctly internal source of loneliness, whereas the other four dimensions specifically refer to external sources. Some aspects of loneliness can be traced to personality features that possibly stand in the way of self-actualization. Shyness, fear of loving and being loved, self-pity, and the development of a schizoid personality are examples of traits that can contribute to loneliness. But one point I emphasize as a sociologist is that *personal troubles often come from outside,* even though the individual experiences them as very private and intimately his own. This sociological analysis helps to get us beyond a narrow psychological and everyday notion that somehow an individual is at fault when he is feeling lonely. On the contrary, if an individual has lost a parent, a friend, or child in death, has moved from home, has changed or lost his job, is rejected by his group, and has lost his religious faith, is confused by his ambiguous American heritage, and does not feel deep, abiding loneliness, then I suspect that something drastic is lacking within him. Much loneliness that I have examined is a normal response to breaks in an individual's important relationships.

In all five dimensions there is the element of a suffering self-recognition of separateness from something, though each general type can be distinguished from the others. In each situation there are different kinds of relationships lacking. Consequently, there are different needs to be met. Recognizing specific needs proper to different dimensions is extremely important when someone is trying to cope with loneliness. For example, a person who sorely misses a special other person will not have the need satisfied by joining a group. Yet in spite of an impressive history of failure, we continue to encourage widows to compensate by joining organizations. That is, we tell

"HIDEWAYS"

6

& THAT KEEPS
YOU AWAY
FROM ME...

11

& IT
HIDES ME FROM
YOU...

12

I WISH I HAD
A THIMBLE...

ᴛᴏᴍ McCain

1

IF I SHUT THE DOOR TO
MY HOUSE, YOU CAN'T
COME INSIDE...

7

MOST OF THE TIME... BUT
WHEN IT DOESN'T, I CRAWL
INTO A SHOE BOX
I KEEP IN THE TV BOX...

2

& EVERYTHING'S FINE
BECAUSE I DON'T
THINK ABOUT YOU....

8

EXCEPT SOMETIMES SO
THEN I CLIMB INTO
A PRESCRIPTION BOTTLE
INSIDE THE SHOE BOX...

3

EXCEPT SOMETIMES &
THOSE TIMES I LOCK
MYSELF IN MY ROOM...

9

& IF IT DOESN'T, I ROLL
UP INTO A BALL
BECAUSE I DON'T HAVE
ANYTHING SMALLER TO GET INTO...

4

BECAUSE NOTHING THERE
REMINDS ME
OF YOU...

5

BUT SOMETIMES SOMETHING
DOES & I HIDE IN A
BOX THE TV CAME IN...

10

WHERE NOTHING YOU
DID OR SAID
CAN REACH ME...

them to look to the social dimension to satisfy an interpersonal need. We offer hand-holding to members of minority groups who suffer from a sense of exclusion, instead of creating a place for them to experience participation. Many attempts to cope with loneliness are unsuccessful because the need of a particular type of loneliness has not been met. The conventional wisdom that recommends lonely people keep busy does not confront the problem of loneliness. It dodges it and instead applies compulsive activity like a narcotic. I have been told by countless widows that they have tried this formula only to find that they return home to an empty house exhausted and all the more vulnerable to the painful void of their lives.

If we recognize loneliness as a significant form of self-perception, consider its context, and identify the dimensions involved, then we will be better prepared to face it realistically and positively. We need to get away from the simplistic notion that for loneliness "all you need is love." Love is often not enough. Social action is sometimes necessary and individual preparation for loneliness is essential.

If more than just an interpersonal dimension is present, then a more complex form of response will be needed. For example, persons suffering from both interpersonal and social loneliness are more prone to low self-esteem. The latter can jeopardize close, interpersonal relationships and discourage persons from taking an active role in a group. Meaningful participation in a group and developing some social role of importance can help combat the troubles stemming from the societal dimension of loneliness. It also can improve self-esteem, and prepare a person to become more ready for mature friendships and love.

If we are to meet the needs of lonely people effectively, we must get at the sources of their loneliness. Too often we treat loneliness merely as a symptom; that's one reason it keeps recurring. To confront loneliness in the modern world, our response will have to be a multi-level one. This concept of the five dimensions of loneliness can be helpful to social scientists, counselors, and anyone in detecting intelligently the types of loneliness we may encounter in the course of our lives. It also suggests the various sources from which it arises, and the multi-dimensional approach needed to cope adequately with the complex problem of loneliness.

Follow-Up

1. *Sadler describes five distinct dimensions of loneliness: interpersonal, social, cultural, cosmic, and psychological. Explain how you have experienced each of these dimensions, or as many as you can; how you handled the particular type of loneliness; and its consequences for you.*
2. *Sadler states that loneliness often strikes us unexpectedly. Not being prepared for it, we become confused, frightened, depressed, or find ways to avoid it. Discuss or write about your reactions to his argument.*
3. *Choose any other aspect of this article and write about or discuss your response.*

My Tyrant

Tom Peyton

In 1776 a handful of hardy and determined souls decided to leave the tyranny of the English government. Their purpose was to find the freedom to live a life they chose, instead of one chosen for them. They sought independence. This past Fourth of July, I discovered the tyrant of my own mind.

I wandered downtown through the crowds of people and watched happy couples embracing. I observed families celebrating together and kids running through the blocked-off city streets. There were smiling faces everywhere—except for mine. The tyrant in my mind spoke: You are alone, Tom. Totally alone. You are all by yourself. Incomplete without a partner, without a spouse. The rest of society is complete. Look at how happy everyone is—it's because they have someone. You, Tom, have no one. The voice beat at my heart and soul. My shoulders tightened and my mood darkened; my body started to feel very tired. My thoughts turned to the incompleteness of the moment and my own incompleteness. My head lowered, heavy with thought. My eyes focused on the blades of grass in front of me, and my thoughts turned to my divorce.

HOPING FOR WHOLENESS

Since my divorce, I have spent more than a year waiting to feel whole again. Waiting for the tyrant in my mind to ease. Waiting for the voice of guilt and shame to quiet. Waiting for something or someone to still the abusive chatter that swirls in your head when you think you have created a situation so ugly, so hideous that you must keep it to yourself. It is a lonely feeling to carry this weight of guilt and shame. This weight is of my own creation, I thought. The guilt is my guilt, and the shame of failure is my shame. I am the one giving it the power to ruin my day. I am the one letting it destroy my mental health. I should be the one to get myself out of this insane dialogue with myself. But I could not. I was trapped, and I surrendered to the rambling in my head. At that moment a drop of rain landed on my forehead, then another and another. In the middle of my self-absorption, it was raining. Perfect, I thought. Perfect?

I looked up and noticed that the sun was still shining. I gazed to the left and saw a beautiful rainbow arching across the sky. A smile crept onto my face.

"Guilt Trip" by Tom McCain. Copyright © 1996.

For a moment, the tyrant stopped. My brain grew quiet, and the only thing that existed was the rainbow. At that moment, my past was in the past, and my future was too far away to see. At that moment, I was completely present with myself. I was no longer searching for my feeling of completeness—I was experiencing it. I was with myself, not by myself.

In the chaos of thousands of people, I understood that I had never been alone. That for 30 years, I have lived this drama we call life, feeling as if I needed someone in my life to feel complete. And for the entire time, that someone was me. I laughed at the irony of it, then felt the sadness of the illusion. To expect someone else to make you whole is a path of misery and depression.

I wrote this very personal column for my own healing. I decided to share it because I know there are people in this world who have the same illusion—that they are alone. I hope, for a moment today, that they understand that they are with themselves, and it's a great place to be. I understand, too, that I will slip and falter along this path of self-acceptance. But, for the rest of the evening, I quietly celebrated with myself. A celebration of independence from the tyranny of my own mind. Freedom on the Fourth of July.

Follow-Up

1. *What is your response to these statements?*
   - *I have lived this drama we call life, feeling as if I needed someone in my life to feel complete. And for the entire time, that someone was me.*
   - *You are alone, Tom. Totally alone. . . . The rest of society is complete. Look at how happy everyone is—it's because they have someone. You, Tom, have no one.*
2. *Do you have an inner "tyrant" at times? How does it influence how you see yourself?*

You Never Know

Nels Goud

There are times when someone does something so totally unexpected, so outside of what you thought possible, that there is no choice but to change the way you think. Here's one such instance.

During my senior year in high school there was a freshman I'll call Joanie. Today Joanie would be placed in a class for the mildly mentally handicapped. But my school had no special education program, so Joanie was put in general curriculum classes where she performed poorly but was passed anyway. Beside her limited intellectual capacity, Joanie was saddled with other qualities that placed her near the bottom of the prevailing status scales. Her face was pocked with pimples and her tongue protruded slightly. She spoke with a lisp. Joanie had a very out-of-date, drab, and baggy wardrobe. She had a strong body odor. Her long, loping strides seemed out of place on her plump, short frame. It was a common sight to see guys following directly behind her mocking her gait. A newcomer, Joanie was cast into high school society with no friends and seemingly no social skills to find any.

Soon Joanie became a laughing stock and scapegoat for the insecure members of the school culture. Strangely it did not affect her behavior. She remained very friendly and smiled a lot. Joanie had one organizing force in her life—to be liked. She would do almost anything to get someone to notice or talk to her. It did not make any difference if the attention was respectful or derogatory. She seemed to exist to belong to someone, something, anything.

Joanie often asked "Do you like me?" This would usually happen after someone told her that "Larry" liked her. She would then seek out Larry and ask him "Do you like me?" Larry, of course, would loudly protest in the midst of a chorus of guffaws and taunts of his buddies. Joanie would just stand there and smile, not completely aware of what was going on, but hanging on to the chance that maybe this time it was true. Besides, it was a human connection.

If students treated Joanie with civility, they did so at a price. They would have a shadow for days that made it impossible for them to have a normal social life. These students soon learned to escape physically or adopt techniques of polite disregard. Then Joanie would hang around the outside of a group—a human satellite.

It was a big deal in those days to attend dances following football games. Everyone was into human connections at these events. There seemed to be a ritual. For the first half hour or so the guys would be slouched against one wall of the gym trying to look "cool" but afraid to dance. The girls would be dancing with each other, or gathered in small groups occasionally stealing glances at some "cool" guy across the floor. It was the slow ballad that awakened a few slouchers to saunter across the floor to ask a girl to dance. Then the others girls grabbed a few wall-huggers. Soon the floor was back-to-back with young adolescents discovering all sorts of human connections. All except Joanie. Surprisingly, she attended these dances knowing she would be isolated for the whole evening. Joanie would stand in the corner alone and stare into the mass of swaying couples. After a couple hours her parents would arrive to take her home.

At one of these dances one of those moments occurred when you know there is hope for the species—all because of a classmate of mine named Lance. Lance was an athlete, very good looking, a senior, and he drove a new white convertible. In addition, he dated girls from out of town (a *big* status point). Lance was a popular guy—so popular that he could go over and ask a girl, any girl, to dance during the first dance of the night. I wasn't jealous at all. I had a better baseball batting average than he, and besides, I could slouch better.

About an hour into the dance Lance was dancing about his 50th dance and, naturally, with the best looking junior girl in the whole world. The song ended and the next song was Elvis's "Love Me Tender." This ballad even brought *me* out of my slouch, and I went over to ask the new clarinetist to dance. I happened to notice that Lance walked over to Joanie's corner. He asked her to dance. She didn't know how to dance, but this did not matter to Lance. He swept her into his arms and led her through the best fox-trot I've ever seen.

Joanie shadowed Lance for at least a week after the dance. He just politely acknowledged her presence and went his way. No one ribbed Lance. They were too astounded, or afraid of getting knots pounded on their heads. Some of us even learned something.

I saw Lance at a high school reunion fifteen years later and told him of my observations. He had forgotten it. He mentioned that Joanie had since married and was living on the edge of town. Joanie finally belonged.

Follow-Up

1. *A strongly felt need to belong can often make individuals act in unexpected ways. Describe how you have experienced this phenomenon.*
2. *In the story Lance showed compassion when no one else did. Have you witnessed or been part of similar acts? If so, describe one and explain how it affected you afterwards.*
3. *Respond to any other aspect of the article.*

Little Joys

Abe Arkoff

When Salman Rushdie was sentenced to death by the Ayatollah Khomeini for writing "The Satanic Verses," he went into hiding. Reminiscing about the life he left behind, he said, "What I miss is ordinary life: walking down the street, browsing in a bookshop, going to a grocery store, going to a movie. I've always been a big movie addict, and I haven't been in a cinema for a year."

"I haven't driven a car for a year," Rushdie continued. "I really love driving, and suddenly I have to sit in the back seat all the time. What I miss is just that, these tiny little things."

The value of little things was what playwright Thornton Wilder had in mind when he wrote *Our Town*, which proved to be his most famous work. The play was, he said, "an attempt to find a value above all price for the smallest events in our daily life." In this simple but moving drama, he eloquently shows what is extraordinary about the most ordinary and commonplace.

In *Our Town*, Emily, who has died in early adulthood, finds she can return to relive a day of her life. When she returns to relive her twelfth birthday, she finds her experience—from the vantage point of death—too poignant and in too great a contrast to the living who move matter-of-factly through the day. Overcome, she returns to death saying:

> Good-by, good-by, world. Good-by Grover's Corners . . . Mama and Papa. Good-by to clocks ticking . . . and Mama's sunflowers. And food and coffee. And new-ironed dresses and hot baths . . . and sleeping and waking up. Oh, earth you're too wonderful for anybody to realize you . . . Do any human beings realize life while they live it?—every, every minute?

My favorite essay on joy is a brief paper by Hermann Hesse. Although written almost 100 years ago, it sounds remarkably up-to-date as it laments the speed of "modern life," with the feverish pursuit of entertainment and ironically less and less joy. Hesse reminds the reader of the little joys available in daily rounds if one will only take a moment for them. He concludes his essay, "It is the small joys first of all that are granted to us for recreation, for daily relief and disburdenment, not the great ones."

Some recent research suggests that Hesse's advice is good psychology. Seek out as many as possible of the small joys each day. Studying both college-age and older persons, Professor Ed Diener of the University of Illinois has found that it is frequent little joys rather than an occasional big joy that make for a general sense of well-being. While less intense positive emotions are common, intense positive emotions are infrequent; furthermore, such intense events are often purchased at the price of past unhappy events and can serve to diminish the sensation of future positive events. Diener found happiness to be associated with those persons who frequently experience positive emotions rather than those whose positive experiences are intense. Thus, Diener and Hesse agree that the key to well-being is to fill one's days with little joys.

More evidence concerning the limited value of big joy was found by a research team who compared the levels of happiness in 22 major lottery winners with the levels of a control group similar in other respects. Each group indicated how happy they were at present, had been earlier (for the winners, before winning, for the controls, 6 months earlier), and expected to be in a couple of years. Significant differences between winners and controls in previous, present, or anticipated levels of happiness: none.

Even more striking results were found when both groups were asked how pleasant they currently found seven activities: eating breakfast, reading a magazine, watching television, talking with a friend, hearing a funny joke, getting a compliment, and buying clothes. Compared to controls, the winners found significantly less pleasure in these activities. Although the emotional big high of winning had not brought a significant, lasting increase in happiness, seemingly, by comparison, everyday little highs had paled.

The Chinese philosopher Lin Yutang passionately described the little pleasures that made his own life joyful. Indeed there were many, and in his enthusiasm, he gave a number of them first place. For example, he wrote, "If there is a greater happiness than lying in the sun, I'd like to be told." But then he noted, "If a man will be sensible and . . . count on his fingers how many things give him enjoyment, invariably he will find food is the first one." Still, later, seemingly to settle the matter, he set down the final truth: "If one's bowels move, one is happy, and if they don't move one is unhappy. That is all there is to it."

There is much in our day we think of as routine that could become little joys if approached in another way. Rushdie noted that he missed things he once thought completely unimportant—even chores—such as shopping for groceries. What once were tasks now were seen as privileges.

George Leonard recommends the Zen strategy of finding joy in the commonplace. What this requires is not a change of activity but rather a change of attitude. Leonard writes, "You might think that the value of Zen practice lies in the unwavering apprehension of the present moment while sitting motionless. But a visit to a Zen retreat quickly reveals that potentially, *everything* is meditation—building a stone wall, eating, walking from one place to another, sweeping a hallway."

Psychologist Frank Dougherty has made an important distinction between the pursuit of relief and the pursuit of delight. Some of us who (perhaps without knowing it) have spent our lives pursuing relief, wonder why we never feel delight, but no amount of relief can produce delight. People whose minds are set on relief work to make sure that everything is taken care of and under control. There will be time for delight, they think, when things settle down, but of course, things never do.

To pursue delight requires a different mindset, and we can pursue delight even though everything isn't in order. We don't let the work waiting on Monday morning interfere with our enjoyment of the picnic this lovely Sunday afternoon.

Sir Alexander Korda recalled talking with Winston Churchill during the war when some bad news arrived. Churchill glanced at his watch and announced he was due back at 10 Downing Street. "It will all look different after a good lunch, a cigar, and a nap," he said. "Besides, Marshall Stalin has sent us some excellent caviar by courier, and it would be a shame not to enjoy it."

Often, the event that produces relief for one person delivers delight to another who approaches it in a very different way. In this connection, one of my students recalled a backpack trip he had been on with a group of others. Each day, the same person was first to reach their destination. One evening, the group was sharing the memories of the day's beautiful vistas, and this person finally spoke and said, "I guess all I really saw today was the top of my shoes."

Years ago, Sol Gordon wrote a brief set of instructions on how to be happy in an unhappy world. It was simply "to be able to enjoy at least the number of things equal to our age." Gordon was 51 years old at the time, and he wrote out the 51 things he enjoyed. The list included bittersweet stories and chocolate, uninterrupted classical music, reading slowly the good novelists, being warm and intimate with people he really cared about, and fantasizing that one of his still unpublished books was number one or number two on the *New York Times* best-sellers list.

Following Gordon's advice, my students and I make up our own lists of little joys when we are on the topic of happiness. I have found that just making up a list and sharing it with others makes one feel good.

As director of a freshman seminar program and coordinator of a program for older persons, I have taught some of the youngest and oldest students on my campus. The older students seem to compose their long lists of joys as easily as the youngest students do their much shorter ones.

My oldest student (and the one most full of fun and joy) was 91 years old when she made out her list and had no trouble in arriving at 91 items. Now 95, she is recovering from open-heart surgery and writes that she is enjoying in anticipation her next trip to Hawaii.*

*Since I wrote this, she has made the trip to Hawaii, and we celebrated her 96th birthday together; she is as full of fun and joy as ever.

After my students compose their little joy lists, I ask them to go back and put a star or asterisk by each item they have actually enjoyed in the past 30 days. What good is something that can bring joy if one doesn't take time to enjoy it? I enjoy reading my students' lists as much as my own. Most of the items cost very little or nothing at all. One of the most common items, of course, is chocolate. It appears on Sol Gordon's list and, I confess, my own. However, other common items are calorie-free, such as music, reading, nature, movies, a favorite TV program or comic strip.

The most uncommon joy producer that I have seen on any list is "Standing in the barn loft—after feeding hay to about 100 cattle—and listening to them crunch or munch the hay." It was on the list of one of my older students—a 64-year-old man from Tennessee. His whole list was quite special and not only because it didn't mention chocolate even once. Other items on his list included giving a flower to a lovely lady and watching her eyes light up; sitting on the patio and watching the fields and valleys and mountains change with the shadows as the sun moves across the sky; looking at—and feeling proud of—the many afghans and quilts his mother made and gave to him; driving a good, responsive car on a curvy mountain road; and after a hard, tiring day outside, a drink of good straight sour mash whiskey, mixed with a little 7-Up and cranberry juice.

Make up your list of little joys today, and make sure that in 30 days, each has a star by it.

Follow-Up

1. *Make a list of all the things you are able to deeply enjoy, and include as many items as you are years old. Put a star or asterisk in front of each item you have actually enjoyed in the past 30 days. Then write an account of your thoughts and feelings as you worked on and read over your list.*

2. *Live an ordinary day as you usually would, except be especially aware of everything in the day that brings you joy. Before you go to sleep, write an account of this experience.*

3. *Live an ordinary day as you usually would, except make the most of each joyful moment or each opportunity for one. Before you go to sleep, write an account of this experience.*

4. *How much is your life a pursuit of relief, and how much a pursuit of delight? Discuss this aspect of your life.*

Jealousy and Envy

The Demons Within Us

Jon Queijo

Rick and Liz seemed to have a wonderful marriage; they did everything together. This changed suddenly, however, when Liz's ex-boyfriend began working at her law firm. Besieged by insecurity, Rick began calling Liz's office at odd hours and at night questioned her suspiciously. In a coup de grace, he burst in on her during a business luncheon and falsely accused her of having an affair.

Ann worked extremely hard to achieve success as a real estate agent. Her satisfaction turned sour, however, when a new agent was hired who managed to work less, yet made more sales. Ann hid her dislike of the new agent by offering to take her phone messages while she was out. When Ann began making more sales than her rival, no one made the connection between this turn of events and Ann's tendency to "accidentally" forget to deliver certain phone messages.

The jealous rage of a lover. The shameful actions of envy. Despite our better intentions, most of us feel these emotions dozens of times in our lifetimes. Pulling us apart from lovers, friends, family members, co-workers and even perfect strangers, jealousy and envy can devastate our lives and cause effects ranging from sadness, anger and depression, to estrangement, abuse and even violence.

Beyond our own lives, the power of these emotions has spawned countless works of poetry and prose and triggered numerous historical events. Perhaps for this reason society proclaimed judgment on jealousy and envy thousands of years ago, with the verdict coming down harder on envy. For example, while the pain of jealousy has been forever immor-

talized in poetry and song, the shame of envy emerges as early as the Ten Commandments: "Thou shalt not covet thy neighbor's house, field, wife or anything that is thy neighbor's." In fact, envy is despicable enough to be considered one of the "Seven Deadly Sins," taking its place alongside pride, gluttony, lust, sloth, anger and greed.

Although we see jealousy and envy arise in numerous situations, their basic definitions are fairly simple: jealousy is "the fear of losing a relationship" (romantic, parental, sibling, friendship); and envy is "the longing for something someone else has" (wealth, possessions, beauty, talent, position).

Despite these definitions and the numerous philosophers, poets and scientists who have pondered these emotions, some remarkably fundamental questions remain: What causes jealousy and envy? Are the emotions actually different? What do they feel like? What are the best ways to cope with these feelings? Why do we often use the terms interchangeably? And what are their implications for society?

Researchers have taken various approaches to answer these questions. The biological view, for example, says that jealousy and envy serve a basic purpose—the emotions lead to biochemical changes that spur the individual to take action and improve the situation. The evolutionary view holds that jealousy may enhance survival by keeping parents together, thus increasing protection of the offspring. Other explanations range from the reasonable—envy stems from parental attitudes that make a child feel inferior; to the bizarre—the emotions begin in infants when the mother withholds breast-feeding.

Probably the most practical understanding of jealousy and envy, however, emerges from the work of social psychologists—researchers who look at the way people react to each other and society. To them, jealousy and envy arise when the right mix of internal *and* external ingredients are present in society.

"I tend to look at jealousy and envy in terms of motivation and self-esteem," explains Peter Salovey, a social psychologist at Yale University. "It's the interaction between what's important to you and what's happening in the environment. The common denominator is this threat to something that's very important to the person—something that defines self-worth."

Richard Smith, a social psychologist at Boston University who has conducted several studies on jealousy and envy, emphasizes external factors, such as how society affects our view of ourselves. "My perspective is from social comparisons," he explains, "which says we have no objective opinion for evaluating our abilities, so we look at others."

Smith, like Salovey, also stresses internal factors—the role of self-esteem, for example—in determining whether we will feel jealous or envious in any given situation. "People who are dissatisfied with themselves are primed for having other people's talents and possessions impinge on them," Smith points out. "If, on the other hand, you're satisfied with yourself, then what other people have or do won't unduly raise your expectations for yourself, and you should be less likely to feel envy."

Embarrassed by his display of jealousy, Rick apologizes to Liz and they discuss the problem. Soon they realize that while Rick loves Liz and fears losing her, something else is at work here. Because Liz's ex-boyfriend is a lawyer, he possesses skills Rick does not. While Rick is proud of his ability as a store manager, he fears Liz's ex-boyfriend could lure her away with other skills.

Feeling guilty about her actions, Ann calls a friend for support. Ann knows she feels inadequate because the new agent is succeeding in a career that is very important to her, but that doesn't explain everything; others have done better whom Ann has not envied. Then it occurs to her: What bothers her is the way the woman was bettering Ann. She was more outgoing and self-confident—two skills about which Ann has always felt insecure.

As Rick and Ann's situations illustrate, if someone is unsure about an ability—such as Rick and his law knowledge or Ann and her communication skills—then a social situation can bring out that insecurity. "In envy," notes Salovey, "the threat may come from someone else's possessions or attributes. In jealousy the situation is the same, except that the other person's possessions or attributes cause you to fear losing the relationship. Either way, somebody else threatens your self-esteem."

Yet Salovey emphasizes that it is not as simple as saying someone is at risk for these emotions if they have a low opinion of themselves. "It's low self-esteem in a specific *area*," he explains. "If you have a low opinion about your physical looks or occupation, then that's the area in which you're more likely to be vulnerable. You feel it when you confront somebody else who is superior to you in that respect."

From Smith's point of view, the key is how that person compares him or herself to others. In one study, for example, he found that envy was strongest among people who performed below their expectation in an area that was important to them and then confronted someone who functioned better. In a related study, Smith also found that a person's "risk" for feeling jealous or envious increases with the increased importance they put on the quality.

While much of this may sound like common sense, in fact little research has been done to establish even the most basic ground rules of jealousy and envy. For example, are the two emotions actually different? What do people feel when they are jealous or envious? Despite centuries of long-held assumptions, only recently have researchers begun to answer these questions scientifically.

Smith and his colleagues, for example, recently conducted a study to see if the classic distinctions between the two emotions are actually true. Their findings—presented last August at the annual convention of the American Psychological Association—validated what we have always suspected. Jealous people tend to feel a fear of loss, betrayal, loneliness, suspicion and uncertainty. Envious people, on the other hand, tend to feel inferior, longing for what another has, guilt over feeling ill will towards someone, shame and a tendency to deny the emotion.

The study was not an idle exercise in stating the obvious. It was designed to help clear an ongoing debate about jealousy and envy and our curious tendency not only to mix up the terms, but to experience an overlap of both emotions.

Consider, for example, the following uses of the word jealousy: Bruce was jealous when his girlfriend began talking to another man at the party; the boy cried in a fit of jealousy when his parents paid attention to the new baby; Ellen became jealous when her friend began spending more time at the health club. Nothing unusual with any of these uses of jealousy—they all refer to someone's "fear of losing a relationship."

Now, however, consider these uses: The professor, jealous of his colleague's success, broke into his lab and ruined his experiment; Mary is always complaining of being jealous of her sister's beautiful blonde hair; Mark admits that he is jealous of John's athletic ability. All of these situations actually refer to envy, "the longing for something someone else has." Researchers have noticed the mix-up and it has led them to question how different the feelings really are.

"In everyday language it's clear that people use the terms interchangeably," notes Smith, adding, "For that reason, there's naturally some confusion about whether they're different." In a recent study, however, Smith and his colleagues found the mix-up only works one way, with jealousy being the broader term. That is, jealousy is used sometimes in place of envy, but envy is rarely used when referring to jealousy. So while you might say, "I'm jealous of Paul's new Mercedes," you would never say, "When she left her husband, he flew into an *envious* rage."

Is there an underlying reason for why the terms are used interchangeably? One reason people may use jealousy in place of envy, and not vice versa, is because of the social stigma attached to envy. But Salovey and Smith both point to another reason for the overlap.

Dave and Marcia had been dating for a year when Marcia decided she wanted to see other men. Dave was devastated—not only because he cared for her, but because he was older and feared his age was working against him. One evening he bumped into Marcia, arm-in-arm with another man. As Dave talked to the couple, sarcasm led to verbal abuse, until finally Dave took a swing at Marcia's date— a man at least 10 years his junior.

In case you haven't guessed, Dave wanted back more than his relationship with Marcia; he also wanted the return of his youth. He was feeling a painful mixture of jealousy *and* envy. Explains Salovey, "The same feelings emerge when your relationship is threatened by someone else as when you'd like something that person has. I think one reason is that in most romantic situations, envy plays a role. You're jealous because you're going to lose the relationship, but you're also envious because there is something the other person has that allows him to be attractive to the person you care about."

Because this overlap occurs so frequently, Salovey has found the best way to understand jealousy and envy is to examine each *situation*. In addition, because jealousy is the more encompassing term, he views envy as a form of jealousy and distinguishes the two

COMPARING OURSELVES TO OTHERS

In Sickness and In Health

Envy, according to Richard Smith, arises when we compare ourselves to others and can't cope with what we see. Indeed, he believes that the way in which we cope with "social comparisons" plays an important role in our physical as well as mental health.

Smith theorizes that we use one of four "comparison styles" to cope with social differences. Two of these styles are "constructive" to well-being, while two are "destructive." "It's a difficult problem to tackle," says Smith, "but we're trying to measure these styles and see if they predict a person's general satisfaction with life or ability to cope with illness." For example, he notes, "There's considerable evidence" that one way people cope with serious illness is by focusing on others who are not doing as well.

Smith has arranged the four comparison styles in a matrix, with the descriptions in each box referring to the characteristics of that style. "*Upward*-Constructive," for example, represents those who compare themselves to others who are better off, and use it as a healthy stimulus. In this category, "You don't feel hostile to others who are better," says Smith, "because you hope to be like them. It suggests that upward comparisons are not necessarily bad."

"*Upward*-Destructive," however, shows how comparing yourself to those doing better can be unhealthy. Envy, resentment, Type A behavior and poor health all fit into this category. Smith points to a study that looked at personalities of people who had heart attacks, "and the only dimension that predicted heart disease was this jealousy-suspicion trait."

What Smith calls "*Downward*-Constructive," refers to people who compare themselves to those worse off, and use it to feel better about themselves. Such people, says Smith, "realize that others aren't doing so well and how lucky they are. There's some solid evidence in the health literature showing the value of that kind of comparison."

Finally, "*Downward*-Destructive," describes those who get pleasure out of comparing themselves to others who are worse off. "I'd call the effect 'schadenfreude,' or joy at the suffering of others," says Smith. "It's akin to sadism and it's probably not conducive to health."

"What's interesting about all four comparison styles," notes Smith, "is that they don't necessarily have any relation to reality. They reflect what people construe and focus on." While Smith stresses, "This is all speculative," he adds that "my feeling is that 'Upward-Destructive' explains people's hostility in terms of their social comparison context. It shows why their relation to people doing better leads to envy and why they'd feel hostile to begin with."

—J. Q.

by the terms "romantic jealousy," the fear of losing a relationship; and "social-comparison jealousy," the envy that arises when people compare traits like age, intelligence, possession and talent.

Smith agrees with Salovey that one reason people confuse the terms may be that envy is present in most cases of jealousy. Nevertheless, he takes issue with Salovey's use of the term "social-comparison jealousy." "It may be true that there's almost invariably envy in every case of jealousy," he notes, "but it doesn't mean there's no value in distinguishing the two feelings. The overlap in usage only goes one way, so there's no reason to throw out the term 'envy.'"

Salovey counters, "I'm not saying we need to stop using 'envy.' The reason we use 'social-comparison jealousy' is to emphasize that the situation that creates the feeling is important." And one reason Salovey stresses the situation —rather than other mood differences—is that romantic jealousy, since it includes envy, is usually very intense, making it difficult to separate distinct feelings.

Nevertheless, Smith believes the distinction should be made, especially because "In its traditional definition, envy has a hostile component to it." Not everyone would agree with that. After all, in envying others, we can also admire *them* and even use *them* as role models to spur ourselves to greater abilities. There is no hostility in that, yet these cases, Smith contends, are not precisely envy. Indeed, Smith believes envy differs from jealousy not only because of its hostility, but because of another distinct ingredient: privacy.

By the time Bill was 40, he was vice president at his firm and owned a luxurious house in an affluent neighborhood. Nevertheless, Bill had never married and was lonely. He envied his brother Jim, who lived a modest but happy life with his wife and children. One day Jim asked Bill to write a reference letter to help him get a bank loan for a new home. Bill said he'd be delighted, but soon realized he could send the letter to the bank without Jim ever seeing it. Bill wrote the letter and his brother, never knowing why, was refused the loan.

Although this anecdote is fictional, Smith has shown in his research that the principles illustrated are probably true. In a recent study, Smith had subjects identify with an envious person. He then gave them the option of dividing a "resource" between themselves and the envied person. Among the many options were: dividing the resource equally; dividing it so the subject kept the most and gave the least to the envied person; and dividing it so they sacrificed the amount they could otherwise keep for themselves if it meant giving the least to the envied person. Most subjects chose the last option, but only when they could do so in private, rather than public, circumstances.

Although Smith admits the findings need to be verified, he believes the results are strongly "suggestive." The envious person's choice, he says, "was unambiguously hostile. Not selfish, but hostile. And the findings verified the conventional wisdom that envy has a secretive quality about it that you wouldn't admit to the person you envy. And under the right circumstances it will lead to actual hostile behavior."

The reason people would be hostile in private seems obvious, given that envy is socially unacceptable. But why the hostility in the first place? Smith theorizes that the envied person's "superiority" emphasizes the envious person's low self-esteem in a specific area— the way the new real estate agent's communication skills affected Ann; Marcia's young date affected Dave; and Jim's happy family life affected Bill. Hostility is a way of putting down the envied person and devaluing his or her "superiority." Whether it takes the form of thought, word or deed, hostility pushes the envied person away, thereby allowing the vious person to restore his self-esteem.

Smith is looking at other implic; envy and hostility in society. For exa

RANKING JEALOUSY AND ENVY

What situations are most likely to evoke feelings of jealousy and envy? In a study published in the Journal of Personality and Social Psychology, Peter Salovey and Judith Rodin asked subjects to rank 53 situations according to the degree of emotion each would evoke. Below are 25 of those situations, listed in decreasing order, that received the highest "jealousy/envy" ratings:

1. You find out your lover is having an affair.
2. Someone goes out with a person you like.
3. Someone gets a job that you want.
4. Someone seems to be getting closer to a person to whom you are attracted.
5. Your lover tells you how sexy his/her old girl/boyfriend was.
6. Your boyfriend or girlfriend visits the person he or she used to date.
7. You do the same work as someone else and get paid less than he or she.
8. Someone is more talented than you.
9. Your boyfriend or girlfriend would rather be with his/her friends than with you.
10. You are alone while others are having fun.
11. Your boyfriend or girlfriend wants to date other people.
12. Someone is able to express himself or herself better than you.
13. Someone else has something you wanted and could have had but don't.
14. Someone else gets credit for what you've done.
15. Someone is more intelligent than you.
16. Someone appears to have everything.
17. Your steady date has lunch with an attractive person of the opposite sex.
18. Someone is more outgoing and self-confident than you.
19. Someone buys something you wanted but couldn't afford.
20. You have to work while your roommate is out partying.
21. An opposite-sex friend gives another friend a compliment, but not you.
22. Someone has more free time than you.
23. You hear that an old lover of yours has found a new lover.
24. Someone seems more self-fulfilled than you.
25. You listen to someone tell a story about things he did without you.

—J. Q.

don't know much about why people are hostile to begin with, but since envy is related to hostility, maybe the way people respond to the way they compare themselves to others is at the root of hostility." And there are other subtle—and even more frightening—implications. For one thing, Smith notes, because envy is socially unacceptable, "It's often not conscious, and as a result people will arrange the details of their situation and their perception of the other person to make envy something they can label as 'resentment'—resentment in the sense of righteous indignation."

Smith goes as far as to propose that many intergroup conflicts in the world—between countries, races and religious groups, for example—may begin with envy. One group is better off economically, for example, than another, and the "inferior" group feels envy as a result. "But if they're just envious," he explains, "no one is going to give them any sympathy. So they tend to see their situation as unfair and unjust. In this way, envy becomes righteous resentment, which in turn gives them the 'right' to protest and conduct hostile—or even terrorist—activity.

This topic raises questions about what is fair or unfair in our society, how people cope with differences and whether, as a result, they feel envy, resentment or acceptance. Smith points out that coping with envy may depend on how well we learn to accept our inequalities. "I think as people mature, they learn to cope with differences by coming to terms with the fact that life *isn't* fair and that it's counterproductive to dwell on things you can't do anything about."

While some of Smith's ideas on coping with envy are speculative, Salovey has found that there are specific strategies—illustrated in the following anecdotes—that work in preventing and easing jealousy and envy. . . .

Rick and Liz are getting along much better these days even though Liz still works with her ex-boyfriend at the law firm. Rick isn't thrilled by this, *but he overcame his jealousy by focusing instead on his relationship with Liz: spending time with her, planning vacations, discussing their future.*

Ann no longer feels envy or hostility towards her co-worker at the real estate agency. She put an end to those negative feelings by simply ignoring her rival's superior communication skills and concentrating instead on her own achievements.

As illustrated here and isolated in a survey Salovey and Yale associate Judith Rodin conducted with *Psychology Today* readers, there are three major coping strategies: *Self-reliance*, in which a person does not give into the emotion, but continues to pursue the goals in the relationship; *Selective ignoring*, or simply ignoring the things that cause the jealousy or envy; and *Self-bolstering*, or concentrating on positive traits about yourself.

Surprisingly, "We found that the first two coping strategies are very effective in helping a person not feel jealousy," reports Salovey. "We thought that self-bolstering would also be good, since if something that's important to you is threatened, then maybe you should think of things in which you do well."

Although self-bolstering was not helpful in preventing jealousy. "Once you were *already* jealous, it was the only thing that kept you from becoming depressed and angry," notes Salovey. "So the first two keep jealousy in check, but if jealousy does emerge, self-bolstering keeps jealousy from its worst effects."

In the same study, Salovey and Rodin also uncovered some interesting data about how men and women experience jealousy and envy. "Men tend to be more envious in situations involving wealth and fame, and women more so in beauty and friendship," reports Salovey, but he emphasizes, "I should put that finding in context. We looked at a lot of variables and very rarely found differences. Men and women were very similar on nearly everything you could measure except that one difference."

Smith and Salovey do agree that while jealousy and envy can be devastating to those experiencing them, in milder forms they can actually be helpful. "I tend to think of jealousy and envy as normal," says Salovey. "In any relationship where you really care about the other person, when your relationship is threatened by someone, you're going to feel negative emotions. If you don't, maybe you don't care that much."

As for envy, Smith points out that, "I don't think it's a bad thing, necessarily. It's a motivator when it's in the form of admiration and hero worship." He does add, however, that at those levels the emotion may not be envy since envy, by definition is hostile. "It's hard to know where one stops and the other begins," he notes.

Nevertheless, Smith stresses that "Coping with differences is something we all do. Some of us do it in constructive ways and others in destructive, and that has implications for who is going to be happy or unhappy. Envy is a sign of not coping well—maybe." He adds that while "some people have a right to recognize that a situation is unfair, the next question

is, what do you do? It may be best to recognize the unfairness and cope with it before it leads to more painful feelings."

Jealousy and envy can have an unpleasant knack of cropping up between the people who care most about each other. Our first reaction is often to blame the other person—my *wife* is the one who is lunching with her ex-boyfriend; my *co-worker* is undeservedly making more sales; why should my *brother* have a happy family *and* a big house? Part of our blame is understandable: life *is* unfair; society and circumstance *do* create differences between us beyond our control.

Nevertheless, the bottom line is not how we view other people, but how we view ourselves. When jealousy or envy become overwhelming, it is as much from passing judgment on ourselves as on others. That's when we owe it to everyone to talk it out, change what needs to be changed and—perhaps most importantly—accept ourselves for what we are.

Follow-Up

1. *Queijo writes that jealousy and envy are most likely to happen whenever individuals are vulnerable and insecure about a specific aspect of their lives. Is this true in your experience?*

2. *Coping strategies for jealousy and envy are: (1) self-reliance, (2) selective ignoring, and (3) self-bolstering. Apply them to prevent or ease jealousy or envy in your current situation, if applicable.*

3. *Analyze your "social comparison styles" according to the explanations given in the boxed section entitled "Comparing Ourselves To Others: In Sickness and In Health." Are you satisfied with your current styles?*

4. *After reading the boxed section entitled "Ranking Jealousy and Envy," circle the three that most likely would cause you high levels of jealousy or envy. Discuss or write about your reactions to these three selections.*

5. *Choose any other idea in the article to write about or discuss.*

Sarcasm and Apathy

When I was young, *Leave It To Beaver* and *Father Knows Best* were topics of household conversations. There was a lot of admiration for straightforward, innocent, polite people. Sarcasm wasn't something people carried like a badge. Although I have no desire to go back to that era and to give up some of the freedoms we have now, I find myself wishing we could do without some of the sarcasm we have developed. Sometimes the sarcasm that has become such a living, breathing part of our daily lives drives me up the wall.

I grew up on a farm in rural Indiana. For years I actually believed that people could talk to each other without "put-downs." This isn't to say that we never gave opinions—Farmers and small town people can be very frank. But when we talked it was from the heart. Possibly our hearts didn't have so many dark spots. Possibly we were more naive.

By the time I reached high school, the sarcastic revolution had started. Our class had the proud distinction of being the first senior class in the town's history to be released a week earlier than every other grade because of the apathy of the entire senior class. For four years it wasn't "cool" to answer questions in class. It wasn't "cool" to get involved. The administration had an assembly for the senior class to tell us that, after four years of struggling to try and please us and being met with apathy, at last they were tired. They wanted us out.

Eventually I moved to the city and though I had maintained my non-sarcastic attitude, I couldn't keep it forever. One day I was with my sister and she commented on how sarcastic I had become. She was right. I spent a week trying to keep from saying anything sarcastic. Oh, it was tough. I told my son how proud I was of him for doing a chore. He was so confused, he actually asked me if I meant it. Amazingly, though, trying not to be sarcastic has rewards. I felt more real. I felt as if I wasn't trying to cover up my real feelings as much. As a result I was much more relaxed that week. Sometimes, on days when I am in a particularly sarcastic mood, I go to bed wishing that the children were still awake so that I could hold them. On those days I wonder if they know how much I love them. During the week that I was trying not to be sarcastic, I didn't have those down feelings. I went to sleep feeling that my day had been fulfilling.

In my graduate education class I interacted with two other teachers. I noticed the amount of their sarcasm. We all find sarcasm funny so we encourage it, but it was odd to me that these teachers acted in ways that my teachers hated so much in the class of 1970. "Do we have to do this?" "How much of this do we have to do?" "I don't want to do this."

I couldn't help wondering how much sarcasm and apathy they tolerated from their students.

One night in class I sat between these two teachers. We had seen the *Griffin and Phoenix* movie, and they were talking about the movie's "over-kill." After several sarcastic comments, one of them turned to me and asked me what I thought. I feigned that I had been too tired to listen to their conversation. The second woman generously filled me in and I replied, "It was pretty sappy." I couldn't believe myself! I thought about the movie all the way home. In fact, I *cried* about the movie—remembering how some people find living harder than dying. So why did I say that? Probably for the same reason that the woman who had a whole notebook full of writing for one of her papers had said that she hadn't started her papers. It isn't "cool" to be non-sarcastic or non-apathetic.

There is probably a good chance that half of the time people are being sarcastic or apathetic it isn't genuine. Some people probably aren't even comfortable being that way. Comedy clubs, friends, books, and all types of resources help us to develop the idea that sarcasm and apathy should be associated with things that are fun. Sarcasm and apathy are more than just a form of humor—they are becoming a way of life.

Leave It To Beaver has been replaced by Bart Simpson. Bart Simpson is more than a sarcastic underachiever. Bart Simpson is proud to be called that.

—A graduate student and teacher

Follow-Up

1. *The author says that she felt more real when not being sarcastic. Do you agree with this idea?*
2. *Describe the source and effects of any sarcasm and/or apathy in your life.*

On the Death of a Father

Sanford Colley

Wednesday April 29, 1992

My father died last night.

For nearly 2 hours I stood at his bedside, held his hand, and watched the digital readout on a heart machine register an increasingly weaker pulse, slower heart rate, and lower blood pressure. Finally, all three blinked zero.

The ventilator was the only intrusion into what was otherwise a peaceful death. It continued to pump air into his lifeless body in a grotesque parody of breathing. When it was over, my sister asked, "May we turn that damned machine off now?"

Dad, a retired minister, was 85, and he had been in declining health for several years. Dylan Thomas would have been proud of him. He did not go gentle into that good night. A few weeks ago I pushed him in a wheel chair through the halls of a retirement center that had been his home for several months. "Look at all these old people," he snorted. "They're pitiful . . . just pitiful." I did not have the heart to point out the obvious; most were more ambulatory than he.

Two days ago, the morning started like a number of others during the last few months. There was an early morning call from the retirement home, "Your father has fallen again . . . we don't know how serious, but he does appear to be in some pain . . . we've sent for an ambulance . . . you should meet us in the emergency room."

I canceled meetings, rearranged classes, called on wonderfully supportive faculty colleagues to cover appointments, and left a long list of things to do with an accommodating and understanding secretary. X-rays revealed that his hip was broken. The options were to remove the hip joint completely and confine him to a wheelchair or to replace the joint and hope he might regain some of his ability to walk. Although surgery was risky because of his weak heart, the physician recommended joint replacement and surgery was scheduled for the next morning.

I arrived at the hospital in time to see him before the operation. The wait during surgery was long—much longer than my sisters and I had been led to expect. The young surgeon finally came out wearing a thin smile that masked his concern. (Was it only last week I warned my counseling students to never assume a smile means all is well?) He told us that during the operation Dad had gone into cardiac arrest. They had him stabilized, but the next few hours would be critical. At first, Dad improved, then he weakened, and finally, his physician told us, "he's not going to make it."

My two sisters and I stayed with Dad in the intensive care cubicle. His eyes were half closed, but once he shifted his gaze to mine and for a long time we looked at each other intently. I tried desperately to read what was in that gaze. Was it fear? Resignation? Love? Whatever he felt at that moment, I *know* he was aware his three children were there with him.

Dad seemed to sense that his life was nearly over. Last week he told me his days were numbered and asked about his will. I assured him everything was in order. The surgeon seemed to be quite moved when he told us of a comment Dad made to the anesthetist just before surgery. "I'm going to have a heart attack," he said. Those were his last words.

When the ventilator was turned off, I embraced my sisters, and we wept. The last time I cried aloud was 3 years ago when Dad was staying at our home. About 3:00 in the morning I had gotten out of bed and spent nearly an hour struggling to help him to the bathroom. He could hardly stand, much less walk, and he was dead weight in my arms. When I finally returned to bed, exhausted, I saw a guide to the Appalachian Trail (AT) on my bedside table. Dad had always talked about wanting to hike the AT, and I had the guide out because we had talked about spending a couple of days on an accessible part of the trail. That night I knew that he would never realize his dream, and I wept because he *could* have done it when he was in better health had he only chosen to do so. I did a hundred miles on the AT just prior to the American Association of Counseling and Development convention in Baltimore, and realized that I was doing it partly for me and partly for him.

A major concern was how my mother would respond to news of the death. She was in reasonably good physical health, but has experienced a significant reduction in her mental functioning as a result of Alzheimer's disease. She lives in a nursing home, seems to be content and happy, and recognizes members of the family, but she is usually unable to structure her thoughts well enough to form a complete sentence.

I decided it would be best to be direct and unambiguous, so I told her in simple language about the fall, the surgery, and the heart attack. "He's dead, Mom," I concluded, my heart aching.

For a fleeting moment, she seemed to understand. "Oh no," she responded, her eyes filling with tears, an incredibly pained look on her face. Then, almost immediately, she relaxed, her dementia seemingly insulating her from intense grief.

She glanced around the room and pointed to an old tennis shoe in her closet. The mate to it had been lost several weeks earlier. "It's gone, but that one is still there." I was stunned. A shoe with a lost mate; the most gifted and creative writers on our faculty would have been hard pressed to come up with a more striking metaphor for the loss of a spouse. Her thoughts confused and scrambled, Mom had seized that image. Perhaps she had understood.

Friday, May 1, 1992

We buried Dad today.

I woke up early this morning and ran—14 long, leisurely, lung-clearing miles. Halfway through I stopped to watch a hazy sunrise over the Tennessee River. I absorbed the beauty and remembered the fishing trips Dad and I took there when I was a boy. I reflected on his active life, my love for him, and how terribly unhappy he had been confined to the retirement home. When I resumed running, I had acknowledged a feeling of relief that I had not wanted to admit before. I was at peace.

The love and concern we felt at the funeral home last night and at the funeral today was a moving experience. I was overwhelmed that university colleagues would drive so far to express their support. Many individuals spoke of how effectively Dad had ministered to them in their times of grief. One young woman told me of seeing him go by her home every morning during his daily walk to the coffee shop.

"I'll never forget that funny old crooked walking cane he used," she said. "He told me once he wanted to be buried with it."

"I'll tell you a secret," I whispered, "It's with him in the casket."

Sunday, June 21, 1992

Father's Day. My first in 53 years without Dad. It has been nearly 2 months since his death, and the wrenching pangs of grief I experienced initially have started to subside. The healing is not complete, but it has started.

Going through Dad's library has been interesting. I found first editions of Rollo May's 1939 *The Art of Counseling* and Carl Rogers's

1942 *Counseling and Psychotherapy*. A real treasure was an 1892 copy of William James's *Principles of Psychology*, the very first book ever published (initially in 1890) with "psychology" in the title.

Although nothing more than coincidental, I was deeply moved by a book of daily devotionals over 20 years old. I started to chuck it because there were no notations or anything else of apparent value, only a single rusty gem clip on a page with the corner turned down. It marked the devotion for April 28.

That was the date of his death.

Follow-Up

1. *If one or both of your parents have died, compare your initial reactions to those of the author.*
2. *If one or both of your parents are alive, what are some things you'd like them to experience, with or without you, before they die? When will these happen?*
3. *If you are a parent, what are some things you can do* now *with your child (children) that won't be realistic years from now? When will you do these things?*
4. *Discuss or write about any other point in this article.*

Loss And Mourning

Judith Viorst

We are separate people constrained by the forbidden and the impossible, fashioning our highly imperfect connections. ~~We live by losing and leaving and letting go.~~ And sooner or later, with more or less pain, we all must come to know that loss is indeed "a lifelong human condition."

Mourning is the process of adapting to the losses of our life.

"In what, now," asks Freud in "Mourning and Melancholia," "does the work which mourning performs consist?" He replies that it is difficult and slow, involving an extremely painful, bit-by-bit inner process of letting go. He is talking, as I will be here, about the mourning we do at the death of people we love. But we may mourn in a similar fashion the end of a marriage, the coming apart of a special friendship, the losses of what we'd once had . . . been . . . hoped might be. For, as we shall see, there is an end, an end to much that we have loved. But there can be an end to mourning, too.

How we mourn and how, or if, our mourning is going to end, will depend on what we perceive our losses to be, will depend on our age and their age, will depend on how ready all of us were, will depend on the way they succumbed to mortality, will depend on our inner strengths and our outer supports, and will surely depend on our prior history—on our history with the people who died and our own separate history of love and loss. Nevertheless, there does seem to be a typical pattern to normal adult mourning, despite individual idiosyncrasies. And it seems generally agreed that we pass through changing, though overlapping, phases of mourning and that after about a year, sometimes less but often far longer indeed, we "complete" a major part of the mourning process.

Now many of us find it difficult to hear about phases of mourning without bristling, without the sense that some Julia Child of sorrow is trying to provide us with a step-by-step recipe for the perfect grief. But if we can hear about phases not as something that we—or others—*must* go through, but as something that may illuminate what we—or others—have gone or are going through, perhaps we can come to understand why "sorrow . . . turns out to be not a state but a process."

And the first phase of this process, whether the loss has been anticipated or not, is "shock, numbness and a sense of disbelief." This can't be happening! No, it cannot be! Perhaps we will weep and wail; perhaps we will sit there silently; perhaps waves of grief will alternate with periods of stunned incomprehension. Our shock may be mild if we've lived long and hard with the dead's impending death. Our shock may be less (let's face it) than our relief. But the fact that someone we love no longer exists in time and space is not yet entirely real, is beyond our belief.

Mark Twain, whose daughter Susy—"our wonder and our worship"—died suddenly at the age of twenty-four, writes in his autobiography of that initial state of benumbed disbelief.

> It is one of the mysteries of our nature that a man, all unprepared, can receive a thunderstroke like that and live. There is but one reasonable explanation of it. The intellect is

stunned by the shock and but groping gathers the meaning of the words. The power to realize their full import is mercifully wanting. The mind has a dumb sense of vast loss—that is all. It will take mind and memory months and possibly years to gather the details and thus learn and know the whole extent of the loss.

Although an expected death will usually stun us less than one we are unprepared for, although with a fatal illness our major shock may come when that illness is diagnosed and although in the time preceding the death we may sometimes engage in "anticipatory mourning," we will initially find it difficult—despite such preparation—to assimilate the death of a person we love. Death is one of those facts of life we acknowledge more with our brain than we do with our heart. And often, although our intellect acknowledges the loss, the rest of us will be trying hard to deny it.

A man whose wife, Ruth, had died was found frantically waxing the floors of their house on the day of her funeral; family and friends would be coming and "if the house is a mess, Ruth will kill me," he earnestly said. When Tina died, her younger brother Andrew inquired, "Why must we say that she's dead? Why can't we just pretend she's in California?" I, when told of the sudden death of a dearly loved young girl, grotesquely replied to her weeping father, "You're kidding!" And sometimes, as in the shared delusion of the family below, the denial of death defies the clinical facts.

An elderly woman was rushed to the hospital by her family following the sudden onset of a stroke. Within a few hours she died, and the attending intern immediately informed the several grown children who had remained at the hospital. Their immediate reaction was disbelief, and together they went in to see their mother. After several minutes they came from her room insisting that she was not dead, and they requested that the family physician be called. Only after the diagnosis was confirmed by a second physician did they accept the obvious reality. . . .

Some disbelief, some denial, may continue well beyond the initial shock. Indeed, it may take the entire mourning process to make of the impossible—death—a reality.

After the first phase of mourning, which is relatively short, we move to a longer phase of intense psychic pain. Of weeping and lamentation. Of emotional swings and physical complaints. Of lethargy, hyperactivity, regression (to a needier, "Help me!" stage). Of separation anxiety and helpless hopeless despair. And of anger too.

Annie, age twenty-nine when her husband and daughter were killed by a truck, recalls how angry she was, "how I hated the world. I hated that man in the truck. I hated all trucks. I hated God for making them. I hated everyone, even John [her four-year-old son] sometimes because I had to stay alive for him and if he hadn't been there I could have died too. . . ."

We are angry at the doctors for not saving them. We are angry at God for taking them away. Like Job, or the man in the following poem, we are angry at our comforters—what right have they to say that time will heal, God is good, it is all for the best, we'll get over it?

> Your logic, my friend, is perfect,
> Your moral most drearily true;
> But, since the earth closed on her coffin,
> I keep hearing that, and not you.
>
> Console if you will, I can bear it,
> 'Tis a well-meant alms of breath;
> But not all the preaching since Adam
> Has made Death other than Death.

There are those who insist that anger—toward others, and also toward the dead—is invariably a part of the mourning process.

Indeed, a great deal of the anger that we focus on those around us is the anger we feel, but won't let ourselves feel, toward the dead. Sometimes, however, we do express it directly. "God damn you! God damn you for dying on me!" a widow recalls having said to her dead husband's picture. Like her, we love the dead, we miss and need and pine for our dead, but we also are angry at them for having abandoned us.

We are angry at, hate, the dead the way an infant hates the mommy who goes away. And like that infant we fear that it is our anger, our hatred, our badness that drove them away. We have guilt about our bad feelings and we also may have great guilt for what we have done—and what we didn't do.

Guilty feelings too—irrational guilt and justified guilt—are very often a part of the mourning process.

For the ambivalence that is present in even our deepest love relationships tainted our love for the dead while they were alive. We saw them as less than perfect and we loved them less than perfectly; we may even have fleetingly wished that they would die. But now that they are dead we are ashamed of our negative feelings and we start berating ourselves for being so bad. "I should have been kinder." "I should have been more understanding." "I should have been more grateful for what I had." "I should have tried to call my mother more often." "I should have gone down to Florida to visit my dad." "He always wanted a dog, but I would never let him have one, and now it's too late."

Of course there are times when we ought to feel guilt for the way that we treated the dead, appropriate guilt for harm done, unmet needs. But even when we loved them very, very well indeed, we still may find grounds for self-recrimination.

Here are a mother's musings on the death of her son at the age of seventeen:

Missing him now, I am haunted by my own shortcomings, how often I failed him. I think every parent must have a sense of failure, even of sin, merely in remaining alive after the death of a child. One feels that it is not right to live when one's child has died, that one should somehow have found the way to give one's life to save his life. Failing there, one's failures during his too brief life seem all the harder to bear and forgive. . . .

I wish we had loved Johnny more when he was alive. Of course we loved Johnny very much. Johnny knew that. Everybody knew it. Loving Johnny more. What does it mean? What can it mean, now?

We feel guilt about our failures toward someone we love when he or she dies. We feel guilt about our negative feelings, too. And what we may do to defend against, or alleviate, our guilt is to loudly insist that the person who died was perfect. Idealization—"My wife was a saint," "My father was wiser than Solomon" —allows us to keep our thoughts pure and to keep guilt at bay. It is also a way of repaying the dead, of making restitution, for all of the bad we have done—or imagined we've done— to them.

Canonizing—idealizing—the dead is frequently a part of the mourning process.

Discussing idealization in her excellent book *The Anatomy of Bereavement*, psychiatrist Beverley Raphael gives us Jack, a forty-nine-year-old widower who described his dead wife Mabel in terms of unremitting adulation. She was, he declared, "the greatest little woman ever . . . the best cook, the best wife in the world. She did everything for me." Dr. Raphael then goes on to observe:

He could say nothing negative of her and insisted their life together had been perfect in every way. The intensity of his insistence on this was harsh and aggressive, as though he dared anyone to prove otherwise. It was only after careful exploration that he revealed his resentment toward her for her coddling and intrusive control of his life, and how much he had longed for his freedom. He then became able to talk in a more realistic way, cheerfully, yet sadly, talking of the good and the bad. . . .

Anger, guilt, idealization—and attempts at reparation—seem to suggest that we do in fact know the dead died. Yet alternately, or even simultaneously, their death may still continue to be denied. John Bowlby, in his book *Loss*, describes this paradox:

"On the one hand is belief that death has occurred with the pain and hopeless yearning that that entails. On the other is disbelief that it has occurred, accompanied both by hope that all may yet be well and by an urge to search for and to recover the lost person." A child whose mother leaves him will deny the departure, will search for her, Bowlby says. It is in a similar spirit that we—as left, bereft adults—search for our dead.

This searching may express itself unconsciously—as restless random activity. But some of us consciously seek the dead as well. Beth looks for her husband by going again and again to all of the places they'd gone to together. Jeffrey stands in the closet among the clothes his wife used to wear, smelling her smell. Anne, the widow of the French movie actor, Gérard Philipe, describes her search for her husband at the cemetery:

> . . . I went to find you. A mad rendezvous. . . . I remained outside reality, without being able to go in. The tomb was there. I could touch the earth that covered you and without being able to help it, I began to believe that you would come, a little late as usual; that soon I would feel you approach me. . . .
>
> There was no point in telling myself that you were dead. . . . You weren't coming, no, you were waiting for me in the car. A mad hope, that I knew to be mad, and still it overtook me.
>
> "Yes, he's waiting in the car." And, when I found it empty, I protected myself once more, as though trying to give myself respite: "He's taking a walk on the hill." I went down to the house, talking to friends the while, looking for you on the road. Without believing in it, of course.

Searching for the dead we sometimes even summon them up: We "hear" their step in the driveway, their key in the lock. We "see" them on the street and eagerly follow them for a block; they turn and we confront . . . a stranger's face. Some of us may bring our dead back to life with hallucinations. Many of us bring our dead back to life in our dreams.

A father dreams of his son—"I dreamed one night that dear More was alive again and that after throwing my arms round his neck and finding beyond all doubt that I had my living son in my embrace—we went thoroughly into the subject, and found that the death and funeral at Abinger had been fictitious. For a second after waking the joy remained—then came the knell that wakes me every morning—More is dead! More is dead!"

A mother dreams of her daughter—"It's very ordinary, my dream. She's just there—and not dead."

A woman dreams of her sister—". . . She often comes to me, you know; we have a laugh. . . ."

A daughter (Simone de Beauvoir) dreams of her mother—"She blended with Sartre, and we were happy together. And then the dream would turn into a nightmare: Why was I living with her once more? How had I come to be in her power again? So our former relationship lived on in me in its double aspect—a subjection that I loved and hated."

A son dreams of his father—"I carried him to the ocean. He was dying. He died peacefully in my arms."

A son dreams of his mother (his first dream about her since her death)—"She was laughing at me sadistically because I couldn't get off a moving train. She was baring her teeth with a really sadistic laugh. I was shocked when I woke up but I told myself that, in the midst of all my wonderful memories, I shouldn't forget about this part of her too."

This same son dreams of his mother some months later—"I was walking somewhere alone; ahead of me were three women in floor-length nightgowns. One of the figures turned; it was my mother, and as clear as can be she said, 'Forgive me.'"

A daughter dreams of her father—"I dreamt he was running away and I wanted to catch him, it was terrible."

A widow dreams of her husband one month after his suicide—"There are two spiral staircases set side by side. I'm going up one and he's going down the other. I reach out my hand to make contact but he pretends he doesn't know me and keeps going down."

In fantasies and dreams, in all of our searchings for the dead, we try to deny the finality of the loss. For the death of someone we love revives our childhood fears of abandonment, the ancient anguish of being little and left. By summoning up the dead we can sometimes manage to persuade ourselves that the person we lost is still here, that we aren't bereft. But sometimes, as in this chilling story told to me by a sensible, down-to-earth friend, summoning up the dead may persuade us they're dead.

Two years to the day after Jordan's young wife had committed suicide, he lay in bed with Myra, a new ladylove. A woman who'd been a friend of his late wife Arlene. A woman he viewed as a stand-in for Arlene. A woman he had been pressing to be like Arlene. A perfectly lovely woman he wasn't quite prepared to marry because she wasn't, after all, Arlene.

That night in bed, however, when he awoke and glanced at Myra's sleeping body, "I didn't see Myra; I saw the corpse of Arlene. I couldn't make it turn back," he said, "I couldn't get back to the reality of Myra. I was laying there, in panic, with this corpse."

He finally got out of bed and fled the apartment.

Now happily married to Myra, Jordan says that his experience was terrifying, but liberating too. It allowed him, at last, to get on with the rest of his life. It made him understand that he couldn't resurrect his wife, that "I couldn't replace Arlene with another Ar-

lene." He says, "After that, I was able to let her die."

In this acute phase of grief some of us will mourn quietly, some vocally—though it isn't our style to rend garments and tear our hair. But in our own different ways we will have to pass through the terror and tears, the anger and guilt. the anxiety and despair. And in our own different ways, having managed somehow to work our way through our confrontations with unacceptable losses, we can begin to come to the end of mourning.

Starting with shock and making our way through this phase of acute psychic pain, we move toward what is called the "completion" of mourning. And although there still will be times when we weep for, long for, miss our dead, completion means some important degree of recovery and acceptance and adaptation.

We recover our stability, our energy, our hopefulness, our capacity to enjoy and invest in life.

We accept, despite dreams and fantasies, that the dead will not return to us in this life.

We adapt, with enormous difficulty, to the altered circumstances of our life, modifying—in order to survive—our behavior, our expectations, our self-definitions. Psychoanalyst George Pollock, who has written extensively on the subject of mourning, has called the mourning process "one of the more universal forms of adaptation and growth . . . " Successful mourning, he argues, is far more than making the best of a bad situation. Mourning, he says, can lead to creative change.

But he and his colleagues warn us that mourning is rarely a straightforward, linear process. So does Linda Pastan in a powerful poem that begins with "the night I lost you" and traces the long hard ascent through the stages of grief until the final stage is approached and . . .

. . . now I see what I am climbing towards: Acceptance

written in capital letters,
a special headline:
Acceptance,
its name is in lights.
I struggle on,
waving and shouting.
Below, my whole life spreads its surf,
all the landscapes I've ever known
or dreamed of. Below
a fish jumps: the pulse
in your neck.
Acceptance. I finally
reach it.
But something is wrong.
Grief is a circular staircase.
I have lost you.

Going through stages of grief, Pastan says, is like climbing a circular staircase—and like learning to climb it "after the amputation." In his record of mourning following the death of his cherished wife, C. S. Lewis uses identical imagery:

How often—will it be for always?—how often will the vast emptiness astonish me like a complete novelty and make me say, "I never realized my loss till this moment"? The same leg is cut off time after time. The first plunge of the knife into the flesh is felt again and again.

In another section he writes:

One keeps on emerging from a phase, but it always recurs. Round and round. Everything repeats. Am I going in circles . . . ?

It sometimes seems that way. And sometimes we do.

And even when, eventually, we accept and adapt and recover, we may suffer from "anniversary reactions"—recurringly mourning our dead, with feelings of pining and sadness and loneliness and despair, on the day in the calendar year that marks their birth or their death or some special shared occasion.

But in spite of setbacks, recurrences and the sense that our sorrow keeps doubling back on itself, there is an end to mourning, to even the seemingly most inconsolable mourning, as this record of a daughter's grieving testifies:

I awake in the middle of the night and tell myself, She's gone. My mother is dead. Never will I see her again. How to grasp this?

Oh, Mama, I don't want to eat, to walk, to get out of bed. Reading, working, cooking, listening, mothering. Nothing matters. I do not want to be distracted from my grief. I wouldn't mind dying. I wouldn't mind at all. I wake from sleep in the middle of every night and say to myself, "My mother is dead!" . . .

Mourning. . . . You seem to be filled with it. Always. In a sense, like a pregnancy. But . . . pregnancy imparts a sense of doing something even while inactive, [whereas] mourning bequeaths a sense of futility and meaninglessness in the midst of activity. . . . Her death is the only thing on my mind. . . .

My everydayness has snapped and I am in quarantine from the world. Want nothing from it, have nothing to give to it. When things get too bad, the whole world is lost to you, the world and the people in it.

It's all a rotten hoax, this life of ours. You go from zero to zero. Why attach yourself to love only to have your beloved ripped from you? The upshot of love is pain. Life is a death sentence. Better not to give yourself to anything. . . .

I have to begin from the beginning and repeat: She's dead. As if it's just struck me. And I find myself drowning, engulfed by the disorder of the current, wanting to seize her hand to bring me to shore. Missing her so. . . .

Some days I can look at her photograph and the image revives me, reinforces her for me. On other days, I gaze at her and am blinded with tears. Newly bereft. . . .

This outpouring of feeling, of self-pity, is . . . a crying on Mama's shoulder, a wailing into the wind, a hiccuping amid sobs against an irrevocable crashing surf. A lament. A dirge. You come. And you go. I had her once, and now she's gone. So, what's new? What's the point?

Am I healing? I'm able to gaze at her photograph without that tourniquet tightening

LIFE LOSSES

When we think of loss we think of the loss, through death, of people we love. But loss is a far more encompassing theme in our life. For we lose not only through death, but also by leaving and being left, by changing and letting go and moving on. And our losses include not only our separations and departures from those we love, but our conscious and unconscious losses of romantic dreams, impossible expectations, illusions of freedom and power, illusions of safety—and the loss of our own younger self, the self that thought it always would be unwrinkled and invulnerable and immortal.

Somewhat wrinkled, highly vulnerable and non-negotiably mortal, I have been examining these losses. These lifelong losses. These necessary losses. These losses we confront when we are confronted by the inescapable fact . . .

that our mother is going to leave us, and we will leave her;
that our mother's love can never be ours alone;
that what hurts us cannot always be kissed and made better;
that we are essentially out here on our own;
that we will have to accept—in other people and ourselves—the mingling of love with hate, of the good with the bad;
that no matter how wise and beautiful and charming a girl may be, she still cannot grow up to marry her dad;
that our options are constricted by anatomy and guilt;
that there are flaws in every human connection;
that our status on this planet is implacably impermanent;
and that we are utterly powerless to offer ourselves or those we love protection—protection from danger and pain, from the inroads of time, from the coming of age, from the coming of death; protection from our necessary losses.

These losses are a part of life—universal, unavoidable, inexorable. And these losses are necessary because we grow by losing and leaving and letting go.

Note: From *Necessary Losses,* by Judith Viorst, 1986, New York: Simon and Schuster. Copyright © 1986 by Judith Viorst. Reprinted with permission.

round my throat, clamping memory. . . . I'm beginning to see her in *her* life, and not only myself bereft of her life. . . .

Piece by piece, I reenter the world. A new phase. A new body, a new voice. Birds console me by flying, trees by growing, dogs by the warm patch they leave on the sofa. Unknown people merely by performing their motions. It's like a slow recovery from a sickness, this recovery of one's self. . . . My mother was at peace. She was ready. A free woman. "Let me go," she said. Okay, Mama, I'm letting you go.

In another passage this daughter talks about being weaned from her mother's material presence, but "filled with her as never before." She is describing, in her own words, the process that psychoanalysts call "internalization." It is by internalizing the dead, by making them part of our inner world, that we can at last complete the mourning process.

Remember that, as children, we could let our mother go, or leave our mother, by establishing a permanent mother within us. In a similar way we internalize—we take into ourselves—the people we have loved and lost to death. The "loved object is not gone," psychoanalyst Karl Abraham writes, "for now I carry it within myself. . . ." And while surely he overstates—the touch is gone, the laugh is gone, the promise and possibilities are gone, the sharing of music and bread and bed is gone, the comforting joy-giving flesh-and-blood presence is gone—it is true nonetheless that by making the dead a part of our inner world, we will in some important ways never lose them.

Follow-Up

1. *Viorst discusses the characteristics of three phases of mourning: shock, intense psychic pain (anger, guilt, idealization), and completion. Discuss or write about the validity of these phases from your experience and observations. Recognize the wide range of individual, varying expressions of the feelings in each mourning phase.*

2. *In the boxed section "Life Losses," Viorst lists several kinds of losses that most of us will (or have) faced. Choose one or more of these losses and describe how you reacted to it. Did any of your reactions fit the phases of mourning? What are some themes or patterns in how you handle loss?*

3. *Choose any other idea or statement to discuss or write a reaction.*

4. *In another section of her book, Viorst discusses how mourning may not come to an end. Some people engage in chronic mourning that can take the form of continual grief or its opposite, complete denial of grief. Because these forms have wide-ranging effects on living a normal life, some professional help is usually recommended. See Viorst's book,* Necessary Losses, *for further reading on this topic.*

THE MADNESS PERSONALITY INVENTORY

Nels Goud

For each item indicate L (like me), or N (not like me). Scoring instructions will be described at the end of the test.

N 1. I wish my feet were higher up on my body.

N 2. Adverbs make me angry.

L 3. I hear voices on my telephone.

N 4. Their should be a number between 5 and 6.

N 5. My cousin married an otter.

N 6. I often wonder what carrots do on weekends.

N 7. I enjoy the company of freeze-dried pets.

L 8. I sleep on my elbows.

N 9. Animal crackers bite me.

N 10. I like to kiss with one lip.

L 11. I'd rather be a plant.

L 12. Large crowds make my thighs sweat.

N 13. I like to talk with my protons.

L 14. Jumping nude into a vat of tapioca appeals to me.

N 15. It is beyond me how bassoons mate.

L 16. My tongue moves when I talk.

N 17. I take pictures of people picking their noses at stoplights.

N 18. All my friends eat algae.

N 19. I don't trust people who say "the."

N 20. Each of my toes has a name.

N 21. I always say "thank you" to my toothbrush after brushing.

N 22. Sometimes I feel like a tadpole.

N 23. Every day at noon I yodel.

N 24. I don't know why, but the letter "Q" excites me.

L 25. I get dizzy from thinking about things such as if nothing lasts forever, then how did infinity get discovered? Why waffle irons? How do elves take giant steps? Why is Waldo always hiding?

Scoring: Every L counts as one point. Any score above 10 means you need a long break. Any score below 2 means you lied.

Applied Activities for Section Four

EMOTIONAL CHARADES

This activity provides experiences in both emotional and nonverbal expression. For best results, have the instructor prepare the emotion cards (described below); do *not* look at the list prior to the activity.

1. Participants should divide into groups of 4–6 members (both genders if possible).
2. Place the emotion cards face down in the middle of the group.
3. Each member selects a card, reads it silently, and then places it face down.
4. Each member has a maximum of 2 minutes to nonverbally act out the emotion on the card. Only body language is permitted by the sender. The other group members are to identify the emotion expressed. If the emotion is *not* correctly identified within two minutes, go to the next person.
5. Complete this procedure until all the cards are correctly identified. To prepare the emotion cards, write the following emotional states on 3 × 5 separate index cards:

Sorry/remorseful	Embarrassed
Afraid	Withdrawn
Encouraging/supportive	Hesitant/unsure
Bored/apathetic	Disappointed/let down
Arrogant/superior	Angry/hostile
Dominant/showing power, authority	Wonder/amazed
Playful/spontaneous	Eager/enthusiastic
Proud/confident	Content/at ease, relaxed
Friendly/warm	Anxious/nervous
Puzzled/baffled	Romantically interested

Follow-Up

1. Which body parts dominated in expressing emotions? Why were some emotions easier to express than others? What were the effects of this activity on how you worked as a group?
2. Discuss your experience with the whole class.
3. Write a reaction paper on your observations.

EMOTIONS AND PERCEPTION

To demonstrate the power of emotions in your life, try the following activity.

1. Choose a common situation in your life (job, college class, driving, free time, interacting with others).
2. Observe and summarize your perceptions of this situation under different emotional states. (Choose at least two of these emotional states.)

Situation: _____

Emotion	Perceptions
Happy	
Angry	
Depressed	
Confused	
Anxious	
Confident	

3. Is your emotional state a main factor in how you interpret any given external event? If yes, what are some applications of this finding?
4. Discuss or write about your thoughts on this subject.

NONVERBAL OBSERVATIONS

1. While watching a dramatic TV or talk show, turn off the sound and focus on the participants' body language (particularly the face and gestures). Try to guess what emotional states are being expressed. Occasionally turn on the sound to check out your hunches. For more accuracy, record the show on a VCR.
2. Observe your own ways of expressing various emotions. Some major nonverbal methods include: facial expressions, eye contact, vocal speed/volume/inflection, body positioning and distance, gestures, use of environmental objects (e.g., where you sit). Consider having someone who knows you well

offer their observations on how you express various emotions. If you find that you are not expressing a certain emotion as well as you would like, experiment with your nonverbal methods.

3. Discuss or write about what you learned from any of these activities.

LISTENING TO EMOTIONS

With positive emotions like joy and wonder, we usually let them be and do not try to change them. With negative emotions, however, there is a tendency to try to avoid or to change them. Few people enjoy feeling anxious, guilty, or inadequate. Even these negative emotions have their gifts for us. In a sense, they are a special kind of teacher. For example, anxiety, can teach us that we need to prepare for whatever we are afraid of facing; anxiety can show us how to be more alert; anxiety tells us that we are alive. Envy can teach us how we judge our own self-worth. Certain kinds of guilt can be helpful in maintaining a life of integrity.

Instead of avoiding or trying to escape negative emotions, it is often helpful to first reflect on what they mean. Reflection enables us to accept and not to deny the teaching power of negative emotions. This does not mean that you have to "like" them. There are several ways to listen to negative emotions as if they were teachers:

1. Ask yourself what is this emotion attempting to tell me? What is this emotion warning me of in this situation?
2. With a person you trust, share your negative emotion and discuss what it could be trying to "teach you."
3. Write a brief letter to your emotion asking why it is there. Have the emotion write back to you. You will have the opportunity to see the emotion's point of view if you do the latter.
4. Thomas Moore's *Care of the Soul* (1992) discusses how emotions can be teachers.

ANGER MANAGEMENT

Anger can be a natural emotional response in the following life situations: physical or emotional hurt, blocked needs, unmet expectations, guilt, loss, helplessness, threats, unfulfilled goals/dreams, injustice. Below are constructive and nonconstructive ways to handle anger. Mark the ones that are your typical anger responses.

Constructive Responses

___ Knowing that anger is a natural human feeling and that *you determine* whether to express it.

___ *Delay* any decision or action until your strong anger has subsided.

____ Using *diversion* techniques: Take a deep breath (or even ten) and exhale slowly; count to ten slowly or count slowly backward from fifty; take a walk; engage in physical exercise; tackle a mundane task like laundry or mow a lawn; listen to or play music.

____ Appropriate *venting:* Talk it out with an understanding friend or colleague; howl at the moon; cry it out, write about it.

____ Engage in an *incompatible behavior:* Laughter (see a funny movie or TV show, romp with a pet, have fun with a friend); relaxation activities (neck or back rub, a hot bath, view something beautiful); do something you like to do that requires full absorption.

____ You can say "Yes" to the question: Is your anger in *proportion* to whatever caused it?

____ Ask and honestly answer: "How much of my life energy is worth being spent in anger at this person or situation?"

____ Start *problem-solving* strategies if warranted. These could include: Understanding the underlying causes of your anger; seeing other points of view; initiating constructive, confrontational conversation with the other party after your anger's intensity has lessened; arranging a group meeting to resolve the issue (if it is a problem important to the group); possibly getting a third party to mediate a dispute.

____ Use the anger as a *positive energy source* and motivation.

____ Seek qualified guidance if the anger persists in ways that negatively affect your life.

____ *Observe* and learn how others handle similar anger situations in constructive ways. Also consider talking with them about their approaches.

Nonconstructive Reactions

____ *Aggression:* Physical attack, ridicule, hostile silence. Aggressive responses almost always evoke strong negative responses in others that add to the problem. Aggressors may even be negatively affected by realizing that their anger increases and/or feelings of guilt result from the aggressive acts.

____ *Displacement:* Taking out your anger on someone who is not the source of the anger (e.g., yelling at someone at home for a problem at work or school).

____ *Denial:* Refusing to acknowledge the feeling of anger. If suppressed for a long period, the angry feeling may result in resentment, volatile explosive acts or words or depression.

____ Inappropriate *blaming:* Individuals unfairly blame someone or something else for whatever is causing the anger, or they unfairly blame themselves when the cause is truly elsewhere.

___ *Disproportional* anger expression: Individuals respond with either excessive anger intensity or duration to whatever caused the anger. Also, it means that appropriate anger has not been expressed.

Follow-Up

1. Keep an anger journal. Record the incident, place and time of any anger experience. Do this for at least 1–2 weeks. Examine your responses using the above guidelines.
2. Add one or more constructive anger management techniques to your repertoire. Decrease or eliminate nonconstructive reactions.
3. Ask people who know you well to describe their perception of your anger management skills. (And don't become angry!)
4. Discuss and/or write about what you've learned about anger management.

HOW DO YOU FEEL?

It is helpful to recognize your individual style of experiencing emotions. One of the best ways is to write about how each emotion affects you. Below are some excerpts concerning this technique as taken from John Wood's *How Do You Feel?* (1974).

Hope   I am beginning to see some light at the end of the tunnel. . . . Good things can happen, whereas before they have been living under a cloud of 'No,' powerless and trapped. . . . It is moving from a negative, nothing, zero point of view into some sort of potentiality, a letting in of the good possibilities.

Guilt   Feeling guilty is a diminishing, belittling, unworthy kind of feeling for me that always makes me think less of myself. Somehow I am smaller and the rest of the world is bigger than me, looking down on me. . . . My guilt is essentially feeling bad about myself because of some offense—real or imagined—that I have committed.

Accepted When I feel accepted, it feels like an emotional sauna. It feels good, warm; it makes me relax. . . . The tension of how I'm going over with others seems to disappear. I think about the difference between being accepted and being liked. Acceptance is bigger than liked; it takes in being liked and disliked. . . . And it takes in more than being tolerated too.

Lonely   I usually know when I'm lonely when I find myself doing a lot of things to take up time, scheduling myself very tightly, filling up time with more than one thing. Like I'm washing dishes, listening to the record player, and watching TV. . . . I go into a lot of fantasies too. . . . It's very hard for me to say that I'm lonely. I tend to let it out in other ways; I tend to get angry, say hurtful things. It seems like the world is against me. . . . Sometimes I can make myself lonely by cutting off those very things I want, by withholding, withdrawing. When I can say "I am lonely" and fully accept it, then I can go about finding out what some of my lonely needs are and try and take care of those.

Follow-Up

1. Select one or more emotions (they may or may not be the same as above) and write a paragraph describing how it exhibits itself in you.
2. Discuss your emotion descriptions in a small group.
3. Gather examples of emotion descriptions from novels, movies, and conversations.
4. Write a reaction paper on what you learned from one or more of these activities.

HUMAN
RELATIONSHIPS

ne of the best ways to learn the function of anything is to do without it. An injury to any part of your body readily shows its taken-for-granted purpose. A power outage highlights our pervasive dependence on electricity. Imagine a life without other people. Sometimes we may want such a thing, but only when we choose it. What we consider to be typical human behavior would not be possible without constant interaction with many persons in our lives. Observations of persons raised in isolation from an early age show great deficits in language, emotional expression, and a marked incapacity for a mature, sustained human interaction.

Most of us cannot escape the influence of our fellow humans even when we are alone—we think of them, we wonder what they are doing, we wonder if they miss us, we may even get mad at them, we might feel lonely. We are so enmeshed in our significant relationships that their influence permeates our existence even after their deaths.

Our human interactions differ according to their type, intensity, frequency, and duration. You can visually capture these dimensions by making a human web. Place a dot in the middle of a blank piece of paper—this dot represents you. Draw lines from the dot to circles with these labels: relatives, friends, colleagues, teachers, professional relationships, authority figures, social groups, neighbors, acquaintances, heroes, mentors, role models, romantic encounters, disliked

245

persons, and you can add any other relationship categories. When you place names by each of these circles, you begin to see how much of your life is spent in human interactions. You, too, are a member of many other webs.

Embedded deep within the human is the need to love and belong, in the dual sense of giving and receiving. Much of our lives is spent in attempting to fulfill these two needs. Abraham Maslow (1968) said that "no psychological health is possible unless the person is fundamentally accepted, loved and respected by others" (p. 196).

The reading selections in this section represent some of our most significant human relationships:

- The differing, and sometimes baffling and hostile, interactions between men and women are explored by Aaron R. Kipnis and Elizabeth Herron in "Ending the Battle Between the Sexes." A strategy for gender peace and understanding is offered.
- The dynamic tension of separateness and closeness is the topic of Harriet Lerner's "The Dance of Intimacy."
- A day of joining and parting is described by Tom Keating in "Sometimes It Rains."
- Len Smith tells the story of a night of attempts to face some fears and revitalize a love life in "The Monster."
- The nature of adult friendships is examined by Phillip Lopate in "What Friends Are For."
- Judith Viorst posits that we have six "Kinds of Friends."
- Mark Murrmann talks about past friends in "Lamenting the Fading of Friendships."
- The impact of brothers and sisters on our lives is the focus of "The Secret World of Siblings" by Erica E. Goode.
- A Little League becomes a mirror of fundamental values and lessons in human relations in Nels Goud's true story of "The Human Potential of Whip Gimby."
- The struggle to become independent from parents and to accept them as distinct persons is the thesis of "Parents" by Martin Shepard. Exercises for parent dialogues are included.
- Steve Regan shares how a next door neighbor became a major role model for him in "Think Nanny."
- A teacher who cared is featured in "The Missing Halloween" by Nels Goud.
- Changes and trends in interpersonal relationships and sexuality are posed by Shervert Frazier in "Psychotrends."

The Applied Activities and the Follow-Up study questions aid in expanding the ideas in the readings and how to apply them to your own life.

Reference

Maslow, A. (1968). *Toward a psychology of being.* New York: Van Nostrand Reinhold Co.

Ending the Battle Between the Sexes

Aaron R. Kipnis
and Elizabeth Herron

Have you noticed that American men and women seem angrier at one another than ever? Belligerent superpowers have buried the hatchet, but the war between the sexes continues unabated. On every television talk show, women and men trade increasingly bitter accusations. We feel the tension in our homes, in our workplaces, and in our universities.

The Clarence Thomas–Anita Hill controversy and the incidents at the Navy's Tailhook convention brought the question of sexual harassment into the foreground of national awareness, but it now appears that these flaps have merely fueled male-female resentment instead of sparking a productive dialogue that might enhance understanding between the sexes.

Relations between women and men are rapidly changing. Often, however, these changes are seen to benefit one sex at the expense of the other, and the mistrust that results creates resentment. Most men and women seem unable to entertain the idea that the two sexes differing perspectives on many issues can be equally valid. So polarization grows instead of reconciliation, as many women and men fire ever bigger and better-aimed missiles across the gender gap. On both sides there's a dearth of compassion about the predicaments of the other sex.

For example:

- Women feel sexually harassed; men feel their courting behavior is often misunderstood.

- Women fear men's power to wound them physically; men fear women's power to wound them emotionally.
- Women say men aren't sensitive enough; men say women are too emotional.
- Women feel men don't do their fair share of housework and child care; men feel that women don't feel as much pressure to provide the family's income and do home maintenance.
- Many women feel morally superior to men; many men feel that they are more logical and just than women.
- Women say men have destroyed the environment; men say the women's movement has destroyed the traditional family.
- Men are often afraid to speak about the times that they feel victimized and powerless; women frequently deny their real power.
- Women feel that men don't listen; men feel that women talk too much.
- Women resent being paid less than men; men are concerned about the occupational hazards and stress that lead to their significantly shorter life spans.
- Men are concerned about unfairness in custody and visitation rights; women are concerned about fathers who shirk their child support payments.

It is very difficult to accept the idea that so many conflicting perspectives could all have intrinsic value. Many of us fear that listening to the story of another will somehow weaken our own voice, our own initiative, even our own identity. The fear keeps us locked in adversarial thinking and patterns of blame and alienation. In this frightened absence of empathy, devaluation of the other sex grows.

In an attempt to address some of the discord, between the sexes, we have been conducting gender workshops around the country. We invite men and women to spend some time in all-male and all-female groups, talking about the opposite sex. Then we bring the two groups into an encounter with one another. In one of our mixed groups this spring. Susan, a 35-year-old advertising executive, told the men. "Most men these days are insensitive jerks. When are men going to get it that we are coming to work to make a living, not to get laid? Anita Hill was obviously telling the truth. Most of the women I work with have been harassed as well."

Michael, her co-worker, replied, "Then why didn't she tell him ten years ago that what he was doing was offensive? How are we supposed to know where your boundaries are if you laugh at our jokes, smile when you're angry, and never confront us in the direct way a man would? How am I supposed to learn what's not OK with you, if the first time I hear about it is at a grievance hearing?"

We've heard many permutations of this same conversation:

Gina, a 32-year-old school teacher in Washington, D.C., asks, "Why don't men ever take no for an answer?"

Arthur, a 40-year-old construction foreman, replies that in his experience, "some women *do* in fact say no when they mean yes. Women seem to believe that men should do all the pursuing in the mating dance. But then if we don't read her silent signals right, we're the bad guys. If we get it right, though, then we're heroes."

Many men agree that they are in a double bind. They are labeled aggressive jerks if they come on strong, but are rejected as wimps if they don't. Women feel a similar double bind. They are accused of being teases if they make themselves attractive but reject the advances of men. Paradoxically, however, as Donna, a fortyish divorcée, reports, "When I am up front about my desires, men often head for the hills."

As Deborah Tannen, author of the bestseller about male-female language styles *You Just Don't Understand,* has observed, men and women often have entirely different styles of communication. How many of us have jokingly speculated that men and women actually come from different planets? But miscommunication alone is not the source of all our sorrow.

Men have an ancient history of enmity toward women. For centuries, many believed women to be the cause of our legendary fall from God's grace. "How can he be clean that is born of woman?" asks the Bible. Martin Luther wrote that "God created Adam Lord of all living things, but Eve spoiled it all." The "enlightened" '60s brought us Abbie Hoffman, who said: "The only alliance I would make with the women's liberation movement is in bed." And from the religious right, Jerry Falwell still characterizes feminism as a "satanic attack" on the American family.

In turn, many feel the women's movement devalues the role of men. Marilyn French, author of *The Women's Room,* said, "All men are rapists and that's all they are." In response to the emerging men's movement, Betty Friedan commented, "Oh God, sick . . . I'd hoped by now men were strong enough to accept their vulnerability and to be authentic without aping Neanderthal cavemen.

This hostility to the men's movement is somewhat paradoxical. Those who are intimately involved with the movement say that it is primarily dedicated to ending war and racism, increasing environmental awareness, healing men's lives and reducing violence, promoting responsible fatherhood, and creating equal partnerships with women—all things with which feminism is ideologically aligned. Yet leaders of the men's movement often evoke indignant responses from women. A prominent woman attorney tells us, "I've been waiting 20 years for men to hear our message. Now instead of joining us at last, they're starting their *own* movement. And now they want us to hear that they're wounded too. It makes me sick."

On the other hand, a leader of the men's movement says, "I was a feminist for 15 years. Recently, I realized that all the men I know are struggling just as much as women. Also, I'm tired of all the male-bashing. I just can't listen to women's issues anymore while passively watching so many men go down the tubes."

Some of our gender conflict is an inevitable by-product of the positive growth that has occurred in our society over the last generation. The traditional gender roles of previous generations imprisoned many women and men in soul-killing routines. Women felt dependent and disenfranchised; men felt distanced from feelings, family, and their capacity for self-care.

With almost 70 percent of women now in the work force, calls for women to return to the home full time seem ludicrous, not to mention financially impossible. In addition, these calls for the traditional nuclear family ignore the fact that increasing numbers of men now want to downshift from full-time work in order to spend more time at home. So if we can't go back to the old heroic model of masculinity and the old domestic ideal of femininity, how then do we weave a new social fabric out of the broken strands of worn-out sexual stereotypes?

Numerous participants in the well-established women's movement, as well as numbers of men in the smaller but growing men's movement, have been discovering the strength, healing, power, and sense of security that come from being involved with a same-sex group. Women and men have different social, psychological, and biological realities and receive different behavioral training from infancy through adulthood.

In most pre-technological societies, women and men both participate in same-sex social and ceremonial groups. The process of becoming a woman or a man usually begins with some form of ritual initiation. At the onset of puberty, young men and women are brought into the men's and women's lodges, where they gain a deep sense of gender identity.

Even in our own culture, women and men have traditionally had places to meet apart from members of the other sex. For generations, women have gathered over coffee or quilts; men have bonded at work and in taverns. But in our modern society, most heterosexuals believe that a member of the opposite sex is supposed to fulfill all their emotional and social needs. Most young people today are not taught to respect and honor the differences of the other gender, and they arrive at adulthood both mystified and distrustful, worried about the other sex's power to affect them. In fact, most cross-gender conflict is essentially *conflict between different cultures.* Looking at the gender war from this perspective may help us develop solutions to our dilemmas.

In recent decades, cultural anthropologists have come to believe that people are more productive members of society when they can retain their own cultural identity within the framework of the larger culture. As a consequence, the old American "melting pot" theory of cultural assimilation has evolved into a new theory of diversity, whose model might be the "tossed salad." In this ideal, each subculture retains its essential identity, while coexisting within the same social container.

Applying this idea to men and women, we can see the problems with the trend of the past several decades toward a sex-role melting pot. In our quest for gender equality through sameness, we are losing both the beauty of our diversity and our tolerance for differences. Just as a monoculture is not as environmentally stable or rich as a diverse natural ecosystem, androgyny denies the fact that sexual differences are healthy.

In the past, perceived differences between men and women have been used to promote discrimination, devaluation, and subjugation. As a result, many "we're all the same" proponents—New Agers and humanistic social theorists, for example—are justifiably suspicious of discussions that seek to restore awareness of our differences. But pretending that differences do not exist is not the way to end discrimination toward either sex.

Our present challenge is to acknowledge the value of our differing experiences as men and women, and to find ways to reap this harvest in the spirit of true equality. Carol Tavris, in her book *The Mismeasure of Women,* suggests that instead of "regarding cultural and reproductive differences as· problems to be eliminated, we should aim to eliminate *the unequal consequences that follow from them.*"

Some habits are hard to change, even with an egalitarian awareness. Who can draw the line between what is socially conditioned and what is natural? It may not be possible, or even desirable, to do so. What seems more important is that women and men start understanding each other's different cultures and granting one another greater freedom to experiment with whatever roles or lifestyles attract them.

Lisa, a 29-year-old social worker from New York participating in one of our gender workshops, told us, "Both Joel [her husband] and I work full time. But it always seems to be me who ends up having to change my schedule when Gabe, our son, has a doctor's appointment or a teacher conference, is sick at home or has to be picked up after school. It's simply taken for granted that in most cases my time is less important than his. I know Joel tries really hard to be an engaged father. But the truth is that I feel I'm always on the front line when it comes to the responsibilities of parenting and keeping the home together. It's just not fair."

Joel responds by acknowledging that Lisa's complaint is justified; but he says, "I handle all the home maintenance, fix the cars, do all the banking and bookkeeping and all the yard work as well. These things aren't hobbies. I also work more overtime than Lisa. Where am I supposed to find the time to equally co-parent too? Is Lisa going to start mowing the lawn or help me build the new bathroom? Not likely."

In many cases of male-female conflict, as with Lisa and Joel, there are two differing but *equally valid* points of view. Yet in books, the media, and in women's and men's groups, we only hear about most issues from a woman's point of view or from a man's. This is at the root of the escalating war between the sexes.

For us, the starting point in the quest for gender peace is for men and women to spend more time with members of the same sex. We have found that many men form intimate friendships in same-sex groups. In addition to supporting their well-being, these connections can take some of the pressure off their relationships with women. Men in close friendships no longer expect women to satisfy *all* their emotional needs. And when women meet in groups they support one another's need for connection and also for empowerment in the world. Women then no longer expect men to provide their sense of self-worth. So these same-sex groups can enhance not only the participants' individual lives, but their relationships with members of the other sex as well.

If men and women *remain* separated, however, we risk losing perspective and continuing the domination or scapegoating of the other sex. In women's groups, male-bashing has been running rampant for years. At a recent lecture we gave at a major university, a young male psychology student said, "This is the first time in three years on campus that I have heard anyone say a single positive thing about men or masculinity."

Many women voice the same complaint about their experiences in male-dominated workplaces. Gail, a middle management executive, says, "When I make proposals to the all-male board of directors, I catch the little condescending smirks and glances the men give one another. They don't pull that shit when my male colleagues speak. If they're that rude in front of me, I can only imagine how degrading their comments are when they meet in private."

There are few arenas today in which women and men can safely come together on common ground to frankly discuss our rapidly changing ideas about gender justice. Instead of more sniping from the sidelines, what is needed is for groups of women and men to communicate directly with one another. When we take this *next step* and make a commitment to spend time apart and then meet with each other, then we can begin to build a true social, political, and spiritual equality. This process also instills a greater appreciation for the unique gifts each sex has to contribute.

Husband-and-wife team James Sniechowski and Judith Sherven conduct gender reconciliation meetings—similar to the meetings we've been holding around the country—each month in Southern California. In a recent group of 25 people (11 women, 14 men), participants were invited to explore questions like: What did you learn about being a man/woman from your mother? From your father? Sniechowski reports that "even though, for the most part, the men and women revealed their confusions, mistrust, heartbreaks, and

bewilderments, the room quickly filled with a poignant beauty." As one woman said of the meeting, "When I listen to the burdens we suffer, it helps me soften my heart toward them." On another occasion a man said, "My image of women shifts as I realize they've been through some of the same stuff I have."

Discussions such as these give us an opportunity to really hear one another and, perhaps, discover that many of our disagreements come from equally valid, if different, points of view. What many women regard as intimacy feels suffocating and invasive to men. What many men regard as masculine strength feels isolating and distant to women. Through blame and condemnation, women and men shame one another. Through compassionate communication, however, we can help one another. This mutual empowerment is in the best interests of both sexes, because when one sex suffers, the other does too.

Toward the end of our meetings, men and women inevitably become more accountable for the ways in which they contribute to the problem. Gina said, "I've never really heard the men's point of view on all this before. I must admit that I rarely give men clear signals when they say or do something that offends me."

Arthur then said, "All my life I've been trained that my job as a man is to keep pursuing until 'no' is changed to 'yes, yes, yes.' But I hear it that when a woman says no, they want me to respect it. I get it now that what I thought was just a normal part of the dance is experienced as harassment by some women. But you know, it seems that if we're ever going to get together now, more women are going to have to start making the first moves."

After getting support from their same-sex groups and then listening to feedback from the whole group, Joel and Lisa realize that if they are both going to work full time they need to get outside help with family tasks, rather than continuing to blame and shame one another for not doing more.

Gender partnership based on strong, interactive, separate but equal gender identities can support the needs of both sexes. Becoming more affirming or supportive of our same sex doesn't have to lead to hostility toward the other sex. In fact, the acknowledgment that gender diversity is healthy may help all of us to become more tolerant toward other kinds of differences in our society.

Through gender reconciliation—both formal workshops and informal discussions—the sexes can support each other, instead of blaming one sex for not meeting the other's expectations. Men and women clearly have the capacity to move away from the sex-war rhetoric that is dividing us as well as the courage necessary to create forums for communication that can unite and heal us.

Boys and girls need regular opportunities in school to openly discuss their differing views on dating, sex, and gender roles. In universities, established women's studies courses could be complemented with men's studies, and classes in the two fields could be brought together from time to time to deepen students' understanding of both sexes. The informal discussion group is another useful format in which men and women everywhere can directly communicate with each other (see *Utne Reader* issue no. 44 [March/April 1991]). In the workplace the struggle for gender understanding needs to go beyond the simple setting up of guidelines about harass-

ment; it is essential that women and men regularly discuss their differing views on gender issues. Outside help is often needed in structuring such discussions and getting them under way. Our organization, the Santa Barbara Institute for Gender Studies, trains and provides "reconciliation facilitators" for that purpose.

These forums must be fair. Discussions of women's wage equity must also include men's job safety. Discussions about reproductive rights, custody rights, or parental leave must consider the rights of both mothers and fathers—and the needs of the children. Affirmative action to balance the male-dominated political and economic leadership must also bring balance to the female-dominated primary-education and social-welfare systems.

We call for both sexes to come to the negotiating table from a new position of increased strength and self-esteem. Men and women do not need to become more like one another, merely more deeply themselves. But gender understanding is only a step on the long road that must ultimately lead to fundamental institutional change. We would hope, for example, that in the near future men and women will stop arguing about whether women should go into combat and concentrate instead on how to end war. The skills and basic attitudes that will lead to gender peace are the very ones we need in order to meet the other needs of our time—social, political, and environmental—with committed action.

Follow-Up

1. *Explain why you agree or disagree with the authors' contention that in cases of male-female conflict there are two differing but equally valid points of view.*
2. *Discuss or write about your views on any two statements in this article.*

3. *What is one major issue or question you would like answered by the opposite gender? Consider asking a few members of the opposite gender and report the responses and your analysis.*
4. *To attempt the authors' strategy for attaining gender peace, see the end of this section and the Applied Activity entitled "Men and Women: A Dialogue."*

The Dance of Intimacy

Harriet Goldhor Lerner, Ph.D.

What does an intimate relationship require of us to be successful? For starters, intimacy means that we can be who we are in a relationship and allow the other person to do the same. By "being who we are," we can talk openly about things that are important to us, we can take a clear position on where we stand on significant emotional issues, and we can clarify the limits of what is acceptable and tolerable to us. If we allow the other person to do the same, we can stay emotionally connected to that other party, who thinks, feels, and believes differently, without needing to change, convince, or fix him.

An intimate relationship is one in which neither person silences, sacrifices, or betrays the self, and each expresses strength and vulnerability, weakness and competence, in a balanced way. Truly intimate relationships do not operate at the expense of the self, nor do they allow the self to operate at the expense of the other. This is a tall order, or, more accurately, a lifelong challenge. But it is the heart and soul of intimacy.

Only when we stay in a relationship over time—whether by necessity or choice—is our capacity for intimacy truly put to the test. Only in a long-term relationship are we called upon to navigate that delicate balance between separateness and connectedness, and only then can we confront the challenge of sustaining both, without losing either, in a way that works for each partner.

WHEN RELATIONSHIPS ARE STUCK

All of us develop our identities through emotional connectedness to others, and we continue to need close relationships throughout our lives. We get into trouble when we distance ourselves from friends, lovers, and kin; pretend we don't need people; ignore a relationship that begins to go badly; or put no energy into generating new options for change.

The challenge of change is greatest when a relationship becomes a source of frustration and our attempts to fix things only lead to more of the same. These stuck relationships are often "too distant," and/or "too intense," precluding real intimacy. Intense feelings—no matter how positive—are hardly a measure of true and enduring closeness. In fact, intense feelings may *prevent* us from taking a careful and objective look at the intimate dance we carry on with significant people in our lives. Intense togetherness can easily flip into intense distance—or intense conflict, for that matter.

Too much intensity means one person, overfocuses on the other in a blaming or worried way or in an attempt to fix him. Or each person may be overfocused on the other and underfocused on the self.

Too much distance indicates there is little togetherness and real sharing of one's true self in the relationship. Important issues go underground rather than get aired and worked on. Many distant relationships are also intense, because distance is one way we manage intensity. If, for instance, you haven't seen your ex-husband in five years and can't talk with him about the kids without clutching yourself inside, then you have a *very* intense relationship.

Once a relationship is stuck, the motivation to change things is not enough to make it happen. For one thing, we may be so buffeted by strong feelings that we can't think clearly and objectively about the problem or our own part in it. When intensity is high we *react* rather than observe and think, we overfocus on the *other* rather than on the self, and we find ourselves in polarized positions where we are unable to see more than one side of an issue (our own) and find new ways to relate. We may navigate relationships in ways that lower our anxiety in the short run but diminish our capacity for intimacy over the long haul.

In addition, we may have a strong wish for change in a relationship but be unaware of, or unwilling to confront, the actual source of anxiety that is fueling a problem and blocking intimacy. How can we gain the courage to discover and confront the real issues? How can we unblock our intimate relationships?

NAMING THE PROBLEM

A couple of years ago my sister came to me with a problem that illustrates this situation. Susan called me one day and confessed she was having a very rough time with her boyfriend, David. Although she felt entirely committed to the relationship, David said he needed more time to work through his own issues in order to make a decision about their living together. Susan and David lived in different cities, making for long and tiring weekend trips; however, this long-distance arrangement (and David's indefiniteness) was nothing new—it had been going on for quite some time.

What was new was my sister's sudden feeling of panic, resulting in her pressuring David for a decision he was not yet ready to make. Because Susan had been working for some time on altering her pattern of pursuing men who were distancers in romantic relationships, she was able to see her behavior like

a red warning flag. She was unable, however, to tone down her reactivity and stop pursuing. By the time Susan called me, she was feeling terrible.

While thinking about my sister's situation, I was particularly struck by the *timing* of the problem. Susan's sense of desperation and her heightened reactivity to David's wish for more time and space followed a trip we took to Phoenix to visit our parents and to see our uncle Si, who was dying from a fast-moving lung cancer. Si's diagnosis had been a shock to us—he'd always been such a vibrant, active man. Seeing him sick reminded our family of past losses, impending losses, and some recent health scares on the family tree. Of all these stresses, the closest to home for Susan and me was the earlier diagnosis of our father's rare, degenerative brain disease. Because our father surprised everyone by regaining his functioning, this devastating diagnosis was replaced with a more hopeful one—but the experience had been very hard on our family.

During our phone conversation, I asked Susan if there might be a connection between her anxious focus on David and all the emotions that were stirred up by our recent visit to Phoenix. This made intellectual sense to her, but it also seemed a bit abstract, since Susan did not feel any connection at a gut level.

A few weeks later Susan visited me for a long weekend and decided to consult a family systems therapist. Afterward, she began to more fully appreciate the link between recent health issues in our family and her anxious pursuit of David. Simply *thinking* about this connection helped Susan to de-intensify her focus on David and reflect more calmly and objectively on her current situation.

Susan was also challenged to think about the pursuer-distancer pattern she was stuck in. It was as if 100 percent of the anxiety and ambivalence about living together was David's. And as if Susan was just 100 percent raring to go—no worries at all, except how they would decorate the apartment. Such polarities (she stands for togetherness, he for distance) are common enough, but they distort the experience of self and other and keep us stuck.

Finally, Susan confronted the fact that she was putting so much energy into her relationship with David, she was neglecting her own family and her career. On the one hand, Susan's attention to this relationship made sense because insuring its success was her highest priority. On the other hand, focusing on a relationship at the expense of one's own goals and life plan overloads that relationship. The best way Susan could work on her relationship with David was to work on her own self. This kind of self-focus is a good rule of thumb for all of us. While Susan's energy was overfocused on David, another woman might find herself overfocusing on another kind of relationship; she might dwell too intensely on a co-worker who undermines her or on a troubled sibling.

BREAKING THE PURSUIT CYCLE

Susan had gained insight and understanding of her problem, but her next challenge was translating what she had learned into action. What could she do differently when she was back home to lower her anxiety and achieve a calmer, more balanced relationship with David? By the time Susan left, she had formulated a plan. Whenever we are feeling very anxious, it can be enormously helpful to have a clear plan, one based not on reactivity and a reflexive need to "do something— anything!" but rather one based on reflection and a solid understanding of the problem.

Susan enacted her plan. First, she shared with David that she had been thinking about their relationship during her trip and had gained some insight into her own behavior. "I came to realize," she told him, "that the pressure I was feeling about our living together had less to do with you and our relationship and more to do with my anxiety about some other things." She filled David in on what these were—family issues related to health and loss. David was understanding and clearly relieved.

Susan also told him that perhaps she was letting him express the ambivalence for both of them, which probably wasn't fair. She reminded David that her own track record with relationships surely provided her with good reason to be anxious about commitment, but she had avoided this pretty well by focusing on *his* problem and *his* wish to put off the decision.

This statement was the hardest for Susan, because when we are in a pursuer-distancer polarity, pursuers are convinced that all they want is more togetherness, and distancers are convinced that all they want is more distance. Sometimes only after the pursuit cycle broken can each party begin to experience the wish we all have for both separateness and togetherness.

Finally, Susan told David that she had been neglecting her work projects and needed to put more time and attention into them. "Instead of driving up next weekend," Susan said, "I'm going to stay at home and get some work done." For the first time in a while, Susan became the spokesperson for more distance, *not in an angry, reactive manner but as a calm move for self.*

The changes Susan made were successful in breaking the pursuer-distancer pattern, which was bringing her pain. If we are pursuers, such moves can be excruciatingly difficult to initiate and sustain in a calm, nonreactive way. Why? Because pursuing is often an unconscious reaction to anxiety. If it is our *usual* reaction, we will initially become *more* anxious when we keep it in check.

From where, then, do we set the motivation and the courage to maintain such a change? We must get it from the conviction that the old ways simply do not work.

Before Susan returned home, she considered another option aimed at helping her to calm things down with David. Whenever she found herself feeling anxious about the relationship and slipping back into the pursuit mode, she would contemplate sitting down and writing a letter to our father instead, or calling home.

This may sound a bit farfetched at first, but it makes good sense. If Susan managed her anxiety about family issues by distancing, she would be more likely to get intense with David. If, instead, she could stay connected to the *actual source of her anxiety,* she would feel more anxious about our parents' failing health, but the anxiety would be less likely to overload her love relationship. Indeed, learning how to stay in touch with our relatives and working on key emotional issues at their source lays the groundwork for more solid intimate relationships in the present or future.

A POSTSCRIPT ON PARTNERS WHO CAN'T MAKE UP THEIR MINDS

What if *your* partner can't make a commitment? What if he's not ready to think about marriage, not ready to give up another relationship, not sure he's really in love? He may or may not be ready in two years—or 20. Does Susan's story imply that we should hang around *forever,* working on our own issues and failing to address our partner's uncertainty? Does it mean that we should never take a position on our partner's distancing or lack of commitment? Certainly not. A partner's long-term ambivalence *is* an issue for us—that is, if we really want to settle down.

We will, however, be *least successful* in addressing the commitment issue, or any other, when we feel reactive and intense. Working to keep anxiety down is a priority, because anxiety drives reactivity, which drives polarities. (*All* he can do is distance. *All* she can do is pursue.) The more we pay attention to the different sources of anxiety that affect our lives, the more calmly and clearly we'll navigate the hot spots with our intimate other.

A CALM BOTTOM LINE

Let's took at a woman who was able to take a clear position with her distant and ambivalent partner, a position relatively free from reactivity and expressions of anxious pursuit. Gwenna was a 26-year-old real estate agent who sought my help for a particular relationship issue. For two and a half years she had been dating Greg, a city planner who had had disastrous first and second marriages and couldn't make up his mind about a third. Gwenna was aware that Greg backed off further under pressure, yet she didn't want to live forever with the status quo. How did she ultimately handle the situation?

As a first step, Gwenna talked with Greg about their relationship, calmly initiating the conversation in a low-keyed fashion. She shared her perspective on both the strengths and weaknesses of their relationship and what her hopes were for their future. She asked Greg to do the same. Unlike earlier conversations, she conducted this one without pursuing him, pressuring him, or diagnosing his problems with women. At the same time, Gwenna asked Greg some clear questions, the answers to which exposed his own vagueness.

"How will you know when you *are* ready to make a commitment?" she asked. "What specifically would need to change or be different than it is today?"

"I don't know," Greg responded. When questioned further, the best he could come up with was he'd "just feel it."

"How much more time do you need to make a decision one way or another?"

"I'm not sure," Greg replied. "Maybe a couple of years, but I really can't answer a question like that. I can't predict or plan my feelings."

And so it went.

Gwenna really loved this man, but two years (and maybe more) was longer than she could comfortably wait. So, after much thought, she told Greg that she would wait until the fall—about ten months—but she would move on if he couldn't commit himself to marriage by then. She was open about her own wish to marry and have a family with him yet equally clear that her first priority was a mutually committed relationship. If Greg was not at that point by fall, then she would end the relationship—painful though it would be.

Having set up a waiting period, Gwenna was able *not* to pursue Greg and *not* become distant or otherwise reactive to his expressions of ambivalence. In this way, she gave him emotional space to struggle with his dilemma, and the relationship had its best chance of succeeding. Her bottom line position (a decision by the fall) was not a threat or an attempt to rope Greg in, but rather a true definition of self and a clarification of the time limits she could live with. Gwenna would not have been able to proceed this way if the relationship were burdened with baggage from her past and present that she was not paying attention to.

Unfortunately, doing our part right does not insure that things turn out as we wish. While my sister and David now live together happily, Gwenna's story has a different ending.

When fall arrived, Greg told Gwenna that he needed another six months to make up his mind. Gwenna deliberated a while and decided she could live with that. But when the six months was up, Greg was still uncertain

and asked for more time. It was then that Gwenna took the painful but ultimately empowering step of ending their relationship.

GETTING TO THE SOURCE

We all know that anxiety impacts on everything from our immune system to our closest relationships. How can we identify the significant sources of emotional intensity in our lives? How can we know when anxiety from source A is causing "stuckness" in relationship B?

Sometimes it's obvious: there may be a recent stressful event, a negative or even positive change we can pinpoint as a source of the anxiety that is overloading a relationship. If *we* miss it, others may see it for us ("No wonder you've been fighting with Jim—you moved to a new city just three months ago and that's a major adjustment!").

Sometimes we think that a particular event or change is stressful, but we aren't fully aware just how stressful it really is. Our narrow focus on one intimate relationship obscures the broader emotional field from our view. For example, we may downplay the emotional impact of significant transitions—a birth, wedding, job change, promotion, graduation, child leaving home, ill parent—because these are just normal things that happen in the course of the life cycle. We fail to realize that "just normal things," when they involve change, will profoundly affect our closest ties.

Paradoxically, couples become less able to achieve intimacy as they stay focused on it and give it their primary attention. Real closeness occurs most reliably not when it is pursued or demanded in a relationship, but when both individuals work consistently on their own selves. By working on the self, I do not mean that we should maintain a single-minded focus on self-enhancement or career advancement; these are male-defined notions of selfhood, which women would do well to challenge. Working on the self includes clarifying beliefs, values, and life goals; staying responsibly connected to people on one's own family tree; defining the self in key relationships; and addressing important emotional issues as they arise.

THE CHALLENGE OF INDEPENDENCE

For women, this presents an obvious dilemma. Only a few of us have been encouraged to put our primary energy into formulating a life plan that neither requires nor excludes marriage. In fact, we may have received generations of training to *not* think this way. Yet this kind of self-focus not only insures our well-being, it also puts us on more solid ground for negotiating in our intimate relationships. We cannot navigate clearly within a relationship unless we can live without it.

Having a life plan means more than working to insure our own economic security. It also means working toward clarifying our values, beliefs, and priorities and then applying them to our daily actions. It means thinking about what talents and abilities we want to develop over the next two—or 20—years. Obviously, a life plan is not written in stone

but is instead open to constant revision over time.

Finally, having a life plan does not mean adopting masculine values and pursuing goals single-mindedly. Some of us may be striving to lighten our work commitments so we can spend more time with our friends and family or in other pursuits, such as spiritual development or the world peace movement. What *is* significant about a life plan is that it can help us live our own lives, not someone else's, as well as possible.

When we do not focus our primary energy on working on a life plan, our intimate relationships suffer. We begin to look to others to provide us with meaning or happiness, which is not their job. We seek a partner who will provide self-esteem, which cannot be bestowed by another. We set up a situation in which we are bound to get overinvolved in the other person's ups and downs because we are underfocused on ourselves.

Intimate relationships cannot substitute for a life plan. And, to have any meaning at all, a life plan must include intimate relationships. Only through our connectedness to others can we really know and enhance the self. And only through working on the self can we begin to enhance our connectedness to others. There is, quite simply, no other way.

Follow-Up

1. *Lerner states that intense feelings, even positive ones, are not a measure of true and enduring closeness, and they can prevent a person from truly observing a relationship. Explain why you agree or disagree with this idea.*
2. *Many partners are caught in a pursuer-distancer polarity. This polarity blocks the necessary balance that everyone needs. Write about and/or discuss your views.*
3. *If some of the ideas in this article hold true for a relationship you are in, attempt the steps Lerner mentions to develop a more balanced intimacy. You might consider reading her book for further ideas.*

4. *Write about and/or discuss your views on one or more of these statements:*
   - *Couples become less able to achieve intimacy as they stay focused on it and give it their primary attention.*
   - *We cannot navigate clearly within a relationship unless we can live without it.*
   - *When we do not focus our primary energy on working on a life plan, our intimate relationships suffer.*
   - *Choose any other statement and respond.*

Sometimes It Rains

Thomas R. Keating

The rain was coming down in solid sheets, but the young man and woman holding hands as they ducked into the revolving door at the Delaware Street entrance to the City-County Building didn't notice at all.

Storms, even tornadoes, are relative on your wedding day.

Shaking the rain out of their hair and laughing, they bounced along the main floor of the building and grinned at each other steadily as they stepped onto the escalator to the basement.

The young man was 20. The girl was 18.

They looked very much like any other young couple except that they were dressed in their best clothes and looked like they had just discovered one of the world's top secrets.

In the basement they met another young man and woman who were even more exuberant. The men shook hands while the girls exchanged hugs and brief kisses on the cheek.

After a minute of excited talk, they all gathered in the chambers of the Center Township justice of the peace for the ceremony.

Six floors up a woman with a streaked red face and tired eyes was standing across a courtroom from a hefty man who minutes before had been her husband. They were listening intently as the judge read the final divorce decree.

The judge explained the particulars of the separate existence they would be living from now on.

He repeated how and when the couple's three children would be shifted about and how much money would exchange hands on what dates and who would get to keep which of the possessions that had accumulated in nine years of marriage.

The man was 30. She was 28.

During the divorce proceedings the wife had charged mental cruelty and infidelity. The husband had not challenged the charges or made any of his own, but he said privately that he felt she was to blame for the breakup.

Both the man and the woman felt a vague embarrassment at airing their most personal failings in public. So the divorce had been handled with little emotion.

As the judge concluded, the man glanced at his wife. He tried to sneer but it came off instead as a look of boredom. The woman alternated between paying polite attention to the judge and searching her husband's face as if to see if he would have a last-minute change of heart.

When the court proceedings were finished, the couple stood separately in the wide hallway, each talking quietly with their respective attorneys. After a few minutes, the woman approached the man who was now her ex-husband.

"Well, good-by," she said. "I hope you'll be happy."

"I will, don't worry," he returned.

After a pause, however, he thought better of what he had said and added, "Well, I hope you're happy too. I don't know what happened, but I guess we'll both be better off."

"Sure, I agree, sure," she said, straining to smile.

With that the man turned and walked across the hallway to a bench where a young woman in a bright blue dress was waiting.

They talked together in whispers for a moment and then disappeared into an elevator. The girl was smiling. The man was not.

The ex-wife watched them go and then sighed deeply, shrugged her shoulders and got onto another elevator alone.

On the main floor, the newly married couple was staring out the high glass doors at the rain with the perspective that only comes when you are young and everything is yet to happen.

"I love storms," the girl said. "Don't you?"

"Let's go then," her husband said. Grabbing her around the waist. They raced down the sidewalk for a few feet and then stopped and leaned against a pole in a tangle, oblivious to the fact they were getting drenched.

A few moments later, the divorced woman peered out the same glass doors.

"This is the lousiest weather I've ever seen in my life," she said. "But, what the hell, maybe I'll catch a cold."

She passed the young couple on the sidewalk but didn't notice them. Her head was down and she was looking for puddles.

Follow-Up

1. *The newly divorced man says to his now former wife, "I don't know what happened, but I guess we'll both be better off." They were married nine years. How could the relationship disintegrate without them knowing what happened? Would you guess that the newly divorced couple were like the newly married couple nine years ago? Offer your views on these questions.*
2. *Write about or discuss any other thought that this article evokes.*

The Monster

Len Smith

It was a Saturday night and I had committed to going out with some friends to a new bar to shake some dust off of my social life. It had been several months since I had broken up with my girlfriend and my calendar was bare, with the exception of a national holiday or two. I was single so the possibility of finding the future "ex" was always looming on the horizon. I began the evening with the usual routine. I showered and then spent 20 minutes in front of a huge mirror in my bathroom using a hair dryer, a brush, three tons of hair gel, and every ounce of patience I could muster to get my hair to look "that certain way." The result probably would have looked the same if I had run a brush through it and called it a day. However, my skewed logic dictated that such attention to my hair builds confidence.

Next, I spent a half an hour trying to figure out what clothes I would wear. I started with a new shirt and jeans. Using a full-length mirror in my bedroom and a hand mirror, I began contorting myself and striking poses. Each move was an effort to determine whether the look I was going for was working. After five angles I determined the shirt wasn't right. I changed the shirt, then the jeans, then brought the shirt back, then the shirt with shorts and sandals, then a sweatshirt with sandals only including socks, then a button-down shirt, then every option only with boots, then a hat worn forward and backwards and after shedding more covering than a snake I found myself back in the original ensemble. The amount of consideration I had given this outfit proved to me that it was the right outfit. I had built more confidence. I doused myself in cologne, brushed my teeth, gargled with mouthwash, practiced my smile, and strutted out to my car.

When I arrived at my buddy's house, he was just getting out of the shower. He threw on a shirt, ran a brush through his hair and in under ten minutes he was ready to go. Ten minutes! I can't even change my mind in ten minutes! Obviously he wasn't as interested in meeting someone as I was. His lack of preparation would almost certainly leave him standing in a corner, one hand in his pocket—alone. Maybe the woman I would meet might have a friend. Finally after I took one last look in the bathroom mirror, we were in the car and heading downtown. Our destination was the Circle Center Mall's bar district, in particular a bar known as Flashbaxx.

When we arrived at the mall I reached up and contorted the rear view mirror so it was facing vertically towards the passenger seat. I had to primp one last time. A stray hair was neatly tucked back in place, the smile was practiced again, and my entire face was checked over to make sure there was nothing out of the ordinary that might cause a perspective date to point and yell, "Freak!" I thought to myself, "Maybe I should have worn a hat." I felt my confidence reaching peak levels. As we walked towards the mall, I brought my shoulders back, sucked in my stomach, swelled my neck muscles, put one hand in my pocket and began the stroll towards Flashbaxx. Mr. Cool.

We arrived at the Flashbaxx and to our delight ran into some friends we did not expect to meet. My little ship was sailing at full speed on a sea of confidence. We cut up a little, had a few beers and began sizing up the crowd. At about 10 o'clock the club was becoming very crowded. Flashbaxx was a thematic bar. Decked out with all the gaudiness and florescence of the 80s, walls adorned with memorabilia from the 60s and 70s, I soon understood that the bar was named Flashbaxx because it played nothing but older tunes. It was when the D.J. fired up "Dancing Queen" by ABBA that I knew it could be a fun night. The bar was comprised of a wide variety of people—young and old, preppy and grunge, athletic and cosmopolitan. The atmosphere was great. Three beers had relaxed me, my attention to my appearance had built my confidence, and I was ready to meet someone.

Then it happened. Out of nowhere, fear came along and torpedoed my happy little boat; within seconds all hands were abandoning ship. I had thought of everything to prepare myself for the moment when I would be required to approach a total stranger and initiate a conversation. What I had not considered, though, was how to actually go up and begin the conversation. Fresh out of a five-year relationship, my conversation skills with unknown women were as sharpened as a wooden spoon. There I stood in a crowded club with "Night Fever" by the Bee Gee's blaring while hundreds of closet disco kings and queens imitated John Travolta. I tried to rehearse what I would say. Phrases like "Hey, isn't this music cool?" or "Great bar, eh!" or even "Do you come here often?" began to race around my head. I could not believe it. It was like my encyclopedia of clever conversation lines came from a *Brady Bunch* episode. After all my preparation, the fear of rejection had reduced me to piece of wet bread. I would have had a better chance of meeting someone if I had been wearing Speed-O's and a biking helmet. I tried to use the smile. I would catch a person's eye and I would think to myself, "I think she smiled back at me!" but the fear had

risen so high that I just stood there. That is, until I had to move out of the way to make room for some guy that wasn't a mental doughnut and didn't have a problem talking to strangers.

During my anxiety attack, my buddy had made his way up to the dance floor and was dancing with three women. I couldn't believe it. He had spent all of ten minutes getting ready. He had slept up until twenty minutes before we were supposed to leave! There he was six-foot-six, hair still a little wet from the shower, jumping up and down with three cute women to the tune of "My Sharona." On the other hand, I was frantically peeling the label off of my beer and striking a pose to look cool. If I had been watching myself from a distance I probably would have pointed and yelled "Freak!"

After a few hours of shifting my weight from one foot to the other, swelling my chest and acting cool I was sure I had made a complete fool out of myself. By about one o'clock we decided to leave. My buddy had a phone number, a good buzz, and an endless amount of stories about dancing for hours with three cute women. On the other hand, I could tell you every way to peel a beer label off and how to stand and look completely ridiculous while trying to meet someone without saying a word. What had I been afraid of? Did I think someone would actually yell "Leave me alone, idiot!" if I tried to make conversation? Or was it a fear that my attempts to make conversation with a woman would cause all the music to stop, the lights to come on, and the entire bar to point and laugh while at the same time chanting, "Look at that guy's outfit, and that hair, and those teeth, and why isn't he wearing a hat?"

As we left Flashbaxx we ran into some friends from college. One of these friends was a young lady I had been attracted to but had not pursued because of my relationship with my ex-girlfriend. After some coy conversation and an exchange of phone numbers I realized that without knowing it I had flirted, had a polite conversation, and had not torn the label off of anything. All of this occurred without even a dry run to practice my smile. I'm not sure how it will go when I call this girl but one thing's for certain, the next time I hear "My Sharona" I'm going to be on a dance floor having fun—well, and maybe trying to look just a little cool.

Follow-Up

1. *The author faces a number of pressures and fears in an attempt to revitalize his romantic life. If you have had a similar circumstance, describe how you handled it. What seems the best way to lessen the fears to a manageable level?*
2. *Write about or discuss any other aspect of this piece that relates to your life and how you face your fears.*

What Friends Are For

Phillip Lopate

Is there anything left to say about friendship after so many great essayists have picked over the bones of the subject? Aristotle and Cicero, Seneca and Montaigne, Francis Bacon and Samuel Johnson, William Hazlitt, Ralph Waldo Emerson, and Charles Lamb have all taken their cracks at it.

Friendship has been called "love without wings." On the other hand, the Stoic definition of love ("Love is the attempt to form a friendship inspired by beauty") seems to suggest that friendship came first. Certainly a case can be made that the buildup of affection and the yearning for more intimacy, without the release of sexual activity, keeps friends in a state of sweet-sorrowful itchiness that has the romantic quality of a love affair. We know that a falling out between two old friends can leave a deeper and more perplexing hurt than the ending of a love affair, perhaps because we are more pessimistic about the affair's endurance from the start.

Our first attempted friendships are within the family. It is here we practice the techniques of listening sympathetically and proving that we can be trusted, and learn the sort of kindness we can expect in return.

There is something tainted about these family friendships, however. My sister, in her insecure adolescent phase, told me, "You love me because I'm related to you, but if you were to meet me for the first time at a party, you'd think I was a jerk and not worth being your friend." She had me in a bind: I had no way of testing her hypothesis. I should have argued that even if our bond was not freely chosen, our decision to work on it had been. Still, we

are quick to dismiss the partiality of our family members when they tell us we are talented, cute, or lovable; we must go out into the world and seduce others.

It is just a few short years from the promiscuity of the sandbox to the tormented, possessive feelings of a fifth grader who has just learned that his best and only friend is playing at another classmate's house after school. There may be worse betrayals in store, but probably none is more influential than the sudden fickleness of an elementary school friend who has dropped us for someone more popular after all our careful, patient wooing. Often we lose no time inflicting the same betrayal on someone else, just to ensure that we have got the victimization dynamic right.

What makes friendships in childhood and adolescence so poignant is that we need the chosen comrade to be everything in order to rescue us from the gothic inwardness of family life. Even if we are lucky enough to have several companions, there must be a Best Friend.

I clung to the romance of the Best Friend all through high school, college, and beyond, until my circle of university friends began to disperse. At that point, in my mid-20s, I also acted out the dark, competitive side of friendship that can exist between two young men fighting for a place in life and love by doing the one unforgivable thing: sleeping with my best friend's girl. I was baffled at first that there was no way to repair the damage. I lost this friendship forever, and came away from that debacle much more aware of the amount of injury that friendship can and cannot sustain. Perhaps I needed to prove to myself that friendship was not an all-permissible resilient bond, like a mother's love, but something quite fragile. Precisely because best friendship promotes such a merging of identities, such seeming boundarylessness, the first major transgression of trust can cause the injured party to feel he is fighting for his violated soul against his darkest enemy. There is not much room to maneuver in a best friendship between unlimited intimacy and unlimited mistrust.

Still, it was not until the age of 30 that I reluctantly abandoned the best friend expectation and took up a more pluralistic model. At present, I cherish a dozen friends for their unique personalities, without asking that any one be my soul-twin. Whether this alteration constitutes a movement toward maturity or toward cowardly pragmatism is not for me to say. It may be that, in refusing to depend so much on any one friend, I am opting for self-protection over intimacy. Or it may be that, as we advance into middle age, the life problem becomes less that of establishing a tight dyadic bond and more one of making our way in a broader world, "society." Indeed, since Americans have so indistinct a notion of society, we often try to put a network of friendships in its place.

If a certain intensity is lost in the pluralistic model of friendship, there is also the gain of being able to experience all of one's potential, half-buried selves, through witnessing all the spectacle of the multiple fates of our friends. As it happens, the harem of friends, so tantalizing a notion, often translates into feeling pulled in a dozen different directions, with the guilty sense of having disappointed everyone a little. It is also a risky, contrived enterprise to try to make one's friends behave in a friendly manner toward each other. If the effort fails, one feels obliged to mediate; if it succeeds too well, one is jealous.

Whether friendship is intrinsically singular and exclusive or plural and democratic is a question that has vexed many commentators. Aristotle distinguished three types of friendship: "friendship based on utility," such as businessmen cultivating each other for benefit; "friendship based on pleasure," like young people interested in partying; and "perfect friendship." The first two categories Aristotle calls "qualified and superficial friendships," because they are founded on circumstances that could easily change. The last, which is based on admiration for another's good character, is more permanent, but also rarer, because good men "are few." Cicero, who wrote perhaps the best treatise on friendship, also insisted that what brings true friends together is "a mutual belief in each other's goodness." This insistence on virtue as a precondition for true friendship may strike us as impossibly demanding: Who, after all, feels himself good nowadays? And yet, if I am honest, I must admit that the friendships of mine that have lasted longest have been with those whose integrity, or humanity, or strength to bear their troubles I continue to admire. Conversely, when I lost respect for someone, however winning he or she otherwise remained, the friendship petered away almost immediately. "Remove respect from friendship," said Cicero, "and you have taken away the most splendid ornament it possesses."

Friendship is a long conversation. I suppose I could imagine a nonverbal friendship revolving around shared physical work or sport, but for me, good talk is the point of the thing. Indeed, the ability to generate conversation by the hour is the most promising indication, during the uncertain early stages, that a possible friendship will take hold. In the first few conversations there may be an exaggeration of agreement, as both parties angle for adhesive surfaces. But later on, trust builds through the courage to assert disagreement, through the tactful acceptance that differences of opinion will have to remain.

Some view like-mindedness as both the precondition and the product of friendship. Myself, I distrust it. I have one friend who keeps assuming that we see the world eye-to-eye. She is intent on enrolling us in a flattering aristocracy of taste, on the short "we" list against the ignorant "they." Sometimes I do not have the strength to fight her need for consensus with my own stubborn disbelief in the existence of any such inner circle of privileged, cultivated sensibility. Perhaps I have too much invested in a view of myself as idiosyncratic to be eager to join any coterie, even a coterie of two. What attracts me to friends' conversation is the give and take, not necessarily that we come out at the same point.

"Our tastes and aims and views were identical—and that is where the essence of a friendship must always lie," wrote Cicero. To some extent, perhaps, but then the convergence must be natural, not, as Emerson put it, "a mush of concession. Better be a nettle in the side of your friend than his echo."

Friendship is a school for character, allowing us the chance to study, in great detail and over time, temperaments very different from our own. These charming quirks, these contradictions, these nobilities, these blind spots of our friends we track not out of disinterested curiosity: We must have this information before knowing how far we may relax our guard, how much we may rely on them in crises. The learning curve of friendship involves, to no small extent, filling out this picture of the other's limitations and making peace with the results. Each time I hit up against a friend's inflexibility I am relieved as well as disappointed: I can begin to predict, and arm myself in advance against repeated bruises. I have one friend who is always late, so I bring a book along when I am to meet her. I give her a manuscript to read and she promises to look at it over the weekend. I prepare for a month-long wait.

Though it is often said that with a true friend there is no need to hold anything back ("A friend is a person with whom I may be sincere. Before him I may think aloud," wrote Emerson), I have never found this to be entirely the case. Certain words may be too cruel if they are spoken at the wrong moment—or may fall on deaf ears, for any number of reasons. I also find with all my friends, as they must with me, that some initial resistance, restlessness, some psychic weather must be overcome before that tender ideal attentiveness may be called forth.

I have a good friend, Charlie, who is often very distracted whenever we first get together. If we are sitting in a café he will look around constantly for the waiter, or be distracted by a pretty woman or the restaurant's cat. It would be foolish for me to broach an important subject at such moments, so I resign myself to waiting the half hour or however long it takes until his jumpiness subsides. Or else I draw this pattern grumpily to his attention. Once he has settled down, however, I can tell Charlie virtually anything, and he me. But the candor cannot be rushed. It must be built up to with the verbal equivalent of limbering exercises.

The friendship scene—a flow of shared confidences, recognitions, humor, advice, speculation, even wisdom—is one of the key elements of modern friendships. Compared to the rest of life, this ability to lavish one's best energies on an activity utterly divorced from the profit motive and free from the routines of domination and inequality that affect most relations (including, perhaps, the selfsame friendship at other times) seems idyllic. The friendship scene is by its nature not an everyday occurrence. It represents the pinnacle, the fruit of the friendship, potentially ever present but not always arrived at. Both friends' dim yet self-conscious awareness that they are wandering conversationally toward a goal that they have previously accomplished but that may elude them this time around creates a tension, an obligation to communicate as sincerely as possible, like actors in an improvisation exercise struggling to shape their baggy material into some climactic form. This very pressure to achieve "quality" communication may induce a sort of inauthentic epiphany, not unlike what sometimes happens in the last 10 minutes of a psychotherapy session. But a truly achieved friendship scene can be among the best experiences life has to offer.

Contemporary urban life, with its tight schedules and crowded appointment books, has helped to shape modern friendship into something requiring a good deal of intentionality and pursuit. You phone a friend and make a date a week or more in advance: then you set aside an evening, as if for a tryst, during which to squeeze in all your news and advice, confession and opinion. Such intimate compression may add a romantic note to modern friendships, but it also places a strain on the meeting to yield a high quality of meaning and satisfaction, closer to art than life. If I see busy or out-of-town friends only once every six months, we must not only catch up on our lives but also convince ourselves within the allotted two hours together that we still share a special affinity, an inner track to each other's psyches, or the next meeting may be put off for years. Surely there must be another, saner rhythm of friendship in rural areas—or maybe not? I think about "the good old days" when friends would go on walking tours through England together, when Edith Wharton would bundle poor Henry James into her motorcar and they'd drive to the south of France for a month. I'm not sure my friendships could sustain the strain of travel for weeks at a time, and the truth of the matter is that I've gotten used to this urban arrangement of serial friendship "dates," where the pleasure of the rendezvous is enhanced by the knowledge that it will only last, at most, six hours. If the two of us don't happen to mesh that day (always a possibil-

ity)—well, it's only a few hours. And if it should go beautifully, one needs an escape hatch from exaltation as well as disenchantment. I am capable of only so much intense, exciting communication before I start to fade; I come to these encounters equipped with a six-hour oxygen tank. Is this an evolutionary pattern of modern friendship, or just a personal limitation?

Perhaps because I conceive of the modern friendship scene as a somewhat theatrical enterprise, a one-act play, I tend to be very much affected by the "set." A restaurant, a museum, a walk in the park through the zoo, even accompanying a friend on shopping errands—I prefer public turf where the stimulation of the city can play a backdrop to our dialogue, feeding it with details when inspiration flags.

I have a number of *chez moi* friends who always invite me to come to their homes while evading offers to visit me. What they view as hospitality I see as a need to control the mise-en-scène of friendship. I am expected to fit in where they are most comfortable, while they play lord of the manor, distracted by the props of decor, the pool, the unexpected phone call, the swirl of children, animals, and neighbors. Indeed, *chez moi* friends often tend to keep a sort of open house, so that in going over to see them—for a tête-à-tête, I had assumed—I will suddenly find their other friends and neighbors, whom they have also invited, dropping in all afternoon. There are only so many Sundays I care to spend hanging out with a friend's entourage before I become impatient for a private audience.

Married friends who own their own homes are apt to try to draw me into their domestic fold, whereas single people are often more sensitive about establishing a discreet space for the friendship to occur. Perhaps the married assume that a bachelor like me is desperate for home cooking and a little family life. I have noticed that it is not an easy matter to pry a married friend away from mate and milieu. For married people, especially those with children, the home often becomes the wellspring of all their nurturing feelings, and the single friend is invited to partake in the general flow. Maybe there is also a certain tendency on their part to kill two birds with one stone: They don't see enough of their spouse and kids, and they figure they can visit with you at the same time.

From my standpoint, friendship is a jealous goddess. Whenever a friend of mine marries, I have to fight to overcome the feeling that I am being "replaced" by the spouse. I don't mind sharing a friend with his or her family milieu—in fact I like it, up to a point—but eventually I must get the friend alone, or else, as a bachelor at a distinct power disadvantage, I risk becoming a mere spectator of familial rituals instead of a key player in the drama of friendship.

A person who lives alone usually has more energy to give to friendship. The danger is investing too much emotional energy in one's friends. When a single person is going through a romantic dry spell, he or she often tries to extract the missing passion from a circle of friends. This works only up to a point: The frayed nerves of protracted celibacy can lead to hypersensitive imaginings of slights and rejections, and one's platonic friends seem to come particularly into the line of fire.

Today, with the partial decline of the nuclear family and the search for alternatives to it, we also see attempts to substitute the friendship web for intergenerational family life. Since psychoanalysis has alerted us to regard the family as a mine field of unrequited love, manipulation, and ambivalence, it is only natural that people may look to friendship as a more supportive ground for relation. But in our longing for an unequivocally positive bond, we should beware of sentimentalizing friendship, as saccharine "buddy" movies and certain feminist novels do, and of neutering its problematic aspects. Besides, friendship can never substitute for the true meaning of family: If nothing else, it will never be able to duplicate the family's wild capacity for concentrating neurosis.

In short, friends can't be your family, they can't be your lovers, they can't be your psychiatrists. But they can be your friends, which is plenty.

When I think about the qualities that characterize the best friendships I've known, I can identify five: rapport, affection, need, habit, and forgiveness. Rapport and affection can only take you so far; they may leave you at the formal, outer gate of goodwill, which is still not friendship. A persistent need for the other's company, for the person's interest, approval, opinion, will get you inside the gates, especially when it is reciprocated. In the end, however, there are no substitutes for habit and forgiveness. A friendship may travel for years on cozy habit. But it is a melancholy fact that unless you are a saint you are bound to offend every friend deeply at least once in the course of time. The friends I have kept the longest are those who forgave me time and again for wronging them unintentionally, intentionally, or by the plain catastrophe of my personality. There can be no friends without forgiveness.

Follow-Up

1. *Lopate says that, for him, having a "Best Friend" only lasted until age 30 when he then developed several friendships of approximately the same intimacy level. What kinds of friendship patterns have you had in your life? Are you satisfied with your friendship connections? Why or why not?*

2. *The author contends that contemporary friendship requires planned efforts and often the contacts are short. Is this true in your experience? If so, is this satisfactory?*

3. *If you are single, what happens to your friendship if a friend marries? If you are married, how have your friendship patterns changed, if at all?*

4. *The author says that single persons can invest too much emotional energy in their friends. Do you agree or disagree with this idea? Explain why.*

5. *What is the best friendship arrangement for you at this time? If you do not have this arrangement, what steps can you initiate to make it happen?*

Kinds of Friends

In her book *Necessary Losses,* Judith Viorst discusses how we form different categories of friendships. A brief description of the kinds of friendships is given below:

1. *Convenience Friends*—Persons with whom we exchange small favors; a friendly, but limited, intimacy relationship.
2. *Special Interest Friends*—Persons with whom we share common interests and activities; regular involvement, but not deep intimacy.
3. *Historical Friends*—Persons who were friends in our past but who we do not see often; there may be little in common now, but there is an intimacy that derives from being able to say, "I knew you when. . . ."
4. *Crossroads Friends*—Significant friends at a special time of our lives (e.g., college, former roommate, military service); little current contact, but the specialness can be quickly regenerated if there is an interaction.
5. *Cross-Generational Friends*—The older–younger relationships that have influence and intimacy. It may be a relationship of a mentor, or a cherished non-family friendship in which the older persons are valued for their counsel and acceptance and the younger persons for their liveliness and eagerness to learn.
6. *Close Friends*—Persons who hear our deeper disclosures; those whom we can trust and with whom we can just "be."

Follow-Up

1. *Do your friends generally fall into the categories listed above? If not, what other friend category(ies) would you add?*
2. *Viorst says we have ambivalent feelings toward close friends. There may be envy and competition, as well as affection and love. We generally are more aware of the positive feelings. Is this true for you?*
3. *How would you (or do you) feel about being classified into these categories by your friends?*
4. *Discuss and/or write about your reactions.*

Lamenting the Fading of Friendships

People change.

I know I'm a different person, in some aspects, than I was just six months ago.

It's hard to deal with people changing, especially when those people are, or used to be, your friends.

Of my good friends in high school, I am still close with exactly none of them. Some of them I see once in a while, and we still get along well. Others I see maybe once a year, passing each other by chance on the street. We haven't got much to say, though.

Most of my old friends and I haven't really got much in common anymore. Thus, our conversations are limited to what we've been doing with our lives, what we plan on doing with our lives and what others are doing with their lives.

That is a boring, tired conversation. I may as well be talking to a stranger.

I am at fault for not seeing many of my old friends, and that makes me mad at myself. One of my best friends in high school lived one block away for the past year. I saw him only a few times—the times he came to my house.

Now that he's moved, I feel dumb for never stopping by.

SHARED PAST NOT ENOUGH

Other friends I have shut out of my life on purpose. We were once friends, and now we're not. We once had a lot in common; now we have little. All we have in common is a part of our past.

It's hard to have a relationship with someone based solely on the past. There is only so much you can reminisce over.

But I'm not going to take full blame for the friends with whom I've lost touch.

People change, but I'm not the only one.

It's sad sometimes, thinking of all the great plans we had for the future, all the "forevers, alwayses, nevers."

Then we drifted apart, for one reason or another. And now sometimes when I see an old friend approaching on the street, I almost wish I could turn invisible.

There are other times when I'd like nothing more than to call an old friend, if nothing else, just to say hello.

But I've lost contact.

Now I have more acquaintances, but fewer friends. And while sometimes I miss my old friends, my new friends are great. Really good friends are hard to come by, and it's sad that so many of mine have been swallowed by shadows.

People change, and so do I.

—Mark Murrmann

Note: "Lamenting the Fading of Friendships" by Mark Murmann originally appeared in the *Indianapolis Star,* August 19, 1995. Reprinted with permission.

Follow-Up

Mark Murrmann discusses how he and his former high school friends now have little in common.

- *Do you feel some sense of guilt when former friendships are not maintained?*
- *What seems to be the norm for changing friends?*
- *How should we act when it is time for a friendship to change?*

The Secret World of Siblings

Erica E. Goode

They have not been together like this for years, the three of them standing on the close-cropped grass, New England lawns and steeples spread out below the golf course. He is glad to see his older brothers, has always been glad to have "someone to look up to, to do things with." Yet he also knows the silences between them, the places he dares not step, even though they are all grown men now. They move across the greens, trading small talk, joking. But at the 13th hole, he swings at the ball, duffs it and his brothers begin to needle him. "I should be better than this," he thinks. Impatiently, he swings again, misses, then angrily grabs the club and breaks it in half across his knee. Recalling this outburst later, he explains, simply: "They were beating me again."

As an old man, Leo Tolstoy once opined that the simplest relationships in life are those between brother and sister. He must have been delirious at the time. Even lesser mortals, lacking Tolstoy's acute eye and literary skill, recognize the power of the word *sibling* to reduce normally competent, rational human beings to raw bundles of anger, love, hurt, longing and disappointment—often in a matter of minutes. Perhaps they have heard two elderly sisters dig at each other's sore spots with astounding accuracy, much as they did in junior high. Or have seen a woman corner her older brother at a family reunion, finally venting 30 years of pent-up resentment. Or watched remorse and yearning play across a man's face as he speaks of the older brother whose friendship was chased away long ago, amid dinner table taunts of "Porky Pig, Porky Pig, oink, oink, oink!"

Sibling relationships—and 80 percent of Americans have at least one—outlast marriages, survive the death of parents, resurface after quarrels that would sink any friendship. They flourish in a thousand incarnations of closeness and distance, warmth, loyalty and distrust. Asked to describe them, more than a few people stammer and hesitate, tripped up by memory and sudden bursts of unexpected emotion.

Traditionally, experts have viewed siblings as "very minor actors on the stage of human development," says Stephen Bank, Wesleyan University psychologist and coauthor of *The Sibling Bond*. But a rapidly expanding body of research is showing that what goes on in the playroom or in the kitchen while dinner is being cooked exerts a profound influence on how children grow, a contribution that approaches, if it may not quite equal, that of parenting. Sibling relationships shape how people feel about themselves, how they understand and feel about others, even how much they achieve. And more often than not, such ties represent the lingering thumbprint of childhood upon adult life, affecting the way people interact with those closest to them, with friends and coworkers, neighbors and spouses—a topic explored by an increasing number of popular books, including *Mom Loved You Best*, the most recent offering by Dr. William and Mada Hapworth and Joan Heilman.

SHIFTING LANDSCAPE

In a 1990s world of shifting social realities, of working couples, disintegrating marriages, "blended" households, disappearing grandparents and families spread across a continent, this belated validation of the importance of sibling influences probably comes none too soon. More and more children are stepping in to change diapers, cook meals and help with younger siblings' homework in the hours when parents are still at the office. Baby boomers, edging into middle age, find themselves squaring off once again with brothers and sisters over the care of dying parents or the division of inheritance. And in a generation where late marriages and fewer children are the norm, old age may become for many a time when siblings—not devoted sons and daughters—sit by the bedside.

It is something that happened so long ago, so silly and unimportant now that she is 26 and a researcher at a large, downtown office and her younger brother is her best friend, really, so close that she talks to him at least once a week. Yet as she begins to speak she is suddenly a 5-year-old again on Christmas morning, running into the living room in her red flannel pajamas, her straight blond hair in a ponytail. He hasn't even wrapped it, the little, yellow-flowered plastic purse. Racing to the tree, he brings it to her, thrusts it at her—"Here's your present, Jenny!"—smiling that stupid, adoring, little brother smile. She takes the purse and hurls it across the room. "I don't want your stupid present," she yells. A small crime, long ago forgiven. Yet she says: "I still feel tremendously guilty about it."

Sigmund Freud, perhaps guided by his own childhood feelings of rivalry, conceived of siblingship as a story of unremitting jealousy and competition. Yet, observational studies of young children, many of them the groundbreaking work of Pennsylvania State University psychologist Judy Dunn and her colleagues, suggest that while rivalry between brothers and sisters is common, to see only hostility in sibling relations is to miss the main show. The arrival of a younger sibling may cause distress to an older child accustomed to

parents' exclusive attention, but it also stirs enormous interest, presenting both children with the opportunity to learn crucial social and cognitive skills: how to comfort and empathize with another person, how to make jokes, resolve arguments, even how to irritate.

The lessons in this life tutorial take as many forms as there are children and parents. In some families, a natural attachment seems to form early between older and younger children. Toddlers as young as 14 months miss older siblings when they are absent, and babies separated briefly from their mothers will often accept comfort from an older sibling and go back to playing happily. As the younger child grows, becoming a potential playmate, confidant and sparring partner, older children begin to pay more attention. But even young children monitor their siblings' behavior closely, showing a surprisingly sophisticated grasp of their actions and emotional states.

PARENTAL SIGNALS

To some extent, parents set the emotional tone of early sibling interactions. Dunn's work indicates, for example, that children whose mothers encourage them to view a newborn brother or sister as a human being, with needs, wants and feelings, are friendlier to the new arrival over the next year, an affection that is later reciprocated by the younger child. The quality of parents' established relationships with older siblings can also influence how a new younger brother or sister is received. In another of Dunn's studies, first-born daughters who enjoyed a playful, intense relationship with their mothers treated newborn siblings with more hostility, and a year later the younger children were more hostile in return. In contrast, older daughters with more contentious relationships with their mothers greeted the newcomer enthusiastically—perhaps relieved to have an ally. Fourteen months later, these older sisters were more likely to imitate and play with their younger siblings and less apt to hit them or steal their toys.

In troubled homes, where a parent is seriously ill, depressed or emotionally unavailable, siblings often grow closer than they might in a happier environment, offering each other solace and protection. This is not always the case, however. When parents are on the brink of separation or have already divorced and remarried, says University of Virginia psychologist E. Mavis Hetherington, rivalry between brothers and sisters frequently increases, as they struggle to hold on to their parents' affection in the face of the breakup. If anything, it is sisters who are likely to draw together in a divorcing family, while brothers resist forming tighter bonds. Says Hetherington: "Males tend to go it alone and not to use support very well."

Much of what transpires between brothers and sisters, of course, takes place when parents are not around. "Very often the parent doesn't see the subtlety or the full cycle of siblings' interactions," says University of Hartford psychologist Michael Kahn. Left to their own devices, children tease, wrestle and play make-believe. They are the ones eager to help pilot the pirate ship or play storekeeper to their sibling's impatient customer. And none of this pretend play, researchers find, is wasted. Toddlers who engage regularly in make-believe with older siblings later show a precocious grasp of others' behavior. Says Dunn: "They turn out to be the real stars at understanding people."

Obviously, some degree of rivalry and squabbling between siblings is natural. Yet in extreme cases, verbal or physical abuse at the hands of an older brother or sister can leave scars that last well into adulthood. Experts like Wesleyan University's Bank distinguish between hostility that takes the form of humiliation or betrayal and more benign forms of conflict. From the child's perspective, the impact of even normal sibling antagonism may depend in part on who's coming out ahead. In one study, for example, children showed higher self-esteem when they "delivered" more teasing, insults and other negative behaviors to their siblings than they received. Nor is even intense rivalry necessarily destructive. Says University of Texas psychologist Duane Buhrmester: "You may not be happy about a brother or sister who is kind of pushing you along, but you may also get somewhere in life."

They are two sides of an equation written 30 years ago: Michèle, with her raven-black hair, precisely made-up lips, restrained smile; Arin, two years older, her easy laugh filling the restaurant, the sleeves of her gray turtleneck pulled over her hands.

This is what Arin thinks about Michèle: "I have always resented her, and she has always looked up to me. When we were younger, she used to copy me, which would drive me crazy. We have nothing in common except our family history—isn't that terrible? I like her spirit of generosity, her direction and ambition. I dislike her vapid conversation and her idiotic friends. But the reality is that we are very close, and we always will be."

This is what Michèle sees: "Arin was my ideal. I wanted to be like her, to look like her. I think I drove her crazy. Once, I gave her a necklace I thought was very beautiful. I never saw her wear it. I think it wasn't good enough, precious enough. We are so different—I wish that we could be more like friends. But as we get older, we accept each other more."

It is something every brother or sister eventually marvels at, a conundrum that novelists have played upon in a thousand different ways: There are two children. They grow up in the same house, share the same parents, experience many of the same events. Yet they are stubbornly, astonishingly different.

A growing number of studies in the relatively new field of behavioral genetics are finding confirmation for this popular observation. Children raised in the same family, such studies find, are only very slightly more similar to each other on a variety of personality di-

"Triplet Sisters" by Greg Mason. Copyright © 1996.

mensions than they are, say, to Bill Clinton or to the neighbor's son. In cognitive abilities, too, siblings appear more different than alike. And the extent to which siblings *do* resemble one another in these traits is largely the result of the genes they share—a conclusion drawn from twin studies, comparisons of biological siblings raised apart and biological children and adopted siblings raised together.

CONTRASTS

Heredity also contributes to the *differences* between siblings. About 30 percent of the dissimilarity between brothers and sisters on many personality dimensions can be accounted for by differing genetic endowments from parents. But that still leaves 70 percent that *cannot* be attributed to genetic causes, and it is this unexplained portion of contrasting traits that scientists find so intriguing. If two children who grow up in the same family are vastly different, and genetics accounts for only a minor part of these differences, what else is going on?

The answer may be that brothers and sisters don't really share the same family at all. Rather, each child grows up in a unique fam-

ily, one shaped by the way he perceives other people and events, by the chance happenings he alone experiences, and by how other people—parents, siblings and teachers—perceive and act toward him. And while for decades experts in child development have focused on the things that children in the same family share—social class, child-rearing attitudes and parents' marital satisfaction, for example— what really seem to matter are those things that are not shared. As Judy Dunn and Pennsylvania State behavioral geneticist Robert Plomin write in *Separate Lives: Why Siblings Are So Different*, "Environmental factors important to development are those that two children in the same family experience differently."

Asked to account for children's disparate experiences, most people invoke the age-old logic of birth order. "I'm the middle child, so I'm cooler headed," they will say, or "Firstborns are high achievers." Scientists, too, beginning with Sir Francis Galton in the 19th century, have sought in birth order a way to characterize how children diverge in personality, IQ or life success. But in recent years, many researchers have backed away from this notion, asserting that when family size, number of siblings and social class are taken into account, the explanatory power of birth ranking becomes negligible. Says one psychologist: "You wouldn't want to make a decision about your child based on it."

At least one researcher, however, argues that birth order does exert a strong influence on development, particularly on attitudes toward authority. Massachusetts Institute of Technology historian Frank Sulloway, who has just completed a 20-year analysis of 4,000 scientists from Copernicus through the 20th century, finds that those with older siblings were significantly more likely to have contributed to or supported radical scientific revolutions, such as Darwin's theory of evolution. Firstborn scientists, in contrast, were more apt to champion conservative scientific ideas. "Later-borns are consistently more open-minded, more intellectually flexible and therefore more radical," says Sulloway, adding that later-borns also tend to be more agreeable and less competitive.

HEARTHSIDE INEQUITIES

Perhaps most compelling for scientists who study sibling relationships are the ways in which parents treat their children differently and the inequalities children perceive in their parents' behavior. Research suggests that disparate treatment by parents can have a lasting effect, even into adulthood. Children who receive more affection from fathers than their siblings do, for example, appear to aim their sights higher in terms of education and professional goals, according to a study by University of Southern California psychologist Laura Baker. Seven-year-olds treated by their mothers in a less affectionate, more controlling way than their brothers or sisters are apt to be more anxious and depressed. And adolescents who say their parents favor a sibling over themselves are more likely to report angry and depressed feelings.

Parental favoritism spills into sibling relationships, too, sometimes breeding the hostility made famous by the Smothers Brothers in their classic 1960s routine, "Mom always loved you best." In families where parents are more punitive and restrictive toward one child, for instance that child is more likely to act in an aggressive, rivalrous and unfriendly manner toward a brother or sister, according to work by Hetherington. Surprisingly, it may not matter who is favored. Children in one study were more antagonistic toward siblings even when *they* were the ones receiving preferential treatment.

Many parents, of course, go to great lengths to distribute their love and attention equally. Yet even the most consciously egalitarian parenting may be seen as unequal by children of different ages. A mother may treat her

"Brothers" by Greg Mason. Copyright © 1996.

4-year-old boy with the same care and attention she lavished on her older son when he was 4. But from the 7-year-old's perspective, it may look like his younger brother is getting a better deal. Nor is there much agreement among family members on how evenhandedly love is apportioned: Adolescents report favoritism when their mothers and fathers insist that none exists. Some parents express surprise that their children feel unequally treated, while at the same time they describe how one child is more demanding, another needs more discipline. And siblings almost never agree in their assessments of who, exactly, Mom loves best.

NATURE VERSUS NURTURE

Further complicating the equation is the contribution of heredity to temperament, each child presenting a different challenge from the moment of birth. Plomin, part of a research team led by George Washington University psychiatrist David Reiss that is studying sibling pairs in 700 families nationwide, views the differences between siblings as emerging from complex interaction of nature and nurture. In this scheme, a more aggressive and active child, for example, might engage in more conflict with parents and later become a problem child at school. A quieter, more timid child might receive gentler parenting and later be deemed an easy student.

In China, long ago, it was just the two of them, making dolls out of straw together in the internment camp, putting on their Sunday clothes to go to church with their mother. She mostly ignored her younger sister, or goaded her relentlessly for being so quiet. By the time they were separated—her sister sailing alone at 13 for the United States—there was already a wall between them, a prelude to the stiff Christmas cards they exchange, the rebuffed phone calls, the impersonal gifts that arrive in the mail.

Now, when the phone rings, she is wishing hard for a guardian angel, for someone to take away the pain that throbs beneath the surgical bandage on her chest, keeping her curled under the blue and white cotton coverlet. She picks up the receiver, recognizes her sister's voice instantly, is surprised, grateful, cautious all at once. How could it be otherwise after so many years? It is the longest they have spoken in 50 years. And across the telephone wire, something is shifting, melting in the small talk about children, the wishes for speedy recovery. "I think we both realized that life can be very short," she says. Her pain, too, is dulling now, moving away as she listens to her sister's voice. She begins to say a small prayer of thanks.

For a period that seems to stretch forever in the timelessness of childhood, there is only the family, only the others who are unchosen partners, their affection, confidences, attacks and betrayals defining the circumference of a limited world. But eventually, the boundaries expand, friends and schoolmates taking the place of brothers and sisters, highways and airports leading to other lives, to office parties and neighborhood meetings, to other, newer families.

ADULT BONDS

Rivalry between siblings wanes after adolescence, or at least adults are less apt to admit competitive feelings. Strong friendships also become less intense, diluted by geography, by marriage, by the concerns of raising children and pursuing independent careers. In national polls, 65 percent of Americans say they would like to see their siblings more often than the typical "two or three times a year." And University of Indianapolis psychologist Victoria Bedford finds, in her work, that men and women of child-rearing age often show longing toward siblings, especially those close in age and of the same sex. Yet for some people, the detachment of adulthood brings relief, an escape from bonds that are largely unwanted but never entirely go away. Says one woman about her brothers and sisters: "Our values are different, our politics diametrically opposed. I don't feel very connected, but there's still a pressure to keep up the tie, a kind of guilt that I don't have a deeper sense of kinship."

How closely sibling ties are maintained and nurtured varies with cultural and ethnic expectations. In one survey, for example, 54 percent of low-income blacks reported receiving help from a brother or sister, in comparison with 44 percent of low-income Hispanics and 36 percent of low-income whites. Siblings in large families are also more likely to give and receive support, as are those who live in close geographical proximity to one another. Sex differences are also substantial. In middle and later life, sisters are much more likely than brothers to keep up close relationships.

So important, in fact, is the role that sisters play in cementing family ties that some families all but fall apart without them. They are the ones who often play the major role in caring for aging parents and who make sure family members stay in touch after parents die. And in later life, says Purdue University psychologist Victor Cicerelli, sisters can provide a crucial source of reassurance and emo-

"Brother and Sister" by Nelson Goud. Copyright © 1996.

tempt at rapprochement—unheard of. One man, asked by a researcher about his brother, shouted, "Don't mention that son of a bitch to me!" and slammed the door in the psychologist's face.

Sibling feuds often echo much earlier squabbles and are sparked by similar collisions over shared responsibility or resources—who is doing more for an ailing parent, how inheritance should be divided. Few are long lasting, and those that are probably reflect more severe emotional disturbance. Yet harmonious or antagonistic patterns established in childhood make themselves felt in many adults' lives. Says psychologist Kahn: "This is not just kid stuff that people outgrow." One woman, for example, competes bitterly with a slightly older coworker, just as she did with an older brother growing up. Another suspects that her sister married a particular man in part to impress her. A scientist realizes that he argues with his wife in exactly the same way he used to spar with an older brother.

For most people, a time comes when it makes sense to rework and reshape such "frozen images" of childhood—to borrow psychologist Bank's term—into designs more accommodating to adult reality, letting go of ancient injuries, repairing damaged fences. In a world of increasingly tenuous family connections, such renegotiation may be well worth the effort. Says author Judith Viorst, who has written of sibling ties: "There is no one else on Earth with whom you share so much personal history."

tional security for their male counterparts. In one study, elderly men with sisters reported greater feelings of happiness and less worry about their life circumstances.

WARMTH OR TOLERANCE?

Given the mixed emotions many adults express about sibling ties, it is striking that in national surveys the vast majority—more than 80 percent—deem their relationships with siblings to be "warm and affectionate." Yet this statistic may simply reflect the fact that ambivalence is tolerated more easily at a distance, warmth and affection less difficult to muster for a few days a year than on a daily basis. Nor are drastic breaches between siblings—months or years of silence, with no at-

Follow-Up

1. *For those who have siblings, how would you describe the ways in which you relate to them and feel about them? How are you alike and different?*
2. *In childhood, sibling relationships often carry over to other people in adulthood (e.g., a colleague may remind you of a brother or sister). Examine your life patterns to see if this is true. If yes, are you content with your behavior or would you like to change?*

3. *If you are a parent of two or more children, which points of the article do you agree and disagree with? Why?*
4. *Studies of only children show that there are few differences, if any, between the overall development of only children and those who have siblings. If you are an only child, what, if anything, has been an advantage? A disadvantage?*
5. *For those with siblings, how have your relationships changed during adulthood?*
6. *Write about or discuss any other main point in this article.*

The Human Potential of Whip Gimby

Nels Goud

While on a picnic my seven-year-old son and I walked over to watch a couple innings of a men's baseball game. It was the end of a close game, the bases were loaded, and the pitcher was nervously pawing the dirt on the mound. The pitcher peered in toward the plate, took a quick look over at third and fired an aspirin fastball. The batter was ready and took a mighty swing and conked the catcher on the back of the head. Everyone on the field and in the stands remained frozen for a few seconds and stared. Except for the catcher. He fell forward and sprawled face down over home plate. His mask had protected his skull but the force of the blow knocked him out. The ump removed his mask and called "Time Out!" Players and coaches from both teams ran toward home plate, some sounding like medical students—"You all right Pete?" Pete slowly rolled over on his back, opened his eyes and looked for the freight train that roared onto the diamond. "Pete, you OK?" yelled the medical teammates. Pete stood up, rubbed his head and hoped it was still connected to his neck. Between home and first base a big argument was brewing. The catcher's coach was shouting at the ump "He swung! It's strike two!" The ump appeared mystified at the sense of priorities here and told the coach to shut up and walked over to the catcher. The coach marched behind the ump and kept yelling "It's a strike!" This guy wanted to win. The catcher staggered to his feet and began slowly rotating his head.

"What's the coach arguing about, Dad?" asked my son.

"Well, he is saying that the batter swung and even though he hit the catcher, it should be called a strike."

"What difference does that make?" responded my son with some anger, "The catcher's hurt!"

A single baseball play escalates into human drama. A young boy becomes puzzled by the lack of agreement on the obvious ethical choice. Once again I realize how life's fundamentals are reflected in almost any activity. All you have to do is look in a certain way. A single wild flower revealed the whole world to the philosopher Suzuki. Since it is summer, baseball seems to fit nicely as a mirror.

During my high school years I had to find the best players for my Little League team, the Decatur Tigers. The selection criteria was simple—choose the best hitters and fielders. You would have been surprised on how many good players were passed over in the general draft. This happened because human bias weaseled its way into the coaches' choices. In Decatur there was a negative image of the "farm kid." Most other coaches selected these players last, and then grudgingly. Maybe this was because most coaches were "town kids." Although I lived in town I knew many farm families through my father's work, truck farming. I also knew who could run, hit, and throw. Seven Tiger regulars were farm kids and even though these players helped win League championships for the Tigers, each year they were passed over by other coaches. It was one of the few times in my life that I applauded bias.

This farm kid prejudice brought disaster to the other teams during one particular year. The Tigers were struggling about half way through the season due to erratic pitching. My third baseman, a farm kid, happened to bring his neighbor Harmon to a practice. Harmon looked like he just finished cleaning barns. He wore baggy pants held up with suspenders, had a long-sleeved work shirt, and his head almost hidden by a floppy wide-brimmed hat. He was a quiet kid and when he did speak it was in a slow drawl. I asked Harmon to help us out by chasing down foul balls during batting practice and throw them back to me. After the fifth foul ball my catching hand was turning red from the force of his throws.

"Hey Harmon, how old are you?" I asked.

"Twelve," he quietly drawled. The upper age for Little League.

"Have you ever played baseball?"

"No."

"How would you like to play for the Tigers?"

"OK."

I walked Harmon over to the other coaches and asked if they minded if I added Harmon to my roster, he being a friend of my third baseman and having nothing to do. They looked over Harmon, barely holding back the wisecracks, and with large smiles generally said, "Go ahead, fine with me." I showed Harmon how to wind up like a pitcher. I told him to throw as hard as he could into the catcher's mitt. Harmon threw hard and straight and the Tigers won every game from there on out.

Harmon was a natural. If he were a flower, he would only have needed a couple inches of dust and an occasional sprinkle to achieve full bloom. But as most coaches know, for every Harmon there is a Whip Gimby.

If Whip was a flower, it would take daily pampering all spring on the finest soil to get his seed to break ground surface. Whip was one of those boys who, not really knowing why or questioning it, was supposed to play baseball because it seemed boys did that sort of thing in the summer. Whip appeared genuinely interested but somewhat baffled by the sport. The first practice sessions quickly revealed that he did not know how to hold a bat, what a shortstop did, or what to do if he happened to stop a ball hit at him. At ten years old his spindly frame had yet to show signs of any musculature, and hand-eye coordination was best classified in the potentials category. The regulation size baseball glove hung from his hand like a heavy saddle. There was only one position for Whip—right field. There was where he earned the nickname. He would stand motionless in right field until a ball flew by him. Tracking it down, he would stand there with a puzzled look. "Throw it to second base!" shouted the other players.

Wide-eyed, he would unfurl a long, skinny arm for a mighty heave. The ball would arch lazily for a few feet and roll to a stop, almost making it to the infield. "Arm like a whip," said the center-fielder. The name stuck. I think he liked it. He had something special— a baseball name.

Whip's first time at bat found him straddling the plate facing the pitcher head on, his hands holding the bat like it was an ax. Whip was a true coaching challenge. We straightened out his batting stance. The remaining problem was that his swing went in the same arc and speed whether the pitch was high or low, fast or slow. No amount of coaching could change this swing. It had to be a genetic fixed action pattern. Whip would make contact only if the ball happened to pass in the space of his lone swing pattern. He was just as surprised as the rest of us when this did occur.

Strangely, it was Whip Gimby who taught us a great deal about positive human character. Blessed with the aptitude of a turnip for baseball and having to prove it each practice and game, I cannot remember a single instance when he was angry, withdrawn, frustrated, or blaming someone. Whip retained an eagerness to learn and attended every practice. An infrequent catch or hitting a weak ground ball was enough to sustain him through many failures. Whip seemed to accept his limited abilities and was proud to be a Tiger. How do you not like a kid like this?

Whip became a key figure for many Tigers on learning the meaning of human respect. During the first practices Whip became the target of jokes and taunts by several good hitters. My lecturing did not seem to stop these wisecracks. It became obvious that another method had to be employed. I called it "empathy training." If a player persisted in making degrading remarks about Whip's hitting, I made sure he would not have a chance to hit the ball when his turn came to practice. For a high school pitcher, this was not hard to do; I could really bring the heat from the Little League mound. The superstars would miss every pitch and I would offer a comment or two on their pathetic hitting prowess. The wisecracking diminished to zero after one empathy session.

The real thrills in Little League baseball came from playing in actual competition. You got a chance to show your stuff in front of family and friends, match skills with opposing players, and even play with a spanking brand new baseball. And if you were on a winning team, it was all magnified. To play in a game as a Tiger you had to attend practice. The Tigers were always in contention for first place and the guys attended practice regularly in order to play. This, of course, made us a better team. The "you practice, you play" rule combined fairness with the work ethic so cherished by the culture. It also produced an ethical dilemma one season.

It was the next to the last game and the Tigers were tied for first place. The final game was against the other first-place team. A win in this game was crucial. Harmon was doing his usual job, sizzling fast balls by batters making them look for holes in their bats. But a few errors and walks and an occasional hit got them enough runs to tie us going into the last two innings. We had two more chances at bat. It was then I realized that I had not played four

Tigers who had attended practice that week. No one said anything and it was common practice to stick with your best players in tight games. I was tempted. But what can you do when your players faithfully follow the practice-play rule? I sent the four out to their fielding positions. Whip loped out to right field.

An inning passes with no change in score. Harmon strikes out the side in the first half of the last inning. Our last chance at bat. Jimmy hits a double. A strike out and a ground out make it two down, but Jimmy has scampered to third. The opposing pitcher is getting tired and wild. He walks the next batter. Two on and two out. Seems like I read a similar baseball story before, but now I'm in it. Yes, it is Whip Gimby's turn at immortality. True to form, Whip doesn't realize it's his turn. "Whip!" I call, "It's your turn to hit." Whip catapults off the bench and runs to homeplate. He has forgotten his bat, and runs back to the bench. Normally a pumped up state can help a player. It's making Whip more confused. I walk over to calm him down. His eyes are wide, darting left and right.

"Should I swing?" he asks.

"Swing if it is a pitch you can hit. Do not swing if it's a bad pitch." Sound advice to a nervous batter if he knows the difference between a bad and good pitch. This is not one of Whip's strengths. "You'll do fine Whip, just watch the pitch." There is another choice. Just tell him to take all pitches because the pitcher is getting wild and there's a good chance of getting a walk. The odds for a walk are considerably higher than Whip hitting a pitch. But what does this coaching advice communicate to a young boy? I'm beginning to hate principles.

Whip swings at the first pitch and misses. The second pitch comes in head high. Whip swings about when the catcher throws it back to the pitcher. He is consistent, though. Both swings were in his fixed lone swing pattern. I can tell he is too pumped up yet. I go over to talk to him, tell him he's doing fine, and to really watch the ball before he swings. He settles back into the batter's box with his wide eyes. The pitcher winds up and a fastball streaks over the middle of the plate. Whip unleashs his only swing. POOF, he misses again. A few groans are heard. As Whip walks back to the bench I think I catch the first look of dejection I've seen on him the whole season. A couple Tigers go out and tell him that it was all right, they struck out earlier too.

The Tigers survived this game and clinched the championship in the final game.

Harmon set a league strikeout record. Whip could say he was on a champion team.

If you happen to watch some baseball you might take a minute to look at the human drama out there. You might also cheer on a kid throwing aspirins or even a skinny one who swings the same way no matter if the pitch is high or low, fast or slow.

Follow-Up

1. *In almost any organized activity—sports, music groups, and so forth—there is a Whip Gimby or two. Not having the aptitude or background of more skilled peers, these persons often have other redeeming qualities that contribute to the group. Try to think of an example of this phenomenon in your life. Offer your analysis of why the less talented are, or can be, needed and valued members of a group.*
2. *The author states that "life's fundamentals are reflected in almost any activity." Discuss another life activity for which this is true, and provide examples.*
3. *Write about or discuss your views on any other aspect of this piece.*

Parents

Martin Shepard

Learning to accept your parents as people in their own right—different and distinct from you—is a task that poses difficulties for quite a large number of people. There should be nothing surprising in all of this. For we all have one very good historical reason—our childhoods.

The infant is born into a world in which he is, literally, *part* of his mother. Without her to comfort, clothe, feed and shelter him, he could not survive. During childhood our little girl and boy still depend greatly on their parents. They have not yet acquired the skills necessary to provide for and sustain themselves. This is a time one learns certain "do's" and "don'ts." You learn how to count and how to read, how to cook and how to sew, how to hammer and how to saw. And you learn *not* to swallow iodine, *not* to put a fork in the electrical outlet, and *not* to cross a street unless you look to make sure there is no traffic approaching.

Typically the child's contract with the parent is one in which he accepts the dependent role in return for the favors/protection/guidance/and support he receives from them. There are, of course, dissatisfactions. He prefers taking things out to play with more than he does putting them away. He wants to do and try things he sees grown-ups doing and resents it when they say "No." He may want to come and go more freely than they are ready to allow. And he'd rather watch television than do his homework or practice the piano.

Adolescence marks the years during which relatively accepting and "sweet" children become adults in their own right. Following the sexual maturation of puberty, adolescents typically reject the dependent con- tracts that as children they had with their parents. It is a period of much storm and strife, both in the inner life of the adolescents and in their relationships to their parents. Opposition/confrontation/argumentation are a natural part of the process as the adolescent seeks to break away and find his or her own adulthood. If it is accomplished smoothly, and the adolescent truly feels adult, he comes to accept his parents as he would other adults. If they share common interests and *if* the parents accept him as an adult (not only as their child), they remain close. If their interests are not similar and/or if the parents cannot transcend their *roles* as parents, there is a polite distance—as any adult would have with people who are on different wavelengths. This second alternative is a more common outcome of maturation.

What I have described thus far is "normal" maturation. Many individuals, no matter how old they are, never make it, psychologically speaking, past either childhood or adolescence when it comes to relating to their parents. Those stuck in the childhood phase remain overly docile and dependent. Those stuck in adolescence relate to their parents in a perpetually rebellious and ill-tempered way.

Given the cultural roles males and females are assigned (males presumably being "aggressive" and females "passive"), one might expect that women are more likely to become stuck in the childhood state and men in the adolescent one. And—although there are many reversals to this expectation—such is usually the case.

Louise is a good example of such a child/ woman. In her childhood and adolescence, her parents were perpetually available to her. They were quick to comfort and pamper her. They always soothed her hurts, took her side, indulged her fancies. She, in turn, pampered their egos by letting them know how exceptional they were, how they were the only people who understood her, how much wisdom and sage advice they had, and how appreciative she was.

At twenty-two she married for the first time. Her husband, Greg, was an insurance salesman and just out of college. He was a decent, responsible, upright young man, who looked forward to supporting Louise and raising a family. But it never worked out that way.

Louise was incapable of accommodating herself to the rigors of a more spartan and independent existence. She consulted her mother daily, both to ask for advice on simple housekeeping chores and for consolation over any minor inconveniences she was having with Greg. She was incapable of sticking to a budget and so, behind Greg's back, ran to her physician father for extra funds to pay her charge-account bills and indulge her passion for clothes, cars (which she insisted on changing yearly), and innumerable redecoration schemes.

When her first and only child was born, her parents hired a maid for her. And Mother came over daily for several months to help out and give advice.

After three years of marriage, Louise left Greg. Marriage didn't conform to her picture of "picket fences and lace curtains." She was interested in playing more and working less. Her parents were sympathetic. They agreed with Louise that Greg was "cheap," "selfish," and that he "always got his way." Besides which, Mother was willing to raise Louise's daughter while Louise went back to school and tried to find a new man.

Now thirty-nine years old and on her fifth husband, Louise lives in another city. But she still phones her family a few times each week.

Sam, who is twenty-eight, is the sort of person who typifies adolescent "stuckness." For he remains continuously close to, yet antagonistic toward, his parents.

While attending a local college, he, like many other students, began smoking marijuana. Not content to do it privately, he naturally let his parents know of his activities. They were frightened, shocked, and strongly disapproving. Sam, rather than dropping the subject, continued to let them know of his usage by smoking at home. Quarrels/insults/ door-slamming occurred frequently on both sides.

Dinner conversations to this day are reminiscent of the popular television series *All in the Family*—with Sam typically attacking his father's political and social points of view and Mother acting as a harassed peacemaker.

Four years ago Sam moved out of his parents' home but continued to bring home his laundry for his mother to wash. His attitude was sullen. If his mother inquired about his life he would give her flippant answers or accuse her of trying to hold on to him. Yet he made it a point to inform his parents of many of his activities that he knew they objected to—his dating a woman of another religion, his intention of quitting a promising job, his experimentation with LSD.

Every now and then he would ask his father for a loan or the use of the family car. He felt it was coming to him. On those occasions when his father refused him, he always had some unkind words for the old man.

Two years ago he married. He made it a point to tell his mother not to interfere when she offered to help care for Suzy, Sam's daughter, who was born eight months ago. But whenever Sam and his wife, Brenda, have a party to attend, Sam calls up his mother, expecting her to be always available for babysitting. When she is not, he accuses her of being a hypocrite for having offered to help out earlier.

How can you tell if you are *stuck*, in any respect, regarding your parents? One way is to see if they embarrass you. Perhaps you don't want your parents to meet your friends because you fear they will act in a way that will humiliate you; that they will treat you as their little girl or boy, correct you, or behave "coarsely" in front of your friends.

Such embarrassment is often related to your still feeling yourself a *part* of—an extension of—your parents. You fail to realize that if your parents do react absurdly, it is *they* who will be laughed at, not you. Unless, of course, you take it as personally as a thirteen-year-old who brings her first date over to the house.

Other indications of dependency are the making of routine daily or weekly telephone calls to your parents, wanting their approval constantly, or finding that there is "no other person as good, wise, and kind to me as my mother (or father)."

Signs of rebelliousness are so self-evident, emotionally, to the sufferer, that they need no further elaboration.

There is a certain validity to a child's blaming a parent when things don't work out to his satisfaction. After all, the parent *is* in charge. If a meal doesn't taste good, the child can't very well cook his own. If the family moves and the child must give up his neighborhood friends, that is the parents' responsibility, not his. *But once you pass the age of eighteen,* those conditions no longer hold true. There is no further need to depend upon your parents.

The task of both the *child-stuck* and *adolescent-stuck* person is to get *un-stuck,* by learning to do things on your own and, in doing so, becoming a more self-sufficient human being. You can't have a very good self-concept—can't very well consider yourself any person's equal—if you remain a child-at-heart in relationship to your parents. Whatever *advantages* there are in taking things from your parents by continuing the "child" or "adolescent" integrations are more than offset by the loss of basic self-esteem that results from staying in that role.

The "child" is reluctant to go *through* the adolescent, rebellious, phase. The "adolescent" is reluctant to achieve total self-sufficiency. He wants all of the advantages of both childhood *and* adulthood, but none of the disadvantages of either. "Adolescents" are too embarrassed to admit how much they still *want* their parents, and how much they might even love them.

Both groups ask for their parents' support and approval (albeit in different ways) long after they are capable of managing their own lives. Not only does this interfere with their lives in general (witness Louise and Sam), but it certainly prevents the possibility of their establishing a realistic present-day relationship with their parents.

I've talked frequently in this book* about living in the *here and now,* and how emotions, people, and relationships change. One of the things that can certainly be said of people who have trouble dealing with their parents is that they are usually reacting to *memories* of both their parents and themselves—as they all were ten, fifteen, or twenty years ago—and *not* in terms of the realities of all of them now. This is always due to the *holding back* of the maturational process.

We are left, therefore, with many adults who still *blame* their parents for the way they have treated them. As if their parents had chosen to make the child's life miserable.

Yet there are very few parents who *intentionally* act cruelly. Every set of parents, if they could choose, would elect to be the world's best parents.

Of course, lack of "intent" does not mean that parents don't occasionally act cruelly. Why shouldn't they? They are primarily *people* before they are parents. All of us are capable of cruelty. Besides, they had parents who "misunderstood" them, too. Parents, like all

*Martin Shepard is referring to his *The Do-It-Yourself Psychotherapy Book* from which this reading was taken.—The Editor

people, can be tight-fisted, generous, disappointing, helpful, indifferent, funny, tender, or short-tempered.

When I was twenty-five and a student in medical school, I was still reacting to my parents as an adolescent. I resented having to go visit them each week. I felt they were still trying to control me. When I was questioned by my analyst whether the situation might not be reversed—whether I might not be trying to control *them*—I realized that I made my weekly sojourns to pick up a weekly allotment that they were generous enough to offer me. And that I could possibly manage to get by with a much lower amount. And that I needn't show up weekly to "pay my dues" for their generosity—that they gave it out of kindness and not for my weekly shows of obeisance. With that realization I stopped my mechanical visits, cut down on what I was receiving and began to relate to them more adultly.

A therapist friend of mine was treating a young man who constantly fought with his mother. He wanted her approval, but she was constantly critical. Mother was an exceptionally irrational woman and never saw how much her son wanted her blessings. He, in turn, could not accept her irrationality.

My friend asked his patient the following question: "If you passed by a mental institution and saw your mother looking through the barred windows on one of the floors, and she was screaming the same things at you, as you passed by, that she now screams at you at home, would it still trouble you?"

"No," said the young man. "I'd discount it, because I'd know she was crazy."

"From now on, then, every time your mother gets on your nerves, I want you to recall that picture of her shouting from that hospital window."

His patient did just that and found his aggravation and frustration subsiding.

A device such as this is I think, a useful tool for people who find themselves continuously fighting with a non-accepting parent.

A rule to bear in mind that will help you to see your parents more realistically, is:
Grown-ups are merely children in aging skin.

When you get to feeling overwhelmed by your parents' (or parent substitutes—such as bosses or teachers) "wisdom" or resentful over their "shortcomings," try to see the child that is hiding and acting inside of them.

I have purposely avoided writing a chapter on *being a parent*—on dealing more effectively with your children—for a number of reasons. One is that there is no way to be a *parent.* You can only be *yourself.* And if you become a mentally healthy adult (as, I'm sure, all of the readers of this book are trying to become), you will do all right both as *yourself* and as a parent.

As a psychiatrist, I have seen hundreds upon hundreds of people complaining about their parents. If they were given a great deal of material advantages, they would complain that "my parents bought me things as a substitute for love." If they were given few things, the complaint was "my parents were cheapskates and didn't love me enough." If they were given a great deal of freedom by their parents, they would lament that their "parents weren't interested in me or what I did." But if they were closely supervised, it was because "my parents were too strict."

Naturally it helps to be kind, tolerant, and understanding of your children. Remembering your own childhood helps. But sometimes a spanking or some punishment may well be in order.

So there are no suggestions I have to offer you as a parent, except to bear in mind that *whatever you do, it is likely to be wrong in your child's eyes.* But when and if your child grows to maturity—if he or she doesn't get stuck in child-like or adolescent behavior—your child will come to appreciate that you did the best that you could.

And further—it is your *child's* responsibility to grow up, to mature—not yours to do it for him. Just as you must realize that you are no longer part of your parents—that things aren't *their fault* —your child has to learn the same things about you.

The exercises that follow attempt to help you continue your own maturational process vis-à-vis your parents. You may need *repeated* work on the exercises in order to abandon your unrealistic views of both yourself and your parents. For you must, eventually, learn to let go of them, give up your demands that they be different than they are, forgive them their faults (and all of the things that they "should" have done, did do, and didn't do)— and come to realize that your parents couldn't possibly have been anything other than what they were and what they are.

SHEPARD'S EXERCISES

1. Work with two empty chairs. Put your father in one and tell him all of the negative things you've held back from him—your resentments, frustrations, hatreds. Be as specific as you can. Then, switch seats, be him, and respond to "you." Say how you feel hearing all of these negative things. Keep the dialogue going by changing chairs once more and telling your father what you needed, now need, wanted, and now want from him. Have him respond by saying what he needs and wants from you (past and present). See whether or not you can achieve any greater understanding of one another's positions, as you keep the dialogue going, as opposed to finding yourselves simply *arguing.*

2. Repeat exercise 1, substituting your mother for your father.

3. Pretend you are your father and write a short composition about "The Difficulties I Had In Raising My Child."

4. Repeat exercise 3, but now write as your mother instead of your father.

5. Place your father back in the empty chair. Tell him all of the things you've appreci-

ated or loved about him. Switch seats and, as your father, say what you *feel* about your child's telling you such nice things. Keep the dialogue going.

6. Repeat exercise 5 with your mother.

7. Be your father and tell your child all the things you've loved and appreciated about her (or him). Switch chairs, be yourself, and say how you feel about hearing these things. Be your father again and respond.

8. Repeat exercise 7 with your mother.

9. List all of the secrets concerning your private life that you would never tell your parents. Place each of your parents in an empty chair in front of you and tell each one, in turn, these secrets. Be your parents and react. Again, keep switching chairs and get a dialogue going See whether you can move toward mutual understanding rather than conflict and confrontation.

10. If your relationship with either parent is characterized by dependent routines, daily or weekly phone calls or visits (if you are living away from home), take a month's vacation from these activities. Don't call. Don't visit. Politely tell your parents that you simply want to see what it's like to live without such regular contact with them. And stick to your word.

If you are over twenty-one and still live with your parents spend the next month living elsewhere, giving the same reasons. Move in with a friend or series of friends, into a Y, a hotel room, with a sibling, or with a different relative. Better still, try all of these different arrangements for a few nights each so that you might see what it is like to live in different spaces.

11. If your relationship with either parent is characterized by aloofness or grumpiness, or if you have not had much contact with them in some time, see what it is like to try to get closer.

Make a date to meet them somewhere and treat them to a dinner. Give them a small gift—a token of your "appreciation" (whether it is felt or not). Ask them details about their lives. Tell them whatever things you appreciate or like about them—and work hard at avoiding unkind words during this experience.

A day later, write about your experience. Describe what it meant to you and what you learned from it.

If either of your parents is dead, do the above exercise in fantasy for the one (or ones) you can't bring along in reality.

Follow-Up

1. *In what major ways are you like and unlike each of your parents (guardians)? How much choice do you have in keeping or changing these qualities?*
2. *If you are a parent of adolescent or adult children, explain why you agree or disagree with some of Shepard's ideas.*
3. *Write about and/or discuss any other main point of this article.*
4. *Attempt one or more of the exercises listed at the end of the article and report what you learned.*

A Life in a Day of Aging

My father tells me
my mother is slowing down.

He talks deliberately and with deep feelings
as stoop-shouldered he walks to his garden
behind the garage.

My mother informs me
about my father's failing health.

"Not as robust as before," she explains,
"Lower energy than in his 50s."

Her concerns arise as she kneads dough for biscuits.

Both express their fears to me
as we view the present from the past.

In love, and with measured anxiety,
I move with them into new patterns.

—Sam Gladding

Note: From *Family Therapy* (p. 137), by Sam Gladding, 1995, Englewood Cliffs, NJ: Prentice-Hall. Copyright © 1995 by Prentice-Hall. Reprinted with permission.

Think Nanny

Stephen D. Regan

Zonona was remarkable. Even her name was remarkable—Zonona. She had been named for an Indian woman who fed her grandfather's family during a terrible Iowa winter when the Sargood stores were depleted. But I couldn't pronounce it so I just called her Nanny. And she was everything a small boy could ever hope to imagine: candy provider, malt maker, bruise comforter. The aroma of her house surrounded guests with wonderful smells of warmth, kindness, and love. As I close my eyes and drift through the years I can still smell Nanny's house.

She lived but two doors away and somehow was always home when I needed her. When I burned my fingers lighting an illicit bonfire in the bushes behind the old barn, she soothed the pain. When I got my first bike, she shared my joy. When I graduated from college she was the first to acknowledge my triumph. And I wrote my dissertation with her in mind.

Nanny always listened. She always understood, when I was little and when I wasn't. And she seemed to have an amazing amount of knowledge. I once discussed at long length the pros and cons of the economic interpretations of the U.S. Constitution, and she asked profound questions and added insights I had not seen in my studies. She had never heard of Abe Maslow but had a good understanding of needs and self-concept and self-actualization though she had never been to college nor studied psychology.

One day when I was hardly ten, I went to Nanny's house and when I discovered no one was home I explored her house as if it was a treasure house filled with magnificent riches. My glance caught the mahogany and cedar cigar box she had given her husband on her first wedding anniversary. Pulling out one of the large green Cuban cigars I went to an upstairs bedroom to smoke and pretend I was grown up. By the time Nanny got home I was quite ill and as green as the cigar butt. Instead of being angry she asked me what lessons I had learned, and was satisfied when I mumbled about not taking things that belong to others and smoking cigars before I was at least fifty years old. Quietly, in a loving voice, Nanny told me that since I had learned my lesson there was no reason to tell my parents and that she had the perfect cure for my illness—a strawberry malt.

No matter how big the hurt or large the scrape, she soothed the pain with care and love. In total acceptance she listened openly and unconditionally. She shared her feelings and cared about mine. Nanny always let you know that occasionally kids did bad things but there were no bad kids. You were always safe at Nanny's house. Sometimes we talked long after my scheduled bedtime. Sometimes in silence we just sat and watched prism-made rainbows stretch across the walls. Sometimes she read poems to me or recited passages from literature.

My first book, *How big are you, baby,* had an inscription from Nanny. My collection of Robert Louis Stevenson came from her. History of war and peace and diplomacy and discovery flowed in volumes. Quietly without ever saying a word she guided my thinking and my beliefs through modeled leadership, care, love, service, loyalty, dedication, devotion, honor, and patriotism. Never a lecture was made about caring for others but her long hours at the camp for handicapped children and the veterans hospital taught powerful lessons. And regardless of planned activities or pleasures, each Memorial Day morning was spent at the cemetery remembering those who paid the full price for the liberties we prized and the rights we have maintained.

Her long, weekly letters were inspirations of gossip, profound thought, curiosity, and ideas that I looked forward to whether I was in a dorm room or barracks or my own home. And try as I might, my responses were but shadows of hers.

When I was grown up and graduated I took a job as a school counselor. Often I was confronted with adolescent burdens of such magnitude I could hardly cope myself, let alone assist my young students. Facing child abuse, incest, poverty, ignorance, and junior high school–aged pregnancy on a daily basis I floundered looking for ways to ease the suffering. In frequent desperation for just the right technique or intervention strategy that would alleviate the aches of these young people, I plowed through text books and lecture notes searching for answers. How could I help these kids? What could I do?

Books and notes were no help. Emulation of idolized professorial mentors failed. Then I thought of the one person who always eased my pain, who brought rainbows through storms. I thought of Nanny. I remembered what she so patiently taught me not through lessons or lectures but through the quiet, behavior of love. On that day I put a small handwritten sign above my worn, brown desk. It simply said THINK NANNY.

From that day on I simply did as Nanny did. I accepted kids for what they were. I listened and cared. I let kids know that occasionally bad things happen but they themselves were special and unique people with infinite capacities of goodness. Slowly, I believe, my students began to realize that though I could not eliminate their problems, my office was a special place of warmth and love. In my office everything was OK.

We buried Nanny in last November's rain beneath an old maple tree in an Iowa cemetery. Much of what I am or shall become, I owe to her. And whatever pain I have helped reduce, I reduced because of her. And when I am depressed or lonely or hurting I sit in my living room and watch Nanny's rainbows cast by her prism now in my window as they bounce off an old mahogany and cedar cigar box. And I THINK NANNY.

Follow-Up

1. *Sometimes, our role models come from unusual places. Regan's came from next door. Have you had a person like "Nanny" or a person similar to her in your life?*
2. *See the Applied Activity entitled "Heroes, Heroines, and Role Models" at the end of this section to discover how much these persons have influenced your life.*

The Missing Halloween

Nels Goud

When you are ten years old, Halloween takes a good four weeks to plan if you want to do it right. For one, you want to make sure your costume is different from the others and this requires some checking around. Then there is the challenge of planning the route. A route which hits the big givers first before they run out of the good stuff. This means several sprints from one neighborhood to the next, swooping in on the target homes, and then hustling back to get the homes you skipped. It is also crucial to play along with the crazy adults. Adults like Mr. and Mrs. Parish who dress up in monster costumes and try to scare the kids by jumping out from behind furniture, but if you scream real loud it is good for at least a Snickers bar. And when you have all the rounds made you and your friends make sure to knock on Mr. Warren's door. We know he is in there, but he will not come to the door, and one of us stands guard while the others soap a few of his windows. After all there is a "trick" in trick-or-treat. And along the way it is mandatory to hide behind a large tree until your sister and her friends come along, and then leap out in the midst of screeches which will echo the nights until December. Advanced Halloween veterans remember their sacrificing parents and share some of the booty with them—things like apples, walnuts, and other assorted items you don't like.

Everything went as planned that Halloween except that I did not get to go. A sore throat and a stiff neck kept me out of school three days before Halloween. The town Doc came over—they did that back then—and checked me over and told my folks "He has polio." I was whisked off to a big hospital in Kalamazoo and spent Halloween looking out a window at the wall of another building.

A ten-year-old does not get depressed about things like this, unlike older persons. Confused and worried, but not bummed out. For one, the pain was not too bad and everyone paid me a lot of attention. Nurses told jokes as they placed steaming hot packs on my back and legs. The doctors just asked me to do simple things like touching my toes, and when I could not do that they said it was OK anyway. My parents came by often and brought a radio, my favorite foods, and acted very normal in the way only parents can when they are afraid but cannot let their children know it. And there were cards, candy, and comic books coming in on a steady basis. In a way I became a small celebrity.

After a week or so I was taken out of isolation and placed in a large room with five other guys who had polio also. Some seemed to have it worse. Johnny had braces and could not walk so I had to drag his bed next to mine to play cards. Then there was Mike, about 6, who never had a visitor. He whined and cried a lot at night and we eventually had to tell him to shut up but he kept crying anyway.

The World Health Organization is predicting that polio will be eliminated from the Western Hemisphere. It was reading this news release that released my memories. I was one of the fortunate ones who eventually fully recovered. Johnny remained permanently impaired. I do not know what happened to the 6-year-old who cried at night. I do know that the year of the missing Halloween was the one Jonas Salk first introduced the polio vaccine. Bad timing for some of us. But Halloween and polio are only background for my real story.

Each day in the hospital I received at least two cards from classmates. There was always one card which had a puzzle and the next day would bring a card with the answer and a new puzzle. Natural fifth-graders do not send cards this reliably. But 10-year-olds in Mrs. Pollack's fifth grade class did.

Mrs. Pollack was a charter member from the traditional school of thought and looked about 90 years old. Adverbs, fractions, and proper punctuation were ecstatic expressions to Mrs. Pollack. No one dared question these life verities. Her face was stern and could contort in a way which even made Max Thundermouth cringe when he got the urge to express his inner being. Even her generous acts had a price. If your birthday fell on a schoolday, Mrs. Pollack would give the lucky student a dime and everyone would get a treat. Then the celebrant would have to walk a gauntlet of classmates for a good ol' birthday spanking and she got in the last lick for good luck. Mrs. Pollack lived in a house on a hill surrounded by trees and no one knew anything about her. I must have thought, back then, that six weeks away from Mrs. Pollack was like an excused vacation. Now I ask—"Why did my classmates send those cards to me?"

Then there was Miss G. Miss G. was our music teacher. Almost all of us liked music until she came along. Other music teachers let us sing like we were spring meadowlarks, like music was to be a joyous occasion and a celestial right of being human. But Miss G. had standards. We were to be the midwest version of the Mormon Tabernacle Choir. I was having problems with Miss G. because of my low voice, a baritone at the time. As I was a short male, Miss G. felt that I should have a higher voice and told me to sing higher. I tried but could only sing louder. I was faking, she said. We argued a lot. I received my first S- from Miss G. Miss G. even gave me an S- during the time I had polio and wasn't in school. I discovered then that teachers, too, had personalities. Some, like Miss G., were awful. Mrs. Pollack was awful tough, but not awful.

Two weeks after I returned from the hospital, I was still at home trying to regain muscle strength. My mother said I should put on my regular clothes and get into the living room.

"Why?" I asked.

"Because," she said, "there is a school bus in front of our house and your whole fifth grade class is coming to the door."

I threw off my pajamas and put on a shirt and pants and tried to run to the living room but my muscles were too weak and I fell down. I got up and made it to the couch just as Mrs. Pollack knocked on the door.

"Mrs. Goud," she asked. "Is it all right if we visit Nelson for a few minutes?"

"Of course, Mrs. Pollack," said my mother. Mrs. Pollack led the troops into the house and asked how I was doing as she gave me a small gift. All I could muster was an "OK . . . uh . . . thank you, Mrs. Pollack."

My classmates also gave me several presents and we goofed around for a while and then they left.

Each year there are studies which try to define "the good teacher." I will now suggest they add Mrs. Pollack to the list.

Follow-Up

1. *Think of your favorite teachers from elementary school to the present. What qualities made them so special? Have you ever let them know what they meant to you? (If not, when will you?)*
2. *What effect have teachers, good and bad, had on your development?*

Psychotrends: Taking Stock of Tomorrow's Family and Sexuality

Shervert H. Frazier, M.D.

Has the sexual revolution been side-tracked by AIDS, and the return to traditional values we keep hearing about? In a word, no. The forces that originally fueled the revolution are all still in place and, if anything, are intensifying: mobility, democratization, urbanization, women in the workplace, birth control, abortion and other reproductive interventions, and media proliferation of sexual images, ideas, and variation.

Sexuality has moved for many citizens from church- and state-regulated behavior to a medical and self-regulated behavior. Population pressures and other economic factors continue to diminish the size of the American family. Marriage is in sharp decline, cohabitation is growing, traditional families are on the endangered list, and the single-person household is a wave of the future.

AIDS has generated a great deal of heat in the media but appears to have done little, so far, to turn down the heat in the bedroom. It is true that in some surveys people *claimed* to have made drastic changes in behavior—but most telling are the statistics relating to marriage, divorce, cohabitation, teen sex, out-of-wedlock births, sexually transmitted diseases (STDs), contraception, and adultery. These are far more revealing of what we *do* than what we *say* we do. And those tell a tale of what has been called a "postmarital society" in continued pursuit of sexual individuality and freedom.

Arguably there are, due to AIDS, fewer visible sexual "excesses" today than there were in the late 1960s and into the 1970s, but those excesses (such as sex clubs, bathhouses, backrooms, swinging singles, group sex, public sex acts, etc.) were never truly reflective of norms and were, in any case, greatly inflated in the media. Meanwhile, quietly and without fanfare, the public, even in the face of the AIDS threat, has continued to expand its interest in sex and in *increased,* rather than decreased, sexual expression.

Numerous studies reveal that women are more sexual now than at any time in the century. Whereas sex counselors used to deal with men's complaints about their wives' lack of "receptivity," it is now more often the women complaining about the men. And women, in this "postfeminist" era, are doing things they never used to believe were "proper." Fellatio, for example, was seldom practiced (or admitted to) when Kinsey conducted his famous sex research several decades ago. Since that time, according to studies at UCLA and elsewhere, this activity has gained acceptance among women, with some researchers reporting that nearly all young women now practice fellatio.

Women's images of themselves have also changed dramatically in the past two decades, due, in large part, to their movement into the workplace and roles previously filled exclusively by men. As Lillian Rubin, psychologist at the University of California Institute for the Study of Social Change and author of *Intimate Strangers,* puts it, "Women feel empowered sexually in a way they never did in the past."

Meanwhile, the singles scene, far from fading away (the media just lost its fixation on this subject), continues to grow. James Bennett, writing in *The New Republic*, characterizes this growing population of no-reproducers thusly: "Single adults in America display a remarkable tendency to multiply without being fruitful."

Their libidos are the target of million-dollar advertising budgets and entrepreneurial pursuits that seek to put those sex drives on line in the information age. From video dating to computer coupling to erotic faxing, it's now "love at first byte," as one commentator put it. One thing is certain: the computer is doing as much today to promote the sexual revolution as the automobile did at the dawn of that revolution.

Political ideologies, buttressed by economic adversities, *can* temporarily retard the sexual revolution, as can sexually transmitted diseases. But ultimately the forces propelling this revolution are unstoppable. And ironically, AIDS itself is probably doing more to promote than impede this movement. It has forced the nation to confront a number of sexual issues with greater frankness than ever before. While some conservatives and many religious groups have argued for abstinence as the only moral response to AIDS, others have lobbied for wider dissemination of sexual information, beginning in grade schools. A number of school districts are now making condoms available to students—a development that would have been unthinkable before the outbreak of AIDS.

Despite all these gains (or losses, depending upon your outlook) the revolution is far from over. The openness that it has fostered is healthy, but Americans are still ignorant about many aspects of human sexuality. Sexual research is needed to help us deal with teen sexuality and pregnancies, AIDS, and a number of emotional issues related to sexuality. Suffice it to say for now that there is still plenty of room for the sexual revolution to proceed—and its greatest benefits have yet to be realized.

THE REVOLUTION AND RELATIONSHIPS

The idea that the Sexual Revolution is at odds with romance (not to mention tradition) is one that is widely held, even by some of those who endorse many of the revolution's apparent objectives. But there is nothing in our findings to indicate that romance and the sexual revolution are inimical—unless one's defense of romance disguises an agenda of traditional male dominance and the courtly illusion of intimacy and communication between the sexes.

The trend now, as we shall see, is away from illusion and toward—in transition, at least—a sometimes painful reality in which the sexes are finally making an honest effort to *understand* one another.

But to some, it may seem that the sexes are farther apart today than they ever have been. The real gender gap, they say, is a communications gap so cavernous that only the most intrepid or foolhardy dare try to bridge it. Many look back at the Anita Hill affair and say that was the open declaration of war between the sexes.

The mistake many make, however, is saying that there has been a *recent* breakdown in those communications, hence all this new discontent. This conclusion usually goes unchallenged, but there is nothing in the data we have seen from past decades to indicate that sexual- and gender-related communication were ever better than they are today. On the contrary, a more thoughtful analysis makes it very clear they have always been *worse*.

What has changed is our *consciousness* about this issue. Problems in communication between the sexes have been masked for decades by a rigid social code that strictly prescribes other behavior. Communication between the sexes has long been preprogrammed by this code to produce an exchange that has been as superficial as it is oppressive. As this process begins to be exposed by its own inadequacies in a rapidly changing world, we suddenly discover that we have a problem. But, of course, that problem was there for a long time, and the discovery does not mean a decline in communication between the sexes but, rather, provides us with the potential for better relationships in the long run.

Thus what we call a "breakdown in communications might more aptly be called a *breakthrough*.

Seymour Parker, of the University of Utah, demonstrated that men who are the most mannerly with women, those who adhere most strictly to the "code" discussed above, are those who most firmly believe, consciously or unconsciously, that women are "both physically and psychologically weaker (i.e., less capable) than men." What has long passed for male "respect" toward women in our society is, arguably, *disrespect*.

Yet what has been learned can be unlearned —especially if women force the issue, which is precisely what is happening now. Women's views of themselves are changing and that, more than anything, is working to eliminate many of the stereotypes that supported the image of women as weak and inferior. Women, far from letting men continue to dictate to them, are making it clear they want more *real* respect from men and will accept nothing less. They want a genuine dialogue; they want men to recognize that they speak with a distinct and equal voice, not one that is merely ancillary to the male voice.

The sexual revolution made possible a serious inquiry into the ways that men and women are alike and the ways that each is unique. This revolutionary development promises to narrow the gender gap as nothing else can, for only by understanding the differences that make communication so complex do we stand any chance of mastering those complexities.

Subtrends

Greater Equality Between the Sexes. Despite talk in the late 1980s and early 1990s of the decline of feminism and declarations that women, as a social and political force, are waning, equality between the sexes is closer to becoming a reality than ever before. Women command a greater workforce and wield greater political power than they have ever done. They are assuming positions, in both public and private sectors that their mothers and grandmothers believed were unattainable (and their fathers and grandfathers thought were inappropriate) for women. Nonetheless, much remains to be achieved before women attain complete equality—but movement in that direction will continue at a pace that will surprise many over the next two decades.

Women voters, for example, who have long outnumbered male voters, are collectively a sleeping giant whose slumber many say was abruptly interrupted during the Clarence Thomas–Anita Hill hearings in 1991. The spectacle of a political "boy's club" raking the dignified Hill over the coals of sexual harassment galvanized the entire nation for days.

On another front, even though women have a long way to go to match men in terms of equal pay for equal work, as well as in equal opportunity, there is a definite *research* trend that shows women can match men in the skills needed to succeed in business. This growing body of data will make it more difficult for businesses to check the rise of women into the upper echelons of management and gradually help to change the corporate consciousness that still heavily favors male employees.

As for feminism, many a conservative wrote its obituary in the 1980s, only to find it risen from the dead in the 1990s. Actually, its demise was always imaginary. Movements make headway only in a context of dissatisfaction. And, clearly, there is still plenty for women to be dissatisfied about, particularly in the wake of a decade that tried to stifle meaningful change.

The "new feminism," as some call it, is less doctrinaire than the old, less extreme in the sense that it no longer has to be outrageous in order to call attention to itself. The movement today is less introspective, more goal oriented and pragmatic. Demands for liberation are superseded—and subsumed—by a well-organized quest for power. Women no longer want to burn bras, they want to manufacture and market them.

The New Masculinity. To say that the men's movement today is confused is to understate mercifully. Many men say they want to be more "sensitive" but also "less emasculated," "more open," yet "less vulnerable." While the early flux of this movement is often so extreme that it cannot but evoke guffaws, there is, nonetheless, something in it that commands some respect—for, in contrast with earlier generations of males, this one is making a real effort to examine and redefine itself. The movement, in a word, is *real.*

Innumerable studies and surveys find men dissatisfied with themselves and their roles in society. Part of this, undoubtedly, is the result of the displacement men are experiencing in a culture where *women* are so successfully transforming themselves. There is evidence, too, that men are dissatisfied because their own fathers were so unsuccessful in their emotional lives and were thus unable to impart to their sons a sense of love, belonging, and security that an increasing number of men say they sorely miss.

The trend has nothing to do with beating drums or becoming a "warrior" It relates to the human desire for connection, and this, in

the long run, can only bode well for communications between humans in general and between the sexes in particular. Many psychologists believe men, in the next two decades, will be less emotionally closed than at any time in American history.

More (and Better) Senior Sex. People used to talk about sex after 40 as if it were some kind of novelty. Now it's sex after 60 and it's considered not only commonplace but healthy.

Some fear that expectations among the aged may outrun physiological ability and that exaggerated hopes, in some cases, will lead to new frustrations—or that improved health into old age will put pressure on seniors to remain sexually active beyond any "decent" desire to do so.

But most seem to welcome the trend toward extended sexuality. In fact, the desire for sex in later decades of life is *heightened,* studies suggest, by society's growing awareness and acceptance of sexual activity in later life.

Diversity of Sexual Expression. As sex shifts from its traditional reproductive role to one that is psychological, it increasingly serves the needs of the individual. In this context, forms of sexual expression that were previously proscribed are now tolerated and are, in some cases increasingly viewed as no more nor less healthy than long-accepted forms of sexual behavior. Homosexuality, for example, has attained a level of acceptance unprecedented in our national history.

More Contraception, Less Abortion. Though abortion will remain legal under varying conditions in most, if not all, states, its use will continue to decline over the next two decades as more—and, better—contraceptives become available. After a period of more than two decades in which drug companies shied away from contraceptive research, interest in this field is again growing. AIDS, a changed political climate, and renewed fears about the population explosion are all contributing to this change.

Additionally, scientific advances now point the way to safer, more effective, more convenient contraceptives. A male contraceptive that will be relatively side-effect free is finally within reach and should be achieved within the next decade, certainly the next two decades. Even more revolutionary in concept and probable impact is a vaccine, already tested in animals, that some predict will be available within 10 years—a vaccine that safely stops ovum maturation and thus makes conception impossible.

Religion and Sex: A More Forgiving Attitude. Just a couple of decades ago mainstream religion was monolithic in its condemnation of sex outside of marriage. Today the situation is quite different as major denominations across the land struggle with issues they previously wouldn't have touched, issues related to adultery, premarital sex, homosexuality, and so on.

A Special Committee on Human Sexuality, convened by the General Assembly of the Presbyterian Church (USA), for example, surprised many when it issued a report highly critical of the traditional "patriarchal structure of sexual relations," a structure the committee believes contributes, because of its repressiveness, to the proliferation of pornography and sexual violence.

The same sort of thing has been happening in most other major denominations. It is safe to say that major changes are coming. Mainstream religion is beginning to perceive that the sexual revolution must be acknowledged and, to a significant degree, accommodated with new policies if these denominations are to remain in touch with present-day realities.

Expanding Sexual Entertainment. The use of sex to sell products, as well as to entertain, is increasing and can be expected to do so. The concept that "sex sells" is so well established that we need not belabor the point here. The explicitness of sexual advertising, however, may be curbed by recent research finding that highly explicit sexual content is so diverting that the viewer or reader tends to overlook the product entirely.

Sexual stereotyping will also be less prevalent in advertising in years to come. All this means, however, is that women will not be singled out as sex objects; they'll have plenty of male company, as is already the case. The female "bimbo" is now joined by the male "himbo" in ever-increasing numbers. Sexist advertising is still prevalent (e.g., male-oriented beer commercials) but should diminish as women gain in social and political power.

There's no doubt that films and TV have become more sexually permissive in the last two decades and are likely to continue in that direction for some time to come. But all this will surely pale alongside the brave (or brazen) new world of "cybersex" and virtual reality, the first erotic emanations of which may well be experienced by Americans in the coming two decades. Virtual reality aims to be just that—artificial, electronically induced experiences that are virtually indistinguishable from the real thing.

The sexual revolution, far from over, is in for some new, high-tech curves.

FROM BIOLOGY TO PSYCHOLOGY: THE NEW FAMILY OF THE MIND

Despite recent pronouncements that the traditional family is making a comeback, the evidence suggests that over the next two decades the nuclear family will share the same future as nuclear arms: there will be fewer of them, but those that remain will be better cared for.

Demographers now believe that the number of families consisting of married couples with children will dwindle by yet another 12 percent by the year 2000. Meanwhile, single-parent households will continue to increase (up 41 percent over the past decade.) And household size will continue to decline (2.63 people in 1990 versus 3.14 in 1970). The number of households maintained by women, with no males present, has increased 300 percent since 1950 and will continue to rise into the 21st century.

Particularly alarming to some is the fact that an increasing number of people are choosing *never* to marry. And, throughout the developed world, the one-person household is now the fastest growing household category. To the traditionalists, this trend seems insidious—more than 25 percent of all households in the United States now consist of just one person.

There can be no doubt: the nuclear family has been vastly diminished, and it will continue to decline for some years, but at a more gradual pace. Indeed, there is a good chance that it will enjoy more stability in the next two decades than it did in the last two. Many of the very forces that were said to be weakening the traditional family may now make it stronger, though not more prevalent. Developing social changes have made traditional marriage more elective today, so that those who choose it may, increasingly, some psychologists believe, represent a subpopulation better suited to the situation and thus more likely to make a go of it.

As we try to understand new forms of family, we need to realize that the "traditional" family is not particularly traditional. Neither is it necessarily the healthiest form of family. The nuclear family has existed for only a brief moment in human history. Moreover, most people don't realize that no sooner had the nuclear family form peaked around the turn of the last century than erosion set in, which has continued ever since. For the past hundred years, reality has chipped away at this social icon, with increasing divorce and

the movement of more women into the labor force. Yet our need for nurturance, security, and connectedness continues and, if anything, grows more acute as our illusions about the traditional family dissipate.

Our longing for more satisfying sources of nurturance has led us to virtually redefine the family, in terms of behavior, language, and law. These dramatic changes will intensify over the next two decades. The politics of family will be entirely transformed in that period. The process will not be without interruptions or setbacks. Some lower-court rulings may be overturned by a conservative U.S. Supreme Court, the traditional family will be revived in the headline from time to time, but the economic and psychological forces that for decades have been shaping these changes toward a more diverse family will continue to do so.

Subtrends

Deceptively Declining Divorce Rate. The "good news" is largely illusory. Our prodigious national divorce rate, which more than doubled in one recent 10-year period, now shows signs of stabilization or even decline. Still, 50 percent of all marriages will break up in the next several years. And the leveling of the divorce rate is not due to stronger marriage but to *less* marriage. More people are skipping marriage altogether and are cohabiting instead.

The slight dip in the divorce rate in recent years has caused some prognosticators to predict that younger people, particularly those who've experienced the pain of growing up in broken homes, are increasingly committed to making marriage stick. Others, more persuasively, predict the opposite, that the present lull precedes a storm in which the divorce rate will soar to 60 percent or higher.

Increasing Cohabitation. The rate of cohabitation—living together without legal marriage—has been growing since 1970 and will accelerate in the next two decades. There were under half a million cohabiting couples in 1970; today there are more than 2.5. The trend for the postindustrial world is very clear: less marriage, more cohabitation, easier and—if Sweden is any indication—less stressful separation. Those who divorce will be less likely to remarry, more likely to cohabit. And in the United States, cohabitation will increasingly gather about it both the cultural acceptance and the legal protection now afforded marriage.

More Single-Parent Families and Planned Single Parenthood. The United States has one of the highest proportions of children growing up in single-parent families. More than one in five births in the United States is outside of marriage—and three quarters of those births are to women who are not in consensual unions.

What is significant about the single-parent trend is the finding that many single women with children now *prefer* to remain single. The rush to the altar of unwed mothers, so much a part of American life in earlier decades, is now, if anything, a slow and grudging shuffle. The stigma of single parenthood is largely a thing of the past—and the economic realities, unsatisfactory though they are, sometimes favor single parenthood. In any case, women have more choices today than they had even 10 years ago; they are choosing the psychological freedom of single parenthood over the financial security (increasingly illusory, in any event) of marriage.

More Couples Childless by Choice. In the topsy-turvy 1990s, with more single people wanting children, it shouldn't surprise us that more married couples *don't* want children. What the trend really comes down to is increased freedom of choice. One reason for increasing childlessness among couples has to do with the aging of the population, but many of the reasons are more purely psychological.

With a strong trend toward later marriage, many couples feel they are "too old" to have children. Others admit they like the economic advantages and relative freedom of being childless. Often both have careers they do not want to jeopardize by having children. In addition, a growing number of couples cite the need for lower population density, crime rates, and environmental concerns as reasons for not wanting children. The old idea that "there must be something wrong with them" if a couple does not reproduce is fast waning.

The One-Person Household. This is the fastest growing household category in the Western world. It has grown in the United States from about 10 percent in the 1950s to more than 25 percent of all households today. This is a trend that still has a long way to go. In Sweden, nearly *40 percent* of all households are now single person.

"Mr. Mom" a Reality at Last? When women began pouring into the work force in the late 1970s, expectations were high that a real equality of the sexes was at hand and that men, at last, would begin to shoulder more of the household duties, including spending more time at home taking care of the kids. Many women now regard the concept of "Mr. Mom" as a cruel hoax; but, in fact, Mr. Mom *is* slowly emerging.

Men *are* showing more interest in the home and in parenting. Surveys make clear there is a continuing trend in that direction. Granted, part of the impetus for this is not so much a love of domestic work as it is a distaste for work outside the home. But there is also, among many men, a genuine desire to play a larger role in the lives of their children. These men say they feel "cheated" by having to work outside the home so much, cheated of the experience of seeing their children grow up.

As the trend toward more equal pay for women creeps along, gender roles in the home can be expected to undergo further change. Men will feel less pressure to take on more work and will feel more freedom to spend increased time with their families.

More Interracial Families. There are now about 600,000 interracial marriages annually in the United States, a third of these are black-white, nearly triple the number in 1970, when 40 percent of the white population was of the opinion that such marriages should be illegal. Today 20 percent hold that belief. There is every reason to expect that both the acceptance of and the number of interracial unions will continue to increase into the foreseeable future.

Recognition of Same-Sex Families. Family formation by gay and lesbian couples, with or without children, is often referenced by the media as a leading-edge signifier of just how far society has moved in the direction of diversity and individual choice in the family realm. The number of same-sex couples has steadily increased and now stands at 1.6 million such couples. There are an estimated 2 million gay parents in the United States.

And while most of these children were had in heterosexual relationships or marriages prior to "coming out," a significant number of gay and lesbian couples are having children through adoption, cooperative parenting arrangements, and artificial insemination. Within the next two decades, gays and lesbians will not only win the right to marry but will, like newly arrived immigrants, be some of the strongest proponents of traditional family values.

The Rise of Fictive Kinships. Multiadult households, typically consisting of unrelated singles, have been increasing in number for some years and are expected to continue to do so in coming years. For many, "roommates" are increasingly permanent fixtures in daily life.

In fact housemates are becoming what some sociologists and psychologists call "fictive kin." Whole "fictive families" are being generated in many of these situations, with some housemates even assigning roles ("brother,' "sister," "cousin," "aunt," "mom," "dad," and so on) to one another. Fictive families are springing up among young people, old people, disabled people, homeless people, and may well define one of the ultimate evolutions of the family concept, maximizing, as they do, the opportunities for fulfillment of specific social and economic needs outside the constraints of biological relatedness.

THE BREAKUP OF THE NUCLEAR FAMILY

It's hard to tell how many times we've heard even well-informed health professionals blithely opine that "the breakup of the family is at the root of most of our problems." The *facts* disagree with this conclusion. Most of the social problems attributed to the dissolution of the "traditional" family (which, in reality, is *not* so traditional) are the product of other forces. Indeed, as we have seen, the nuclear family has itself created a number of economic, social, and psychological problems. To try to perpetuate a manifestly transient social institution beyond its usefulness is folly.

What *can* we do to save the nuclear family? Very little.

What *should* we do? Very little. Our concern should not be the maintenance of the nuclear family as a *moral* unit (which seems to be one of the priorities of the more ardent conservative "family values" forces), encompassing the special interests and values of a minority, but, rather, the strengthening of those social contracts that ensure the health, well-being, and freedom of individuals.

Follow-Up

1. *Discuss or write about a trend in family life that you find encouraging. Discuss or write about a trend which you dislike or question.*

2. *Frazier contends the breakup of the nuclear family is not the root of social problems and that the nuclear family is often the cause of these problems. Additionally, we should not be concerned with the maintenance of the nuclear family as a moral unit. Why do you agree or disagree with these positions?*

3. *Select one or more other trends or ideas from this article and offer your evaluation.*

Applied Activities for Section Five

MEN AND WOMEN: A DIALOGUE

The intent of this activity is to perceive the different worlds of men and women.

1. Form all-men and all-women groups. If possible, each group should have 4–7 members.
2. The groups are to discuss a common topic concerning the *opposite* gender. Some sample topics are:
   - The advantages and disadvantages of being a man/woman.
   - Things I *don't* understand, like, or agree with about most men/women. (Why do they. . . ?)
   - Identity transformation. See the Applied Activity entitled "A New Identity" at the end of Section I.
   - A current national or local issue concerning gender rights.
3. Spend at least 20 minutes discussing the common topic. Have someone record the main points of the discussion and appoint a spokesperson who will present these points to the whole group.
4. Have each group spokesperson summarize the main points and questions raised for the whole group. Other groups listen and try to understand these points and do *not* offer their views. Once all groups have presented their findings, post the lists of each group's main points on a wall. Take a few minutes to let all participants look at these lists.
5. Depending on time constraints, try one or both of the following:
   (a) Form mixed gender groups of 4–8 members. Discuss one or more of the points mentioned in the earlier steps. The intent is to have each gender *understand* a point of view, not to persuade or to argue it.
   (b) Have the whole group meet. Address one of the points generated in the earlier steps—especially if a participant does not understand why someone feels a certain way. Again, the intent of the exercise is to understand, not to argue, lecture, or persuade. It may be helpful to appoint a facilitator to make sure this intent is followed (this person is usually the instructor).
6. Write about your reactions and what you learned from this experience.

HEROES, HEROINES, AND ROLE MODELS

A person who has attained the highest human possibilities we value is our hero or heroine. These persons serve as ultimate guides and inspirations for our own strivings. Our heroes or heroines may even have a flaw or two, but this can make them even more powerful to us because we, too, have flaws. A hero/heroine has qualities that often transcend a particular discipline. One of my heroes is Maynard Ferguson, a jazz trumpeter. While he inspires my trumpet-playing, he has an enduring exuberance and commitment that I admire and that I try to emulate in my work as a professor. Our heroes and heroines provide clear standards and ways of being for our lives.

Role models demonstrate highly valued skills and personal qualities in a specific life role. More often than not, we know them. They are the people we strive to be like in our careers, as parents, or as citizens. Like heroes and heroines, role models are inspirational, but their influence may or may not extend beyond a specific role.

Our heroes/heroines and role models help define us as a person and shape our values. Try the following activities to see their effects on your life:

1. Briefly list the heroes/heroines from your early childhood until now. These may have been fictional as well as real life persons. They may have been historical figures or contemporary persons. Who really inspired you in ways you admired and imitated?
2. Examine your list. What qualities do these heroes/heroines represent? How do your current heroes/heroines influence your life?
3. Imagine that one of your heroes/heroines talked with you for five minutes. What do you think they would say to you?
4. Identify some of your role models. Which of their qualities do you also have, and which qualities do you need to work on more?
5. Discuss and/or write about your responses and what you learned.

SIGNIFICANT OTHER PERCEPTION INVENTORY

Significant others are persons who influence how you perceive yourself. Some significant other categories include: family members, lovers, spouses, friends, colleagues, teachers, supervisors, mentors. Each person determines who is a significant other to them.

This activity asks your significant others to offer their perceptions of you. One of the strengths of significant others is that they can often see something we are not aware of or that we believe are hidden. They can often provide some helpful hints on how to approach life. Look at the sample Significant Other Perception Inventory at the end of this activity.

If you choose to try this activity, follow these guidelines:

1. Try to get at least seven significant other responses. This is necessary to get a minimum number of reactions for analysis and interpretation.
2. Make sure that the significant other is comfortable in filling out the inventory—this helps to attain genuine responses. Sometimes, a significant other

is not willing to complete the inventory for a number of reasons (it may lead to awkward conversations for some, or they place too much pressure on themselves to please you). You may be asked to complete an inventory on them. Do *not* require the significant other to discuss their responses—only do so if they seem willing.

3. Allow sufficient time for significant others to respond to the activity (sometime these are mailed). If necessary, provide a stamped envelope addressed to you or the instructor.

4. Complete a Significant Other Perception Inventory on yourself from your point of view.

5. Analysis and interpretation suggestions:

   a. After all the inventories have been collected, list all responses to each item.

   b. Examine each list for patterns and common responses. Note these themes. Circle any response or theme that has impact for you in any way (positive or negative).

   c. Attempt to really "listen" to your significant others. Try not to dismiss a response if it bothers you or if you disagree with it. Be open to any message before judging or criticizing it.

   d. How did your inventory compare with those of your significant others? Which (if any) responses surprised you or were unexpected? Are there any observations that need further exploration on your part? Are any specific action steps indicated?

6. Discuss or write about what you learned.

You have been selected by _____ as having an important influence on his or her life. As part of a group activity, this person has been asked to obtain *your personal perceptions* of him or her as indicated by your completion of this inventory. Your observations and comments will be valuable and appreciated. You do *not* have to sign your name to this inventory.

Your comments will *not* be used in determining any type of grade for this person or as a personal reference. Try to be as open and genuine as you can in answering each item. Also, answer according to *your* point of view, *not* according to the way you think others see this person.

You can approach the inventory in one of two ways:

1. Complete it and return it directly to the person.

2. Type your responses and do not write your name on the inventory. Send the completed form by mail to the group facilitator. (The person who asked you to complete the inventory will provide you with an addressed, stamped envelope.) The facilitator will then give your inventory to the appropriate person without revealing the source.

Directions

Keeping the above-named person in mind, complete each of the following unfinished sentences as honestly as you can. If you cannot think of an appropriate completion or if you choose not to complete an item, do not write anything in the blank provided.

1. *Three adjectives* (traits) that immediately come to mind when I think of this person are . . .

2. At least *three* strengths consistently manifested by this person are . . .

3. a. A potential or ability that this person possesses, but has *not* fully developed yet . . .

   b. One way to further develop this ability would be to . . .

4. a. One obstacle (originating either from outside or from within the person) to this person's realization of full personal growth is . . .

   b. One way to overcome this obstacle would be to . . .

5. Within the next year I believe that it will be very important for this person to . . .

6. If I could give this person a gift (either tangible or intangible) that would make a difference in his or her life right now, it would be . . .

Thank you for your efforts and cooperation.

:tions: Complete the quiz individually before checking the answers (you
l also discuss your answers with a small group prior to checking the an-
;).

1. What is the age of first sexual intercourse for the average American?

    (a) 11–12 (b) 13–14 (c) 16–17 (d) 18–19

2. How many sex partners, on average, do American *males* report during their
   lifetime?

    (a) 3 (b) 6 (c) 12 (d) 19

3. How many sex partners, on average, do American *females* report during their
   lifetime?

    (a) 2 (b) 4 (c) 5 (d) 8

4. Which category below reports the lowest incidence of sexual intercourse?

    (a) married couples (b) single persons (c) unmarried couples who
    live together (d) professors

5. The approximate percentage of *men* who claim to be virgins at the time of
   marriage is (as of 1995).

    (a) 10% (b) 20% (c) 30% (d) 40%

6. The approximate percentage of *women* who claim to be virgins at the time
   of marriage is (as of 1995).

    (a) 15% (b) 25% (c) 35% (d) 45%

7. Which category is most responsive to cultural shifts in sexual attitudes and
   practices over several decades?

    (a) unmarried females (b) unmarried males (c) married couples
    (d) neurotic rabbits

8. Both males and females experience a four-stage sexual response during intercourse. Out of order these stages are: resolution, plateau, excitement, and
   orgasm. What is the correct order?

9. Which of the following contraceptive techniques has the *lowest* failure rate
   (i.e., is most reliable)?

    (a) condom (b) diaphragm with spermicide (c) combined oral
    contraceptive pills (d) spermicidal foam (e) coitus interruptus

10. Using lubricants such as petroleum jelly enhances the effectiveness of a condom or diaphragm.

  True   ~~False~~

11. Which group is statistically more likely to contract an STD (sexually transmitted disease) after a single act of intercourse with an infected person?

  Males   ~~Females~~

12. The most common STD in the United States is:

  (a) gonorrhea   (b) chlamydia   (c) acquired immune deficiency syndrome   (d) syphilis   (e) genital herpes

13. A woman or teenage girl can get pregnant during her menstrual flow.

  ~~True~~   False

14. Menopause causes the majority of women to lose interest in sex.

  ~~True~~   False

15. Erection problems are most often started by *physical* factors.

  True   ~~False~~

16. Approximately what percent of persons in their 60s are sexually active?

  (a) 15%   (b) 25%   (c) 40%   (d) 80%

17. Most women prefer a partner with a larger-than-average penis.

  True   ~~False~~

18. Below are common sexual fantasies. Try to identify the top three fantasies for males and females. Place M's beside your choices for men and W's beside your choices for women.

  ¬(a) __W__ having sex with a complete stranger (by choice)
  (b) __M__ being forced to have sex with a chosen partner
  (c) __M__ group sex
  (d) __W__ sex with a celebrity
  (e) __W__ sex in front of an audience
  (f) __W__ oral sex
  W (g) __M__ sex with a friend's spouse
  (h) __W__ sex with a person of the same gender
  (i) __M__ watching two members of the opposite gender have sex

Answers to Sexuality Quiz

1. c

2. b

3. a

4. b

5. a

6. b

7. a.   Studies show that unmarried females are the most responsive to shifts in cultural sexual attitudes and practices.

8. Excitement, plateau, orgasm, and resolution.

9. c.   Here are the failure rates for selected contraceptive techniques:

Method	Failure Rate
Tubal sterilization	0.4%
Vasectomy	0.4%
Combined oral Pill	0.5%
Progestin-only Pill	1.0%
Condom	2.0%
Diaphragm with spermicide	2.0%
Spermicidal foam/cream	3.0–5.0%
Coitus interruptus	16%

10. False.   Lubricants erode a condom or diaphragm, allowing STD organisms to pass through.

11. Females.

12. b.   Chlamydia is a bacterial disease transmitted during intercourse. It often goes unnoticed. Experts estimate that as many as 10% of sexually active women have chlamydia. It is effectively treated with antibiotics.

13. True.

14. False.   Some women report a lowered sex drive, but this can be treated with hormone replacement therapy.

15. True.   Physical factors include disease (e.g., diabetes), drug or alcohol abuse, and medications. Most erections problems can be successfully treated.

16. d.   Additionally, approximately two out of three women and four out of five men are sexually active in their 70s.

17. False.   Most surveys show that women are not as concerned with penis size as are men. Some women even consider a larger-than-average penis as a problem.

18. The top three *male* fantasies are b, c, and i. The top three *female* sexual fantasies are a, d, and g. If you do not agree, then list your own!

References
Items 1, 9, 10, 11, 13, 14, 15, and 17 are from Reinisch, J. (1990). *The Kinsey Institute New Report on Sex.* New York: St. Martin's Press.
Items 2, 3, 4, 5, 6, 8, 12, and 16 are from Lefrancois, G. (1996). *The Lifespan.* Belmont, CA: Wadsworth Publishing.
Item 7 is from Brehm, S. (1992). *Intimate Relationships.* New York: McGraw-Hill, Inc.
Item 18 is from Walker, R. (1996). *The Family Guide to Sex and Relationships.* New York: Macmillan.

INTIMATE RELATIONSHIP CHOICES

Below are brief descriptions of five models of pairing or, in one case, nonpairing. Read each description, and complete the incomplete statements following it by giving as many reasons as you can. If a model is generally unattractive to you, try to find something about it that you like. If a model is generally attractive to you, try to find something about it that you *don't* like.

1. The traditional model: The male is primarily the breadwinner while the female is primarily the homemaker.

   This model is attractive to me because

   This model is unattractive to me because

2. The shared-roles model: The parties share equally in the breadwinning and homemaking activities.

   This model is attractive to me because

   This model is unattractive to me because

3. The reversed-roles model: The female is primarily the breadwinner while the male is primarily the homemaker.

This model is attractive to me because

This model is unattractive to me because

4. The living-together model: The parties live together without being formally married and possibly with no intention to have children or permanency.

This model is attractive to me because

This model is unattractive to me because

5. The singlehood model: The person lives alone.

This model is attractive to me because

This model is unattractive to me because

Identify the pairing model that you prefer for yourself and explain in detail why it is your preference.

Note: "Intimate Relationship Choices" taken from Arkoff, A. (1988). *Exploration in personal growth.* Boston: Allyn and Bacon.

SECTION

six

A QUALITY LIFE

I f asked what it is we want most from life, most of us shuffle our feet and mumble some words about "happiness," "fulfillment," or "meaning." Whatever "it" is, we feel empty if we do not have it, and if we do have it, the meaning has great difficulty working its way out of our mouths. Many of our best writers have attempted to explain what people want from life. See if you can find an answer close to yours in the following attempts:

The only ones among you who will be truly happy are those who will have sought and found how to serve.

—Albert Schweitzer

How simple and frugal a thing is happiness: a glass of wine, a roasted chestnut, a wretched little brazier, the sound of the sea.

—Nikos Kazantzakis

One should not search for an abstract meaning of life. . . . Life can be made meaningful in a threefold way: first, through what we give to life . . . second, by what we take from the world . . . third, through the stand we take toward a fate we no longer can change. . . .

—Viktor Frankl

This is the true joy in life—being used for a purpose recognized by yourself as a mighty one; being thoroughly worn out before you are thrown on the scrap heap; being a force of nature instead of a feverish, selfish little clod of ailments and grievances complaining that the world will not devote itself to making you happy.

—George Bernard Shaw

317

He who dies with the most toys wins.

—Contemporary slogan

Look at every path closely and deliberately. . . . Does this path have a heart? If it does, the path is good; if it doesn't, it is of no use.

—Carlos Castaneda

If you have the guts to follow the risk . . . if one follows what I call one's "bliss"—the thing that really gets you deep in the gut and that you feel is your life—doors will open up . . . if you follow your bliss, you'll have your bliss, whether you have money or not.

—Joseph Campbell

You must want to be first-class . . . meaning the best, the very best you are capable of becoming. If you deliberately plan to be less than you are capable of being, then I warn you that you'll be deeply unhappy for the rest of your life. You will be evading your own capacities, your own possibilities.

—Abraham Maslow

Something has to matter. Otherwise, a person's life will be miserable and empty. Am I the last one to figure that out? The what that matters is unimportant—God, Coke-bottle collecting, track and field—all are equally useful in staving off the uselessness. For my stepfather, Don, bowling matters. Napoleon wanted to conquer Russia. Lana Sue's mom thinks the quality of her life is directly dependent on the meat prices at Kroger's. Career and love life may be a little trite, but they seem to work as well as anything.

To someone on the outside, your basis may look like a joke, but if you know it's important, really know and go on knowing, you'll never fall into despair.

—Tim Sandlin

Outside he stood for a while on the sidewalk, just breathing deeply and feeling the pleasure of being alive in the fall. A sharp breeze tingled his flesh and made his eyes get a little watery, and when he blinked and opened them, it seemed for a moment as if everything was bathed in a soft gold light, like a blessing. It was just for a moment but it gave Sonny a sudden sense of joy that seemed to spread through his whole being. He had known those moments before, in different times and places, and they had seemed so intense and so real that everything else was like sleep. Such moments made you feel completely alive, reminded you of being alive, and Sonny wondered if perhaps that's what "real life" was after all—those moments.

—Dan Wakefield

Perhaps you found one or two guides from these passages that speaks to what *you* call a quality life. If not, then add your own to the list. There seems to be two tendencies in discovering and creating a quality life: striving and being. It just may be that the wisest philosophy is to know when to strive, and when to immerse yourself in being.

Unlike the previous sections, you are urged to complete one or more of these Applied Activities *prior* to reading the articles: The Someday List, Talking To Wise Persons, Evolution of A Person #2. By doing so, you should get some ideas on what a quality life means to you. The readings for this section suggest several ideas and strategies for living a quality life:

- The award-winning science fiction author, Ray Bradbury, tells the story of a man who built "The Happiness Machine."
- Nels Goud contends that how we use time affects our quality of life, in "Having the Time of Your Life."
- Novelist James A. Michener offers his ideas on how time which seems to be wasted may not be that at all, in "On Wasting Time."
- Carin Rubenstein and Phillip Shaver explain how "Active Solitude" is important for a balanced life.
- It may appear contradictory to talk about death in the context of a quality life, but Abe Arkoff tells us that how we view death is crucial for a quality existence in "The Dying-Readiness/Freedom-to-Live-Test."
- Some of our most illuminating and enjoyable life moments become the topic of the pioneering psychologist, Abraham Maslow, in "Lessons from the Peak-Experiences."
- How our quality of life relates to computers is the focus of one of our foremost computer experts, Clifford Stoll, in "Silicon Snake Oil."
- James Fearing provides a quiz on computer addiction in "Ten Symptoms of Computer Addiction."
- Pianist and author Michael Jones ends this section—and the book—with a lyrical essay on discovering our inner essence in "Who Will Play Your Music?"

The Happiness Machine

Ray Bradbury

On Sunday morning Leo Auffmann moved slowly through his garage, expecting some wood, a curl of wire, a hammer or wrench to leap up crying, "Start here!" But nothing leaped, nothing cried for a beginning.

Should a Happiness Machine, he wondered, be something you can carry in your pocket?

Or, he went on, should it be something that carries you in *its* pocket?

"One thing I absolutely *know*," he said aloud. "It should be *bright!*"

He set a can of orange paint in the center of the workbench, picked up a dictionary, and wandered into the house.

"Lena?" He glanced at the dictionary. "Are you 'pleased, contented, joyful, delighted'? Do you feel 'Lucky, fortunate'? Are things 'clever and fitting,' 'successful and suitable' for you?"

Lena stopped slicing vegetables and closed her eyes. "Read me the list again, please," she said.

He shut the book.

"What have I done, you got to stop and think an hour before you can tell me? All I ask is a simple yes or no! You're *not* contented, delighted, joyful?"

"Cows are contented, babies and old people in second childhood are delighted, God help them," she said. "As for 'joyful,' Leo? Look how I laugh scrubbing out the sink. . . ."

He peered closely at her and his face relaxed. "Lena, it's true. A man doesn't appreciate. Next month, maybe, we'll get away."

"*I'm* not complaining!" she cried. "*I'm* not the one comes in with a list saying, 'Stick out your tongue.' Leo, do you ask what makes your heart beat all night? No! Next will you ask, What's marriage? Who knows, Leo? Don't ask. A man who thinks like that, how it runs, how things work, falls off the trapeze in the circus, chokes wondering how the muscles work in the throat. Eat, sleep, breathe, Leo, and stop staring at me like I'm something new in the house!"

Lena Auffmann froze. She sniffed the air.

"Oh, my God, look what you done!"

She yanked the oven door open. A great cloud of smoke poured through the kitchen.

"Happiness!" she wailed. "And for the first time in six months we have a fight! Happiness, and for the first time in twenty years it's not bread, it's charcoal for supper!"

When the smoke cleared, Leo Auffmann was gone.

The fearful clangor, the collision of man and inspiration, the flinging about of metal, lumber, hammer, nails, T square, screwdriver, continued for many days. On occasion, defeated, Leo Auffmann loitered out through the streets, nervous, apprehensive, jerking his head at the slightest sound of distant laughter, listened to children's jokes, watching what made them smile. At night he sat on neighbors' crowded porches, listening to the old folks weigh and balance life, and at each explosion of merriment Leo Auffmann quickened like a general who has seen the forces of darkness routed and whose strategy has been reaffirmed. On his way home he felt triumphant until he was in his garage with the dead tools and the inanimate lumber. Then his bright face fell away in a pale funk, and to cover his sense of failure he banged and crashed the parts of his machine about as if they really did make sense. At last it began to shape itself and at the end of the ten days and nights, trembling with fatigue, self-dedicated, half starved, fumbling and looking as if he had been riven by lightning, Leo Auffmann wandered into his house.

The children, who had been screaming horribly at each other, fell silent, as if the Red Death had entered at the chiming of the clock.

"The Happiness Machine," husked Leo Auffmann, "is ready."

"Leo Auffmann," said his wife, "has lost fifteen pounds. He hasn't talked to his children in two weeks, they are nervous, they fight, listen! His wife is nervous, she's gained ten pounds, she'll need new clothes, look! Sure—the machine is ready. But happy? Who can say? Leo, leave off with the clock you're building. You'll never find a cuckoo big enough to go in it! Man was not made to tamper with such things. It's not against God, no, but it sure looks like it's against Leo Auffmann. Another week of this and we'll bury him in his machine!"

But Leo Auffmann was too busy noticing that the room was falling swiftly up.

How interesting, he thought, lying on the floor.

Darkness closed in a great wink on him as someone screamed something about that Happiness Machine, three times.

The first thing he noticed the next morning was dozens of birds fluttering around in the air stirring up ripples like colored stones thrown into an incredibly clear stream, gonging the tin roof of the garage softly.

A pack of multibred dogs pawfooted one by one into the yard to peer and whine gently through the garage door; four boys, two girls, and some men hesitated in the driveway and then edged along under the cherry trees.

Leo Auffmann, listening, knew what it was that had reached out and called them all into the yard.

The sound of the Happiness Machine.

It was the sort of sound that might be heard coming from a giant's kitchen on a summer day. There were all finds of hummings, low and high, steady and then changing. Incredible foods were being baked there by a host of whirring golden bees as big as teacups. The giantess herself, humming contentedly under her breath, might glide to the door, as vast as all summer, her face a huge peach-colored moon gazing calmly out upon smiling dogs, corn-haired boys and flour-haired old men.

"Wait," said Leo Auffmann out loud. "I didn't turn the machine on this morning! Saul!"

Saul standing in the yard below, looked up.

"Saul, did you turn it on?"

"You told me to warm it up half an hour ago!"

"All right, Saul, I forgot. I'm not awake." He fell back in bed.

His wife, bringing his breakfast up, paused by the window, looking down at the garage.

"Tell me," she said quietly. "If that machine is like you say, has it got an answer to making babies in it somewhere? Can that machine make seventy-year-old people twenty? Also, how does death look when you hide in there with all that happiness?"

"Hide!"

"If you died from overwork, what should I do today, climb in that big box down there and be happy? Also tell me, Leo, how is our life? You know how our house is. Seven in the morning, breakfast, the kids; all of you gone by eight-thirty and it's just me and washing and me and cooking and socks to be darned, weeds to be dug, or I ran to the store or polish silver. Who's complaining? I'm just reminding you how the house is put together, Leo, what's in it! So now answer: How do you get all those things I said in one machine?"

"That's not how it's built!"

"I'm sorry. I got no time to look, then."

And she kissed his cheek and went from the room and he lay smelling the wind that blew from the hidden machine below, rich with the odor of those roasted chestnuts that sold in the autumn streets of a Paris he had never known. . . .

A cat moved unseen among the hypnotized dogs and boys to purr against the garage door, in the sound of snow-waves crumbling down a faraway and rhythmically breathing shore.

Tomorrow, thought Leo Auffmann, we'll try the machine, all of us, together.

Late that night he awoke and knew something had wakened him. Far away in another room he heard someone crying.

"Saul?" he whispered, getting out of bed.

In his room Saul wept, his head buried in his pillow. "No . . . no . . ." he sobbed. "Over . . . over . . ."

"Saul, you had a nightmare? Tell me about it, son."

But the boy only wept.

And sitting there on the boy's bed, Leo Auffmann suddenly thought to look out the window. Below, the garage doors stood open.

He felt the hairs rise along the back of his neck.

When Saul slept again, uneasily, whimpering, his father went downstairs and out to the garage where, not breathing, he put his hand out.

In the cool night the Happiness Machine's metal was too hot to touch.

So, he thought, Saul was here tonight.

Why? Was Saul unhappy, in need of the machine? No, happy, but wanting to hold onto happiness always. Could you blame a boy wise enough to know his position who tried to keep it that way? No! And yet . . .

Above, quite suddenly, something white was exhaled from Saul's window. Leo Auffmann's heart thundered. Then he realized the window curtain had blown out into the open night. But it had seemed as intimate and shimmering a thing as a boy's soul escaping his room. And Leo Auffmann had flung up his hands as if to thwart it, push it back into the sleeping house.

Cold, shivering, he moved back into the house and up to Saul's room where he seized the blowing curtain in and locked the window tight so the pale thing could not escape again. Then he sat on the bed and put his hand on Saul's back.

"*A Tale of Two Cities?* Mine. *The Old Curiosity Shop?* Ha, that's Leo Auffmann's all right! *Great Expectations?* That *used* to be mine. But let *Great Expectations* be his, now!"

"What's this?" asked Leo Auffmann, entering.

"This," said his wife, "is sorting out the community property! When a father scares his son at night it's time to chop everything in half! Out of the way, Mr. Bleak House, Old Curiosity Shop. In all these books, no mad scientist lives like Leo Auffmann, none!"

"You're leaving, and you haven't even tried the machine!" he protested. "Try it on, you'll unpack, you'll stay!"

"*Tom Swift and His Electric Annihilator*— whose is that?" she asked. "Must I *guess?*"

Snorting, she gave *Tom Swift* to Leo Auffmann.

Very late in the day all the books, dishes, clothes, linens had been stacked one here, one there, four here, four there, ten here, ten there. Lena Auffmann, dizzy with counting, had to sit down. "All right," she gasped. "Before I go, Leo, prove you don't give nightmares to innocent sons!"

Silently Leo Auffmann led his wife into the twilight. She stood before the eight-foot-tall, orange-colored box.

"That's *happiness?*" she said. "Which button do I press to be overjoyed, grateful, contented, and much-obliged?"

The children had gathered now.

"Mama," said Saul, "don't!"

"I got to know what I'm yelling about, Saul." She got in the machine, sat down, and looked out at her husband, shaking her head. "It's not me needs this, it's you, a nervous wreck, shouting."

"Please," he said, "you'll see!"

He shut the door.

"Press the button!" he shouted in at his unseen wife.

There was a click. The machine shivered quietly, like a huge dog dreaming in its sleep.

"Papa!" said Saul, worried.

"Listen!" said Leo Auffmann.

At first there was nothing but the tremor of the machine's own secretly moving cogs and wheels.

"Is Mama all right?" asked Naomi.

"All right, she's fine! There, now . . . there!"

And inside the machine Lena Auffmann could be heard saying, "Oh!" and then again, "Ah!" in a startled voice. "Look at that!" said his hidden wife. "Paris!" and later, "London! There goes Rome! The Pyramids! The Sphinx!"

"The Sphinx, you hear, children?" Leo Auffmann whispered and laughed.

"Perfume!" cried Lena Auffmann, surprised.

Somewhere a phonograph played "The Blue Danube" faintly.

"Music! I'm dancing!"

"Only *thinks* she's dancing," the father confided to the world.

"Amazing!" said the unseen woman.

Leo Auffmann blushed. "What an understanding wife."

And then inside the Happiness Machine, Lena Auffmann began to weep.

The inventor's smile faded.

"She's crying," said Naomi.

"She can't be!"

"She is," said Saul.

"She simply can't be crying!" Leo Auffmann, blinking, pressed his ear to the machine. "But . . . yes . . . like a baby . . ."

He could only open the door.

"Wait." There his wife sat, tears rolling down her cheeks. "Let me finish." She cried some more.

Leo Auffmann turned off the machine, stunned.

"Oh, it's the saddest thing in the world!" she wailed. "I feel awful, terrible." She climbed out through the door. "First, there was Paris . . ."

"What's wrong with Paris?"

"I never even *thought* of being in Paris in my life. But now you got me thinking: Paris! So suddenly I want to be in Paris and now I'm not!"

"It's almost as good, this machine."

"No. Sitting in there, I knew. I thought, it's not real!"

"Stop crying, Mama."

She looked at him with great dark wet eyes. "You had me dancing. We haven't danced in twenty years."

"I'll take you dancing tomorrow night!"

"No, no! It's not important, it *shouldn't* be important. But your machine says it's important! So I believe! It'll be all right, Leo, after I cry some more."

"What else?"

"What else? The machine says, 'You're young.' I'm not. It lies, that Sadness Machine!"

"Sad in what way?"

His wife was quieter now. "Leo, the mistake you made is you forgot some hour, some day, we all got to climb out of that thing and go back to dirty dishes and the beds not made. While you're in that thing, sure, a sunset lasts forever almost, the air smells good, the temperature is fine. All the things you want to last, last. But outside, the children wait on lunch, the clothes need buttons. And then let's be frank, Leo, how long can you *look* at a sunset? Who *wants* a sunset to last? Who wants perfect temperature? Who wants air smelling good always? So after awhile, who would notice? Better, for a minute or two, a sunset. After that, let's have something else. People are like that, Leo. How could you forget?"

"Did I?"

"Sunsets we always liked because they only happen once and go away."

"But Lena, that's sad."

"No, if the sunset stayed and we got bored, that would be a real sadness. So two things you did you should never have. You made quick things go slow and stay around. You brought things faraway to our backyard where they don't belong, where they just tell you, 'No, you'll never travel, Lena Auffmann, Paris you'll never see! Rome you'll *never* visit.' But I *always* knew that, so why tell me? Better to forget and make do, Leo, make do, eh?"

Leo Auffmann leaned against the machine for support. He snatched his burned hand away, surprised.

"So now what, Lena?" he said.

"It's not for me to say. I know only so long as this thing is here I'll want to come out, or Saul will want to come out like he did last night, and against our judgment sit in it and look at all those places so far away and every time we will cry and be no fit family for you."

"I don't understand," he said, "how I could be so wrong. Just let me check to see what you say is true." He sat down inside the machine. "You won't go away?"

His wife nodded. "We'll wait, Leo."

He shut the door. In the warm darkness he hesitated, pressed the button, and was just relaxing back in color and music, when he heard someone screaming.

"Fire, Papa! The machine's on fire!"

Someone hammered the door. He leaped up, bumped his head, and fell as the door gave way and the boys dragged him out. Behind him he heard a muffled explosion. The entire family was running now. Leo Auffmann turned and gasped, "Saul, call the fire department!"

Lena Auffmann caught Saul as he ran. "Saul," she said. "Wait."

There was a gush of flame, another muffled explosion. When the machine was burning very well indeed, Lena Auffmann nodded.

"All right, Saul," she said. "Run call the fire department."

Everybody who was anybody came to the fire. There was Grandpa Spaulding and Douglas and Tom and most of the boarders and some of the old men from across the ravine and all the children from six blocks around. And Leo Auffmann's children stood out front, proud of how fine the flames looked jumping from the garage roof.

Grandfather Spaulding studied the smoke ball in the sky and said, quietly, "Leo, was that it? Your Happiness Machine?"

"Some year," said Leo Auffmann, "I'll figure it and tell you."

Lena Auffmann, standing in the dark now, watched as the firemen ran in and out of the yard; the garage, roaring, settled upon itself.

"Leo," she said, "it won't take a year to figure. Look around. Think. Keep quiet a little bit. Then come tell me. I'll be in the house, putting books back on shelves, and clothes back in closets, fixing supper, supper's late, look how dark. Come, children, help Mama."

When the firemen and the neighbors were gone, Leo Auffmann was left with Grandfather Spaulding and Douglas and Tom, brooding over the smoldering ruin. He stirred his foot in the wet ashes and slowly said what he had to say.

"The first thing you learn in life is you're a fool. The last thing you learn in life is you're the same fool. In one hour, I've done a lot of thinking. I thought, Leo Auffmann is blind! . . . You want to see the *real* Happiness Machine? The one they patented a couple thousand years ago, it still runs, not good all the time, no! but it runs. It's been here all along."

"But the fire—" said Douglas.

"Sure, the fire, the garage! But like Lena said, it don't take a year to figure; what burned in the garage don't count!"

They followed him up the front-porch steps.

"Here," whispered Leo Auffmann, "the front window. Quiet, and you'll see it."

Hesitantly, Grandfather, Douglas, and Tom peered through the large windowpane.

And there, in small warm pools of lamplight, you could see what Leo Auffmann wanted you to see. There sat Saul and Marshall, playing chess at the coffee table. In the dining room Rebecca was laying out the silver. Naomi was cutting paper-doll dresses. Ruth was painting water colors. Joseph was running his electric train. Through the kitchen door, Lena Auffmann was sliding a pot roast from the steaming oven. Every hand, every head, every mouth made a big or little motion. You could hear their faraway voices under glass. You could hear someone singing in a high sweet voice. You could smell bread baking, too, and you knew it was real bread that would soon be covered with real butter. Everything was there and it was working.

Grandfather, Douglas, and Tom turned to look at Leo Auffmann, who gazed serenely through the window, the pink light on his cheeks.

"Sure," he murmured. "There it is." And he watched with now-gentle sorrow and now-quick delight, and at last quiet acceptance as all the bits and pieces of this house mixed, stirred, settled, poised, and ran steadily again. "The Happiness Machine," he said. "The Happiness Machine."

A moment later he was gone.

Inside, Grandfather, Douglas, and Tom saw him tinkering, make a minor adjustment here, eliminate friction there, busy among all those warm, wonderful, infinitely delicate, forever mysterious, and ever-moving parts.

Then smiling, they went down the steps into the fresh summer night.

Follow-Up

1. *Written over 40 years ago, Bradbury's* The Happiness Machine *foreshadows contemporary virtual reality technology. Many thinkers have warned if you "seek happiness for its own sake, you will not find it" (Tyron Edwards). Have your attempts to directly find happiness also been unsuccessful? Try to find the underlying reasons for when you feel happiness, and why.*

2. *Leo Auffmann was driven to build his machine even though it created large problems between him and those closest to him. Have you ever been so driven that similar results occurred? If yes, describe the reasons why, the effects, and whether you will do that again.*

3. *The story implies that happiness is meant to be shortlived, that permanently happy conditions would eventually get boring, and that one's Happiness Machine is essentially where you are and those most important to you. Write about or discuss your reactions to these points.*

4. *Select any other aspect of the story to write about or discuss.*

Having the Time of Your Life

Nels Goud

Driving to work I found myself switching music stations whenever a commercial or lousy song came on, going over a couple of lesson plans, giving my opinion on the gene pools of a few fellow drivers, gazing at the bare limbs of some maple trees for signs of spring buds, and chomping down an apple.

During one 15-minute interval at a faculty meeting I sat next to a colleague who was writing a letter, eating lunch, jotting down dates in a daily planner, looking up and nodding at a point made, making notes on a student's paper, asking a question, and probably wondering why I was observing all of this.

These are examples of "multi-tasking," the simultaneous performance of multiple activities. Some of our more revered persons were multi-taskers. Burns (1993) describes a scene of a typical work day in 1621 of the artist Peter Paul Rubens who was simultaneously painting, dictating a letter, having a book read to him, and coherently carrying on a conversation. Rubens was a master multi-tasker. Burns describes the Busy/Body Syndrome, which is characterized by an intense drive to jam the most activities possible into a single time frame. Underlying this drive is the belief that one of life's most valued commodities, time, is becoming increasingly scarce. Stephan Rechtschaffen (1993) asks people "Do you feel that you have enough time in your daily life?" If you are like 90% of his sample, you would not have the time to answer him. You have what is called time-poverty.

We not only do many things at once, but we like to do things quickly. Social observer Jeremy Rifkin (1987) describes the American cultural pace under one word, speed. "We are a nation in love with speed. We drive fast, eat fast, make love fast. We are obsessed with breaking records and shortening time spans. We digest our life, condense our experiences, and compress our thoughts . . . we are convinced that speed reflects alertness, power, and success" (pp. 58–59). It is like living a life on fast-forward.

Our quality of living is greatly influenced by how we choose to perceive and use time. One choice is the fast-forward, multi-tasking philosophy. But if it is your *only* choice for how to use time, then you will have restricted life options and, probably, a lower quality of life.

What's so bad about a fast-forward, multi-tasking approach to life? We get more things done—besides, sometimes there appears to be no other feasible way. In some instances this answer would be right. In other instances this approach works against us. We must be able to distinguish between these instances and employ different time-use strategies.

THE TEMPO OF LIFE EXPERIENCES

Every life experience expresses itself in a particular tempo. If it is to be fully understood, one must be in step with this tempo. Enjoying baseball, for example, requires a different mental tempo than enjoying basketball—as does reading Hemingway versus TV channel surfing. Each experience has its preferred and characteristic pace.

The fast-forward, multi-tasking time strategy is in synch with life experiences which call for instantaneous, multiple responses. Some examples are: a waiter at a popular restaurant during peak times; any first-grade teacher with 25 first graders with the energy of caffeine-crazed gerbils; a stock/exchange broker; a wedding consultant handling details one week prior to the wedding; a customer service clerk of a busy department store during the holidays. You can probably think of many others. These activities favor a state of heightened arousal, of adrenaline-pumping intensity, of eyes that can dart like those of a cobra surrounded by hungry mongooses.

The fast-forward, multi-tasking strategy is completely out of synch with other life experiences. One of my students wanted a book to help her from always feeling overwhelmed and harried by work, school, and family demands. I recommended Anne Morrow Lindbergh's book *Gift from the Sea*. Here was a small book on this very topic that discussed how to center instead of fragment your life. She returned the book the very next class. I asked her if it hadn't been right for her. "Oh it was easy to read." she replied. "I finished reading it in under two hours." After a brief discussion it became apparent that she could not change how she approached life tasks. To complete this reading quickly took precedent over everything else, including her main reason for wanting the book. We then talked about that.

Maybe you are a fast-forward reader and have already finished this article. How did it end? Here is a question for you: How many animals of each species did Moses take on the Ark? Now that is an odd query at this state of the article. But maybe, just maybe it might slow down any fast-forwarders. The answer, incidentally, is none. It was Noah who built the Ark, not Moses. Ah, a trick question you say. How can it be when it is sitting right there on the page? It is how you approach the question that counts. A fast-forwarding glance at this question will most likely trigger the number two.

Here are some life events which cannot be fully experienced using a fast-forward, multi-tasking strategy: eating good food; dancing to a ballad with someone special; watching clouds while lounging on the grass; meditating or praying; showing a person that you are really listening to him or her; viewing an art exhibit; rock climbing; holding a newborn infant; watching the sun set over the ocean. Can you think of some others?

HAVING A CHOICE

To be able to adapt your tempo to different kinds of life experiences is essential for a balanced life. In short, we must be able to choose the most appropriate time strategies. Modern life seems to encourage the fast-forward, multi-tasking time strategy over others. It is the norm to say "I'm so busy" and expect if from others. The busyness syndrome often becomes habitual. Worse, it may eventually control you. Let's say, for example, that you finally have time for a leisurely lunch with a friend. One time choice is to fully absorb yourself into the conversation and the food. Another choice, often when we do not want it, is having the lunch and simultaneously planning your afternoon schedule, gazing around the room, glancing at the TV above your friend, and looking at your watch every ten minutes. Here we have the mismatch between a time strategy and the natural tempo of an experience—and we may even know it but can't stop it. Our internal engine is stuck on full throttle even when we're idling.

For many, the fast-forward, multi-tasking time approach has become a habitual reflex.

Life becomes a giant *Things To Do* list with the goal of crossing off an event as quickly as possible and going on to the next. We are in a hurry to get somewhere, but we never arrive. The fast-forward, multi-tasking life is one where each moment is completed and then erased. This produces gaping holes in one's life memory bank. Rechtschaffen (1993) says it this way: "By cramming each moment so full of events, we leave ourselves no time to actually experience them in any meaningful way . . . the past is, in effect, absent from our lives."

Just having had an experience does not mean you will remember it. Without time to savor it, to talk about it, to recall the major aspects and the nuances—without this kind of processing, the experience becomes a memory trace. I have toured Japan twice with a music group within a three-year period. I can remember one tour in vivid detail. The other is basically a blur, except for a grueling 14-hour train ride standing up. What was the difference? Was it too much Japanese beer on the forgotten tour? No, I actually had more on the remembered tour. The tour that I remember in detail was one where I kept a journal and took many photos; where musicians and singers talked about their daily experiences with each other; where I discussed the trip often with friends upon my return.

It takes time to remember.

One final clue to whether you are in control of time-use strategies. Think of a situation where you have no immediate demands, no expected tasks. Down time. For a fast-forward, multi-tasking person this situation produces anxiety. Instead of enjoying this time with a slower tempo activity, this person is likely to crowd out the anxiety by engaging in a flurry of tasks. Even leisure is pursued with the same relentless intensity. Viktor Frankl, the founder of Logotherapy, calls this the "Sunday neurosis."

The eventual consequences for most people who live full-time in the fast-forward, multi-tasking mode are physical and emotional exhaustion and/or breakdowns. It may take a while for some, even years, but usually there are heavy costs. Some seek help or develop new time strategies when they cannot satisfactorily answer this question for themselves—What is the purpose of living this way? Or, "I accomplish a lot—so why do I feel deep down that something fundamental is missing?"

Throughout it has been emphasized that a quality life requires the ability to adapt to the different tempos of life experiences. We must be able to control these time use strategies instead of being controlled. The fast-forward, multi-tasking time philosophy strategy is appropriate for some experiences and ill advised for others. It also has a tendency to crowd out and take over all other time use strategies. In the next section, some ideas on how to implement alternative time use strategies are presented.

SIMPLIFYING LIFE

Even in 1850 Henry Thoreau was criticizing the hurriedness of people—"Why should we live with such hurry and waste of life? We are determined to be starved before we are hungry. . . . Simplify, simplify . . . I say, let your affairs be as two or three, and not a hundred or a thousand" (in Krutch, (1962), pp. 128, 173). Well, you may comment, this would be easy for him to say, since all he had to do was wander around the woods and look at a pond. That's what old philosophers do. But Thoreau was about 30 when he wrote these remarks and he lived only two years at Walden Pond.

It is possible to simplify. Two primary time strategies do this: one is to focus, and the other is to slow down. Focusing means to devote your attention and energies to one thing at a time. The phrase that helps me is "Be where you are." The key is to bring your body and mind into the present moment. Do not let yourself wander off into past or future time zones. Be where you are. If you are talking with someone you value, be right there with him or her and show it. For a start, try focusing on a mundane chore; if you are grocery shopping, just do that, be *there*.

Here is a very simple but powerful way to focus, but few can do this the first few times (this is a gentle challenge). The task: Get comfortable and if possible, close your eyes. Take a deep breath and slowly exhale. Do this naturally for 10 breaths. Just observe your breathing. If at any time you become distracted and lose count, start over.

How did it go? This breathing focus activity not only is helpful in learning to "be where you are," but is an excellent relaxation and centering experience. Choosing one focusing activity each day will enable you to add this time-use strategy to your repertoire.

SLOWING DOWN

I Need To Stop So I Can Get Somewhere. Countering the fast-forward time strategy means to let up on the accelerator when appropriate. Focusing is often helpful in adjusting your speed. Here are some other ideas for slowing down:

- Apply the concept of *savoring* to selected life activities. While normally referring to taste, savoring can be generalized to other domains also. It is the gradual experiencing of an event. Gulping is the opposite of savoring. You gulp Big Macs and savor fine wine. You gulp administrative memos and savor a well-written letter or essay. You gulp local news and savor the stories of a friend or family member. See other examples at the end of the section entitled "the tempo of life experiences."

He seemed to have a routine. Fly around the Sebastian Inlet of Florida for a bit, then light on a rock. A rock which had all the appearances of good fishing. And so it was. He would sit there very quietly and very relaxed, but alert. A fish of his liking would swim by and be chosen for a mid-afternoon snack. Sometimes the pelican would let a fish swim by untouched. He was in no hurry. The pelican knew that if he waited just right, whatever he needed would come along.

Sometimes we need to let life come to us.

"Waiting" by Nelson Goud. Copyright © 1996.

- Be aware of (and beware) the *paradox* of *time-saving technology.* Electronic communication devices like E-mail, fax, Internet, and voice-mail allow us to send and receive more messages in a shorter period than any time in our history. The drawback is that speed has greatly increased the number of messages we receive, consequently creating more demands on our time than ever before. Try to be selective as to which messages really require your quality efforts.

- Let experiences reveal themselves *to you* without imposing your needs and expectations on them first. One of my true life joys is to listen to the jazz trumpeter Maynard Ferguson. If he comes to town, I'm there (even my students call me to let me know, in case I missed the notice). I can remember waiting during a concert with great anticipation for his band to play a certain number that had just appeared on his latest album. Maynard calls out the number. The band roared as usual and Maynard was doing things that only all the rest of us trumpeters can do in dreams. But I was somewhat disappointed. The live version did not sound like the recorded one. I wanted to hear it played like the one on the album. I had fallen into the trap I am writing about. I refused to "let" Maynard play how he felt that night, with that song, at that moment. He did not fit my preconceived expectation. Once I realized this, I could kick back and really get into whatever he and his band were doing that night. I sometimes find myself falling into this trap in meeting friends, or visiting favorite places expecting them to be exactly like they were when . . . , and on it goes until I remember to let others or even nature reveal themselves as they truly are at that moment. So, even if you know how your friend's or parent's story will end, let them finish it, not you. It might be the telling that is important, not that you know the ending.

Solomon observed that there is a time to be born and a time to die. There is a time between also. We have choices how we conduct ourselves in this interval called life. One of these choices is to enjoy and find meaning in the journey itself. We can take our time.

References

Burns, L. (1993). *Busy bodies.* New York: W. W. Norton & Co.

Krutch, J. (1962). *Thoreau: Walden and other writings.* New York: Bantam Books.

Rechtschaffen, S. (1993). Time-Shifting: Slowing down to live longer. *Psychology Today*, November/December, 32–36.

Rifkin, J. (1987). *Time wars.* New York: Henry Holt and Co.

Follow-Up

1. *Goud claims that a fragmented hurriedness is a norm for many in modern times and is used even when not appropriate. Write about or discuss your reactions to this statement based on personal experiences.*

2. *A main idea in the article is that every life experience expresses itself in a particular tempo. Provide some examples of this from your life and describe what happens when you are in synch or out of synch with these tempos.*
3. *The author states that unless we try to remember and communicate major experiences, they become blanks in our memories. Describe a time or two when this has happened to you.*
4. *Attempt the focusing and slowing-down ideas mentioned at the end of the article and report the results.*
5. *Select any other ideas from the article and report your reactions.*

On Wasting Time

James A. Michener

We all worry about wasting time, about the years sliding past, about what we intend to do with our lives. We shouldn't. For there is a divine irrelevance in the universe that defies calculation. Many men and women win through to a sense of greatness in their lives only by first stumbling and fumbling their way into patterns that gratify them and allow them to utilize their endowments to the maximum.

If Swarthmore College in 1925 had employed even a halfway decent guidance counselor, I would have spent my life as an assistant professor of education in some Midwestern university. Because when I reported to college it must have been apparent to everyone that I was destined for some kind of academic career. Nevertheless, I was allowed to take Spanish, which leads to nothing, instead of French or German, which as everyone knows are important languages studied by serious students who wish to gain a Ph.D.

I cannot tell you how often I was penalized for having taken a frivolous language like Spanish instead of a decent, self-respecting tongue like French. In fact, it led to the sacrifice of my academic career.

Still, I continued to putter around with Spanish, eventually finding a deep affinity for it. In the end, I was able to write a book about Spain which will probably live longer than anything else I've done. In other words, I blindly backed into a minor masterpiece. There are thousands of people competent to write about France, and if I had taken that language in college I would have been prepared to add no new ideas to general knowledge. It was Spanish that opened up for me a whole new universe of concepts and ideas.

Actually, I wrote nothing at all until I was 40. This tardy beginning, one might say delinquency, stemmed from the fact that I had spent a good deal of my early time knocking around this country and Europe, trying to find out what I believed in, what values were large enough to enlist my sympathies during what I sensed would be a long and confused life. Had I committed myself at age 18, as I was encouraged to do, I would not even have known the parameters of the problem, and any choice I might have made then would have had to be wrong.

It took me 40 years to find out the facts.

As a consequence, I have never been able to feel anxiety about young people who are fumbling their way toward the enlightenment that will keep them going. I doubt that a young man—unless he wants to be a doctor or a research chemist, in which case a substantial body of specific knowledge must be mastered within a prescribed time—is really capable of wasting time, *regardless* of what he does. I believe you have until age 35 to decide finally on what you are going to do, and that any exploration you pursue in the process will in the end turn out to have been creative.

Indeed, it may well be that the years observers describe as "wasted" will prove to have been the most productive of those insights which will keep you going. The trip to Egypt. The two years spent working as a runner for a bank. The spell you spent on the newspaper in Idaho. Your apprenticeship at a trade. These are the ways in which young persons ought to spend their lives . . . the ways of "waste" that lead to true knowledge.

Two more comments. First, I have recently decided that the constructive work of the world is done by an appallingly small percentage of the general population. The rest simply don't give a damn . . . or they grow tired . . . or they fail to acquire when young the ideas that would vitalize them for the long decades.

I am not saying that such people don't matter. They are among the most precious items on earth. But they cannot be depended upon either to generate necessary new ideas or to put them into operation if someone else generates them. Therefore, those men and women who do have the energy to form new constructs and new ways to implement them must do the work of many. I believe it to be an honorable aspiration to want to be among those creators.

Second, I was about 40 when I retired from the rat race, having satisfied myself that I could handle it if I had to. I saw then that a man could count his life a success if he survived—merely survived—to age 70 without having ended up in jail (because he couldn't adjust to the minimum laws that society requires) or having landed in the booby hatch (because he could not bring his personality into harmony with the personalities of others).

I believe this now without question: income, position, the opinion of one's friends, the judgment of one's peers and all the other traditional criteria by which human beings are generally judged are for the birds. The only question is, "Can you hang on through the crap they throw at you and not lose your freedom or your good sense?" I am now 67¾, and it looks as if I've made it. Whatever happens now is on the house . . . and of no concern to me.

Follow-Up

1. *Have you worried about wasting time while deciding what to do with your life? Discuss this aspect of your life.*
2. *What "wasted time" has proven to be useful in your own case?*
3. *Have you "wasted" enough, too much, or too little time before making some of your major life decisions (for example, leaving or returning home, going to college, choosing a college major or a career direction, getting married, having children, and so on)? Discuss this aspect of your life.*
4. *Have you been pressured from without or from within to make one or more major commitments prematurely? Discuss this aspect of your life.*

Active Solitude

Carin Rubenstein
and Phillip Shaver

For some people, being alone automatically implies loneliness; for them, the word *solitude* evokes images of isolation, panic, fear, inability to concentrate, numbness, or boredom. For others—poets and artists, for example—solitude carries almost the opposite meaning: bliss, relaxation, personal integration, a feeling of warm connectedness with the world and other people, creativity, and reflection. What are the differences between these people—or between times in the life of a particular person when one rather than another reaction predominates?

The difference is partly one of perspective. Sometimes, because of past or recent experiences, we conceive of aloneness as being cut off, bereft, alienated from others, the way a child feels after being sent to his or her room for punishment. (As the poet Coleridge put it in "The Rime of the Ancient Mariner": "Alone, alone, all, all alone, / Alone on a wide wide sea! / And never a saint took pity on / My soul in agony.") In this state of mind, we feel a keen sense of loss and powerlessness—loss of other people's approval and company, and powerlessness to do anything about it. The loss calls attention to deficiencies in ourselves; we are "bad," unworthy of love, deserving of rejection, vulnerable and helpless. In this state, self-esteem is diminished; we become frightened and defensive. We can't relax or be creative.

In contrast, the orientation we call active solitude emphasizes the positive side of being alone. In solitude, you are together with yourself, physically but not psychologically cut off from other people; free to explore thoughts and feelings without regard for anyone else's immediate reactions. You can hear your own mental voice and react to your own subtle desires and moods. Oddly enough, the result is often a deeper affection for other people. One of our respondents in Billings, Montana, wrote us, for example, that she spends ten days in total solitude each year—causing rumors among her neighbors that her marriage is on the rocks. Leaving husband, children, dog, and three canaries back home, she retreats to a mountain cabin by herself—to think, read, and write. "I have a ball—no obligations and no distractions. No radio, no TV, no screaming kids or pesky husband. For ten days I have just me. I love being away from it all for those days. Funny thing is though, I appreciate them a whole lot more when I get back—a year's worth of appreciation builds up in just ten days."

One of the people we interviewed told us: "Odd as it sounds, I'm more able to be by myself when I feel most in tune with my lover. It's easier to concentrate on work, to be creative. I know when we're apart that we'll soon be together, that she's there if I need her. And we're more valuable to ourselves and get along better when we've spent time alone."

Although the words "alone" and "lonely" come from the same middle English root—meaning "all one" (or only one)—they are not psychological synonyms. Many people—for example, those trapped in unhappy marriages or forced to live with relatives who "don't understand"—are much lonelier living with others than are the hundreds of thousands who live alone but have close ties with friends and family. It's clearly possible to be lonely without being alone and alone without being lonely.

Many people find that the first few minutes or hours of solitude are unsettling. While working individually on this book, for example, having set aside time for reflection and writing, we often spent the first half hour (at least) with unnecessary phone calls, irrelevant reading, and distracting, time-wasting trips to the bathroom or refrigerator. The urge to avoid self-confrontation, to escape the feeling of aloneness that solitary thought requires, is powerful indeed. In the first few moments of solitude, many people make a hasty decision to go shopping or turn on the television set, and they immediately lose the opportunity for creativity and self-renewal. If this pattern becomes habitual, their sense of identity and personal strength is eroded and they become chronically afraid of solitude.

The writings of religious hermits throughout history reveal that they too suffered an initial period of doubt, agitation, and panic when they first got out into the wilderness by themselves. Most of them, however, like most of us in our successful attempts at creative solitude, waited out this temporary anxiety and found themselves moved and enriched by the rewards of solitude.

In extreme forms, solitude has often been used in *rites de passage* to transform boys into men. In many primitive societies, pubertal boys were sent off into the forest, jungle, or plains, and ordered to remain alone for periods ranging from overnight to several months. The boys were thought to die a symbolic death and become transformed: when they returned to the world of the living as men, their boyhood ignorance and dependence were gone forever. If this sounds barbaric, consider that Outward Bound, a popular American recreation group for men and women of all ages, requires its participants to take solo wilderness trips; the experience of solitary survival is assumed to foster independence and self-sufficiency.

Some researchers have tested the idea that solitude can be strengthening. During the sixties and seventies, John Lilly experimented with "restricted environmental stimulation" by placing people in immersion tanks full of warm salt water, asking them to remain inside for hours, even days, at a time. Psychologist Peter Suedfeld claimed more recently that REST, or *Restricted Environmental Stimulation Therapy,* calms mental patients, helps overweight people lose weight, smokers quit smoking, alcoholics reduce their drinking, and stutterers speak more clearly. REST simply places patients in dark, sound-proof rooms for about eight hours without radios, books, or other diversions.

Strangely enough, meditation and reflection—although usually solitary activities—are almost the opposite of what we normally think of as self-consciousness or self-preoccupation. When properly pursued, they aren't at all narcissistic. When we are self-conscious in the usual sense (anxious or embarrassed), the self that occupies our attention is, meditation experts say, a figment of our social imagination; it is the self of the adolescent conformist wondering nervously if he is accepted by the group. Surprisingly, when we are alone and allow ourselves to pass through the initial period of agitated discomfort, this social pseudo-self eventually evaporates, revealing a more relaxed and substantial self underneath. This genuine self needs no outside approval and is not simply a social creation. People who make contact with this deeper self find that their subsequent social relations are less superficial, less greedy, less tense. They have less need to defend their everyday social selves, their social masks.

Our first piece of advice, then: *When you are alone, give solitude a chance. Don't run away at the first sign of anxiety, and don't imagine yourself abandoned, cut off, or rejected.* Think of yourself *as with yourself, not without* someone else. Allow yourself to relax, listen to music that suits your feelings, work on something that you've been neglecting, write to a friend or for yourself in a journal, or just lie back and be at peace. If you are religious, your solitude may take the form of conversations with God or meditation on religious ideas. Whatever the content of your solitude, if you allow the first burst of anxiety to fade, you will open a door to many rewarding hours: of quiet prayer or contemplation; full enjoyment of music, sketching, or painting; total involvement in a novel or book of poetry; recording your own thoughts, feelings, songs, or poems. This solitude is a far cry from loneliness.

If you think about this, you can begin to see why active solitude and intimacy are related. In solitude, we experience our most genuine needs, perceptions, and feelings. We listen to our deepest selves. Intimacy involves the disclosure of this deeper self to trusted friends or lovers, and really listening, in turn, to their needs, thoughts, and feelings. In other words, in solitude we are intimate with ourselves in a way that enhances our intimacy with other people.

If you find that you can't be comfortable with yourself, you are probably a dissatisfying friend and lover as well. Perhaps you fear there is really nothing very interesting about you; your value is assured only when you are with and approved by someone else. This idea was taken to a supernatural extreme by Henry James, in a story called "The Private Life." Lord Mellifont completely vanishes when he is left alone. "He's there from the moment he knows someone else is." Mellifont is "so essentially, so conspicuously and uniformly the public character" that he is simply "all public" and has "no corresponding private life." Discovering this horrible fact, the narrator of the story feels great sympathy for Mellifont. "I had secretly pitied him for the perfection of his performance, had wondered what blank face such a mask had to cover, what was left to him for the immitigable hours in which a man sits down with himself, or, more serious still, with that intenser self his lawful wife."

We know from our research that adults who have suffered painful losses or rejections in the past are more likely to feel this way and to panic when they are alone; we also know that such people tend to have self-esteem problems. But as long as they cling desperately to others rather than confronting and overcoming their fears and feelings of inadequacy, they are unlikely to become confident and independent. For these people, spending time alone is an essential part of overcoming loneliness.

We don't want to oversell solitude. In fact, for some people solitude replaces normal social life, causing them to become self-contained, fussy, and rigid. Psychiatrist George Vaillant described such a man, in his late forties at the time they talked: "During college he had dealt with his very real fear of people by being a solitary drinker. He enjoyed listening to the radio by himself and found math and philosophy his most interesting courses. Although afraid to go out with girls, he was very particular about his appearance.... Thirty years later, [he] was less interested in clothes, but had become terribly preoccupied with keeping fit. He admitted that in his life 'things had taken the place of people' and that he loved to retreat into the 'peace and quiet of a weekend alone.' Approaching old age with no family of his own, he daydreamed of leaving his rare book collection to a favorite young cousin; but he had made only a small effort to get to know this cousin personally." Vaillant went on: "Not only had he never married, but he never admitted to being in love. Unduly shy with women in adolescence, at forty-seven [he] was still put off by 'eager women' and still found 'sex distasteful and frightening.' He had gone through life without close friends of any kind, male or female, and . . . still found it difficult to say good-bye to his mother."

How can you tell if solitude is leading you toward or away from other people? In general, if you find yourself soothed and strengthened by solitude, more *aware of your love for other peo-*

ple, and less frightened or angry in your dealings with them, then solitude is a healthy part of your social balance. If you find, on the other hand, that you use solitude as a chronic escape from other people, and if people generally seem to you to be scary, selfish, cruel, or too messy, then you are retreating into a shell of solitude. We say this not because we wish to impose some superficial standard of sociability on everyone, but because studies like Vaillant's indicate that long-term defensive withdrawal from other people leads to unhappiness, alcohol and [other] drug abuse, underachievement, and vulnerability to illness.

Practice active solitude, then, *but not to the detriment of intimacy, friendship, or community.* Let active solitude be the ground from which your feelings of intimacy and community grow.

Follow-Up

1. *Write about or discuss your views to one or more of these statements:*
   - *It is clearly possible to be lonely without being alone and alone without being lonely.*
   - *The urge to avoid self-confrontation, to escape the feeling or aloneness that solitary thought requires, is powerful.*
   - *If you find that you can't be comfortable with yourself, you are probably a dissatisfying friend and lover as well.*
2. *The authors warn that solitude can become a vice in the form of chronic escape from other people. Write or discuss your reactions to this idea.*
3. *Attempt one or more periods of active solitude. If you are not used to being alone, start with a period of two hours. Gradually increase the duration of your solitude. Take note of any resistance in the form of doubt, anxiety, or "antsiness." For some interesting insights, try a 24-hour "solo," where you spend a full day and night away from normal activities and distractions. Report your reactions and what you learned from any of these activities.*
4. *For further reading on this topic see Anne Morrow Lindbergh's* Gift from the Sea *and* The Stations of Solitude *by Alice Koller.*

The Dying-Readiness/ Freedom-to-Live Test

Abe Arkoff

In our lives, we move through many turning points. Some are small and taken in stride. Others are large and very affecting. And then one day, we reach a point whose immensity cannot be disputed: death. Death is the ultimate turning point.

Why is the consideration of death and dying so important as we seek to illuminate our lives? Death is a turning point that casts its influence far in advance of its occurrence. How differently we might lead our lives if we knew we would never die. How differently some of us lead our lives as we pretend we never will.

For 10 years (1980–1990), I was a volunteer working with hospice patients and those with life-threatening illnesses. I have also given workshops on preparation for death which I call "Dying Readiness/Freedom to Live." This, I think, is an apt title because it is my experience that those of us who face our mortality and prepare for it free ourselves to live more fully. In getting our house in order and readying ourselves for death, we ironically open wider the door to life. Following are some reasons that this is so.

1. The realization that we are mortal makes life precious.

Suppose that there was an account into which $1,440 was deposited every day for you to spend. However, at the end of the day, the unspent portion is forfeited because no balance can be carried forward. Furthermore, you are given no idea when the account will be closed. How much of your account would you leave unspent?

We each have an account—a true one, not a fantasy. Each day there is a deposit of 24 hours or 1,440 minutes. At the end of the day, all the wasted minutes are forfeited because no time can be carried forward to the next day. Furthermore, you are given no idea when the account will be closed. How much of this account do you forfeit, waste, and throw away?

The full realization that we are mortal, that we will die one day, and indeed might die at any moment, makes life more precious. Persons who have been very near death but recovered frequently report a new appreciation for life and even the smallest joys of life.

When Orville Kelly learned he was incurably ill with cancer, he spearheaded the formation of a self-help group for cancer patients and their close relatives, called "Make Today Count." It now has chapters all over the country and aims "To promote the simple goal of living each day as fully and completely as possible." Kelly (1979) wrote that it took the "specter of death" to make him aware of the preciousness of life.

2. The full realization that we are mortal makes life purposeful.

Suppose that you knew you were going to live forever, what would you get busy and do right now? There might not be much point in getting a move on if you had until the end of time—which is how long death-denying folks seem to think they have. Elisabeth Kübler-Ross writes, "It is the denial of death that is partially responsible for people living empty, purposeless lives; for when you live as if you

There it stands alone. The last leaf of autumn. At the top of a branch of a young broadleaf oak, it is hanging on for a while longer than the others. Maybe it likes the view. It does not seem to mind that its edges are frayed and that you can even see through it. But soon it will join its comrades below. Below, where it will add a little color to the ground. Then slowly, very slowly, get smaller until it becomes part of the soil. It will not be forgotten. In the spring the bare oak branch will gather sustenance from the soil. It will sprout buds and then leaves—leaves which exist because of the last leaf of autumn.

You will leave a legacy. What will it be?

"Ode to the Last Leaf" by Nelson Goud. Copyright © 1996.

would live forever, it becomes too easy to postpone the things that you must do" (p. 164).

Never-ending life has been given considerable attention by writers of imaginative and science fiction. Merritt Abrash reviews this writing in an essay entitled "Is There Life After Immortality?" and concludes there is general agreement that immortality "would not be merely undesirable for various social and philosophical reasons, but a curse upon the so-called beneficiaries" (p. 26). Immortality is seen as destroying life's pleasure, creativity, and significance and as such, ironically, becomes "a fate worse than death."

Suppose that you knew you probably had no more than 6 months of life to live, what would you get busy and do right now? This supposition is not so far-fetched. Quite a number of us will be seated in a doctor's office one

day and learn—if our physician is candid—that we probably have little time to live. The question that opened this paragraph is sometimes asked in workshops dealing with death and dying. Many folks respond by saying that with only 6 months to live, they would get busy and do some things they were letting slide or planning to do some indefinite day. Having only 6 months to get things done filled them with purpose and made them shake a leg and get busy.

Kübler-Ross (1975) writes that when we awaken each morning, it is important to understand that that day may be the last day we have. This understanding or thought might be especially helpful on those days that we have trouble getting a move on. Not forever, not 6 months, just 24 hours. What is it you are going to do today for sure, knowing this is the only day you have for sure?

3. The full realization that we are mortal gives us a useful perspective.

The saying: "I complained that I had no shoes until I met a man who had no feet," suggests that large matters give us some useful perspectives on small ones. There is much in life to fuss and fret about until we separate what is petty or trivial from what is important. One sign of maturity is that we have experienced enough of life so that we are able to tell the difference between the two.

Nothing gives us a better perspective on life than death. In the presence of death, unimportant things indeed seem unimportant, and important things are more easily given their due. "When I thought I might be terminally ill, I thought, my God, how much I love my wife and kids," a man told me, and added, "and I realized how screwed up my values were since I spent so little time with them." Further tests were fortunately negative; he's still alive and living his life more lovingly.

Nobody has written more eloquently or usefully about this matter than Carlos Castaneda. In *Journey to Ixtlan*, Castaneda describes a conversation concerning death with his mentor, don Juan, who is a Yaqui medicine man:

> "Death is our eternal companion," don Juan said with a most serious air. "It is always to our left, at an arm's length. . . . It has always been watching you. It always will until the day it taps you. . . . The thing to do when you're impatient," he proceeded, "is to ask advice from your death. An immense amount of pettiness is dropped if your death makes a gesture to you, or if you catch a glimpse of it, or if you just have the feeling that your companion is there watching you. . . . Death is the only wise adviser that we have. Whenever you feel . . . that everything is going wrong and you're about to be annihilated, turn to death and ask if that is so. Your death will tell you that you're wrong; that nothing matters outside its touch. Your death will tell you, 'I haven't touched you yet.'" (pp. 54–55)

In my own life, I have found don Juan's image of death at arm's length a very powerful one. With death the measure, cataclysms become tremors, whirlwinds whispers, and much pettiness does indeed fall away.

4. The full realization that we are mortal allows us to make the most of the end of our lives.

"To everything there is a season, and a time for every purpose under heaven." These are familiar words from Ecclesiastes, and, indeed, every season of life has its special reasons for being. To have a full life, one would want to live each season fully.

Kübler-Ross titled one of her books *Death: The Final Stage of Growth.* Sometimes, when I talk about dying as an important stage of life, someone will say something like, "No thanks. I would just as soon skip it. I'm hoping to depart suddenly as the result of a massive heart attack at the age of 85."

Every stage of life offers us an opportunity to grow and none more so than the stage called "dying." When I first began to work with terminally ill patients, I thought my visits would be filled with talk of dying and death. Instead, I found my patients more occupied with living and life. Some of them seemed to be living life more fully (if more effortfully) than ever before.

I came to see that dying folks who openly confronted their approaching deaths had freed themselves to live and grow. They were free to regard this part of their lives as a completion to be lived rather than a catastrophe to be denied. They were free to get their house in order, to catch up on all the things that needed to be done, and to say goodbyes. They were free to realize the preciousness of each remaining day.

I remember visiting a man who had cancer throughout his body. When we began to work together he seemed to be nearing death but managed to hang on and even get a little better. As we sat together, enjoying our cups of hot chocolate, he said to me, "I'm grateful. That may seem strange to hear from a man who has had my troubles the past few years. But my wife and I are closer than we have ever been. I'm still working on my relationship with my sons, but at least I have some time to work on it. I like myself better. I'm a lucky man."

THE DYING-READINESS/ FREEDOM-TO-LIVE TEST

As indicated earlier, my work has led me to believe that those of us who ready ourselves to die also free ourselves to lead our lives more fully than ever before. Typically, in my workshops on dying readiness, I administer my "Dying-Readiness/Freedom-to-Live" Test. I give it item by item, discussing each item as I go, so that the participants may have some basis for their answers.

The 10 items of the test are presented in the material that follows, and each item is briefly delineated. You are invited to take the test now. After you have read each item and delineation, answer by drawing a circle around "Yes" or "No" as is appropriate in your own case. If your answer isn't clearly yes or no, circle the question mark.

Yes   ?   No   1. I have allowed myself to think deeply about death and my own death and to experience the feelings that this engenders.

Edna St. Vincent Millay wrote a beautiful poem about death entitled *Childhood is the Kingdom Where Nobody Dies*. Distant relatives die; cats die; but mothers and fathers don't die, and any thought of our own death is far away. But the innocence of childhood is soon lost as we grow and develop an increasing acquaintance with death. We come to know that we too will die. How do we deal with that awesome knowledge?

J. William Worden (1982), a psychologist who has worked with many dying patients and their families, has concluded that many of the problems we face in life stem from our inability to confront the simple fact that we will one day die. He drew up the concept of "personal death awareness" or PDA, for short, which describes the extent to which we are mindful of our mortality, accepting of it, and living our life in accordance with this mindfulness and acceptance.

Although it is possible to be overly preoccupied with death, Worden feels that most of us have PDAs that are too low because we tend to shy away from thoughts of our own mortality; we tend to deny and live in accordance with the denial that our lives will end. His experience is that if we *willingly* increase our PDA and face our mortality, we seldom want to go back to our former state of low awareness.

Worden believes there are two main reasons we keep our PDA at a low level. The first is that we find it anxiety-provoking to think about our own death. Second, we believe it's useless to think about death because there's nothing we can do about it. "That's where you're wrong" Worden writes—and Worden's right. There's a lot we can do about death. There are choices and options open to us, which will become apparent as we proceed with our test.

Your response to this chapter may be a good indication of the level of your PDA. If it makes you quite anxious or you wish it hadn't been included, your PDA may be on the low side. If you ordinarily avoid conversation about death (except to joke) or visiting persons near death or attending funerals, this may be a further indication.

At this point, go back and answer Item 1 if you haven't already. Circle the alternative that best describes your situation. Each of the succeeding items will encourage you to think a little more deeply about your own death and to experience the feelings that this engenders. If in all honesty, you now have to answer Item 1 "no," perhaps by the end of this test you will be a little closer to answering it "yes."

Yes   ?   No   2. I have made out a will.

Picasso left a huge fortune in art works, real estate, investments, and bank accounts, but he left no will. He predicted that after his death there would be a scramble among his legitimate heirs and illegitimate children and children's children. He said, "It will be worse than anything you can imagine." And it was.

Why don't people make out wills? One important reason is that a will is associated with the idea of our death. As was already indicated, thoughts of our mortality can be anxiety-provoking and whatever provokes anxiety may be pushed aside or avoided.

Some of us find it comforting to assume a kind of immortality for ourselves—or at least a nonmortality—and this is inconsistent with making out a will. Somerset Maugham once wrote that if one were small, one might hope to be overlooked by death. For some, making out a will is like registering to die and signing a will is like signing a death certificate or, at least, a promissory note. By not making out a will or not signing it, we feel we haven't put ourselves in jeopardy.

A second reason for not completing a will is that we assume this is something that can be delayed. Because we don't expect to die soon (if at all), why bother now? We can take care of this when we're old and gray.

A third reason for not making out a will is the assumption that one is not leaving much of value. (But if you die a "wrongful death," you may be worth a lot more dead than alive—and who gets it?) A fourth reason is the wishful thought that somehow things will work out all right and that those who should inherit will inherit; because making out a will is an expense and bother, why not just hope for the best?

Dying without a will may save you some effort and momentary anxiety, but it creates problems for those you leave behind. If you die without leaving a valid will, you are said to have died "intestate." Here is what David Larsen (1980), an attorney specializing in wills, trusts, and estate planning, has to say about - intestacy:

> The main problem with intestacy is, of course, that you have no say where your property goes. Your spouse, your children, your adopted children, your parents—all of them may get more, or less, of your property than you might have expected or wanted. That special heirloom may go to a person whom you'd rather not have it. Your funeral and burial wishes may not be carried out. (Will anyone know what they are?) If you and your spouse both die so that your minor children are orphans, the court-appointed "guardian of the person" and "guardian of the property" may be people you'd rather not have watching after your children and their property. The executor of your estate may be some person you wouldn't want. Your executor and the guardian of your children's property may have to post bond, thereby costing your estate money, meaning that your heirs get less. You could end up pay-

ing a lot more in death taxes than you need to: the federal government and the [state] can steamroller your estate because you didn't put up any tax-saving defenses. Finally, dying intestate shows a lack of planning, meaning more than likely that your affairs will be a mess when you die. And who's left to straighten out your mess when you're gone? Your family— and at just the time when they are least able, emotionally, to do it. (p. 12)

It seems a bit curious that folks who care for their loved ones and who also care about their own hard-earned or carefully acquired possessions would leave both in limbo upon death. Making out a will shows that you care. It also shows that you weren't afraid to face your own demise. It's an important step in getting your house in order. Before proceeding further, answer Item 2 by circling one of its three alternatives.

Yes   ?   No   3. I have made known my choice between having and not having my life extended through artificial or heroic measures in the event that there is no reasonable expectation of my recovery from physical or mental disability. (Or I have made out a living will or executed a durable power of attorney.)

Advances in medicine often make it possible to delay death in terminally ill patients and to keep nonterminal but irreversibly comatose patients indefinitely alive. Sometimes the days that technology adds are of little use or quality, and the additional time is purchased at considerable cost and discomfort. The case against maintaining life at all costs is vividly made in Reverend Robert Fraser's adaptation of the Twenty-third Psalm.

Competent adults have the right to refuse life-sustaining treatment, but what happens if one becomes incompetent to make one's wishes known? In this litigious age, physicians run into few problems if they continue to treat a patient, but there can be considerable danger in stopping treatment. In the absence of specific instructions, it is unlikely that life-support systems would be withdrawn and much less likely in the case of a relatively young patient.

By planning ahead, we can have a say concerning artificial or heroic measures that might be used to prolong our own lives. There are various advance directives that can be employed for this purpose, but the two most important are the living will and the durable power of attorney for health care. Living wills are now recognized by statute in more than half the states, although provisions vary considerably. All states and the District of Columbia have statutes recognizing durable powers of attorney, and in most states, such powers can be worded to create a document covering (and limited to) health care. (Unlike an ordinary power of attorney, which terminates if the principal becomes incapacitated, a *durable* power of attorney continues despite the principal's condition.)

A *living will* (not to be confused with a living trust) is a written, signed, witnessed, and possibly notarized declaration that specifies your wishes concerning the use of life-sustaining procedures in your own case if you become terminally ill and incompetent. A *durable power of attorney for health care* is a written, signed, witnessed, and possibly notarized document in which you (the principal) give another (the agent) the legal authority to make health-care decisions on your behalf if you become terminally ill and incompetent. Because some living wills also provide for a health proxy who, in effect, can serve as an agent, and some durable powers of attorney also specify your health-care wishes, there can be a great deal of overlap in these two approaches. State laws vary, so it is important that a local attorney or some other knowl-edgeable authority be consulted for assistance as you weigh your options and devise your own plan.

Yes ? No 4. I have planned my own funeral or planned to dispense with a funeral and made these plans known.

Yes ? No 5. I have chosen and made known a plan for the disposal of my body after death.

Although we don't plan our entrance into this world, we have an opportunity to plan our departure. In our plans, we will want to consider our own wishes and also the needs of our survivors and what would be helpful and convenient for them. Careful planning can avoid a situation like this one described by Robert Kavanaugh (1974):

> Not long ago I attended a funeral of incredible ugliness. The minister kept referring to the deceased by the wrong name, totally unaware of frantic cues from the pews, mistaking our winces and near groans for tears of muffled grief. The eulogy by this insensitive last-minute hireling had obviously been canned for any occasion. His suavity hinted he could be speaking to any luncheon club anywhere, except for his rude and impertinent insistence on forcing his religious assumptions on the semi-religious friends of a dead nonbeliever.
>
> I wondered then and still wonder what purpose such a funeral was thought to serve. Who needed it? Nearly everyone departed in humiliation and anger, pitying the family too distraught to accept our sympathies. I wondered about that man of God who could be paid to talk so glibly about death without touching a single unifying spark in his saddened congregation beyond anger for himself. I wondered why the family needed this hollow and decrepit ritual and why anyone allowed them to put themselves through such a travesty after six months of watching their daughter die. (pp. 187–188)

Here, in sharp contrast, is a recollection of a member of the Older Women's League:

> I'd like to tell you about a memorial service I once attended at a senior center. I didn't know the woman who had died. I was visiting a friend in another city and she invited me to go to the senior center for a memorial service for one of the active members. There was nothing solemn about the occasion—the feeling of the group was warm and friendly. The group leader started by telling about the deceased—some of her special contributions and a couple of amusing anecdotes illustrating her lively character. Another person told a similar story, and soon the conversation was moving along, bringing laughter and an occasional tear. Family members talked of what she had meant to them. One person sang a song, another read a brief poem. A display of pictures and a few clippings were on the wall. The service lasted about 45 minutes, followed by much hugging and then refreshments.
>
> I felt privileged to have heard this re-creation of a remarkable woman's life, told by those who had shared it. The loss was evident, but the group was healing itself and would carry on, with their deceased friend living in their hearts and memories.

What will your funeral or memorial service be like? Or do you want a service at all? Are you leaving this all up to others? In making our own final plans, we help ourselves, in that (1) we can contemplate making a departure appropriate to the wishes of both ourselves and our survivors, (2) we can experience in anticipation this departure just as we preexperience a well-planned trip, and (3) we can gain a sense that we have done what needs to be done and therefore are free to go on to the business of living.

In our final planning, we also help those we leave behind in two ways: (1) We remove the necessity of decision making just at the time when our survivors might be least able to make decisions, guess at what we would have wanted, or resolve differences among themselves. (2) We may ameliorate a common tendency of bereaved persons to overspend on funeral arrangements.

Simplicity is what London schoolmaster Ken James sought in his final arrangements. When he died of cancer, he left an estate of $40,800 but no funds for a funeral. In his will, he wrote, "I specifically forbid a conventional funeral. There must be no ceremony of any kind, religious or otherwise, no floral tributes or mourners or any fuss whatsoever. My ashes are not to be buried or sentimentally scattered, but are to be inconspicuously deposited in any convenient dustbin for refuse collection in the usual way." (That proved to be a bit much for the officials; they had James's ashes buried under a bed of flowers at the crematorium.)

For those of us who wish simplicity and economy in our final disposition (but perhaps not quite so simple and economical as Ken James), joining a memorial society is a good option. These societies are cooperative, democratically run, nonprofit organizations that contract with funeral directors on behalf of their members. By practicing simplicity and by bargaining collectively, the members of the society save 50 to 75 percent of usual funeral costs. These memorial societies have low fees to join (rarely over $25), sell no services of their own, and should not be confused with private companies calling themselves societies. For a directory of cooperative societies, contact their national organizations: Continental Association of Funeral and Memorial Societies, 6900 Lost Lake Road, Egg Harbor, WI 54209, or the Memorial Society of Canada, Box 96, Station A, Weston, Ontario M9N 3M6.

Benevolence is what poet Robert Test (1976) seeks in his final disposition. As a last act, he wants to give himself away:

> The day will come when my body will lie upon a white sheet neatly tucked under four corners of a mattress located in a hospital busily occupied with the living and the dying. At a certain moment a doctor will determine that my brain

has ceased to function and that, for all intents and purposes, my life has stopped.

When that happens, do not attempt to instill artificial life into my body by the use of a machine. And don't call this my death-bed. Let it be called the Bed of Life, and let my body be taken from it to help others lead fuller lives.

Give my sight to the man who has never seen a sunrise, a baby's face or love in the eyes of a woman. Give my heart to a person whose own heart has caused nothing but endless days of pain. Give my blood to the teenager who was pulled from the wreckage of his car, so that he might live to see his grandchildren play. Give my kidneys to one who depends upon a machine to exist from week to week. Take my bones, every muscle, every fiber and nerve in my body and find a way to make a crippled child walk.

Explore every corner of my brain. Take my cells, if necessary, and let them grow so that, someday, a speechless boy will shout at the crack of a bat and a deaf girl will hear the sound of rain against her window.

Burn what is left of me and scatter the ashes to the winds to help the flowers grow.

If you must bury something, let it be my faults, my weaknesses and all prejudice against my fellow man.

Give my sins to the devil. Give my soul to God.

If, by chance, you wish to remember me, do it with a kind deed or a word to someone who needs you. If you do all I have asked, I will live forever.

For those of us who, like Test, would like to give ourselves away, we can do so by completing a Uniform Donor Card, which is a binding legal document in every state through laws based on the Uniform Anatomical Gift Act. This card permits us upon death to make one or more of our body organs available for transplantation or research. For a card or further information, call the nearest organ and tissue bank (look in the phone book yellow pages under "Organ & Tissue Banks"). Some states offer you the opportunity to complete a card when you are applying for or renewing your drivers license. If you wish to donate your body for medical education, call a school of medicine.

For our final disposition, we may choose among a funeral service (held in the presence of the body, with an open or a closed casket), a memorial service (held after the body has been removed for final disposition), a committal service (held at gravesite or in the chapel of a crematory), some combination of these services, or no service at all. Ernest Morgan (1984) has listed some options of disposition in approximate order of their cost, least to most expensive:

1. Immediate removal to a medical school, followed by a memorial service.
2. Immediate cremation, followed by a memorial service.
3. Immediate earth burial, followed by a memorial service.
4. A funeral service in the presence of the body, followed by removal to a medical school.
5. A funeral service in the presence of the body, followed by cremation.
6. A funeral service in the presence of the body, followed by earth burial. (p. 44)

Before proceeding, return to Questions 4 and 5, and answer them.

Yes   ?   No   6. I have made out a survivor's guide.

Dear Ann:

I am perplexed by a problem that I have run across three times in the past few years—secretive husbands.

In one case, an older cousin's husband died and the woman had no idea of the state of their finances. He always provided her with plenty of household and pocket money, but became apoplectic when asked about financial matters, even after he became terminally ill. When he died, his widow was unable to find any assets.

In the second case, a successful physician is unwilling to share information about the family finances. His wife (my sister) has no inkling of their financial status. He has a highly successful practice, is chief of staff of the community hospital and a pillar of the medical community, but totally secretive about financial matters. They have recently reconciled after nearly breaking up over this situation. My sister is a successful professional person in her own right and has had to run the household with her own funds, not paying much attention until recently when it became a bone of contention.

The third example is a sister-in-law. Her husband died suddenly last December. She was unable to find any resources except a small stock account and an apartment in London, which was in both names. He never spoke of business matters, even though they appeared to have a solid marriage.

What do you have to say about such peculiar behavior? How can a woman protect herself against a man who is secretive?

—Perplexed In The West

Dear Perp:

It is hard to imagine a woman being so ignorant and passive about family finances in this day and age, especially since so many females are knowledgeable and involved in business.

Any wife who reads this and does not know what she can count on if her husband dies before her (and most of them will) should open the subject before another day goes by. If her husband refuses to talk about it, she should tell him he owes her that consideration and if he persists in being uncooperative, she will be forced to see a lawyer. She should not hesitate to make good her threat.

The same goes for men whose wives control the purse strings. They, too, have a right to know what goes on. A marriage in which such information is withheld indicates a serious lack of trust and mutual respect.

—Ann Landers

There is often very much that needs to be done when a person dies and the people who need to do it may be in shock or upset and scarcely able to manage. Sometimes it may even be impossible to complete everything that needs doing because vital information is incomplete or unavailable. And yet much of this work could have been easily done long before death by the subject person herself or himself.

The problem noted in the letter written by "Perplexed in the West" is only one of many that can be avoided by filling out a survivor's guide (sometimes called a family guide). This guide is simply a listing of the data necessary to attend to funeral, obituary, legal, financial, and tax matters upon and after your death. You are the best person to gather your own data. You can do in a relatively short period of time what your survivors may be able to do only with difficulty or perhaps not at all.

Survivor's guides take various forms. A typical guide contains the information relative to your death certificate and obituary, desired funeral arrangements, will, safety deposit box, insurance, social security benefits, pensions, annuities, checking accounts, property, and other financial assets and liabilities.

Some funeral homes or mortuaries will provide you with a complimentary survivor's or family guide. To receive a copy of a guide by mail, send $2.00 to the Continental Association of Funeral and Memorial Societies, Inc., 6900 Lost Lake Road, Egg Harbor, WI 54209. Answer Item 6 before continuing on to the next item.

Yes ? No 7. I have made my relationships with "significant others" current by "clearing the past."

We want, of course, to be treated fairly. We want our world to be just. We want what is due to us. We want to get as good as we give. We want others to treat us as nicely as we treat them and to pay us back for all we've done for them.

Alas, our world is not always just and the people in it who are most important to us—our "significant others"—are not always fair. When we are treated unfairly, unjustly, we may build up a good deal of anger and resentment. The raw deals, the things that others did to us and shouldn't have, the things they didn't do, but should have—these things may fester in our minds and memories.

It is important to distinguish between two kinds of wrongs. There are the wrongs to work on and the wrongs to let go of. It takes some wisdom to know the difference.

Some of us become resentment collectors. We are unable to forgive or forget the wrongs done to us. This kind of collecting accomplishes nothing and can become self-destructive. Our resentment consumes energy and keeps us stuck in the past. Like other persistent negative emotions, resentment can have corresponding physiological reactions that wear down the body and make us ill.

Why do we sometimes choose the heavy burden of resentment rather than the liberation that comes with forgiving? What do we get out of it?

Some persons don't forgive because they confuse forgiveness with condonation. They think that to forgive is to condone or overlook or even give approval to a wrong. By being unforgiving they continue to bear witness to the wrong. They keep the offender on the hook (and perhaps themselves as well). But to forgive does not require one to overlook or approve a wrong. Forgiveness notes there is something to be forgiven and also something to be gained by letting go and moving along.

Some persons don't forgive because no retribution has been made. There appears to have been no punishment, no repayment. To pardon the offender might set a bad example. Or would it present a good model? In any case, what may be more important is the effect of forgiveness on the forgiver and on the relationship of the forgiver to the one forgiven.

If we forgive others, we find it easier to forgive ourselves for what we may have done in the past, whether wittingly or unwittingly. If others don't have to be perfect, we don't have to be perfect either. If others can be forgiven, we can forgive ourselves.

The solution to the burden of resentment is forgiveness. When we forgive, we "clear the past" and write off all outstanding emotional debts. We let go of our resentment and let go of the past. In doing so, we free ourselves to come fully into the present and to make the most of it.

In his wise and helpful book *Forgive & Forget,* Lewis Smedes suggests we look upon our hurts with "magic eyes." Such eyes allow one to see things in a new light so that hurts flowing from the wounds of yesterday may heal.

Smedes asks, "What do you do when you forgive someone who hurts you? What goes on? When is it necessary? What happens afterward? What should you expect it to do for you? *What is forgiving?*" Here are his answers:

> The act of forgiving, by itself, is a wonderfully simple act; but it always happens inside a storm of complex emotions. It is the hardest trick in the whole bag of personal relationships.
>
> So let us be honest with each other. Let us talk plainly about the "magic eyes" that are given to those who are ready to be set free from the prison of pain they never deserved.
>
> We forgive in four stages. If we can travel through all four, we achieve the climax of reconciliation.
>
> The first stage is *hurt:* when somebody causes you pain so deep and unfair that you cannot forget it, you are pushed into the first stage of the crisis of forgiving.
>
> The second stage is *hate:* you cannot shake the memory of how much you hurt, and you cannot wish your enemy well. You sometimes want the person who hurt you to suffer as you are suffering.
>
> The third stage is *healing:* you are given the "magic eyes" to see the person who hurt

you in a new light. Your memory is healed, you turn back the flow of pain and are free again.

The fourth stage is the *coming together:* you invite the person who hurt you back into your life; if he or she comes honestly, love can move you both toward a new and healed relationship. The fourth stage depends on the person you forgive as much as it depends on you; sometimes he doesn't come back and you have to be healed alone. (p. 18)

I would make two amendments to what Smedes has written. First, I don't think it is necessary to forget wrongs. In fact, not forgetting the hurt of a wrong done to us may keep us from inflicting similar hurt onto others. But it is necessary for us to remember the wrong differently—perhaps with sadness rather than anger or with a generosity that is above revenge and resentment.

Second, with "magic eyes," we may see the person who hurt us in a new light, but these eyes may also help us to see ourselves differently. We may respect ourselves more as generous, forgiving persons than as vengeful, resentful ones, and also find ourselves easier to live with.

When we have done all the necessary emotional work and "cleared the past," our house is in better order. We are ready to die—and we are ready to live our lives without the burden of resentment. Answer Item 7 before continuing on.

Yes ? No 8. I keep my relationships with "significant others" current by manifesting my love.

Immediately following are instructions for an exercise you can administer to yourself, based on Perlin (1982). Pause after reading each paragraph, and imagine or simply think about yourself as being in that situation. Answer the questions to yourself. Then go to the next paragraph and continue in the same way until you have completed the exercise.

You are seated in a doctor's office. You are waiting for the doctor to come in with the results of your medical examination. It has been rather a long wait. Take a little time to imagine how the office looks or just think about how it looks. How does it smell? What thoughts am going through your mind? What do you feel? (Pause)

The doctor comes in and sits down. There are a number of laboratory reports and some x-rays. You wait for the doctor to speak up. Why doesn't the doctor speak up? Finally, the doctor starts to go over the medical findings with you. You begin to realize that the findings are serious, very serious. You must check into the hospital immediately for more tests. What is going through your mind now? What are you feeling? To whom do you want to talk? Or be with? What would you say to them? (Pause)

Some months have gone by. You are at home and in bed. You are aware that you have only a short time to live. Your body is wasted and weak, but your mind is lucid and you can communicate with others. What are you thinking? What are you feeling? With whom do you want to be? What do you want to say to them? (Pause)

You are back in the hospital. There is only a little time left. People have come to see you and be with you, but the nurse has suggested only one or two approach you at a time. Whom do you want to see the most? Imagine or think of them standing there by your bed. What is being said? (Pause)

Now you have died. Your body remains on the hospital bed. Although the medical staff has left, some people have stayed to be with you a little longer. Who are they? If you could speak to them now, what would you say? (Pause)

In one of his newspaper columns, Charles McCabe (1975) wrote movingly about a dear friend who had died the previous week. McCabe deeply regretted that he had never been able to tell this friend how much he loved him. McCabe added, "I do not know how common this affliction is, this inability to express love. I know that it has been with me nearly all my life, and has caused me many moments of regret."

Many of us are like McCabe. After completing the preceding exercise, many persons report that somewhere in the process, they expressed their love and appreciation to a number of significant others—something they had not done recently, very much, or at all. They did not want to die without manifesting their love. But why—if the declaration of love is so important—were they living without manifesting it?

Marshall Hodge points out in his book *Your Fear of Love* that we all fear closeness, although some are much more frightened of it than others. Our fear is based on the fact that caring always involves vulnerability. Hodge writes, "When we open ourselves and permit another person to know that we love him, we risk being hurt. And because we know how it feels to be hurt, this risk is frightening" (p. 7).

Some of us have trouble in expressing our love because we have grown up in cold or undemonstrative families and have never learned how. Some consider love a kind of reward to be administered only when someone performs up to standards. Some are wary of love because it can interfere with independence.

Hodge writes that although love seems to ebb and flow like the ocean, it is not caring itself but rather the *experience* of love and the *expression* that are intermittent. He notes that moments of love are followed by periods of withdrawal. To keep our relationships with others current, we need to continually manifest our love. We need to keep our expression lines open.

It will be helpful to run a check on yourself now. In the space below make a list of all the people in your life whom you love (names, initials, or symbols will do). Then cross out every one to whom you haven't manifested your love in the past half year. (My dictionary says that *to manifest* means to make clearly apparent to sight or understanding; obvious. So just knowing they know that you love them doesn't qualify.)

Persons Whom I Love

Now, based on the preceding exercise and everything else you know about yourself, answer Item 8. Then continue with remaining two items.

Yes ? No 9. I have learned to die my "little deaths" in preparation for my "big death."

Plato, on his death bed, gave this advice to a visiting friend: "Practice dying." Life gives us plenty of opportunity for this practice because life is filled with a number of little deaths. These are the times when we lose not life but something very important to it. Perhaps someone dear to us dies or we are permanently disabled or we lose a relationship or position of many years or we suffer a great financial reversal or we come to the realization that something we have dreamed of and hoped for will never come to pass.

Stanley Keleman (1974) described life as a migration through many little dyings. In each dying, something old is lost, and something new is born. Keleman writes, "Growth, change and maturing occur by deforming the old and forming the new. In these little dyings we can learn how to live our big dying" (p. 26).

Keleman believes that big dying—death itself—is similar to little dying. If we want to know how we will face big death, we can review our little deaths. If we find we haven't died well or learned from our little dyings, we can change the way we live our dying and better prepare ourselves for big death.

How can we manage our little dyings better? An answer lies in the research and writing on mourning, which, according to psychiatrist George Engel, is like healing. If we do our "grief work" properly, we are healed and become healthy. Psychiatrist Will Menninger spoke of troubled people who healed so well they became "weller than well." In effectively managing our little deaths, we can become sturdier than sturdy —more and more able to face and manage big death or the prospect of it.

William Worden (1982) has identified four tasks involved in mourning or in the adaptation to loss. The first task is to accept the reality of the loss. One of the primary responses to loss is denial. We refuse to believe what has happened has happened, we deny that it is irreversible, or we minimize the full meaning of the loss. Our first task requires us to face the facts and realize what has happened, to know that it can't be undone, and to acknowledge its full importance to us.

The second task is to experience the pain of the grief. In grieving, we may feel shock, anger, sadness, guilt, anxiety, loneliness, helplessness, depression, or a combination or alternation of these states. Instead of acknowledging our grief, we may try to deny it, shut it off, and busy ourselves with other matters. Friends and relatives may support our tactics, encouraging us to keep a stiff upper lip and look on the bright side. Various authorities on mourning believe it is necessary for bereaved persons to go through the pain of grief. If we avoid this pain, the course of mourning is prolonged. Some bereaved persons constrict their lives in an effort to prevent painful memories from arising.

The third task of mourning or adaptation to loss is to adjust to the new reality. We need to pick ourselves up and make a go of it with whatever we have left. This may be enormously difficult—to face life without whoever or whatever it was that made life worth living. But what choices do we have? Judith Viorst (1987) minces no words as she spells out our alternatives when a loved one dies: "To die when they die. To live crippled. Or to forge, out of pain and memory, new adaptations" (p. 295).

Picking ourselves up may mean setting new goals, learning new skills, or playing new roles. Very often it means compromise. But there is also an opportunity for growth and development that otherwise might not have occurred.

A fourth task applies to those situations in which there has been an emotional attachment. Its requirement is that this emotional energy be detached and reinvested in new relationships or enterprises. It is not easy to let go of old attachments. It may, for example, appear disloyal or it may seem that nothing could replace what was lost. And there can be the fear that what was lost once and with so much pain might be lost again.

What little deaths have you suffered? And how have you managed them? What have you learned? Have you learned to accept the reality of your losses? Can you allow yourself to feel the pain of your griefs? Are you able to accommodate your deprivation? Have you invested your emotional energy anew? Consider your responses to these questions, and answer Item 9 before you continue.

Yes ? No 10. I make it a point to appreciate and deeply enjoy the "little joys" of life.

None of us—whether seriously ill or seemingly hale—can count on endless tomorrows. Our lives could end at any moment. Are we fully living our lives; or are we saving our lives to be lived at a later date?

If we don't think of ourselves as mortal, if it's inconceivable to us that we will ever die, then we have forever. What's one day, if we have forever? We can throw it away. What's a little joy, if we have forever? We can keep pursuing big joys, whatever they may be.

One unfortunate notion of life is that it is a staircase. We climb up step by step, and when we get to the top we can be happy. If we are not happy at the top, maybe it isn't the top—maybe it's just a landing—so we need to resume climbing until we get to some place where happiness is.

Hermann Hesse (1988) wrote of the little joys available to us as we make our daily rounds. These are small things to which we may pay little notice but which can give us some moments of delight if we give them their due. A flower, a stretch of sky, a piece of fruit, children's laughter. His advice was that we seek out each day as many as possible of these small joys. He wrote, "It is the small joys first of all that are granted us for recreation, for daily relief and disburdenment, not the great ones."

Happiness, according to Jacques Henri Lartigue, is not an elusive bird that requires work to catch. Instead, happiness is an element—like air—that is everywhere. Lartigue wrote that if "you don't run after it too hard and too long, you'll find it right there, within reach, all the time . . . waiting for you to take it."

When we are ready to die, we are not so focused on large and distant pleasures. We do not primarily pursue the two elusive birds in the distant bush; we attend the one within reach or earshot. We take time to delight in the little joys that present themselves here and now.

Take a moment to recall the little joys you have delighted in today. How about yesterday? What about the day before? Do the memories of little joys come easily to mind, or are you drawing a blank? What about your life as a whole? Are you waiting for some Big Joy to make it all worthwhile? Think about this, and answer Item 10 before you go on.

Take a few moments to review your responses to all 10 items of the test. In your own estimation (there is no exact passing score), do your responses indicate you are ready to die? If so, congratulations because then your house is in order, and you are free to live. If your answers indicate you have more work to do, get busy and do it—not for death's sake but for life's sake.

Kenneth Woodward wrote that "there is no such thing as a good death except for those who have achieved a good life." To M. V. Kamath, the art of living and the art of dying are not different; neither can they be separated, for one flows into the other. He writes, "He who has mastered the art of living has already mastered the art of dying; to such, death holds no terrors."

References

Abrash, M. (1985). Is there life after immortality? In C. B. Yoke & D. M. Hassler (Eds.), *Death and the serpent: Immortality in science fiction and fantasy*. Westport, CT: Greenwood Press.

Castaneda, C. (1972). *Journey to Ixtlan*. New York: Simon & Schuster.

Hesse, H. (1988). On little joys. In A. Arkoff (Ed.), *Psychology and personal growth* (3rd ed, pp. 270–271). Boston: Allyn and Bacon.

Hodge, M. B. (1967). *Your fear of love*. Garden City, NY: Doubleday/Dolphin.

Kalish, R. A. (1985). *Death, grief, and caring relationships* (2nd ed.). Monterey, CA: Brooks/Cole.

Kavanaugh, R. E. (1974). *Facing death*, Baltimore, MD: Penguin.

Keleman, S. (1974). *Living your dying*. New York: Random House/Bookworks.

Kelly, O. E. (1979). Making today count. In L. A. Bugen (Ed.), *Death and dying* (pp. 277–283). Dubuque, IA: Wm. C. Brown.

Kübler-Ross, E. (1975). *Death: The final stage of growth*. Englewood Cliffs, NJ: Prentice-Hall.

Landers, A. (July 1, 1986). Share financial data. *The Honolulu Advertiser*, p. D-2.

Larsen, D. C. (1980). *Who gets it when you go?* Honolulu: University Press of Hawaii.

McCabe, C. (1975, September 16). Love untold. *San Francisco Chronicle*.

Morgan, E. (1984). *A manual of death education and simple burial* (10th ed.). Burnsville, NC: Celo Press.

Perlin, S. (1982). Death visualization: A teaching and learning device. *Death Education*, 6, pp. 294–298.

Smedes, L. B. (1986). *Forgive & forget: Healing the hurts we don't deserve*. New York: Pocket Books.

Test, R. (1976, November). The day will come . . . *Reader's Digest*, p. 142.

Viorst, J. (1987). *Necessary losses*. New York: Fawcett Gold Medal.

Worden, J. W. (1982). *Grief counseling and grief therapy*. New York: Springer.

Worden, J. W., & Proctor, W. (1976). *PDA: Personal death awareness*. Englewood Cliffs, NJ: Prentice-Hall.

Follow-Up

1. *Is your Personal Death Awareness (PDA) at an optimal level? How does your personal awareness of death affect the way you live your life?*

2. *Have you made out a will? Why or why not? Concerning personal items or property with sentimental value or special meaning, who would you like to inherit these items in the event of your death, why them, and have you ensured that this will be so? Concerning damages that might be paid your estate because of your "wrongful death" (for example, through accident), who would you like to inherit this money, why them, and have you ensured that this will be so?*

3. *Are there any conditions under which you would consider measures to prolong or shorten your life if you were terminally ill or irreversibly comatose? What have you done to ensure that your wishes in this regard are respected?*

4. *What plans for funeral or memorial services or for the disposal of your body after death do you prefer? Why? What have you done to ensure that your wishes in this regard are respected?*
5. *Have you made your relationship with "significant others" current by "clearing the past"? If so, give your proof. If not, why not?*
6. *Do you keep your relationships with "significant others" current by manifesting your love? If so, give your proof. If not, why not?*
7. *How have you dealt with a little death or some great loss in your life? What did you learn from this experience?*
8. *Do you make it a point to appreciate and deeply enjoy the little joys of life? If so, give your proof. If not, why not?*

Lessons from the Peak-Experiences

Abraham H. Maslow

What I'm going to talk about tonight is an excursion into the psychology of health, or of the human being at his best. It's a report from the road, of a job not yet done—a kind of commando raid into the unknown in which I have left my scientific flanks very much exposed. This is a warning to those of you who like neatly finished tasks. This is far from finished.

When I started to explore the psychology of health, I picked out the finest, healthiest people, the best specimens of mankind I could find, and studied them to see what they were like. They were *very* different, startlingly different in some ways from the average. The biologist was right who announced that he had found the missing link between the anthropoid apes and civilized man. "It's *us!*"

I learned many lessons from these people. But one in particular is our concern now. I found that these individuals tended to report having had something like mystic experiences, moments of great awe, moments of the most intense happiness or even rapture, ecstasy or bliss (because the word happiness can be too weak to describe this experience).

These moments were of pure, positive happiness when all doubts, all fears, all inhibitions, all tensions, all weaknesses, were left behind. Now self consciousness was lost. All separateness and distance from the world disappeared as they felt *one* with the world, fused with it, really belonging in it and to it, instead of being outside looking in. (One subject said, for instance, "I felt like a member of a family, not like an orphan.")

Perhaps most important of all, however, was the report in these experiences of the feeling that they had really seen the ultimate truth, the essence of things, the secret of life, as if veils had been pulled aside. Alan Watts has described this feeling as, "This is *it!*" as if you had finally gotten there, as if ordinary life was a striving and a straining to get someplace and this was the arrival, this was *Being There!*; the end of straining and of striving, the achievement of the desire and the hope, the fulfillment of the longing and the yearning. Everyone knows how it feels to want something and not know what. These mystic experiences feel like the ultimate satisfaction of vague, unsatisfied yearnings. They are like a sudden stepping into heaven; like the miracle achieved, like perfection finally attained.[1]

But here I had already learned something new. The little that I had ever read about mystic experiences tied them in with religion, with visions of the supernatural. And, like most scientists, I had sniffed at them in disbelief and considered it all nonsense, maybe hallucinations, maybe hysteria—almost surely pathological.

But the people telling me or writing about these experiences were not such people—they were the healthiest people! That was one thing

1. "If a man could pass through paradise in a dream, and have a flower presented to him as a pledge that his soul had really been there, and if he found that flower in his hand when he awoke, ay, what then!" Coleridge.

learned! And I may add that it taught me something about the limitations of the small (not the big) orthodox scientist who won't recognize as knowledge, or as reality, any information that doesn't fit into the already existent science. ("I am the master of this college; what I know not is not knowledge.")

These experiences mostly had nothing to do with religion—at least in the ordinary supernaturalistic sense. They came from the great moments of love and sex, from the great esthetic moments (particularly of music), from the bursts of creativeness and the creative furor (the great inspiration), from women giving natural birth to babies—or just from loving them, from moments of fusion with nature (in a forest, on a seashore, mountains, etc.), from certain athletic experiences, e.g., skindiving, from dancing, etc.

The second big lesson learned was that this was a *natural*, not a *supernatural* experience; and I gave up the name "mystic" experience and started calling them peak-experiences. They can be studied scientifically. (I have started to do this.) They are within reach of human knowledge, not eternal mysteries. They are in the world, not *out* of the world. They belong not only to priests but to all mankind. They are no longer questions of faith but are wide open to human inquisitiveness and to human knowledge. Observe also the implication of naturalistic usages for the words "revelation," "heaven," "salvation," etc. The history of the sciences has been one science after another carving a chunk for itself out of the jurisdiction of religion. It seems to be happening again here. Or to put this all another way, peak-experiences can be considered to be *truly* religious experiences in the best and most profound, most universal, and most humanistic sense of that word. It may turn out that pulling religion into the realm of science will have been the most important consequence of this line of work.

The next big lesson learned was that peak-experiences are far more common than I had ever expected: they were *not* confined to healthy people. These peak-experiences occurred also in average and even in psychologically sick people. As a matter of fact, I now suspect they occur in practically everybody although without being recognized or accepted for what they are.

Think for a minute how crazy this is in its implications. It's taken a long time for it to soak in on me. *Practically everybody reports peak-experiences if approached and questioned and encouraged in the right way. Also I've learned that just talking about it, as I'm doing now, seems to release from the depths all sorts of secret memories or peaks never revealed to anyone before, not even to oneself perhaps.* Why are we so shy about them? If something wonderful happens to us, why do we conceal it? Someone pointed out once, "Some people are scared to die; but some are scared to live." Maybe this is it.

There is considerable overlap between the characteristics of peak-experiences and the characteristics of psychological health (more integrated, more alive, more individual, less inhibited, less anxious, etc.) so I have been tempted to call the peak-experience a transient or temporary episode of self-actualization or health. If this *guess* turns out to be correct, it is like saying almost everyone, even the sickest people, can be psychologically healthy part of the time.

Still another lesson that by now I'm very sure of: Peak-experiences come from *many, many* sources and to every kind of person. My list of sources seems to keep on getting longer and longer as I go on with these explorations. Sometimes I am tempted to think that almost any situation where perfection can be attained, or hope fulfilled, or perfect gratification reached, or where everything has gone smoothly, can produce in some people, at some times, a peak-experience. These can be very humble areas of life or of the workaday world; or the situation may have been repeated a thousand times before without producing a peak-experience.

"If your everyday life seems poor to you," wrote Rilke in his *Letters to a Young Poet,* "do not accuse it; accuse yourself, tell yourself you are not poet enough to summon up its riches, since for the creator there is no poverty and no poor or unimportant place."

For instance, a young mother scurrying around her kitchen and getting breakfast for her husband and young children. The sun was streaming in, the children clean and nicely dressed, were chattering as they ate. The husband was casually playing with the children; but as she looked at them she was suddenly so overwhelmed with their beauty and her great love for them, and her feeling of good fortune, that she went into a peak-experience. (This reminds me of my surprise of getting such reports from women. The surprise taught me how much we had masculinized all this.)

A young man working his way through medical school by drumming in a jazz band reported years later, that in all his drumming he had three peaks when he suddenly felt like a great drummer and his performance was perfect.

A hostess after a dinner party where everything had gone perfectly and it had been a fine evening, said good-bye to her last guest, sat down in a chair, looked around at the mess, and went into a peak of great happiness and exhilaration.

Milder peaks have come after a good dinner with good friends as a man sat smoking a fine cigar, or in a woman after she had done a really good cleaning up in her kitchen and it shone and sparkled and looked perfect.

Thus it is clear that there are many paths to these experiences of rapture. They are not necessarily fancy or occult or arcane or esoteric. They don't necessarily take years of training or study. They are not restricted to far-out people, i.e., to monks, saints, or yogis, Zen Buddhists, orientals, or people in any special state of grace. It is not something that happens in the Far East, in special places, or to specially trained or chosen people. It's available in the midst of life to everyday people in everyday occupations. This is a clear support for the writers on Zen and their concept of "nothing special."

Now another generalization which I'm fairly sure of by now. No matter what the source of the peak-experience, all peak-experiences seem to overlap, to tend to be alike. I can't say they're identical—they're not. But they're much *closer* to being identical than I had ever dreamed. It was a startling thing for me to hear a mother describing her ecstatic feelings during the birth of her one child and using some of the same words and phrases that I had read in the writings of St. Theresa of Avila, or Meister Eckhardt, or in Japanese or Hindu descriptions of *satori* or *samadhi* experiences. (Aldous Huxley makes this same point in his "Perennial Philosophy.")

I haven't done this very carefully yet— these are so far only pilot or preliminary explorations—but I do feel safe in generalizing all peak-experiences to some extent. *The stimuli are very different: the subjective experience tends to be similar.* Or to say it in another way: our *kicks* are the same; we just get them from different paths, perhaps even from rock and roll, drug addiction and alcohol in less strong people. I feel more sure of this after reading in the literatures of mystic experiences, cosmic consciousness, oceanic experiences, esthetic experiences, creative experiences, love experiences, parental experiences, sexual experiences, and insight experiences. They all overlap; they approach similarity and even identity.

One main benefit I've gotten from this discovery, and that we all may get, is that it will help us to understand each other better. If a mathematician and a poet use similar words in describing their peak-experiences from a successful poem and a successful mathematical proof, maybe they're more alike subjectively than we have thought. I can make such parallels between a high school athlete running to a touchdown, a business man describing his feelings over plans for a perfect fig canning factory, a college student catching on to the Adagio movements of Beethoven's Ninth Symphony. I feel men can learn more about women's inner life (and vice versa) if they learn about the things that give them their highest satisfaction and feelings of creativeness. For instance, college women significantly more often than college men report their high moments to come from *being* loved. The men significantly more often get their happiest moments from success, conquest, achievement, winning. This finding conforms both to common sense knowledge and to clinical experience.

If our inner experiences of happiness are very similar no matter what stimulates them and no matter how different the people these experiences happen to (that is, if our insides are more like each other than our outside) then this may furnish us a way of being more sympathetic and understanding with people who are very different from ourselves; athletes and intellectuals, women and men, adults and children, etc. An artist and a housewife are not 1000 miles apart. In some moments they speak a common language, have common experiences, and live in the same world.

Can you bring about these experiences at will? No! Or almost entirely no! In general we are "Surprised by joy," to use the title of C. S. Lewis's book on just this question. Peaks come unexpectedly, suddenly they *happen* to us. You can't count on them. And, hunting them is a little like hunting happiness. It's best not done directly. It comes as a by-product—an epiphenomenon, for instance, of doing a fine job at a worthy task you can identify with.

Of course we can make it more likely, or less likely, out of our experiences in the past. Some fortunate people can almost always have a peak-experience in sex. Some can count on certain pieces of music, or certain favorite activities like dancing or skindiving. But none of these is ever *guaranteed* to bring on a peak-experience. The most propitious frame of mind for "receiving" them is one of receptivity, almost a kind of passivity, or trust, or surrender, a Taoistic attitude of letting things happen without interfering or butting in. You have to be able to give up pride, will, dominance, being at the wheel, being in charge. You have to be able to relax and let it happen.

I think this will do for you what it did for me—renew my interest in Taoism and the lessons it has to teach. So also for Zen. (On the whole, I can say that my findings conform more with the Zen and Tao philosophies than with any of the religious mysticisms.)

I'm very sure now that the ineffability of such experiences has been overstated. It *is* possible to talk about them, to describe them, and to communicate them. I do it all the time now that I've learned how. "Ineffable" really means "not communicable by rational, logical, abstract, verbal, analytic, sensible language." The peak-experience can be described and communicated fairly well if: (1) you both have had such experiences yourselves, and (2) you are able to talk in poetic or rhapsodic language, to let yourself be archaic in Jung's sense, to think-feel in a metaphorical or primary process way—or what Heinz Werner has called physiognomical language.

It's true the psyche *is* alone, encapsulated—cut off from all else—and for two such isolated psyches to communicate across the great chasm between them seems like a miracle. Well, the miracle happens.

What is the relation between the peak and the peaker is my next question. Already it seems evident to me that there is some kind of dynamic isomorphism at work, some kind of mutual and parallel feedback or reverberation between the characteristics of the perceiver and of the perceived world so that they tend to influence each other. To put it very briefly, the perceiver has to be worthy of the percept. Or better said, they must deserve each other like well-married or badly married couples. Kindness can *really* be perceived only by a kind man. A psychopathic personality will never be able to understand kindness, conscience, morality, or guilt since he himself lacks them entirely. But the person who is good, true, and beautiful is more able to perceive these in the world outside—or the more unified and integrated we are, the more capable we are of perceiving unity in the world.

But there is also an effect in the other direction. The more integrated the world, or the more beautiful or just, the more the world tends to make the perceiver more integrated, or beautiful or just, etc. Seeking out the highest values in the world to look at helps to produce or strengthen them in us. For instance, an experiment we did at Brandeis University proved that in a beautiful room people's faces look more alive and alert and higher in well-being, than they do in an ugly room. Or to put it another way, peak-experiences are more apt to come to nicer people, and they are more likely to happen to a particular person the better world conditions are.

This position needs many more examples to make it clear. I intend to write about this at greater length. It's a very important point.

In the peak-experiences, the "is" and the "ought" merge with each other instead of being different or contradictory. The perception is that what *is, ought* to be just that way. What *is* is just fine. This raises so many difficult questions that I don't want to make too much of it at this point, beyond recording that it *does* happen.

Finally, one finding that contradicts some of the mystics, especially of the East: I found all peak-experiences to be transient experiences—temporary not permanent. Some of the effects or after-effects may be permanent but the high moment itself is not.

PROBLEMS AND PUZZLES

Peak-experiences have been highly therapeutic for some people; and for others, a whole outlook on life has been changed forever by some great moment of insight or inspiration or conversion. This is easy to understand. It's like having been in Heaven for a moment and then remembering it in the dull moments of ordinary life. One person said characteristically, "I know life *can* be beautiful and good, and that life can be worth living; and I try to remember that when I need it during the grim days." One woman after natural childbirth, still breathless with the wonder of it said to her husband, "This has never happened to anyone before!" Another one, recalling the same experience said, "Once I was a queen, the most perfect queen of the earth." A man recalled his experience of awe from being in a wartime convoy at night with no lights. He melted into the whole vast universe and was not separate from all its beauty. A man recalled a burst of exuberance going over into sheer crazy, childish joy as he cavorted in the water like a fish, all alone so that he could yell out his great happiness at being so perfectly physical. And, of course, good and beautiful sex under the right circumstances is *often* reported to have this sort of effect.

It is easy to understand how such beautiful experiences should leave therapeutic effects, ennobling and beautifying effects, on the character, on the life outlook, on the way the world looks, on the way that the husband looks, or the baby. What is difficult to understand is why so often this does *not* happen. Practically everyone can be brought to realize he has been through such experiences. Why is it, then, that human beings are such a feeble lot, so full of jealousy, of fear, of hostility, of sheer misery? *This* is what I can't figure out.

One clue may come from a current investigation some of us are making on "Peakers" and "Non-Peakers"; i.e., the ones who reject or deny or suppress their peak-experiences, or who are afraid of them. It is our hunch that the peaks will do no good when they are rejected in this way.

At first it was our thought that some people simply didn't have peaks. But, as I said above, we found out later that it's much more probable that the non-peakers have them but repress or misinterpret them, or—for whatever reason—reject them and therefore don't use them.

Some of the reasons for such rejection so far found are: (1) a strict Marxian attitude, as with Simone de Beauvoir, who was persuaded that this was a weakness, a sickness (also Arthur Koestler). A Marxist should be "tough." Why Freud rejected his is anybody's guess; perhaps (2) his 19th-century mechanistic-scientific attitude, perhaps (3) his pessimistic character. Among my various subjects I have found both causes at work sometimes. In others I have found (4) a narrowly rationalistic attitude which I considered a defense against being flooded by emotion, by irrationality, by loss of control, by illogical tenderness, by dangerous femininity, or by the fear of insanity. One sees such attitudes more often in engineering, in mathematicians, in analytic philosophers, in bookkeepers and accountants, and generally in obsessional people.

The effects of refusing to recognize peak-experiences must be many. We are now trying to work them out.

One thing I have already learned is that authoritative approval lifts the lid off these experiences for many people. For instance, whenever I lecture to my classes or other groups about these peaks, obviously in an approving way, it always happens that many peak-experiences come into consciousness in my audience, or are "remembered" for the first time; or—as I prefer to think today—emerge out of chaotic, unorganized preconscious experience to be given a name, to be paid atten-

tion to, to stand out as figures against the background. In a word, people then "realize" or "understand" what's been happening to them. Many of you who are now listening to me will find this to be so. It's a very close parallel to the emergence of sexual feelings at puberty. But this time, Daddy says it's all right.

A recent subject has taught me something else that may be relevant here; namely that it is possible to have a peak experience as the woman did in childbirth, without recognizing that this is like other peak-experiences—that they all have the same structure. Perhaps this is a reason for lack of therapeutic transfer of peaks, a reason why sometimes they have no generalized effects. For instance, the woman finally realized that her feelings when her husband had once made her feel needed and important to him were very much like her feelings while giving birth, and also like the great gush of motherliness and love when confronted by an orphaned child. Now she can generalize the experiences and use them throughout life, not just in one isolated corner of it.

This work is also beginning to shed some light on an old puzzle noted by many religious writers—especially by those who have written about conversion, like William James or Begbie, as well as many of the old mystics. They implied often that it was *necessary* to go through a "dark night of the soul," to hit bottom—to experience despair as a prerequisite to the mystic ecstasy. I get the feeling from some of this writing that it is as if human will, pride, and arrogance first have to express themselves to the fullest. After will and pride have been proven to yield only total misery, the person in the depths may *then* be able to surrender, to yield, to become humble, to bow his head and bend his knee; to offer himself on the altar; and to say "not my will, but thine be done." I should stress that this is not *only* a religious phenomenon; something of the same sort can happen to the alcoholic, to the psychotic, to the female in her struggle with the male, or to the youngster in his struggle with his parent.

The trouble with this problem has been, I now think, that it can take *either* a healthy *or* a sick form. For instance, this whole scheme works not only for religious conversion or mystic experience, but also for sexuality. It's very easy to pick out sexual elements in mystical literature and you can see how a sex-denying religious would have to reject anything of the sort, and how a debunker like H. L. Mencken would snicker out loud at the whole business. For *all* people for whom sex and religion (in the "higher" life) didn't mix, this was a dilemma they got hung up on. Well, *this* part of the problem is certainly no problem any longer, at least not for those who think sex (or love-sex at least) is a wonderful and beautiful thing, and who are perfectly willing to think of it as one of the gates to Heaven.

But there are other problems. Pride can easily be a sick thing, but so also can the *lack* of pride be, i.e., masochism. It looks as if human beings must be able *both* to affirm themselves (to be stubborn, stiff necked, vigilant, alert, dominant, aggressive, self-confident, etc.) and *also* to be able to trust, to relax and be receptive and Taoistic, to let things happen without interfering, to be humble and surrender. For instance, we now know that *both* in proper sequence are necessary for creativeness, for good thinking and theorizing, for interpersonal relations, and certainly for sexual relationships. It seems true that females have to be extra good at trusting and yielding and males at asserting and affirming, but both must be able to do both.

We have seen that so far as the peaks are concerned, apparently most of them are *receptive* phenomena. They invade the person and he must be able to *let* them. He can't force them, grasp them, or command them. Will power is useless; so is striving and straining. What's necessary is to be able to let go, to let things happen. I can give you some very homely examples to show what I mean. It was Angyal who told me that, in his experience, really obsessional people couldn't "float" in the water. They just couldn't let go or be *non*-controlling. To float you must trust the water. Fight it and down you go. The same is true for urination, defecation, going to sleep, relaxing, etc. All these involve an ability to let go, to let things happen. Will power only interferes. In this same sense it begins to look as if the intrusion of will power may inhibit peak-experiences.

A final word on this point. "Letting go," "trusting," and the like does *not* necessarily mean a "dark night of the soul," or "black despair," or breaking down of pride or being forced to one's knees. Healthy pride goes very nicely with healthy receptivity. It is unhealthy pride only that has to be "broken."

This, by the way, is another point of difference between mystic experience and these peak-experiences.

I have elsewhere pointed out an unsolved problem, that peak-experiences make some people more alert, excited, "high," while others relax, grow quiet, and more serene. I don't know what this difference means, or where it comes from. Perhaps the latter means more complete gratification than the former. Perhaps it doesn't. I have run across at least one subject who gets tension headaches from peak-experiences, especially esthetic ones. She reports stiffness, tension, and great excitement in which she gets very talkative. The headache is not unpleasant and she doesn't avoid it but rather goes looking for more. This headache goes together with other more usual reports. For instance, I quote, "the world looks nice and I feel friendlier. I have a feeling of hopefulness (which is not usual for me). These are the moments when I *know* what I want—sure, less doubt; I'm more efficient and make faster decisions, less confusion. I know better what I want—what I like. I feel not only more hopeful but more understanding and compassionate," etc., etc.

The questions I asked were about the moments of rapture, of greater happiness. They, therefore, observed the well-known fact that tragedy, pain, and confrontation with death all may produce the same cognitive or therapeutic effects in people with sufficient courage and strength. So also the fusion of happiness with sadness—of laughter's closeness to tears—have to be investigated. I was told often enough of the tears that came with tremendous happiness (e.g., weeping at the happy wedding) or with the triumph of justice (e.g., tears at the happy ending), or the lump rising in the throat (e.g., at the peak of an especially beautiful dance performance), or the chills, goose flesh, shivering—and in one case—even incipient nausea, at musical peaks. These questions call for intensive and extensive investigation.

The study of peak-experiences inevitably brings up a very difficult problem that must occupy psychology for the next century. This is what some of the old mystics and some theologians called the "Unitive Consciousness" and by other names as well. The problem as the religionists phrased it was how to live a godly life in an ungodly world, how to live under the aspect of eternity, how to keep the vision of perfection in an imperfect world, how to remember truth, goodness, and beauty in the midst of falsehood, evil, and ugliness. In the past, all sorts of people left the world behind in order to achieve this vision, e.g., immured themselves in monasteries, or lived ascetic lives, etc. And many have tried to subdue the flesh, the body, the appetites out of the mistaken belief that these contradicted the eternal, the perfect, the divine, the realm of Being.

But think! Peak-experiences can very meaningfully be assimilated to—or even replace—the immature concepts in which Heaven is like a country club in some specific place, perhaps above the clouds. In peaks, the nature of Being itself is often perceived nakedly and the eternal values then seem to be attributes of reality itself, or to say it another way, Heaven is all around us, always available in principle, ready to step into for a few minutes. It's anywhere—in the kitchen or the factory, or on a basketball court—*any*place where perfection can happen, where means become ends or where a job is done right. The Unitive Life is more possible than was ever dreamed of, and one thing is very clear—research will bring it closer and make it more available.

One last word. It must by now be obvious to those who are familiar with the literature of mystical experiences that these peak-experiences are very much like them, and overlap them but are not identical with them. What their true relationship is, I do not know. My best guess is that they are different in degree but not in kind. The total mystical experience, as classically described, is more or less approached by greater or lesser peak-experiences.

Follow-Up

1. *Provide some responses to this statement used by Maslow in his studies of peak-experiences.*

   I would like you to think of the most wonderful experience or experiences of your life: happiest moments, ecstatic moments, moments of rapture, perhaps from being in love, or listening to music or suddenly "being hit" by a book or a painting, or from some great creative moments. . . . Try to tell how you feel in such acute moments, how you feel differently from the way you feel at other times, how you are at the moment a different person in some ways (Maslow, Toward A Psychology of Being, *1968, p. 71).*

2. *Maslow found that people cannot seek or bring about peak-experiences by will; they just happen. However, there are certain circumstances that often trigger peak or near peak-experiences. What are your most likely triggers for a peak-experience? Are you active or receptive? What kinds of activities are most likely to produce a peak? Analyze the circumstances of your own peak-experiences.*

3. *Select any other idea(s) in the article to write about or discuss.*

Silicon Snake Oil

Clifford Stoll

Me, an Internet addict? Hey—I'm leading a full life, with family, friends, and a job. Computers are a sideline, nor my life.

Jupiter is rising in the east, looking down on the Connecticut farm where I'm vacationing. On one side, a forest; on the other, a cornfield. Three guys are talking about the Knicks in the next room; in the kitchen, several women are buttering popcorn. One of them just called my name. But I don't care.

Fingers on the keyboard, I'm bathed in the cold glow of my cathode-ray cube, answering e-mail. While one guy's checking the sky through binoculars, and another's stuffing himself with popcorn, I'm tapping out a letter to a stranger across the continent. My attention's directed to the Internet.

Tonight, twenty letters want replies, three people have invited me to chat over the network, there's a dozen newsgroups to read, and a volley of files to download. How can I keep up?

I see my reflection in the screen and a chill runs down my spine. Even on vacation, I can't escape the computer networks.

I take a deep breath and pull the plug.

For fifteen years, I've been online, watching as thousands of computers joined hands to form a ubiquitous global network. At first, the nascent Arpanet seemed like an academic toy, a novelty to connect inanimate computers across the continent. Later, this plaything began supplying electronic mail and an occasional data file from other astronomers.

As the Arpanet grew into the Internet, I began to depend on e-mail to keep up with colleagues and friends. The Usenet brought news from around the continent. It became a whole new way to communicate.

Then, in 1986, while managing a computer system in Berkeley, I stumbled on a group of hackers breaking into computers. No ordinary cyberpunks, these: they sold their discoveries to the Soviet KGB.

It took a year to chase them down. During that time, I realized that our networks aren't simple connections of cables and computers; they're cooperative communities.

Since then, the Internet has become a most inviting and intriguing neighborhood. E-mail and chat lines keep me in touch with friends around the world; data transfers let me exchange information with colleagues. I join in discussions over the Usenet, posting queries and answering questions. One click of the mouse and I can read the daily news or a monthly report. At once it's fun and challenging.

But what a price! Simply keeping track of this electronic neighborhood takes a couple of hours every night. I find myself pawing through internet archives or searching for novelties over the World Wide Web. I spend still more time downloading files and following newsgroups. Bit by bit, my days dribble away, trickling out my modem.

But for all this communication, little of the information is genuinely useful. The computer gets my full attention, yet either because of content or format, the network doesn't seem to satisfy.

I can't turn my back on the network. Or can I? Right now, I'm scratching my head, wondering.

Perhaps our networked world isn't a universal doorway to freedom. Might it be a distraction from reality? An ostrich hole to divert our attention and resources from social problems? A misuse of technology that encourages passive rather than active participation? I'm starting to ask questions like this, and I'm not the first.

And so I'm writing this free-form meditation out of a sense of perplexity. Computers themselves don't bother me, it's the culture in which they're enshrined.

What follows, I suppose, shows my increasing ambivalence toward this most trendy community. As the networks evolve, so do opinions toward them, and my divergent feelings bring out conflicting points of view. In advance, I apologize to those who expect a consistent position from me. I'm still rearranging my mental furniture.

I suspect I'll disappoint science-fiction romantics as well. Nobody can offer utopia-on-a-stick, the glowing virtual community that enhances our world through discovery and close ties while transcending the coarseness of human nature.

Oh, I care about what happens to our networked neighborhood. However, I care more about—and am affected more by—what's happening in our larger society. So do parents, professors, teachers, librarians, and, yes, even politicians.

When I put on my cone-shaped thinking cap, I wonder what I would have said fifty years ago, when the interstate highway system was first proposed. Plenty of people favored it: truckers, farmers, and shippers wanted to break the railroad monopoly. Political subdivisions, car makers, and construction unions knew it would generate money. Politicians from every state felt highways were universally good things.

Who spoke out against the superhighway system? I don't remember anyone saying, "Hey, these beltways will destroy our cities.

They'll pave over pristine lands and give us hour-long commutes. They'll change our society from one of neighborhoods to that of suburbs."

In advance, then, here are my strong reservations about the wave of computer networks. They isolate us from one another and cheapen the meaning of actual experience. They work against literacy and creativity. They will undercut our schools and libraries.

Forgive me. I don't want to pontificate. But I do want people to think about the decisions they're making. It'd be fun to write about the wonderful times I've had online and the terrific people I've met through my modem, but here I'm waving a flag. A yellow flag that says, "You're entering a nonexistent universe. Consider the consequences."

It's an unreal universe, a soluble tissue of nothingness. While the Internet beckons brightly, seductively flashing an icon of knowledge-as-power, this nonplace lures us to surrender our time on earth. A poor substitute it is, this virtual reality where frustration is legion and where—in the holy names of Education and Progress—important aspects of human interactions are relentlessly devalued.

End of philippic. I don't mean to lay down an unwelcome mat. Nor do I feel that I'm entitled to technogoodies and others aren't. Quite the contrary: I look forward to the time when our Internet reaches into every town and trailer park. But the medium is being oversold, our expectations have become bloated, and there's damned little critical discussion of the implications of an online world.

The popular mythos tells us that networks are powerful, global, fast, and inexpensive. It's the place to meet friends and carry on business. There, you'll find entertainment, expertise, and education. In short, it's important to be online.

It ain't necessarily so.

Our networks can be frustrating, expensive, unreliable connections that get in the way of useful work. It is an overpromoted, hollow world, devoid of warmth and human kindness.

The heavily promoted information infrastructure addresses few social needs or business concerns. At the same time, it directly threatens precious parts of our society, including schools, libraries, institutions.

No birds sing.

For all the promises of virtual communities, it's more important to live a real life in a real neighborhood.

I began this meditation with a perplexed ambivalence toward computers, networks, and the culture that enshrines them.

At first, I wanted to think about technical issues. But I found myself returning to the same themes: real life and authentic experience mean much more than anything the modem can deliver. The culture of information isn't knowledge. Electronic networks erode important parts of our community.

Computer networks, like cars and televisions, confer a most seductive freedom, the "freedom to." As I step back from the insistent messages beckoning from across my computer, I'm beginning to wonder about a different kind of freedom—call it a "freedom from."

Certainly, few will toss out their computers or back away from their keyboards. Our networks are far too useful, and there's so much available over the modem.

Oh?

It's late on an October evening in Oakland; I smell popcorn in the kitchen.

I'm done meditating.

Follow-Up

1. *Stoll is one of the most famous and skilled computer experts in America. He now sees the computer and Internet as both a help and a hindrance. Choose one or more of these statements and offer your views:*
   - *Real life and authentic experience mean much more than anything the modem can deliver.*
   - *Simply keeping track of this electronic neighborhood takes a couple of hours every night.*
   - *Perhaps our networked world isn't a universal doorway to freedom. Might it be a distraction from reality? A diversion from social problems? A misuse . . that encourages passive rather than active participation?*
2. *How does the "electronic neighborhood" influence (positively and negatively) the way you live?*

Ten Symptoms
of Computer Addiction

1. A demonstrated "loss of control" when trying to stop or limit the amount of time on the computer. (Breaking promises to self or others. Promising to quit or cut down and not being able to do so.)
2. Being dishonest or minimizing the extent of the time you stay on the computer, or covering up or being dishonest about what activities you participate in when on the computer.
3. Negative consequences experienced by the computer user or his/her friends or family as a direct result of time or activities spent on the computer.
4. Participation in high risk or normally unacceptable behaviors when using the computer. Compromising your morals and values based on the opportunity to remain anonymous and protected on the computer. (A good test for this is to ask yourself if your spouse, partner or family would approve of what you were doing on the computer.)
5. An overdeveloped sense of importance for the computer in your life. Defending your right to use the computer as much as desired, regardless of the fact that people in your life are feeling left out and neglected. (Denial of the problem and justification; not being able to hear or feel what the other people are saying regarding your computer behavior.)
6. Mixed feelings of euphoria (a "rush"), combined with feelings of guilt, brought on by either the inordinate amount of time spent on the computer or the abnormal behavior acted out while using the computer.
7. Feelings of depression or anxiety when something or someone shortens your time or interrupts your plans to use the computer.
8. Preoccupation with the computer and computer activities when you are not using the computer. (Thinking about the computer and its activities when doing something else; i.e., having a family dinner, working on project deadline, etc.)
9. Finding yourself using the computer at times when you are feeling uncomfortable, irritated, or sad about something happening in your life. (Feeling uncomfortable in your relationship, so you will self-medicate and "hide out" on the computer.) Using time on the computer to become externally focused as a way to avoid facing what is happening in your life and avoid feeling the appropriate feelings inside yourself (self-medicating).

10. Experiencing financial concerns or problems in your life as a result of money being spent on computer hardware, computer on-line charges, or any other costs associated with computers.

After honestly answering, if you said yes to one question you *may* have a problem with computer addiction. If you said yes to two questions, there is a *good chance you do* have a problem with computer addiction. If you answered yes to three or more, you are demonstrating a pattern of behavior which would suggest that *you are addicted to your computer* and/or the activities you participate in when you are using it. If you are experiencing problems in this area of your life, it is important for you to contact a psychotherapist in your area who has experience in working with addictive behaviors. A safe place to start would be to have an assessment done to help you and your therapist gain insight into what's happening in this area of your life. Based on this evaluation, the appropriate plan can be formulated for help in your specific situation.

—James Fearing

Note: For further information on this topic contact the author at Net Web Site: http://www.uslink/-ncis/ or email: ncis@uslink.net

Who Will Play Your Music?

Michael Jones

Although I spent long periods of time playing my own music, I was uncomfortable performing for others, with the exception of close friends. Instead, I did covers of other people's music and relied upon these arrangements when I played in public.

It was one of these arrangements I was exploring while sitting at a piano in a hotel lobby one quiet evening. I had been at the hotel for several days, leading a management seminar. We had given ourselves the night off. Now, I sat for a time, lost in my musings. The building around me appeared to be so quiet and empty that I even felt free to let some of my own music weave in and out of these musical conversations.

It wasn't *that* empty, however. Soon an old man walked unsteadily out of the nearby lounge and plopped himself into a big easy chair beside the piano. There, he slowly sipped his wine and watched me play. I felt distracted and uneasy, trapped on the bench, where any moment he might request one of his favorite tunes, one I most likely did not know how to play.

"What's that?" he asked when I was done.

"Oh, a little bit of 'Moon River,'" I replied.

"Yeah, I recognized that," he said. "But there was something else before it, what was that?"

"That was some of my own music," I replied. "I don't have a name for it yet."

"You should," he said. "It deserves one." He looked thoughtful for a moment, then he said, "Your music is beautiful, but you're wasting your time with that other stuff."

His comment dropped into my lap so quickly I wasn't sure I fully understood what I'd just heard.

"What do you mean?" I asked.

"It's *your* music that brought me out here."

"But . . ." I said, cutting him off. "It's the other music that people want to hear."

"Not when they hear this," he replied. "Please, play some more." Then he closed his eyes and sat back in his chair.

When I am being deeply heard, playing my music feels less like a performance and more like an intimate act of love. I become more conscious of being carried along by a current of feelings, and following these feelings becomes more important than holding to the accuracy of the notes. Perhaps it is when we are in the company of another, particularly one whose appreciation for our work knows no bounds, that this love is most likely to be found.

When I finished playing, he and I sat together quietly for a long time. Slowly, he opened his eyes and sipped again from his glass.

"What are you doing with your music?" he asked.

"Nothing," I said. "It's just something I do for myself."

"Is that *all?*" he replied, surprised by my words.

Then I explained briefly what had brought me to the hotel.

"But how many others can do this consulting work?" he asked.

'Oh, perhaps twenty or thirty," I said, adding quickly, "but I don't want to give it up; my mission through this work is to change the world."

"I'm sure it is," he said. He seemed unmoved by the forced conviction of my words. Then he set his wineglass down on the table and looked directly at me.

"But who will play your music if you don't do it yourself?"

"It's nothing special," I protested.

"No," he agreed. "But it's you, and the world will be poorer without it."

I was about to offer other excuses when, with fire in his eyes and a voice sober and clear, he said, "This is your gift—don't waste it."

With that, he stood up, steadied himself by resting his hand on my shoulder for a moment, raised his glass in a silent toast, and then weaved slowly back to the lounge.

I sat frozen on the bench. Who will play my music? I asked myself over and over again. An hour or so passed, but I was still in shock. In his memoirs, Chilean poet Pablo Neruda speaks of how people who have lived unfulfilling lives sometimes complain that no one gave them any advice. No one warned them in advance that they were off course. But this was no longer true for me—I had just been warned.

Later, I went in search of this man, to insist that he tell me more. But he was gone, and a part of me suspected that perhaps he had never been there. If I had not heard his advice on the bench that evening, something else might have happened—a dream, perhaps, or an accident—to get my attention. For some people, it is the ending of a relationship or the onset of an unexpected illness—something comes along that brings our lives up short. What we had always thought secure suddenly becomes finite. In that moment, the larger universe, of which we have always been a part but often ignored, has our full attention. Its presence can be as dramatic and frightening as a raging storm at sea or as gentle as the intimate act of kissing the princess awake. It knows how to find the weak point, the undefended part where we are most likely to yield. This one wake-up call is enough to set us on a path. Following this path as it spirals inward and outward, and honoring it, even though the purpose of it and the final result may remain unclear, becomes our new work. "The truth dazzles gradually," as Emily Dickinson says, "or else the world would go blind."

Often, I imagined that my true vocation was to be a painter, or a poet, or something else equally remote or extraordinary. When friends asked about the music, I was emphatic in my reply. "No," I would say. "This is something *special*." But there is no mystery to the work that is ours to do. Although it may appear to be some attribute situated in the heavens somewhere, it is often found in the familiar and ordinary and located close at hand. Indeed, it is the idea that it should be special and extraordinary, that it is something out there—remote, elusive, and difficult to do—that throws us off track.

What is ours to do comes so easily, because from the very beginning it has always been there. It may not necessarily be a special talent like writing or music; it may instead be a quality of caring that we offer, a capacity for listening deeply to others, or simply the wonder and beauty we bring to the world through how we give our attention to a piece of music, a flower, or a tree. Our purpose is to give ourselves to the world around us—including people, musical instruments, trees, and words—and through the attention we bring to them help them blaze to life. When we offer ourselves to the world, the world gives itself back to us. In the words of D. H. Lawrence, "Life rushes in."

What is it that we desire to do that brings an increase to life? This often offers a clue as to where our gifts are to be found. Beneath the long list of things we *must* do is a deeper purpose, one that involves being present with ourselves and, in so doing, bringing some aspect of the world to life. But we cannot do it alone, for the recognition of who we truly are is most often found through the other. "The mystery of creation was always between two," Laurens van der Post writes, "in an awareness that there was always both a 'thou' and an 'I.'" We all need at least one other person to recognize this spark in ourselves, to make us the one we were meant to be. For me, it was that man in the lobby of the hotel.

Who is it that offers the act of confirmation in your life, the one willing to hold the match to light the fire to set your gift to the world ablaze? And who, or what, does your gift serve? As Laurens van der Post says, "most of us indeed have become distorted into knowing only the 'I' of ourselves and not the 'thou.'" Yet, once ignited, the flame that burns within us does so with such intensity that we would go blind if we looked upon ourselves directly. Our "thou" is seen through the actions of others in relation to us; they are the moons that reflect back to us the intensity of our sun.

When I said yes to that moment, I was re-learning how to say yes to the pleasure I knew the music would bring. But I was also opening myself to the fulfillment of larger intentions, ones that were not entirely my own. I trembled at the thought. Sometimes others have already tried to set our lives ablaze, and we have not accepted the match. We know that once the genie is out of the bottle, our lives will never be quite the same. There is burning that takes place, burning that has the power to transform to ashes old, limiting beliefs and everything else that we hold to be true. Nothing is exempt; everything may change, including even the smallest of acts.

I could neither push forward nor go back. When we reach this step in our creative life, we are often asked to go beyond our skills, to do the opposite of what has gone before. If we have been unfocused, it's time to focus; if we have been driven, as I had been from time to time, it's time for space. Nourish the longing, Kabir says to us, for it is the intensity of the longing that does all the work.

Yet we cannot be casual about this step, either. To turn our attention from our longing, even for a moment, may be one moment too long.

How many of us have turned away from living an imaginative life? How many of us would rather sacrifice ourselves to the security of institutional life than engage with the volatility of a soulful one? What is it that so often compels us to turn away from our longing rather than into it? Perhaps the dream seems so distant from the reality we live with day to day that we simply don't know where to begin or how to find a convenient time to start. There is also an awkwardness in our initial attempts to put ourselves into our art. We can feel unsure and self-conscious—quick to judge our progress and ready to admit defeat in the presence of those who say what we are doing is silly or frivolous, or through the constant pesterings of our own self-doubt.

When we take these first tender and delicate steps into our own imaginative life, we often need a bold and fiery image, one large and intense enough to make it a part of ourselves until our own small, gentle fire is strong enough to burn on its own.

The encounter with the old man had encouraged my return to music, but it offered

"Trumpet" by Nelson Goud. Copyright © 1996.

something more. Being at the piano had opened a pathway in which I could feel once again the tenderness that lay deep within my heart. And as my heart opened, it, in turn, offered an invitation to a wedding—a marriage between the ambitions of my intellect and the yearning for a deeper truth that was emerging within my soul. I was learning to love the other half of my self.

Could I, like Beethoven, hold a vision large enough to fill the entire span of my life? Could I say yes to it all despite the setbacks and confusion and self-doubt? Could I not only accept but embrace the uncertainty, not only tolerate but engage the ambiguity? Could I step forward and meet the suffering, the bliss, and the frustration? Could I willingly receive the future with a humble and prayerful acceptance and say, as philosopher Rudolph Steiner once said, that "whatever the next hour or day may bring, I cannot change it by fear or anxiety, for it is not yet known"? The terrors I feel may simply be shadow images from a more limiting past, not predictors of times to come.

When I left consulting to begin sitting at the piano again, I believed that I played poorly. And I had little experience with writing when I later took time from music to begin working on this book. Perhaps this is what life asks of us—to step faithfully into that very place in our lives where we can no longer fall back on our cleverness or wits. To serve the impulse to create is to accept that it may ask everything from us and offer little assurance in return. Moses guided his people into the Red Sea on faith; they were apparently up to their necks before the sea finally parted. Perhaps it is only when we have emptied ourselves of all guarantees that life finds us.

As I experienced their joining together, I was saddened by the years that had been lost, the times I had willfully struggled to try to get everything right when I didn't know what right was. They were times of planting seeds and then impatiently digging them up to see if they had grown, of trying to figure out what others wanted from me instead of asking what I most wanted for myself, of feeling the fear of not knowing where this was all going to lead, of believing that I needed to rely upon the individualistic and achieving parts of my nature to do all of the work, because I did not believe in asking for help.

Learning to trust that these terrifying leaps of faith are in fact *of* life and not *against* it came slowly for me. And I am grateful now for knowing that perhaps it is when we feel truly lost, groping our way somewhere between the in breath and the out breath that the gods are most near.

How do we discover in words the same depth of truth and inspiration that flows from our hands when we paint or our dancing when our feet touch the floor? Is it possible to suspend our schedules and routines to experiment with the deeper insights that can emerge when we are free to bring our different voices forward without fear of embarrassment or concern? Can we share our most deeply held beliefs with the possibility that behind them lies an even greater truth, one which, once revealed, might allow us to live in a more imaginative and peaceful world?

When I set aside my consulting practice to return to music, I could not foresee where it would lead. But over time, the painful uncertainties have evolved into a wonderful dance that elegantly weaves together all of the various significant but seemingly separate strands of my life. Finding the marriage between my intellect and my soul could not have been planned, at least not by me. It would have been too complex and perhaps too terrifying for my strategic mind to grasp. But perhaps, just as Wagner spoke of Beethoven's spontaneous and deeply felt performances as being "child's play" for him, creating our lives so that they are a reflection of what we love is child's play for the heart.

So now when I join these groups, I don't bring charts and theories and projectors as I did before. Instead, I simply bring myself and a nine-foot-six-inch concert grand. And as we form into a circle, I'm careful to save a place beside the piano for the old man from the lobby of the hotel.

Note: Michael Jones, pianist and composer, is a founding artist of Narada Productions and has re-leased ten recordings. He is also an organizational consultant with DIA Logos in Cambridge, MA. "Who Will Play Your Music?" is excerpted from his book *Creating An Imaginative Life* (Conari Press, 1995) and used with permission of the author.

Follow-Up

1. *Choose one or more of these statements and apply them to your life:*
   - *There is no mystery to the work that is ours to do . . . because from the very beginning it has always been there.*
   - *Our purpose is to give ourselves to the world around us—including people, musical instruments, trees, and words. . . . When we offer ourselves to the world, the world gives itself back to us. What is it that we desire to do that brings an increase to life?*
   - *Perhaps this is what life asks of us—to step faithfully into that very place in our lives where we can no longer fall back on our cleverness or wits. . . . Perhaps it is only when we have emptied ourselves of all guarantees that life finds us.*
2. *Jones states that we all need at least one other person to recognize our gifts, our life work. Comment on this idea and explain if it is true for your life.*
3. *Select any other idea(s) from the article and write about and/or discuss your reactions.*
4. *Who will play your music?*

Applied Activities for Section Six

THE SOMEDAY LIST

Between now and your death there are (and will be) many things you hope to experience and accomplish. Listing some of these often reveals some themes which can be helpful as you seek to understand your life. Below is a technique for finding these themes:

1. List at least twenty things you would like to experience or accomplish before you die that you have not started or completed at this time. Note that an accomplishment is a goal-oriented effort while an experience refers to just being there (letting something happen). Here are a few examples to clarify the difference:

   Accomplishment—earning a degree, writing an article/book, mastering a skill, building something, changing a habit.

   Experiencing—attending a concert or art exhibit, having a child or grandchild, feeling inner harmony, standing on a mountain top, riding in a hot air balloon.

   It may be difficult to complete this list at one sitting. Do as many as you can in a free-associating manner. No one will see your list. Include "unrealistic" items as well as expected ones. Include fantasies and dreams. Leave this task for awhile or even a few days and go back to it. Try to list items from several categories of life.

2. Analysis and interpretation suggestions:

   a. Identify common themes (patterns or clusters) among your listed items. For example, you may have a few items with the theme of physical challenge and excitement, or creativity, or family/interpersonal relationships, or professional goals, or inner states of being, and so on. In a list of twenty-five items, there are usually four or five themes. Some individual items may fit under more than one theme. Once you have identified the themes, label them.

   b. Think of your themes as *unmet needs* which are present *now* (instead of the future). Do you think this list would be the same as one written five years ago? Why or why not?

   c. When will you begin to do these things on your list? Some will, realistically, have to be started later. Others though can be started now. Beware of the "Wait-until" illusion. People keep putting off desired life actions until certain conditions occur—but they may never occur just by waiting. The most common Wait-until conditions are time and money. "I'll be able to *X* when I finish school." Five years later—"When I don't have so many demands at work," or "When the kids are grown." This can continue until the "Wait-until" becomes a "Wish-I-had. . . ," or "If-only. . . ."

If an item has existed for a few years, it probably falls under the Wait-until illusion.

Consider items with short time frames. Physical challenges such as high-level athletics or performance dancing have short lifespans. Many items are very difficult to do with family responsibilities. In short, pay close attention to valuable experiences that have small windows of opportunity.

d. *Activate your themes* in some manner. Remember that the themes act as unmet needs that call for some attention. Choose one or two themes that seem to shout the loudest. If the actual items under the theme are not truly feasible, think of a substitute activity that fulfills the spirit of this theme. For example, if you cannot begin a book, start a chapter or even a short story. If you cannot travel to Europe with a loved one for two months now, plan a nice escape weekend in a location you both like. Any theme can be activated by creating similar, substitute activities.

e. Try at least one activity per theme over the next month.

3. Discuss your Things To Do list and themes in small groups and/or with the whole class. Write about your themes, possible Wait-until traps, and your attempts to activate the themes.

For further reading on this activity and additional ideas, see *Strategies for Experiential Learning: Book Two* (1981) by Louis Thayer (Ed.), published by LT Resources, 8594 Sleepy Hollow Dr., Saline, MI 48176.

TALKING TO WISE PERSONS

A wise person has deep knowledge and understanding and is capable of profound insight and judgment. A wise person may or may not be a highly educated person in the traditional sense. A wise person is one from whom we seek some guidance that will aid us in moments when wisdom is needed. There are many ways in which we can hear from those who are wise. One of these ways is described below. All that is required is a willingness to hear what these wise persons have to say to you.

1. Think of three persons who have the qualities of wise persons as described above. You may have known them as a grandparent, aunt, parent, teacher, neighbor, or mentor. Or, they may be known indirectly to you as a philosopher, religious leader, writer, or historical figure. Somehow these persons connect with you on a deep, inner level. Name these three wise persons:

   _____ , _____ , _____ .

2. Select one of these wise persons with whom you would like to talk at this time. This wise person would be able to offer answers for a current decision, dilemma, or just life in general.

3. Recall the qualities of this person whom you respect so much. Try to remember a couple of instances when he or she was helpful to you in the past. Sense his/her presence with you now.

4. On a sheet of paper start a dialogue by first greeting this wise person and stating why you are requesting guidance. Continue the dialogue with the wise person's imagined response. Continue your conversation in a natural manner. Do not force any words. Let the conversation flow in the manner you think it actually would with this person. You may reach a natural stopping point. If this happens, stop the conversation and pick it up at a later time.

5. If desired, complete steps 2–4 with other wise persons in your life.

6. Follow-up ideas: What ideas or actions resulted from your dialogue(s) with this wise person? Can you now contact this wise person more readily?

This idea is an adaptation of a technique from *A Journal Workshop* by Ira Progoff (1992), Jeremy Tarcher/Perigee Books.

EVOLUTION OF A PERSON #2

1. *Lifeline* (from now to death). List the events you *expect* and *want* to occur during the rest of your life. Try to estimate your age at each event (including your death). Consider the following major events: career/education changes; marriage/family plans; loss of significant others; lessening mental/physical powers; places you want to visit; special goals or dreams.

2. Follow-up questions: What are the one or two things that stand out to you on your projected lifeline? Which part of your life has the most incomplete predictions and what do you think this means? How does your estimate of your age at death influence how you are living now and in the near future?

3. Consider completing this activity during some time of "active solitude" (see the article entitled "Active Solitude" in this section).

4. Discuss or write a reaction paper on what you've learned from this activity.